Psychoanalysis and Women

Contemporary Reappraisals

Psychoanalysis and Women

Contemporary Reappraisals

Edited by
JUDITH L. ALPERT

THE ANALYTIC PRESS

The Analytic Press

Distributed solely by

Lawrence Erlbaum Associates, Inc., Publishers
365 Broadway
Hillsdale, New Jersey 07642

Library of Congress Cataloging-in-Publication Data
Psychoanalysis and women.
   Includes bibliographies and index.
   1. Women — Mental health. 2. Women psychoanalysts.
3. Psychotherapist and patient. I. Alpert, Judith L.
[DNLM: 1. Psychoanalysis. 2. Women. WM 460 P9743]
RC451.4.W6P76 1986   155.6'33   86-1241
ISBN 0-88163-039-X

Printed in the United States of America
10 9 8 7 6 5 4 3 2 1

Contents

Female Patient

Female Analyst

Contributors

JUDITH L. ALPERT, Ph.D., Professor, Doctoral Programs in School Psychology and Professional Child/School Psychology, New York University; Graduate, New York University Postdoctoral Program in Psychotherapy and Psychoanalysis; private practice.

JESSICA BENJAMIN, Ph.D., Graduate, New York University Postdoctoral Program in Psychotherapy and Psychoanalysis; Fellow, New York Institute for the Humanities; has written widely on psychoanalysis, feminism, and social theory; private practice.

RUTH-JEAN EISENBUD, Ph.D., Professor and Supervisor, New York University Postdoctoral Program in Psychotherapy and Psychoanalysis and Adelphi University Institute of Advanced Psychological Studies; Faculty member, Long Island Institute of Psychoanalysis.

ZENIA ODES FLIEGEL, Ph.D., Fellow and faculty member, Institute for Psychoanalytic Training and Research.

RUTH FORMANEK, Ph.D., Professor of Education, Hofstra University; Chief Psychologist, Jewish Community Services of Long Island; Clinical Associate Professor, Adelphi University Postdoctoral Program in Child and Adolescent Psychotherapy.

LISA K. GORNICK, M.Phil., Doctoral Candidate in Clinical Psychology, Yale University.

DOROTHY LITWIN, Ph.D., Graduate Division of Pastoral Counseling, Iona college, New Rochelle, N.Y.; private practice.

ESTHER MENAKER, Ph.D., Professor and Supervisor, New York University Postdoctoral Program in Psychotherapy and Psychoanalysis and National Psychological Association for Psychoanalysis.

RUTH MOULTON, M. D., Fellow, Supervising and Training Analyst, William Alansom White Institute; Assistant Clinical Professor of Psychiatry, Emerita, Columbia University; private practice.

LINDA S. PENN, Ph.D., Associate Professor, Doctoral Program in Clinical Psychology, Long Island University; Director, Long Island University Psychology Clinic; Graduate, New York University Post Doctoral Program in Psychotherapy and Psychoanalysis; private practice.

ZEBORAH SCHACHTEL, Ph.D., Supervisor, Institute of Contemporary Psychotherapy; private practice; Fellow, A. K. Rice Institute.

ADRIA E. SCHWARTZ, Ph.D., Adjunct, Yeshiva University Graduate Program in Psychology and New York University's Gallatin Division; has written widely on women's issue and psychoanalysis; private practice.

JODY BOGHOSSIAN SPENCER, M. A., Doctoral candidate in Professional Child/School Psychology, New York University; Advanced Fellow, Cambridge Hospital and Harvard University Medical School, Department of Psychiatry; Staff Psychologist, Tufts-New England Medical Center, Department of Child Psychiatry.

SUSAN SPIELER, Psy.D., Supervisor and Adjunct Faculty Member, Rutgers University, Graduate School of Applied and Professional Psychology; Adjunct faculty member, New School for Social Research; Faculty member, Training Institute for Mental Health Practitioners; author on gender issues in psychoanalysis; private practice.

Foreword

The appearance of this volume, in which are gathered together a number of essays covering the psychoanalytic psychology of women, is an historic event. Although recent years have seen many books on the psychology of women — indeed, some excellent ones — few have addressed the issues of female psychology specifically from a psychoanalytic viewpoint. The wealth of material concerning the life of women in its many aspects — sexual, emotional, professional, intellectual and artistic — is largely the result of profound social changes in our time, especially those inspired and implemented by the women's movement. This movement began in the eighteenth century with the writings of women such as Mary Wollstonecraft and Ellen Keyes, who were concerned principally with the political, social, and economic rights of women. It burgeoned under the impact of many social forces to meet the need of our psychological age while itself bringing about social and psychological change. From the latter years of my own childhood, when women were about to gain the right to vote in the United States, I recall the remark of a classmate, who said, "Above all, first and foremost I am a girl!" thereby expressing growing pride and affirmation in the self-awareness of femaleness.

While the women's movement has given rise to many of the situations and issues that are the subject of these essays and could thus be considered the *raison d'etre* of this work, its psychoanalytic emphasis springs from a very different source, namely, Freud's illusory conception of the development of woman, which he attempted to derive from and fit into his theories regarding male psychology. "One is *born* a man, but one *becomes* a woman" was the byword among early psychoanalysts. It is the resulting skewed theory of feminine psychology propounded by the founder of psychoanalysis and his early followers that is in large measure responsible for the questions and answers contained in these essays.

With the sociological changes that have taken place, psychoanalysts have been faced with new theoretical and therapeutic problems. One hears less about wishes and their gratification or frustration and more about conflicts of identity, of autonomy, of self-esteem, and of anxiety about separation, the inability to relate to others or to make commitments. Patients are bringing different core problems. This book addresses many of these issues as they relate to women.

It also presents an historical review of the stormy controversy within psychoanalytic circles over norms in the psychological development of woman. Social and historical forces, however, are not static, and the controversies that seemed important and relevant within the framework of Freudian thought have been complicated by shifts and changes within psychoanalysis itself. With increasing opportunity for the observation and treatment of individuals and groups within a rapidly changing society, some of the basic premises of psychoanalysis have been challenged. Whether penis envy in the development of woman is as universal and inevitable a phenomenon as Freud considered it to be is no longer as central an issue as whether indeed the whole of drive theory should be the point of departure for understanding human psychology. For in the evolution of psychoanalysis — resulting largely from social pressures calling for change — the primacy of instincts has been called into question by those emphasizing the development of interpersonal relationships or the importance of the self. The controversies concerning female development thus find themselves played out within a much larger framework that disputes some fundamental premises of psychoanalysis itself. What once were controversies of doctrine have become products of sociopsychological observation, albeit within the context of a psychoanalytic situation.

In his search for universal truths about human development Freud neglected the cultural context in which people grow and function. It is one of the merits of this book that it accepts the mandate of social change to refocus the angle of observation to include the cultural dimension and thus to illuminate the relativity of truths about human development.

One might imagine that a work dealing specifically with the theory of female development and the treatment of women would limit insight into more general problems of human psychology. Quite the opposite is the case. For example, by acknowledging the influence of the analyst's gender on the nature of the transference and countertransference in the therapeutic situation, we open up a much broader issue: the effect of *reality* on the therapeutic procedure and its outcome. The focus on gender as a functioning reality within the psychoanalytic situation makes it clear that other realities, such as ethnic background, subculture, social position, and language, must influence the emotions, interactions, and levels of understanding of both analyst and patient. Although the psychoanalytic situation is conducive to the formation of transference reactions, psychoanalysis can no longer be envisaged exclusively as a procedure in which highly subjective reactions of the patient are projected onto the person of an objective observer. All is not in the mind of the patient; reality is a factor to be reckoned with, and the myth of the neutral therapist, if indeed it still prevails, has been further exploded by, among other things, an awareness of the effects of gender.

By bringing the specific problems of women into focus, this book has done much more than it intended: it has opened up a dual perspective. It makes patently clear that social expectations, norms, codes and mores — probably in every culture — are paramount influences in molding the character, behavior, and self-feeling of women. But by delineating and bringing into relief what is specific and characteristic for women, this book also creates an awareness of the universality of certain human problems. Men, too, can have difficulty in identity formation or can fear success. The nature of such problems is idiosyncratic for women in form, content, and course of development, but the problems are existentially universal. There are, of course, issues of development and conflict that are exclusively female because of the specific nature of woman's life cycle and biological function. This does not mean that "anatomy is destiny," in Freud's narrow sense of genital difference, but that there are biological, psychological and sociological differences that result in a specific psychoanalytic psychology of women that is no longer derivative of the male model of development. Such a psychology accepts and studies differences without the value judgment that for so long has dominated psychoanalytic thinking, equating women's differences from men with inferiority. Not only does this book contribute to a deeper and fairer understanding of women, but it enlarges the scope of psychoanalytic theory and clinical practice by illustrating how much can be gained by shifting the position from which observations are made while simultaneously taking into account the cultural timeframe in which they are made.

Esther Menaker, Ph.D.

Introduction

JUDITH L. ALPERT

Within the psychoanalytic framework, there is a growing body of research and thinking about female development. In addition, there is ongoing research within other areas of psychology, such as developmental psychology and social psychology, which has important implications for an understanding of women's adult development. Often these research findings are not readily available to the analytic community, nor has much of the research been incorporated into a psychoanalytic framework.

The intent of this book is to broaden analytic thinking by integrating contemporary literature from psychoanalysis with that of other areas, both within and outside psychology, which has implications for the understanding of women's development. This literature is conceptualized within a psychoanalytic framework. A basic premise underlying this book is that psychoanalysis needs continuing review and revision in terms of what women and men are about and a continuing focus on whether and how unfounded biases prevent analysts from understanding patients. The present volume considers how sexism and feminism are affecting psychoanalysis and exemplifies how the emerging field of psychoanalysis of women and the issues its existence raises should be conceptualized. The book exemplifies some of the positive contributions that a feminist outlook gives to the study of human behavior and should expand the range of hypotheses that we have about people.

Other books have focused on women and psychoanalysis. They include Mitchell's (1974) *Psychoanalysis and Feminism;* Strouse's (1974) *Woman and Analysis;* Miller's (1976) *Toward a New Psychology of Women;* Blum's (1977) *Female Psychology;* Gallop's (1982) *The Daughter's Seduction: Feminism and Psychoanalysis;* Van Herik's (1982) *Freud: On Femininity and Faith;* Bernstein and Warner's (1984) *Women Treating Women;* Eichenbaum and Orbach's (1983) *Understanding Women: A Feminist Psychoanalytic Approach;* Mendell's (1982) *Early Female Development;* Fast's (1984) *Gender Identity: A Differentiation Model;* and Bernay and Cantor's (1986) *The Psychology of Today's Woman.* The last eight books are the most recent. The books by

Gallop, Van Herik, Bernstein and Warner, Eichenbaum and Orbach, Mendell, and Fast are more focused than the present volume.
While Bernay and Cantor consider a broad picture of women's development, they organize their book from a sociological perspective.
The present volume is unique in that it includes an up-to-date critical
review and integration of literature and is organized around issues,
some of which have received relatively little attention in the literature. In addition, the introductory and concluding sections point to
some parameters, issues, and themes relevant to the emerging field of
psychoanalysis of women, and this, too, has received little previous
attention.

Although the authors of the present volume vary in orientation,
most are practicing psychoanalysts; many have written extensively
in the area of psychoanalysis and gender. The authors hold that a
feminist outlook can offer positive contributions to the study of
human behavior and should expand our range of ideas about people
and their development. They hold further that the issue is no longer
whether males and females are different, but how maleness and
femaleness are represented in varying degrees in men and women,
and how analysts can understand and work with this difference in
order to attain analytic goals. The authors have considered the following with respect to their topics:

1. What are the limitations of earlier psychoanalytic conceptualizations of women?

2. What is present-day understanding about women's development?

3. How can mental health and mental illness be conceptualized
with respect to the topic?

4. What are implications for treating women?

Beginning the first of the book's four sections, Fliegel presents a
historical consideration of feminine psychosexual development in
Freudian theory. She reviews and places into historical perspective
the 1920s–1930s debate between Horney and Jones versus Freud.
She shows that Freud's 1925 paper, "Some Psychological Consequences of the Anatomical Distinctions Between the Sexes," did not
mark the beginning of the controversy but, rather, was written in a
polemical context. She relates some results and formulations from
contemporary work to the positions in the historic controversy. She
points out that many contemporary views are similar to views voiced
by Horney and Jones and that some of the contemporary views
either directly confront the difficulties with Freud's writings on
women or rigidly try to salvage Freud's formulations, even at the

expense of internal logic. In addition, she indicates that there are attempts to make Freud's theories more plausible by construing them in metaphorical terms. Fliegel concludes by calling for both the recognition that Freud's developmental theories of femininity are the weakest component of his thought and the redirection of energies to those aspects of his theory that further our understanding of people.

Spieler, in chapter two of this volume, offers and develops the following hypotheses: The feminine dimensions of the self are insufficiently valued by both women and men because femaleness is unconsciously associated with fallibility; maleness is defensively overvalued by both women and men in order to keep maleness "uncontaminated" by the fallibility associated with femaleness; maleness is used to promote self-esteem; and an overreliance on this form of self-restoration represents a developmental arrest. Spieler holds that this developmental arrest is related to women's rearing children and being undervalued. Spieler also develops the point that psychoanalytic theory is limited in its ability to represent women positively and that psychoanalytic development theory is androcentric, its structure and content being more representative of "male" thinking.

In the third chapter, Schwartz considers the feminist critique of traditional psychoanalytic models of female psychosexual development. The major focus of this chapter is on three key stages in the development of female gender role identity: the rapprochement subphase of the separation-individuation process, triangulation, and adolescence. Included also are discussions of such relevant clinical issues as the symptomatic nature of penis envy and castration fantasies, disidentification from mother as female, and the emergence of stereotypic feminine behavior.

The three chapters in the section "Freudian Theory and Beyond" concern controversial aspects of Freud's theory of femininity — female superego development, masochism, and narcissism. In each chapter there is a review of early analytic theory as well as a consideration of more contemporary analytic, and in some cases nonanalytic, views. In this section, each author presents a critical analysis of the literature, an integrated view or a new conceptualization, and theoretical and clinical implications.

Chapter four considers four conceptualizations of moral development, two from analytic perspectives (Freud and Horney) and two from nonanalytic perspectives (Kohlberg and Gilligan). The two men, Freud and Kohlberg, share some assumptions and values, while the two women, Horney and Gilligan, hold a different set of assumptions and values. Specifically, Freud and Kohlberg assume that a developmentally more advanced moral position involves justice, fairness, and a perspective within which it is possible to rank order traits. In contrast, Horney and Gilligan stress a perspective within which flexibility is maintained and different perspectives are acknowledged as well as valued. Some of the major differences between the male and female theorists are consistent with both Gilligan's finding of sex differences in orientation and the general public's perception that males and females are different. Spencer and I propose that there are gender differences in orientation to moral issues and that these differences are related to different early experiences of attachment, bonding, autonomy, and individuation. The chapter concludes by questioning the impact of these tendencies toward gender differences in orientation on psychotherapeutic work and asks how psychoanalysis, which was created by a male and his mostly male followers, reflects an orientation that is more characteristic of males.

Chapter five concerns masochism. Benjamin suggests that a reconsideration of masochism is indicated by contemporary theories of preoedipal gender identity formation and by contemporary understanding of its function for the ego and the self-structure. In addition, she notes how issues of separation-individuation, in particular the relationship to the father in rapprochement, underlie the longing for ideal love. Benjamin points out that it is difficult for the girl to integrate male and female identifications and that adult ideal love can therefore be seen as a solution to problems in the early struggle to individuate from mother and identify with father.

Formanek's chapter concerns developmental theories of aging, societal perceptions of women and their effect on women's self-esteem, differential experiences of aging according to gender, and narcissistic operations designed to maintain high self-esteem in old age. Her main thesis is that pejorative societal views of aging women contribute to women's negative feelings about themselves. She notes that types of narcissistic operations to raise self esteem, utilized successfully at younger ages, are unsuccessful with increasing age and that older women's attempts to raise self esteem include a relation to things representing people, depersonified abstract ideals and interests, and, for women at any age, intimate relationships to family and friends.

The third section comprises chapters focusing on issues pertinent to the female patient. Here there is consideration of success, autonomy, and lesbian choice. These are salient areas for women. Moulton makes the point that with the emphasis on the role of men in keeping women down, not enough attention has been paid to competition between women or between mother and daughter. Moulton indicates that success is often seen as a defiance of mother and as a threat to early symbiotic bonds with her. It may also arouse an early sense of maternal deprivation covered by a façade of self-sufficiency and pseudoindependence. Moulton points out that the girl may have turned to her father for encouragement, which, when given, added oedipal guilt to preoedipal conflicts. The father may also have deserted the adolescent daughter when he felt threatened by her femininity, received less gratification from her, and lost control over her. Guilt because of oedipal triumph over mother may leave the woman very vulnerable to female criticism. Her efforts to be a "good girl" may interfere with her administrative abilities. There is also guilt about rising above the educational or socioeconomic level of the family of origin. Moulton presents case material to show the effects of different kinds of parents. In addition, she presents a brief review of current literature to compare with some outdated concepts of the past. New emphasis is placed on women's fear of loneliness, separation anxiety, and problems with their sense of self.

In chapter eight Litwin details how autonomy is a conflict for women in our society. Early object relations for females, who are brought up primarily by their mothers, cast them in the role of nurturer, a role reinforced by society. However, society values autonomy as an essential characteristic of maturity and denigrates affiliative inclinations. These conflicting roles put women in a quandary. Another facet of this conflict is the result of internalizing autonomy as an ego ideal. Litwin concludes by indicating that psychoanalysis can be helpful to women in reconciling their conflicts around autonomy by enabling them to accept the rewards of friendship.

In the last chapter in this section, Eisenbud compares her 1969 paper, "Female Homosexuality," with her 1982 work, "Early and Later Determinants of Lesbian choice," with regard to reliance on psychoanalytic theory and its changes. She discusses the implications of the use of regression and fixation and focuses on oedipal defensive manoeuvers in the earlier essay. She explores the results of recognition of internalization and preoedipal experience in the later essay. She reviews her hypothesis that the ego in the preoedipal time could use romantic erotic feelings in its struggles for relatedness and autonomy and thus establish a primary nondefensive lesbian orientation. This reappraisal discusses the implications of each essay and changes in psychoanalytic theory from a feminist point of view. Eisenbud also raises the question of early internalization of negative experience and suggests that the therapist confront internalized distrust, flight, competition, and disgust toward self and others, as well as conflict over bisexual feelings. She concludes by presenting and discussing two dreams of a lesbian patient.

The focus of the fourth section is on the female analyst. There is consideration of the experience of male and female analysts, the female analyst working with the male patient, and transference and countertransference issues relevant to the pregnant therapist. Schachtel holds that women's socialization leads to greater availability of themselves and their personal experience, while men's socialization leads to more separateness and greater emphasis on role rather than person. She holds too that socialization around gender roles affects how some analysts experience and work within their analytic role, particularly in the early stages of professional life. Schachtel considers how gender interacts with and affects the analytic work role. She particularly considers the tensions and contradictions between gender and analytic roles and tasks and focuses on such issues as authorization, power, status, and levels of responsibility. Selected examples from male and female supervisees throw light on the interaction of the gender and analytic roles.

In chapter eleven, Gornick considers the male patient-female therapist dyad. She begins by reviewing rationales and motivations for the classic psychoanalytic position that the sex of the analyst does not significantly effect the analytic process in general or the transference in particular. Further, she discusses female authority, particularly the relationship between power and sexuality for women; and female intimacy, particularly the heightened threat of merging posed by intimacy with women. Transference themes characteristic of and distinctive to the female therapist-male patient dyad are considered; these include the preoedipal maternal transference, feelings of shame in response to the woman therapist's authority, the erotic transference, and the hostile transference. Her consideration of the woman therapist-male patient dyad suggests that the psychoanalytic method relies on male authority. The female-clinician vantage point leads to our viewing some theoretical points as less critical or different and to our considering some aspects of male development differently. For example, this vantage point exhibits the ways in which the relationship of boys to their mothers may condition other relationships to women.

In the last chapter, Penn discusses the significance of the therapist's pregnancy on a psychoanalytically oriented treatment. A review of the sparse literature in the area is followed by a presentation of the major transference and countertransference themes evoked by the therapist's pregnancy. Means of dealing with these as well as other issues arising during the pregnancy are then considered. Penn develops the position that a therapist's pregnancy involves a loss of her anonymity as she is revealed to be a mother, a sexual being, and a person with a separate life. Penn points out that this is a stimulus for powerful transference and countertransference reactions. While reactions to a therapist's pregnancy are tied to the patient's unique dynamics and situation, there are common themes which the pregnancy tends to evoke. Preoedipal aspects of the transference involving issues of attachment, separation, fears of abandonment or loss, and sibling rivalry are frequently mobilized, and oedipal issues highlighting concerns involving the patient's sexuality or sexual identification are frequently triggered. In the countertransference, Penn states, the therapist must deal both with her own reactions to her pregnancy and with her responses to the intense and sometimes primitive transferential reactions of her patients.

As editor, I close the book with some concluding comments.

|I| *Overview*

1 Women's Development in Analytic Theory
Six Decades of Controversy

_____ZENIA ODES FLIEGEL

The last two decades have witnessed a resurgence of interest in the issues, first raised in the 1920s, surrounding Freud's formulations on feminine development. In the intervening period, the historic controversy around this subject was seemingly all but forgotten, with classical literature generally reflecting on unquestioning acceptance of the validity of Freud's views. Even Horney's followers tended to neglect her pertinent early work — perhaps because much of it was written in a Freudian idiom incompatible with her later formulations. Her scattered papers on feminine psychology were not collected and reissued until 1967, posthumously.

Within the mainstream of Freudian analysis, it is only with the current reexamination of this area of psychoanalytic theory that earlier questions and dissents have been rediscovered. In recent years references to Horney and Jones, the central figures in the original debate, have become almost routine in writings on this subject; yet there is great variation in the way they are referred to and in what aspects of their views are chosen for citation. Relatively few Freudian analysts, even if in substantial disagreement with Freud in this area, acknowledge any merit to the views of the early analytic dissenters.[1] Yet the influence of those dissenters is still felt indirectly. Often, nuances in current formulations can be better understood when related to the early history and to earlier polarized positions; in fact,

Parts of this chapter previously appeared in _The Psychoanalytic Quarterly_ (1973) and in _The Psychoanalytic Review_ (1982). The author wishes to thank the editors of both journals for permission to reprint.

[1]An outstanding exception here is Robert Stoller, who has since 1968 consistently pointed out the ways in which the dissenters' views proved more tenable than Freud's.

Freud's own formulations can best be grapsed in that light, since they were forged in the context of the early polemics. In addition, as a result of the original controversy and the fact that it eventually became schismatic, positions in this area were codified and hardened to an extraordinary degree, becoming almost a matter of doctrinaire loyalty.

As is by now well known, in the 1920s and early 1930s there was within Freud's inner circle an intense controversy over feminine psychology — a controversy more extensive than is quite apparent from the printed record. The original debate, much of it conducted out of print, was recorded in a fragmentary and partly submerged way.[2] More important, without scrutinizing the dates of the relevant papers or their original presentations at various congresses, it is not always clear who is answering whom or where. The import of the various contributions to the debate is by no means self-evident; they can easily be misapprehended and they often are.

The most common misapprehension is to regard Freud's "revolutionary"[3] 1925 paper as marking the beginning of the controversy. The present chapter attempts to show that the 1925 paper was written in what was already a polemical context. After some of the relevant sequences are described, a sampling of contemporary research reports and their conceptualizations are placed in relation to the views of the original participants in order to offer a perspective on the current literature.

THE GREAT DEBATE

The main protagonists in the early controversy were Karen Horney, Ernest Jones, and, of course, Freud. Jeanne Lampl-de Groot, Helene Deutsch and Otto Fenichel played important parts; others were involved peripherally. The key papers were two by Horney (1924, 1926), three by Jones (1927, 1933, 1935) and three by Freud (1924, 1925, 1931). There were important papers by Lampl-de Groot (1927) and Helene Deutsch (1930, 1932); Fenichel's (1930, 1934) role was interesting, and Melanie Klein (1928) was an important background figure.

---

[2]Jones makes several references to unpublished letters from Freud on the subject (1933, pp. 467, 472; 1957, p. 263).

[3]Described by Strachey as "somewhat revolutionary" in his editor's note introducing Freud's subsequent (1931) paper on the subject (p. 223).

The Polemics

We start with Horney's first paper, "On the Genesis of the Castration Complex in Women" (1924), originally delivered at the 1922 Berlin Congress. On the face of it, nothing in its contents is incompatible with Freudian theory as articulated up to that point, though the formulations on feminine psychic development are richer and more complete than those Freud had been able to offer; ideas presented here anticipate some very modern contributions.[4]

Among the central points of the later controversy were Horney's suggestion that early pregenital penis envy (later designated as "primary penis envy") be differentiated from a subsequent, more intense form. For the latter she posited different origins within the vicissitudes of the female oedipus complex and regarded it as the more important nucleus of what might develop into a neurotic "castration complex" or "masculinity complex" in adult women. What represented a new departure was that she undertook to analyze both the primary and the secondary forms of penis envy into their psychic components, rather than taking them as self-evident and self-explanatory reactions to the girl's factual constitutional inferiority. Thus Horney saw the origins of primary penis envy in the little girl's relative disadvantage in relation to three pregenital components: (1) urethral erotic omnipotent fantasies arising out of children's narcissistic overvaluation of excretory processes; (2) exhibitionistic and scoptophilic wishes in which the little boy has an advantage due to the visibility of his genital; and (3) suppressed masturbatory wishes, since the girl may interpret the boy's ability to handle his genital during urination as permission for him to masturbate.

This primary penis envy was distinguished by Horney from a later, more complex defensive formation in which, as a step in the resolution of the girl's oedipal attachment, she attempts to identify with the father. This step may be only a transitory phase in her development, or it may become fixed in a neurotic masculinity complex. Crucial to these formulations is the underlying idea, later to be argued forcefully by Jones (1935), that the little girl's oedipal attachment develops out of her innate femininity undergoing its own matu-

---

[4]See, for example, Edgcumbe and Burgner (1975); new formulations are often advanced without apparent recognition of their congruence or similarity to those of the original dissenters.

rational processes.[5] According to Horney's thesis, supported by extensive case material, the little girl, both disappointed and threatened by her oedipal attachment to her father, later renounces her oedipal wishes and replaces them with an identification. This in turn reinforces preexisting preoedipal penis envy. Such defensive oedipal resolution is seen as the more potent force in keeping the "masculinity complex" alive in adult women; Horney assigned a secondary role to the regressive factor, whereby early preoedipal penis envy is revived by such an identification.

Also important to the subsequent debate was Horney's emphasis on the oedipal girl's disappointment in her wish to be given a child by the father, illustrated with a case where "by a process of displacement the penis had become the object of envy in place of the child" (p. 59). One more element among Horney's many reported observations should be mentioned: she regarded as fundamental a "basic fantasy of having suffered castration through the love relation with the father" and designated it as "the second root of the whole castration complex in women" (p. 63). Here, the girl defends against her wishful but guilt- and anxiety-laden castration fantasies with the opposite fantasy of possessing a penis: "The identification with the father doesn't carry with it . . . guilt but rather a sense of acquittal. For . . . from the connection . . . between the ideas of castration and the incest fantasies relating to the father . . . being a woman is in itself felt to be culpable" (p. 65).

In comparing this work with some of Freud's subsequent formulations, one can hardly escape the judgment that Horney is more "Freudian" here than Freud. She stresses the importance of infantile sexual fantasy; Freud is to cling to "reality" in search for explanations. Freud showed no recognition of how consistent Horney's work was with the main lines of psychoanalytic theory. One can only guess why he found this remarkable paper so unacceptable; masculine narcissism as a factor in shaping psychoanalytic formulations, explicitly referred to by Horney, may have played a part. Perhaps more important, her thesis also implies the existence of an intrinsic, pleasure-oriented feminine sexuality. Despite his well-known stress on the importance of sexuality generally, this idea was apparently profoundly alien to Freud's thought. As early as 1905 Freud defined

---

[5]This idea has since become one of the focal points in the currently revived controversy. Some authors, for example, Mitchell (1974), Grossman (1976), and Chodorow (1978), regard the early dissenters' views as too biologistic; the same authors attempt to portray Freud as being less so — or not at all.

"invariably and necessarily of masculine nature, whether it
men or in women" (p. 219). This he reiterated several
ater (1933): "The juxtaposition 'feminine libido' is without
fication" (p. 131).

responded to Horney's 1924 paper with two of his own
1925).[6] The first of these, "The Dissolution of the Oedipus
ex," written within a year of Horney's publication in German
and still rather sketchy as concerns girls, marked a new departure.
As the editors of the *Standard Edition* noted, Freud (1924) for the first
time stressed differences in oedipal development in boys and girls.[7]
Although in turning his attention to girls Freud confesses that here
his material "becomes more obscure and full of gaps" (p. 177), he
nevertheless goes on to outline aspects of his subsequent theory. He
declares: "Anatomy is Destiny" (p. 178), and reasons that for the
girl, without the castration threat "a powerful motive also drops out
for the setting up of a superego and for her breaking off of the
infantile genital organization" (p. 178). He further asserts that it is
the girl's wish for a penis which leads to her wish for a baby: "She
slips — along the line of a symbolic equation . . . from the penis to a
baby" (pp. 178–179) — an exact reversal of Horney's (1924) suggested "process of displacement" from baby to penis. Freud's idea
that the girl lacks a powerful motive for renouncing the oedipal
position similarly counters Horney's thesis, based as that was on the
girl's need to retreat from oedipal guilts and anxieties. Freud concludes his discussion by reiterating: "It must be admitted, however,
that in general our insight into these developmental processes in girls
is unsatisfactory, incomplete and vague" (1924, p. 179).

This abrupt reversal of his own previous ideas, bounded by two
disclaimers of insight, suggests that something other than ordinary
evolution of thought was involved. Following so closely upon
Horney's paper, it suggests rather a move to stake out territory and
possibly also to signal displeasure. The latter possibility is supported
by an interjected remark: "Here the feminist demand for equal rights
for the sexes does not take us far" (p. 178). Freud reemphasized this
sentiment a year later: "We must not be deflected from such conclusions by the denials of the feminists, who are anxious to *force us* to

---

[6]Aside from their temporal proximity, these papers are regarded as reac-
tive to Horney's for reasons that become clear on examination of their
contents.

[7]In so doing Freud reversed his own position of just one year earlier,
where he saw the dissolution of the Oedipus complex in girls taking place
"in a precisely analogous way" (1923a p. 32).

regard the two sexes as completely equal in position and worth"
(1925, p. 258, italics added).

Freud's (1925) landmark paper, "Some Psychological Consequences of the Anatomical Distinction Between the Sexes," develops
further the themes sounded in 1924. Like its antecedent, it is bounded by disclaimers, both within and outside its actual text. As late as
December 1924, Freud wrote to Abraham, in response to a related
question: "I do not know anything about it. As I gladly admit, the
female part of the problem is extraordinarily obscure to me" (Abraham and Freud, 1965, p. 379); and a year *after* offering his definitive
formulation (one he would reaffirm in all subsequent writings on
femininity), he elsewhere stressed once again the limits of his understanding in this area: "We know less about the sexual life of little
girls than of boys. But we need not feel ashamed of this distinction;
after all, the sexual life of adult women is a 'dark continent' for
psychology" (Freud, 1926, p. 212).

In 1925, however, Freud offered his theory of the girl's psychosexual development. A juxtaposition of relevant passages from
Freud's 1925 paper with Karen Horney's thesis again shows a reversal of the latter; this time it is more complete — an almost faithful
mirror image of Horney's thesis. Freud wrote:

> In girls the Oedipus complex is a secondary formation. The
> operations of the castration complex precede and prepare for
> it. . . . there is a fundamental contrast between the two sexes.
> *Whereas in boys the Oedipus complex is destroyed by the castration
> complex, in girls it is made possible and led up to by the castration
> complex* [p. 256, emphasis in the original].

Here, the girl develops her oedipal wishes and feminine attitude
towards her father as a consequence of frustrated phallic jealousy,
and by way of forced resignation to her castrated condition.[8]

The only explicit reference to Horney occurs in the final para-
graph of Freud's 1925 paper:

> In the valuable and comprehensive studies on the masculin-
> ity and castration complexes in women by Abraham (1921),
> Horney (1923), and Helene Deutsch (1925) there is much that
> touches closely upon what I have written but nothing that coin-
> cides with it completely, so that here again I feel justified in
> publishing this paper [p. 258].

---

[8]For a more detailed comparison of the two papers see Fliegel, 1973, pp.
389–392.

It is difficult to guess here whether, as Jones (1933) was to suggest with reference to another point, Freud actually misunderstood Horney sufficiently not to recognize how antithetical their formulations were, or whether this was Freud's way of being polite. Freud's introduction to his paper clearly shows that without allowing time to verify his ideas through further clinical observation, he now felt under pressure to offer his own formulations on questions he had for a long time kept in abeyance; it also shows a need to offer justification for taking such an uncharacteristic course. Freud explained this departure from his usual procedures on the basis of his limited life expectancy, reduced case load, and the availability of collaborators to confirm or deny the validity of his proposed formulations. There was an invitation here, along with an effort to preserve scientific objectivity: "On this occasion, therefore, I feel justified in publishing something which stands in urgent need of confirmation before its value or lack of value can be decided" (p. 249).

An insightful comment about himself made in a letter to Ferenczi may be relevant here; Freud acknowledged: "I know that I am not very accessible and find it hard to assimilate alien thoughts that do not quite lie in my path" (Jones, 1957, p. 57). Freud's self-described inaccessibility may have been expecially pertinent to the ideas Horney advanced. There were two related areas where Freud's genius strained against its limitations until the end of his life. One was his understanding of feminine development, and the other, articulation of postphallic stages for both sexes. Earlier, Freud (1923b) had attempted to differentiate the phallic-castrated phase from a later one, where it is replaced by a masculine–feminine polarity — a task he would resume again years later (cf. Brunswick, 1940). Yet that final postphallic phase was never quite articulated by Freud. This is not surprising, in view of his persistent sense of sexuality and libido as intrinsically masculine and his long-standing conviction of the essential masculinity of the clitoris. He wrote as early as 1908 that the clitoris "behaves in fact during childhood like a . . . penis. . . . it becomes the seat of excitations which lead to its being touched. . . . [and] its excitability gives the little girl's sexual activity a masculine character" (p. 217). For Freud, masturbation, excitability, and libido were all quintessentially masculine; his inability to envision their feminine counterparts inevitably left one end of the "polarity" defined solely in negative terms. At the end of his life, Freud found his own deeply rooted conceptions unsatisfactory. He writes in his posthumously published "Outline of Psycho-Analysis": "For distinguishing between male and female in mental life we make use of what is obviously an inadequate empirical and conventional equa-

tion: we call everything that is strong and active male, and everything that is weak and passive female" (1940, p. 188).

Freud's skewed conception of sexual polarities interconnects with
his at times overtly expressed recoil from identifying even fleetingly
with women's roles or feminine positions.[9] Such recoil from imagina-
tively entering women's subjectivity inevitably left femininity a "dark
continent" for Freud. It also left its mark on the early debate, where
the impression often obtains of their talking past each other and
never connecting.[10]

Whatever motivated Freud to counter Horney as he did, and
despite an admitted dearth of clinical evidence, she did not take
kindly to his response. Her second (1926) paper is frankly polemical,
in contrast to the first, which had respectful references to other
analytic writers and to Freud in particular. In this paper Horney
elaborates some of her earlier ideas and stresses the importance of
motherhood envy in men; she develops further the theme of little
girls' oedipal anxieties and points to fears of internal injury due to the
disproportions in size.

But the main thrust of the paper is polemical. Under the influence
of Simmel, she discusses the masculine orientation of the culture
within which psychoanalysis developed and of psychoanalytic formulations themselves. In a table, she compares the phallic little boy's
notions of femininity and the corresponding psychoanalytic formulations and concludes that they are identical. A note of bitterness
creeps in at times: "Men are evidently under greater necessity to
depreciate women than conversely" (p. 331). Her later sociocultural
bent is also foreshadowed: "It seems to me impossible to judge to
how great a degree the unconscious motives for flight from wom-

---

[9]There are Freud's own statements about mother transferences being
less accessible to him (see Freud, 1931); in addition, HD (1974) quotes him
as saying to her: "I do *not* like to be the mother in transference — it always
surprises and shocks me a little, I feel so very masculine" (pp. 146–147).

[10]Recognizing such recoil as a limiting factor can help make some otherwise puzzling statements of Freud's, in other contexts as well, more intel-
ligible. Thus we have the reiterated assertion that the individual's first
primary identification is "with the father in his own personal prehistory"
(1923a, p. 31). Freud adds in a footnote that "perhaps it would be safer to
say 'with the parents.' " The mother is never considered as a possible object
for the first prehistoric identification. Greenson's (1968) and Stoller's
(1968, 1976a) work on the need to "disidentify" from a close tie to the
mother (known to have been very close in Freud's case) is most likely
relevant here, as are Buxbaum's (1951) and Erikson's (1954) speculations
on Freud's incomplete self-analysis.

anhood are reinforced by the actual social subordination of women" (p. 338).

A year later, Ernest Jones (1927) entered the fray, strongly supporting Horney. While he introduced a number of observations and concepts of his own, in terms of the controversy under discussion, he explicitly agreed with Horney, whom he cited repeatedly. Along with her, he regards the girl's femininity as primary: *"Freud's 'phallic phase' in girls is probably a secondary, defensive construction rather than a true developmental stage"* (p. 451). Jones elaborates on the dangers of girls' incestuous wishes by considering the rival mother as a factor and records his impression that vaginal awareness may develop much earlier than had been assumed (p. 443). Melanie Klein (1928) expressed a conviction of very early vaginal awareness in girls; in her writings, however, the issues around femininity are peripheral to the larger theoretical controversies she generated. The existence of this larger controversy in the background no doubt played a part in shaping the subsequent debate among Freudians.[11]

Freud did not respond to the new Horney and Jones papers until 1931, but in the interval there were other contributions stimulated by the debate. Jeanne Lampl-de Groot (1927) offered confirmation:

> In the first years of her development . . . [the girl] behaves exactly like a boy not only in the matter of onanism but in other respects of her mental life: *in her love aim and object choice she is actually a little man.* When she has discovered and fully accepted the fact that castration has taken place, the little girl is forced once and for all to renounce her mother as love object and therewith to give up the active, conquering tendency of her love aim . . . [pp. 186–187, emphasis added].

Lampl-de Groot posits the regular occurrence of a masculine "negative oedipus complex" in girls, with the mother as sexual object and the father as rival; this, in her view, normally precedes the oedipal interest in the father (p. 189).

In 1930, somewhat belatedly, Helene Deutsch's paper on masochism provided further support; in it after Freud's thesis is cited, comes an italicized sentence: *"My view is that the oedipus complex in girls is inaugurated by the castration complex"* (p. 200). Yet she also credits Horney with "a very illuminating description" of flight from femininity (p. 202). The ambiguities in Deutsch's position become more

---

[11]Jones' final (1935) paper on the subject was originally presented to the Vienna Society as part of a proposed series of exchange lectures intended to promote better understanding between "London" and "Vienna."

evident in her subsequent (1932) paper, where she refers to Freud's 1925 formulation as follows: "In that paper he *demonstrates* the fact that the oedipus complex is not established in girls until after the phallic phase" (p. 222, italics added). This is remarkable considering not only the tentative way in which the 1925 formulations were initially advanced, but his statement, in the interval, that he was relying in part on Deutsch's along with Lampl-de Groot's findings (see Freud, 1931). Her earlier, untranslated work was apparently closer to Horney's (see Jones, 1927, p. 444; see also footnote 12, this chapter); and in this paper, while supporting Freud, she avoids accepting credit for independent confirmation of his thesis.

Otto Fenichel's position in all of this was to attempt (unsuccessfully) to moderate the controversy and to attentuate the differences. In 1930, referring to the ongoing debate, he suspends judgment, emphasizing the need for "exhaustive analysis of very many instances" (p. 185). He offers his own paper as "a modest contribution to the collection of such material." In his discussion of his detailed case reports he agrees on various points with Freud, Horney, and Jones but emphatically not with Lampl-de Groot's "little girl is a little man" formulation or her notion of a universal negative oedipal phase: " . . . . nothing in our material bore out the suppositions of A. Lampl-de Groot. The original mother attachments were, most markedly, exclusively pregenital" (p. 201). Four years later, Fenichel (1934) still sought to keep the relevant questions open; he continued to disagree with Lampl-de Groot's masculine definition of the preoedipal girl and with her concept of a normative negative-oedipus phase (p. 279). These ideas had by then been fully endorsed by Freud. Of this Fenichel indicates no awareness, and he continues to ascribe the negative oedipal thesis to Lampl-de Groot alone (p. 279n). Yet he could not have overlooked Freud's clearly expressed agreement with her, especially since Freud, after endorsing her position, explicitly took note of Fenichel's 1930 rejection of it (see Freud, 1931, p. 242). Fenichel's only acknowledged disagreement with Freud concerns the masculine nature of the preoedipal girl and the phallic nature of the clitoris. While demurring on this point, Fenichel appears not to recognize that this is a key issue in the debate. Since Horney and Jones never denied primary penis envy, and Freud granted its later defensive reinforcement, arguments about their relative strength should not have proved insuperable, except insofar as they related to the question whether the girl was psychologically in effect a castrated boy, or whether there was such a thing as 'primary femininity.'

Jones' (1935) final summation on the subject may serve to re-capitulate the implications of the two antagonistic positions. Refer-ring to his view that oedipal feelings arise spontaneously in girls, who may then temporarily take flight in a phallic position, he continues:

> This view seems to me more in accord with the ascertainable facts, and also intrinsically more probable than one which would regard her femininity to be the result of an external experience (viewing the penis). . . . I do not see a wom-an . . . as a permanently disappointed creature struggling to console herself with secondary substitutes alien to her nature [p. 495].

In contrast, Freud's (1933) final words on the subject still repeat: "We are now obliged to recognize that the little girl is a little man" (p. 118). In short, Freud continues to deny the girl any intrinsic *difference*; it is insufficiency as a man that leads her to develop a compensatory femininity. To growing evidence of early vaginal awareness Freud was to respond by doubting first its existence (1931, 228), later its possible importance (1933, p. 118).

There is no indication that Freud, while incorporating the "little man" formulation, stopped to reflect on the meaning of 'masculinity' prior to the discovery of sexual differences. He also seems oblivious to his own notion of bisexuality. In this new theory, bisexuality no longer applies where it could be presumed to be most relevant — in the earliest undifferentiated phase, which turns out to be masculine for both sexes.

To return briefly to the history: With his 1925 paper, Freud had temporarily left the field to his collaborators. In 1931, his definitive paper on "Female sexuality" was published. It was a comprehensive restatement of his earlier position, citing as evidence the work of Lampl-de Groot and Deutsch. Freud stressed the limitations of his own clinical material: "Women analysts — as for instance Jeanne Lampl-de Groot and Helene Deutsch — have been able to apprehend these facts more easily and clearly because they were helped . . . by transference to a suitable mother substitute. *Nor have I succeeded in seeing my way through any case completely*" (pp. 226–227, emphasis added). Throughout that paper, Freud carefully delineates his own observations from those he accepts from others. After disclaiming knowledge, from his *own* observations, of the sexual content of the "phallic" phase (p. 239), he later cites Lampl-de Groot's (1927) report, which he henceforth incorporates into his own formulations:

> I am in agreement with Jeanne Lampl-de Groot's . . . important
> paper. In this, the complete identity of the pre-Oedipus phase in
> boys and girls is recognized and the girl's sexual (phallic) activity
> towards her mother is affirmed and *substantiated by observa-*
> *tions*. . . . The whole development is summed up in the for-
> mula . . . of the 'negative' Oedipus complex before . . . the
> positive one [p. 241, italics added].

In contrast, Lampl-de Groot's own claims for her empirical bases
were considerably more modest (see Fliegel 1973, p. 399, Note 14).
More generally, Freud's absolute scrupulousness about his own observations is not matched by the claims he makes for his supporters.
Though he does not explicitly ascribe corroborating observations to
Helene Deutsch, these are implied for her as well — both in the
passage on "women analysts" and in his subsequent discussion of her
work. In the latter, he agrees with her 1930 views, without acknowledging that they were in turn based on *her* agreement with *his* earlier
(1925) views.[12]

Conspicuously, Freud does not mention that the papers he now
cites as the clinical foundation for important parts of his thesis came
in response to his own 1925 paper. The editors of the *Standard Edition*
twice call attention to what they regard as a curious omission in the
1931 paper: they note that in referring to various papers published in
the interval "he seems to treat them as though these papers had
arisen spontaneously and not, as was clearly the case, as a reaction to
his own . . . paper of 1925 — to which, indeed, he makes no reference whatever" (p. 223, editor's note; see also p. 240, Note 2).

The final two paragraphs of that paper are the only place where he
discusses the formulations of Horney and Jones in print. He dis-
misses them both, but this time acknowledges differences with
Horney. His dismissal of Jones is rather curt. Jones was to claim in
his next (1933) paper that in his criticism of Horney, Freud had not
adequately understood her position:

> Freud, in criticizing Karen Horney describes her view as being
> that the girl . . . *regresses* to the (deutero)-phallic stage. So sure
> is he that the earliest (clitoris) stage can only be a phallic one.
> But this is just one of the questions at issue. . . . And it is a

---

[12]To compound matters, Freud also refers to Deutsch's earlier work,
which had common features with Horney's, and in effect retracts it for
her — on the grounds that she had been working on mistaken assumptions:
"In her earlier book (1925) the author. . . . [continued] to apply the
Oedipus pattern to the pre-Oedipus phase . . ." (p. 242).

question to be discussed. . . . The clitoris is after all part of the
female genitals. . . . For all these reasons . . . the question of
the alleged clitoric and therefore masculine primacy of the
female infant may well be kept in suspense . . . [pp. 470–471].

This unheeded plea by Jones marks the beginning of the end of the
Great Debate. Freud's 1931 paper effectively closed the discussion,
at least in print. Fenichel (1934) and Jones (1935) each made an
attempt to keep the questions open longer, but after a while they too
kept their peace. Horney, of course, soon went her own way and for
some decades became a nonperson in the mainstream literature (see
Fliegel, 1973, pp. 401–402). The effect of that new schism, along
with the growing controversies around Melanie Klein, was to pol-
iticize the issues even more.

The Historical Setting

Writing on this topic in 1973, I speculated on some special factors
that may have contributed to Freud's 1925 hypothesis hardening into
dogma, and with so little empirical support:

> Freud, threatened in his survival, shaken in his trust in his
> closest collaborators, worried about the cohesion of the psycho-
> analytic movement and the survival of his life's work, re-
> sponded to the "alien thoughts" emanating from Horney and
> then Jones as a threat to the integrity of his theory. He reacted
> with what was perhaps the most dogmatic stand of his career,
> despite an often reiterated awareness of limited insight and
> understanding in this area [p. 406].

While those factors may have played a part, further study of Freud's
interactions with his followers suggests that, ill or well, he was often
inhospitable to "alien thoughts" or to others' taking the lead in matters of fundamental theory.

Whether or not Freud's illness affected his own stance in the
debate, it is likely to have played a part in its aftermath among his
followers. Their manifold and complicated reactions to Freud's cancer, as described in some incidental remarks by Siegfried Bernfeld
(1962, pp. 466–467), make it easier to understand how most of
Freud's followers — the leading authorities in the field for the next
generation — accepted so quickly his strange new insights as received
truths. Neither Jones nor Fenichel were to have much impact, nor
would the issues remain openly recognized as controversial.

THERAPEUTIC IMPLICATIONS

The opposing views carry therapeutic implications. Freud's position is discussed in "Analysis terminable and interminable" (1937):

> We often have the impression that with the wish for a penis and the masculine protest we have penetrated all the psychological strata and reached bedrock, and that thus our activities are at an end. This is probably true, since for the psychical field, the biological field does in fact play the part of underlying bedrock. The repudiation of femininity can be nothing else than a biological fact, a part of the great riddle of sex [p. 252].

If penis envy and "the repudiation of femininity" are regarded as biologically irreducible "bedrock," there can be no purpose to looking beyond them, and all that can be offered is resigned acceptance. Yet, if explored, penis envy may be found to screen other early losses and privations (as Freud recognized in other contexts), deeper feminine wishes (as urged by Jones and Horney), and developmental failures in other areas.

This last point was demonstrated in a case report by Zetzel (1965, pp. 106 ff.). Her illuminating discussion broke new ground in this area. More recently, it was developed further by Grossman and Stewart (1976), who presented two cases to illustrate their views of penis envy "as the manifest content of a symptom that needs analysis, rather than as 'bedrock' . . ." (p. 211). Their case reports were on the re-analyses of two women patients, whose first analyses demonstrate clearly that the clinical situation is not impervious to distortion due to theoretical misconceptions.

Claims for such imperviousness are sometimes made. For example, Barglow and Schaefer (1976) dismiss concerns about analysts' attitudes' intruding into their interventions; they confidently assert that "psychoanalysis, after all, is not an ideology . . ." (p. 410). This glosses over the important question of where objectivity ends and ideology begins; it can be argued that despite striving for neutrality, analysts' theoretical convictions guide their interventions. In the very same volume, Stoller (1976b) points to the therapeutic implications of the varying positions and concludes: "We find that a theoretical issue is likely to become a living pressure in the analyses of women" (p. 75). Similarly, Serebriany (1976), reporting on a "Dialogue" on the subject held at the 1975 London Congress, notes:

> Regarding countertransference . . . the way in which the analyst solved, on a personal level, his own conflict with the archa-

ic mother imago, is vital . . . since this particular point is later to weigh on his theoretical standpoints and can make itself felt in concepts such as femininity equated to "castrated" or "incomplete" sex [p. 313].

THE QUIESCENT INTERVAL

After Horney's defection, published criticisms of Freud's theories of femininity all but disappeared within the mainstream. There were exceptions — each decade saw renewed attempts by prominent authors to confront the more doubtful aspects of Freud's position. These included Jacobson (1937), Zilboorg (1944), Greenacre (1950), Zetzel (1965), and Stoller (1968). With the exception of the last author, whose work helped initiate the current discussions, their impact was slight, their views largely ignored. On the whole, the literature reflected neither continued controversy nor awareness of past disagreements.

The published literature, however, did not fully represent the range of attitudes among Freudian analysts during this period; a dubious theory did not completely dominate clinical practice, though it no doubt had impact and with individual practitioners might have been decisive. There was also another current, carried by an oral tradition, at variance with the prevailing literature and considerably more benign. Describing the then current situation just over a decade ago, I wrote:

> Many analysts convey the impression that what is written on the topic does not accurately reflect their current views. Thus, to take one example, not many analysts would now view masochism . . . as the inevitable concomitant of normal adult femininity. . . . Similarly, few analysts would expect women to regard the acceptance of a generalized passivity and of feelings of inferiority as suitable therapeutic goals for themselves. Yet a reading of the standard literature on the subject could easily convey just such notions. We thus observe a curious phenomenon, namely . . . a difference between contemporary attitudes and the standard literature. This split is . . . striking . . . [1973, p. 385].

A brief example may illustrate the kinds of notions that until recently permeated the literature: Hanns Sachs writes on the feminine "ideal": "The woman . . . does not attain a superego at all unless the necessary renunciation of her claim to the penis leads her to accepting deprivation as a lifelong ideal" (1929, p. 50).

CURRENT STATUS OF FREUD'S
THEORY OF FEMININITY

Today, with accumulating contrary empirical evidence increasingly reflected in contemporary formulations, it seems unlikely that the pattern of official adherence to dogma would be revived. Yet active interest in this area of theory is two-sided. Along with attempted revisions, some significant countercurrents may also be observed. This section attempts to sketch in the range of current formulations in their relation to available evidence, on one hand, and to the historic controversy, on the other.

First, a few comments on the nature of the evidence and of the formulations themselves: the data derive both from direct observations of children and from clinical reports; each of these sources presents its own difficulties and limitations, and the findings of both must be viewed with caution, especially if broad generalizations are to be drawn from them. For their part, the formulations vary greatly in the degree of universality claimed for them. The question of universal applicability becomes one of the issues examined, since current viewpoints differ on whether a single developmental pattern applies to all girls.

Contemporary discussions sometimes lose sight of the fact that Freud's posited developmental sequence was meant to be normative, that is, invariably applicable to normal feminine development; whether or not one might find something resembling it in any one case was never at issue. In it, to recapitulate, the initially masculine girl develops "negative oedipal" wishes towards the mother; these are relinquished, along with masturbation, upon the discovery of sexual differences ("castration"); the girl then turns to the father — at first with the wish to be given a penis, which is transformed into a wish for a child within a positive oedipal constellation; the last step marks the achievement of femininity. Consistent with this theory, as Freud clearly indicated, was the absence of inner genital awareness in childhood (the vagina to be discovered at puberty) or of feminine maternal wishes prior to the completion of the above transformations. The various steps in this postulated sequence have recently been subject to intense scrutiny.

In what follows, a sampling of current research findings bearing on these propositions leads to a discussion of the various resulting conceptualizations. Such a split in the presentation of current work is necessary because similar observations sometimes lead to very different conclusions. However, since inferences and interpretations are often intermingled with reported observations, there will be some departures from this intended format.

A Sampling of the Evidence

On a number of points, the results of observational studies converge and are fairly clearcut. Observers agree that girls cannot accurately be described as "masculine" in earliest childhood, nor can the early genital ("phallic") phase be properly described as such, since self-stimulation often includes the opening to the vagina (Barnett, 1968, Kestenberg, 1975; Galenson and Roiphe, 1976; Kleeman, 1976); self-stimulation does not generally cease in the oedipal phase (Barnett, 1968; Kleeman, 1976) nor during latency (Barnett, 1968; Clower, 1976); maternal interest is shown early preoedipally (Kestenberg, 1975; Kleeman, 1976); and an instance of an explicit wish for a baby *prior* to indications of castration anxiety was noted in a careful study by Parens, Pollock, Stern, and Kramer (1976, p. 102). Kleeman reports preoedipal turning towards the father, with girls showing such attachment earlier than boys (1976, p. 17).

These findings contradict directly many of Freud's assumptions; they tend to invalidate Freud's central postulate, that in girls the positive oedipal constellation develops secondarily, out of the castration complex. By implication they also challenge the idea of a negative oedipal phase regularly preceding the positive — the centerpiece of the old controversy.

As a dynamic concept representing wishes and fantasies, the negative-oedipal phase is not accessible to direct observation; however, predicated as it is on the girl's assumed masculinity, it might be expected to be dropped as a normative concept along with that assumption. This is by no means always the case. What makes this concept inaccessible to observation also makes it relatively immune to disproof, and several authors who find no support for the notion of initial masculinity nevertheless attempt to retain a universal negative oedipal phase. For example, Moore does so "for heuristic reasons" (1976, p. 292); Kestenberg (1975), by inserting still additional steps into Freud's postulated sequence; Galenson (1976) somewhat ambiguously infers a negative oedipal phase from her and Roiphe's observations.

In her report on a 1974 panel on "The Psychology of Women," Galenson (1976) acknowledges that Kleeman's observations are similar to those in her own and Roiphe's studies; she indicates, however, "differences in interpretations of these findings" (p. 148). At first glance, these "differences in interpretations" are a bit puzzling, since they consist of conjectures about the contents of a surmised masturbation fantasy in a 15-month-old child: "Galenson and Roiphe have stressed that . . . the genital manipulation that emerges . . . between the fifteenth and eighteenth month is connected at its onset with erotic thoughts and feelings concerning the mother. . . ." And what is this conjecture based on? "Galenson cited the use of soft toys and transitional-object blankets . . . as evidence for a maternal component of the fantasy" (p. 148). This inferred fantasy is evidently meant to represent a precursor of the negative-oedipus-preceding-the-positive tenet of Freud's theory. Indeed, in her discussion, Galenson goes on to assert that "These findings tend to substantiate Freud's position. . . ." (p. 148). Such "substantiation" is achieved at the expense of the internal logic of his theory, since these observers also find a quality of femininity emerging from the beginning of life.[13]

Disregard for the inner coherence of Freud's conception can be found with some regularity in contemporary writing. Kestenberg (1975), who observed very early parenting wishes in children of both sexes, posits for the girl an early maternal phase, which is expressed through doll play (pp. 26–27). She also finds evidence of early inner-genital awareness and differs from Freud on the girl's initial masculinity. Yet beyond this, she retains Freud's developmental sequence intact and resolves the inner contradiction by interposing additional steps in the girl's path towards femininity. In Kestenberg's

---

[13]In their subsequent work, Roiphe and Galenson (1981) again affirm the correctness of "Freud's original position" on the crucial role of penis envy in feminine development (p. 285). Space will not permit an attempt to disentangle selective observations, "findings," conjectures, inferences, interpretations, and generalized conclusions in this work. Mayer (1983), in a generally appreciative review of the 1981 volume, nevertheless raises some serious questions in her thoughtful discussion of all these issues (see pp. 366–368). Roiphe and Galenson's careful presentation of the physical and mechanical aspects of their research design is not matched by their treatment of the data. These authors' reported findings have varied over time (see Fliegel, 1982, p. 25, Note'a'); their generalized conclusions have remained invariably fixed.

theory, the girl, at around age three to four, discovers that her doll is not a live baby, and reacts with depression, guilt, and fantasies of having killed her doll (pp. 16 and 47);[14] she consequently represses both her maternal and inner-genital feelings and at that point enters Freud's masculine phallic negative-oedipal phase (pp. 18 and 47); the sequence thereafter follows Freud. Thus, while Galenson preserved Freud's sequence by transposing it to infancy, Kestenberg advances it to begin at age three or four. Both authors generalize their observations to *the girl*, much as Freud did originally.

Moore (1976), after considering a number of studies, concludes that both Freud's notion of the girl's initial masculinity and the clitoral-vaginal transfer theory are untenable (p. 289); he nevertheless proposes to retain the negative-oedipal phase as a normative concept, asserting that "a more positive oedipal attachment would require a fuller development of her internal as well as external representations. This can come only after puberty" (p. 292). The implication here, that the girl's positive-oedipal phase is deferred until puberty, makes a most drastic revision in Freud's theory of infantile sexuality — for the sake of preserving its weakest component.

It is evident that available observational data allow much room for inferences, preconceptions, and biases in their interpretation. Yet there are as many difficulties in attempting to confirm or deny a *normative* theory through clinical research. If a particular clinical situation seems to confirm it, that would not prove its universality; failure to confirm would mean as little, since no analysis can ever claim to be absolutely complete. It was in an attempt to overcome some of these difficulties that Anna Freud instigated the establishment of the Hampstead Clinic Research File. The purpose, as she described it, was "to construct . . . something of a 'collective analytic memory,' i.e., a storehouse of analytic material . . . transcending the narrow confines of individual experience" (Preface to Bolland and Sandler, 1965, p. x).

Edgcumbe (1976) and her coworkers made use of that file for as systematic a clinical test of Freud's hypotheses as might be obtainable. Culling the pooled clinical data derived from the child analyses conducted at the Hampstead Clinic, they found that the negative

---

[14]The "death of the doll" fantasy at age three or four is regarded by Kestenberg as part of a normative sequence. The notion that until that age the doll is regularly regarded as a live baby is called into question by the observations of Parens *et al.* (1976), who found that even at age two-and-one-half "A real baby is treated very differently now from a doll" (p. 106).

oedipus category was seldom used; in three of the eight cases where it *was* used, it was to note the paucity or absence of such manifestations. In all eight cases, an examination of the original data suggested that the relationship to the mother was actually preoedipal; on that basis, Edgcumbe concludes that if the concept of a negative oedipal phase is seldom used, ". . . this is because the concept does not accurately fit the observable clinical evidence . . ." (p. 57). Thus, on this key issue in the original controversy, Freud's theory is not supported by pooled data from child analyses, which would be in the best position to supply confirming evidence.

The Conceptualizations

Turning from this sampling of reported findings to the range of conceptualizations offered: the convergence of direct observational and clinical findings is by no means reflected in a similar convergence of the resulting conclusions. The conceptualizations range from Stoller's (1968, 1976) theory of primary femininity, which virtually reverses Freud's theory of phallic primacy, to Nagera's (1975) unqualified reiteration of Freud's theory. A step even beyond Nagera is Lacan's (1958) transposition of "Freudian doctrine" into his own language — one quite impervious to disproof. Lacan's ideas have been popularized by Mitchell (1974).

Barglow and Schaefer (1976) regret that "published criticism of the psychoanalytic formulations of female psychology fail to make the crucial distinction between Freud's theory and contemporary psychoanalysis" (p. 395). In this, they show no recognition that the fault lies partly in contemporary psychoanalysis itself, which as a whole has failed to make that distinction clearly enough. Further, "contemporary psychoanalysis" speaks in many voices: Stoller and Nagera, Galenson, and Kleeman are all part of contemporary psychoanalysis.

Barglow and Schaefer themselves (1976), though they specify their own differences with some of Freud's ideas, follow the common practice of dismissing prior criticism both by analysts and by feminist writers (some of whose objections are in fact sustained by current work). They rely on Mitchell's (1974) dictum that feminist writers all "deny the unconscious," though they go on, quite correctly, to question Mitchell's own notion of the unconscious as representing a considerable modification of Freud's (p. 394).

Barglow and Schaefer (1976) regard Horney's ideas on the phallic phase as "a concession to Freud's anatomical and physiological emphases" (p. 398) and note that she later abandoned them. Yet the distinction Horney proposed in her early work (between "primary" narcissistic and later defensive phallic manifestations) figures significantly in current reformulations. It also formed the nucleus of the subsequent "Freud–Jones" debate and was thus instrumental in codifying this aspect of Freudian theory, now so laboriously being reexamined. In their dismissive attitude towards the early dissenters, Barglow and Schaefer are fairly representative. Though Horney and Jones are now commonly cited, it is often to point to their less plausible (biological or cultural) assumptions, rather than those views that have since acquired new pertinence.[15] This tendency to dismiss the first analytic dissenters, while at times advancing ideas similar to theirs, compounds the ambiguities in this area.

An example of the reemergence of an idea very similar to Horney's but under a slightly different name may be found in Edgcumbe and Burgner's (1975) paper on "The Phallic-Narcissistic Phase"; it is subtitled: "A differentiation between preoedipal and oedipal aspects of phallic development." The distinction they make is very similar to the one advanced by Horney (1924) and Jones (1927), differentiating primary narcissistic (preoedipal) penis envy from later defensive reactions to oedipal anxieties (to which Horney subsequently added the effects of cultural factors). Edgcumbe and Burgner use the term "phallic-narcissistic" (a term suggested to them by Anna Freud) to denote the earlier phase. Their description of that phase shares with Horney's primary penis envy the same emphasis on exhibitionistic, narcissistic, and scoptophilic components.[16] Edgcumbe and Burgner differ explicitly with Mahler (and implicitly with Freud) in their placement of the formation of sexual identity in that earlier, preoedipal phase; for Mahler, sexual identity hinges on the resolution of oedipal conflicts — a position clearly more compatible with Freud's than is Edgcumbe and Burgner's (pp. 165–166).

The similarities with earlier conceptions are not recognized by Edgcumbe and Burgner, nor is there a reference to Horney in that paper. In her subsequent paper on the negative oedipal phase,

---

[15]Those authors who are eager to prove that Horney and Jones were in even greater error than Freud may cite either their biological assumptions (Mitchell, 1974; Grossman, 1976) or Horney's one-sided cultural emphasis (Barglow and Schaefer, 1976) as representing their total contribution.

[16]The main difference between the "phallic-narcissistic" phase and Jones' and Horney's conception is in its name; Jones especially questioned the appropriateness of the "phallic" designation for preoedipal girls.

Edgcumbe (1976) does include a brief section on past "Dissenting viewpoints" (p. 59) with references to Fenichel, Horney, and Jones. Even there, Horney's 1924 paper — the most relevant to the author's work — is not included (perhaps because it predates Freud's 1925 paper, still regarded by many as the opening of the debate).

In the second paper, Edgcumbe suggests that "it might . . . be more appropriate to describe the early phallic phase as narcissistic, for both sexes, rather than as negative oedipal for the girl (and positive oedipal for the boy)" (1976, p. 58). She emphasizes the distinction between preoedipal "preference for mother over father" (p. 48) and the classical concept, where masculine attitudes "resemble in all respects those of the boy in his positive oedipal phase" (p. 57). Fenichel, incidentally, in rejecting this normative concept, repeatedly pointed to the same distinctions (1930, p. 201; 1934, p. 279); thus, because of past failures to integrate corrective viewpoints, analysts seem destined repeatedly to rediscover the same issues and contradictions.

Judging by some of the references to the negative-oedipus in the current literature, it may be worth stressing that even a diffusely eroticized relation to the mother would not per se imply a negative Oedipus in the classical sense. As Jones and Fenichel both emphasized, that concept implied a fantasy of the girl using the clitoris as an organ of penetration, or, in Fenichel's (1930) words, "the little girl really begins as a little boy and desires a penis in order to have coitus with the mother" (p. 200).

Edgcumbe (1976) is clear in her conclusions: "Rather than postulating that recognition of her lack of a penis forces the girl to abandon a masculine position for a feminine one, we suggest a less biased view that awareness . . . of sexual differences . . . aids both boys and girls in consolidating their sexual identity" (p. 59). Such clarity is not the rule. Many authors are more ambiguous, and some tend to explain away, rather than incorporate, new evidence. Moore (1976), for example, after weighing a number of studies and conceding considerable deviation from Freud's expectations, nevertheless concludes that in his theories of femininity, Freud "was right about most of them" (p. 298). Grossman (1976), in an ambiguous paper purporting to recast the terms of the discussion, explains that "in offering this way of thinking . . . I have merely dressed some of Freud's old principles in new formulations" (p. 303). The impulse to "dress" Freud's theory rather than revise it where necessary is evident in a significant segment of the literature.

Galenson and Roiphe on the one hand and Kleeman on the other, though working with very similar observations, reach opposite conclusions on a number of issues. According to Galenson and Roiphe (1976): "penis envy and the feminine castration complex do exert crucial influences upon feminine development" (p. 55). For Kleeman (1976), on the other hand, "penis envy and feelings of inferiority are relegated to a less universal and less *necessary* place in the onset of femininity" (p. 18).

They also differ in the degree of universality they strive for in their formulations. Galenson and Roiphe seek a normative theory, while Kleeman states explicitly: "Observation denies the single routine pattern Freud claimed to be universal and which he felt answered so many issues" (p. 18). At a more abstract level, they differ in their degree of reliance on instinct theory. Galenson and Roiphe write: "Freud's original position that sexual drive organization exerts an exemplary role . . . remains a valid one . . . (p. 53).[17] Contrast this with Kleeman: "Observation suggests that object-relations theory is more primary than instinct theory in this regard" (p. 18).

Object Relations and Drives — New Conceptions

Stoller (1968, 1976b, 1979a), one of the few authors to recognize the common ground between current reformulations and earlier dissents, arrives at a relatively new and increasingly influential conception of the process of sexual differentiation — one that departs considerably from *all* previous views. He offers the concept of a "core" gender identity to designate the conviction the child acquires early in life of belonging to one or the other sex. This conviction is strongly influenced by parental attitudes and expectations. The core identity is seen as evolving with the child's emergence from the symbiotic phase: for girls, it continues the primary identification with the mother; for boys, it requires "disidentifying" from the mother (Greenson, 1968). In Stoller's conception, the girl's gender identity flows more naturally out of the primary identification of the symbiotic phase. The boy, in order to acquire and maintain his masculine core identity, must establish a firm and strongly defended differentiation from his primary object. This contrasts with Freud's view, which saw the establishment of a feminine identity as the more com-

---

[17]While the authors' wish to reassert "Freud's original position" cannot be doubted, it is less clear how "the exemplary role" of drive organization fits into their thinking in this respect. For Freud, innate drives give rise to initial *masculinity*; femininity comes about through an *experiential* factor ("viewing the penis," as Jones (1935) put it).

plicated task, involving a change of object and, Freud thought, a change of sexual orientation as well.

Whatever the girl's advantages in having her gender more firmly rooted in her primary identification, there are also costs. Such unchallenged primary identification may mean greater difficulty in establishing autonomy, independence, and a clearly delineated self-representation. A number of authors stress the importance of the girl's struggle to emancipate herself from the archaic preoedipal mother. That struggle may intensify the girl's penis envy, since she regards the boy's distinguishing physical attributes as helpful to him in gaining separateness (Chasseguet-Smirgel, 1970). In this view, issues of identification and self-object differentiation become crucial to understanding the psychology of sex differences, while drive considerations take a secondary place.

Freud's theories on femininity are currently being reaffirmed from opposite vantage points as regards the role of biological drives. There are those who, in contrast to Galenson and Roiphe, would define psychoanalysis as a strictly psychological system, concerned solely with symbolic expression and especially with the function of language in defining psychological meanings. This point of view was first articulated by Lacan (1958). Though critical of Freud's (and especially his followers') "scientism," Lacan nevertheless went on to reaffirm Freud's universal generalizations, rephrased as "Freudian doctrine" (p. 283), immune to the hazards of empirical refutation. Lacan and, following him, Mitchell (1974) have concentrated their critiques of Horney and Jones on their biological assumptions, while all but absolving Freud, the author of the now famous "bedrock" of any undue "biologism." Similar ideas have since been expressed by Moore (1976) and Grossman (1976). The question of who out-biologized whom deserves to be examined, since it has become one of the focal points of the current reassessments.

Biologism and Metaphor

Paradoxically, this is an area of both growing current concensus and most clearly focused controversy. Stoller's empirical studies, as well as Lacan's antiempirical reinterpretations of Freud point in the same direction: that the old debate, in the terms it was couched, did not do justice to the complex interplay of social and biological factors and, in particular, to the crucial role of earliest object relations in establishing sexual differentiation. Though Jones and Horney contributed many valuable insights, Jones' "a woman is born" (1935, p. 485) would not withstand current scrutiny any better than Freud's "biological fact" of repudiated femininity.

There is this to be said for those who insist that Freud knew better: Indeed he did — most of the time — but he did not apply that understanding to his theory of femininity. From his earliest pre-analytic days, Freud grappled with the relation of constitutional (i.e., biological) to "incidental" (i.e., environmental and social) factors. In 1896, he proposed the idea of what he was later to call a "comple-mental series," that is, a relationship wherein the same effects may obtain if slight "loading" of one factor is compensated by heavier loading of the other (p. 147). This may remain as close an approx-imation to the existing state of affairs and, simultaneously, as good a statement of the limits of our knowledge as is attainable. On the intrinsically insoluble problem of separating definitively constitu-tional from environmental influences, current data also leave an area of indeterminacy. Stoller, though he sees social factors in the form of initial sex assignment as generally overruling biology in gender for-mation (1968), nevertheless presents instances where the reverse is true (1976a, 1979b). Though the limits of what is known may ex-pand, an irreducible area where the issues remain indeterminate is likely to remain. Freud's idea of a complemental series would de-scribe this situation of residual uncertainty perfectly; yet Freud spe-cifically exempted an disputed issues around femininity from the workings of his principle of complementarity.

Addressing once again the derivation of penis envy in adults, Freud (1933) acknowledged that the issue was controversial and, further, that in such cases he generally invoked the idea of a "com-plemental series"; he went on, however, to specify that in this in-stance he favored "decidedly" the "infantile" factor (pp. 125–126), that is, the presumed invariable psychological effects of perceived anatomy. This suspension of the "complemental" principle becomes necessary, starting with Freud's assumption of the girl's initial mas-culinity. A universal factor would be required to reverse the original biological mishap of the infant-girl, who is "a little man." What is confusing about Freud's position is that while he rejects biology as a determinant of femininity, he simultaneously affirms it for mas-culinity (for both sexes); in addition, he treats an experiental factor (i.e., "viewing the penis") as no less immutable in its effects than might be any biological given.[18]

---

[18]Phylogenetic inheritance, occasionally advanced by Freud, could help account for such universality. Mitchell (1974) uses that idea freely. Op-posed as she is to "biologizing," Mitchell appears unaware that in relying on a theory of inherited mental contents, biology is being replaced by . . . biol-ogy; Lamarkian theory, though scientifically doubtful, is a theory within biology (see also Stoller, 1979a, p. 44, on inherited memories.

Some authors (beginning with Lacan) who discount Freud's evident biologisms in this area as misunderstandings, at the same time attempt to preserve his developmental theory of gender formation by construing it as metaphorical. In so doing, they claim to be closer to Freud's true meaning than those who assume that Freud meant what he said. Aside from disregarding his outstanding command of language and capacity for communicating his ideas, such a gloss on his theory ignores both Freud's commitment to empiricism and his quest for universal principles. Metaphors may or may not be apt, but they are certainly not designed to articulate normative theories or universal generalizations.

CONCLUSION

The ongoing reexamination of Freud's theory of femininity remains under the shadow of the historic controversy. At present, two opposing currents may be observed: there is a good deal of continuing research in this area, some of which is used to confront directly the difficulties with Freud's writings on women; there are also, however, continued efforts to salvage everything possible of Freud's formulations, even if at the expense of internal logic (as when his most clearly untenable premises are discarded, while concepts based on the discarded assumptions are retained). There are, in addition, attempts to lend his theories greater plausibility by construing them in metaphorical terms, disregarding both his clear intended meaning and his lifelong quest for universal and empirically testable principles. Elusive as this goal may be, Freud's commitment to it cannot be doubted; it is in fact demonstrated in his manner of presenting his proposed normative theory in 1925.

The attempts to preserve at all costs Freud's developmental theories of femininity are potentially more damaging to Freudian psychoanalysis than would be the recognition and acknowledgment that this area (which he admittedly found obscure) was one where his genius encountered its limits. By recognizing these limitations rather than tinkering with the weakest component of Freud's thought as though the whole structure of psychoanalysis rested on it, the way could be cleared for redirecting energy and attention to those aspects of his rich heritage that have undiminished relevance to the understanding of both men and women.

REFERENCES

Abraham, H. C., & Freud, E. L., eds. (1965), *A Psycho-Analytic Dialogue: The Letter of Sigmund Freud and Karl Abraham.* New York: Basic Books.

Barglow, P., & Schaefer, M. (1976). A new female psychology? In: *Female Psychology*, ed. H. P. Blum. New York: International Universities Press, 1977, pp. 393–438.

Barnett, M. C. (1968). "I can't" versus "he won't": Further considerations of the psychological consequences of the anatomic and physiological differences between the sexes. *J. Amer. Psychoanal. Assn.*, 16:588–600.

Bernfeld, S. (1962). On psychoanalytic training. *Psychoanal. Quart.*, 31:453–482.

Brunswick, R. M. (1940). The preoedipal phase of libido development. In: *The Psychoanalytic Reader*, ed. Robert Fliess. New York: International Universities Press, 1948, pp. 261–284.

Buxbaum, E. (1951). Freud's dream interpretation in the light of his letters to Fliess. *The Yearbook of Psychoanalysis*, 8:56–72, 1952.

Chasseguet-Smirgel, J. (1970). Feminine guilt and the Oedipus complex. In: *Female Sexuality*, ed. J. Chasseguet-Smirgel. Ann Arbor: University of Michigan Press, pp. 94–134.

Chodorow, N. (1978). *The Reproduction of Mothering*. Berkeley: University of California Press.

Clower, V. (1976). Theoretical implications in current views of masturbation in latency girls. In: *Female Psychology*, ed. H. P. Blum. New York: International Universities Press, 1977, pp. 109–125.

Deutsch, H. (1930). The significance of masochism in the mental life of women. In: *The Psychoanalytic Reader*, ed. R. Fliess. New York: International Universities Press, 1948, pp. 195–207.

_____ (1932). On female homosexuality. In: *The Psychoanalytic Reader*, ed. R. Fliess. New York: International Universities Press, 1948, pp. 208–230.

Edgcumbe, R. (1976). Some comments on the concept of the negative oedipal phase in girls. *The Psychoanalytic Study of the Child*, 31:35–61. New Haven: Yale University Press.

_____ and Burgner, M. (1975). The phallic-narcissistic phase. *The Psychoanalytic Study of the Child*, 30:161–180. New Haven: Yale University Press.

Erikson, E. H. (1954). The dream specimen in psychoanalysis. *J. Amer. Psychoanal. Assn.*, 2:5–56.

Fenichel, O. (1930). The pregenital antecedents of the Oedipus complex. In: *The Collected Papers of Otto Fenichel, First Series*, ed. H. Fenichel & D. Rapaport. New York: Norton, 1953, pp. 181–203.

_____ (1934). Further light upon the preoedipal phase in girls. In: *The Collected Papers of Otto Fenichel, First Series*, ed. H. Fenichel & D. Rapaport. New York: Norton, 1953, pp. 241–288.

Fliegel, Z. O. (1973). Feminine psychosexual development in Freudian theory: A historical reconstruction. *Psychoanal. Quart.*, 42:385–409.

_____ (1982). Half a century later: Current status of Freud's controversial views on women. *Psychoanal. Rev.* 69:7–28.

Freud, A. (1965). Preface to J. Bolland & J. Sandler, *The Hampstead Psychoanalytic Index*. New York: International Universities Press.

Freud, S. (1896). Heredity and the aetiology of the neuroses. *Standard Edition*, 3:143–156. London: Hogarth Press, 1962.

―――― (1905). Three essays on the theory of sexuality. *Standard Edition*, 7:135–243. London: Hogarth Press, 1953.

―――― (1908). On the sexual theories of children. *Standard Edition*, 9:209–226. London: Hogarth Press, 1959.

―――― (1923a). The ego and the id. *Standard Edition*, 19:12–66. London: Hogarth Press, 1961.

―――― (1923b). The infantile genital organization of the libido. *Standard Edition*, 19:141–153. London: Hogarth Press, 1961.

―――― (1924). The dissolution of the Oedipus complex. *Standard Edition*, 19:173–179. London: Hogarth Press, 1961.

―――― (1925). Some psychological consequences of the anatomical distinction between the sexes. *Standard Edition*, 19:248–258. London: Hogarth Press, 1961.

―――― (1926). On the question of lay analysis. *Standard Edition*, 20:183–254. London: Hogarth Press, 1959.

―――― (1931). Female sexuality. *Standard Edition*, 21:225–243. London: Hogarth Press, 1961.

―――― (1933). New introductory lectures on psycho-analysis. *Standard Edition*, 22:7–182. London: Hogarth Press, 1964.

―――― (1937). Analysis terminable and interminable. *Standard Edition*, 23:216–253. London: Hogarth Press, 1964.

―――― (1940). An outline of psychoanalysis. *Standard Edition*, 23:144–207. London: Hogarth Press, 1964.

Galenson, E. (1976). Panel report on the psychology of women. *J. Amer. Psychoanal. Assn.*, 24:141–160.

―――― & Roiphe, H. (1976). Some suggested revisions concerning early female development. In: *Female Psychology*, ed. H. P. Blum. New York: International Universities Press, 1977, pp. 29–57.

Greenacre, P. (1950). Special problems of early female sexual development. In: *Trauma, Growth, and Personality*. New York: Norton, 1952, pp. 237–258.

Greenson, R. E. (1968). Disidentifying from mother: Its special importance for the boy. In: *Explorations in Psychoanalysis*. New York: International Universities Press, 1978, pp. 305–312.

Grossman, W. I. (1976). Discussion of "Freud and female sexuality" *Internat. J. Psycho-Anal.*, 57:301–305.

―――― & Stewart, W. (1976). Penis envy: From childhood wish to developmental metaphor. In: *Female Psychology*, ed. H. P. Blum. New York: International Universities Press, 1977, pp. 193–212.

Horney, K. (1924). On the genesis of the castration complex in women. *Internat. J. Psycho-Anal.*, 5:50–65.

―――― (1926). The flight from womanhood: the masculinity complex in women as viewed by men and women. *Internat. J. Psycho-Anal.*, 7:324–339.

HD (1974). *Tribute to Freud*. Boston: Godine.

Jacobson, E. (1937). Ways of female superego formation and the female castration complex. *Psychoanal. Quart.*, 45:525–538, 1976.

Jones, E. (1927). Early development of female sexuality. In: *Papers on Psychoanalysis*. Boston: Beacon Press, 1961, pp. 438–451.

_____ (1933). The phallic phase. In: *Papers on Psychoanalysis.* Boston: Beacon Press, 1961, pp. 452–484.

_____ (1935). Early female sexuality. In: *Papers on Psychoanalysis.* Boston: Beacon Press, 1961, pp. 485–495.

_____ (1957). *The Life and Work of Sigmund Freud,* Volume III. New York: Basic Books.

Kestenberg, J. (1975). *Children and Parents: Psychoanalytic Studies in Development.* New York: Aronson.

Kleeman, J. (1976). Freud's views on early female sexuality in the light of direct child observation. In: *Female Psychology,* ed. H. P. Blum. New York: International Universities Press, 1977, pp. 3–27.

Klein, M. (1928). Early stages of the Oedipus complex. *Internat. J. Psycho-Anal.,* 9:167–180.

Lacan, J. (1958). The Signification of the phallus. In: *Ecrits: A Selection,* New York, Norton: 1977, pp. 281–291.

Lampl-de Groot, J. (1927). The evolution of the Oedipus complex in women. In: *The Psychoanalytic Reader,* ed. R. Fliess. New York: International Universities Press, pp. 180–194, 1948.

Mayer, E. L. (1983). Review of H. Roiphe & E. Galenson, *Infantile Origins of Sexual Identity. Internat. J. Psycho-Anal.,* 64:365–369.

Mitchell, J. (1974). *Psychoanalysis and Feminism.* New York: Vintage, 1975.

Moore, B. E. (1976). Freud and female sexuality: A current view. *Internat. J. Psycho-Anal.,* 57:287–300.

Nagera, H. (1975). *Female Sexuality and the Oedipus Complex.* New York: Aronson.

Parens, H., Pollock, L., Stern, J., & Kramer, S. (1976). On the girl's entry into the Oedipus complex. In: *Female Psychology,* ed. H. P. Blum. New York: International Universities Press, 1977, pp. 79–107.

Roiphe, H. & Galenson, E. (1981). *Infantile Origins of Sexual Identity.* New York: International Universities Press.

Sachs, H. (1929). One of the motive factors in the formation of the super-ego in women. *Internat. J. Psycho-Anal.,* 10:39–50.

Serebriany, R. (1976). Report on dialogue on "Freud and female sexuality." *Internat. J. Psycho-Anal.,* 57:311–313.

Stoller, R. J. (1968). *Sex and Gender: On the Development of Masculinity and Femininity.* New York: Science House.

_____ (1976a). *Sex and Gender, Vol II: The Transsexual Experiment.* New York: Aronson.

_____ (1976b). Primary femininity. In: *Female Psychology,* ed. H. P. Blum. New York: International Universities Press, 1977, pp. 59–78.

_____ (1979a). *Sexual Excitement: Dynamics of Erotic Life.* New York: Pantheon.

_____ (1979b). A contribution to the study of gender identity: Follow-up. *Internat. J. Psycho-Anal.,* 60:433–441.

Zetzel, E. (1965). The incapacity to bear depression. In: *The Capacity for Emotional Growth.* New York: International Universities Press, 1970, pp. 85–114.

Zilboorg, G. (1944). Masculine and feminine. In: *Psychoanalysis and Women,* ed. J. G. Miller. Baltimore: Penguin, 1973, pp. 96–131.

2   The Gendered Self:
A Lost Maternal Legacy

SUSAN SPIELER

> *Because he loves as man only, not as human being, for this reason there is in his sexual feeling something narrow, seeming wild, spiteful, time-bound, uneternal. . . . The girl and the woman, in their new, their own unfolding, will but in passing be imitators of masculine ways, good and bad, and repeaters of masculine professions. . . . Easygoing man . . . presumptuous and hasty undervalues what he thinks he loves. . . . Some day there will be girls and women whose name will no longer signify merely an opposite of the masculine, but something in itself. . . . This advance will change the love-experience, which is now full of error, will alter it from the ground up, reshape it into a relation that is meant to be of one human being to another, no longer of man to woman.*
> — Rainer Maria Rilke (1903/1904)

The psychoanalytic community is divided and constrained by a general adherence to dichotomous and linear theorizing. With few exceptions, psychoanalytic theorists have generally conceived of development as a linear progression from dependence to independence and have *either* focused on how people become able to relate to and love others (e.g., Freud, Mahler, Klein, Sullivan), *or* on narcissistic development, self regulation, and the striving for individual fulfillment of "creative/productive potential" (Kohut, 1984).

Psychoanalytic theory is limited both by its linearity and by several of its dichotomies. A theory that portrays development as progressing in linear fashion from merger and dependence to independence fails to address the normal syncopation of states of oneness and of separateness that more realistically characterize human experience throughout life (Silvermann, Lachmann, and Milich, 1982). A theory that conceives of separateness as the hallmark of mental health assigns a lesser place to the individual's desire and capacity to form attachments (Silverman, 1985) or to cooperate and to enjoy interdependence.[1] This skewed and artificially dichotomous vision fails to incorporate the fact that even in infancy experiences of interrelatedness alternate with experiences of differentiation (Stern, 1983). Although the importance of attachment, cooperation, and interdependence — *all qualities that are often associated with femaleness* — is widely recognized, these qualities have found little place within psychoanalytic theory.

Current infant research (e.g., Stern, 1983; Beebe, 1985) shows that infants relate to others both as differentiated objects (for purposes of "object relating") and as selfobjects[2] (for the "narcissistic" purpose of self-regulation and psychic structuralization). Just as the failure in psychoanalytic theory to encompass experiences of oneness and of separateness distorts reality, so does the failure to encompass developments in object relations and in narcissism.

The failure to encompass these experiences and strivings within a single psychoanalytic theory reveals a limitation of dichotomous thinking. The tendency to depict separation — far more than on attachment and interdependency — as a normal human striving is a limitation arising from linear thinking and a fuller representation of male concerns than of female concerns. *In its tendencies both toward linearity and toward dichotomous thinking, the structure of psychoanalytic theory is "masculine."* Although enormous strides have been made by using an essentially male approach, the neglect of a female approach limits the explanatory potential of psychoanalytic theory. *Both the structure and the content of psychoanalytic developmental theory reflect the influence of "male" thinking almost to the exclusion of "female" thinking.* Thus, on both counts, psychoanalytic theory is androcentric. "Female" thought tends to allow more of a commingling of boundaries between subject and object (Fox Keller, 1985) in contrast to the linearity and dichotomous reasoning commonly associated with male thought. Female content is more likely to focus on relational issues than on separateness (Gilligan, 1982).

Androcentrism permeates the content of Freud's theory of personality (1931, 1933). Thus, the feminine sense of self is seen as essentially crippled because it is not masculine. Freud's personal psychology seemed to interfere with his ability to recognize that girls and

---

[1]Fairbairn (1946) recognized the need for "mature dependence."

[2]Kohut (1971) introduced the concept of selfobject to discuss objects experienced as part of our self. "The expected control over such [selfobjects] is then closer to the concept of the control which a grownup expects to have over his own body and mind than to the concept of the control which he expects to have over others" (pp. 26–27).

women might not think as he did about life and sexuality. He assumed they must feel as he imagined he would, had he lacked a penis. Taking masculinity as a standard, he did not seem able to imagine women capable of valuing, in their own right, their unique sexual and reproductive capacities, and the fact of their similarity to an idealized mother who, like themselves, is female. Although he conceived of women as striving to repair the wound at "discovering" their genital "inferiority" by replacing what they lacked with babies and men to love, it is now clear (Chasseguet-Smirgel, 1964; Blum, 1977; Lerner, 1982; Mendell, 1982) that female desires to love men and to bear children are, for many women, primary, rather than compensatory.

Again taking masculinity as a standard, Freud considered the female sense of conscience inferior to that of males because it is, he claimed, insufficiently impersonal when compared with the male sense of conscious. Recent research (Gilligan, 1982) studying girls and women from their own perspective finds female moral concerns qualitatively different from those of men. One is hard put, however, to rate as inferior solutions to moral dilemmas that revolve around care and attachment, in contrast to those of men, who more commonly value abstract/impersonal moral principles (for example, the image of "blind justice"). Freud's conclusion about female conscience was androcentric. He believed that girls would never be compelled by castration anxiety to repress oedipal desires, as boys do, and that they would therefore never achieve the autonomy and strict kind of conscience he considered hallmarks of a well-structured personality. Clearly, these were, rather, hallmarks of Freud's model of *male* personality.

Freud's view of male development is also androcentric. With the "resolution" of the Oedipus complex and its reworking during adolescence, boys relinquish association with their maternal roots.[3] To reinforce their resolve, many forfeit their nurturant capacities and longings and come to experience them as unnatural. This kind of "resolution" is better understood as an early stage in a process through which the self increasingly assimilates the many contributions to its organization. Fear, disavowal, and devaluation of the feminine dimensions of the self are signs that this process of assimilation has been arrested.

Psychoanalytic tenets whose primary emphasis is on separation/individuation as a goal (Mahler, Pine, and Bergman, 1975)

---

[3]Greenson (1968) saw the "disidentification from mother" as occurring preoedipally.

signify the continued influence of androcentrism. Usually the person from whom separation is to be achieved is female. When mothers are reduced to persons from whom separation is to be accomplished, those values and qualities commonly associated with women and the female dimensions of the self are inadequately acknowledged, even devalued. A person who values separateness, autonomy, and objectivity may not do so out of defensiveness; but when adherence to these values interferes with appreciation of another value system in which caring, attachment, and interdependency are central and equally valid, the imbalance must be seen as self-protective.

The difficulty of encompassing the structures and the contents of femaleness within psychoanalytic theory is paralleled in difficulties of men and women to reconcile the pursuit of their individual fulfillment with the pleasure that is derived when one is concerned about another person. Until the 1970s, when women and men began to share more of the responsibility for the care of children and for the breadwinning, these functions had become divided along stereotypic sex role lines, with women embodying relational matters, such as care and concern for others, and men embodying narcissistic matters, such as the individualistic pursuit of goals and ambitions.

The changes in the roles of women and men have contributed to some intermingling of strivings that formerly were strictly distinct. Women, through careers, have increasingly begun to enjoy the individualistic pursuit of goals and ambitions; men, sharing the care of children, have increasingly begun to enjoy experiences of care and connection.

Because of their previous emphasis on difference (generally a male concern), men and women were often unnaturally separated from one another, limited in their ability to accept and appreciate the fundamental similarity of their concerns and to love one another as human beings as Rilke suggests. Likewise, in *their* emphasis on difference, adherents of particular psychoanalytic theories are sometimes limited in their ability to look beyond the boundaries between theories to discover the useful contributions of alternative formulations. Clearly, there are considerable differences between men and women, as there are between the major theories that shape psychoanalytic thought. While awareness of those differences can enhance exchanges between men and women and help to clarify the implications of individual theoretical contributions, however, an overemphasis on differences often serves defensive and self-restorative functions. These functions have not generally been recognized.

Self psychology offers a particularly useful perspective for analyzing ways that people maintain and restore their vulnerable selves, such as through androcentrism generally, and more specifically, through a defensive emphasis on difference. Since one of the strengths of self psychology lies in its examination of how mental activity maintains and restores self-cohesion and self esteem (Stolorow and Lachmann, 1980), some of the basic concepts of this theory will be reviewed briefly.

Kohut (1966, 1971), introduced an exploration of the "forms and transformations of narcissism" in much the same way that Freud (1905) introduced an exploration of the forms and transformations of object/instinctual life. Kohut disagreed with the previous view of narcissism as an early developmental phase from which it was hoped the healthy person would emerge able to be separate and to love others as distinct from the self. Rather, he suggested that the self must love itself and provide for its own normal narcissistic needs throughout life. Optimally, the archaic narcissism of childhood is transformed to more mature forms of narcissism.

According to Kohut, one is motivated to realize one's creative-productive potential.[4] People may be sought for assistance in realizing these goals, not necessarily as differentiated others but as selfobjects, or extensions of the self that serve narcissistic functions such as mirroring of the self's grandiosity or merger with what is strong, powerful, uplifting, and thus idealizable, to sustain one. This self needs suitable selfobjects throughout life to facilitate the fulfillment of its "creative-productive potential." When needed selfobjects are missing, as when the person does not have access to an idealized parental imago (either in the external or internal world), for example, the self may suffer developmental arrest. Narcissism is not to be renounced or outgrown. A person who strives to renounce narcissistic needs, as many in our culture do, becomes alienated from available sources of sustenance.

Cultural gender patterns are often judged in moral and political terms by those who believe that these patterns diminish human relationships and self-esteem. The tenets of self psychology encourage consideration of the ways that patterns sustain the self and the ways that they interfere with the self's ability to realize its goals. Thus, self psychology enables a nonjudgmental examination of what people need to do to maintain themselves — in this instance, why men and

---

[4]Neither self psychology nor object/instinctual theory alone succeeds in portraying the considerable tension that is often experienced by healthy men and women between individualistic desires to realize creative/productive potential and desires for mutuality and love.

women are androcentric and maintain what appear to be damaging gender patterns.

One self-maintaining function of androcentrism and of its emphasis on difference and dichotomy is to permit the fantasy that one's gender (or one's theory) is "untouched" and independent. The need to believe that one's gender is "untouched" or "uncontaminated" is a phenomenon associated more with male than with female development. Greenson (1968), for example, notes that the boy achieving a masculine identity "disidentifies from mother." Radical disidentification is not characteristic of normal female development. The male tendency to exclude women from "masculine activities" in order to protect masculine identity from the felt danger of dependency on women has been described by Dinnerstein (1976). In a sense, heroic or idealized maleness seems to be needed by many men as a protection against the potential loss of identity that mother unconsciously represents for them. Idealized maleness also serves restorative functions for women in the protection it seems to afford from vulnerability.

A belief in the purity and power of one's selfobject can enhance security and self-esteem. Just as both men and women sometimes need men and maleness to serve as idealizing selfobjects, psychoanalysts sometimes need their theories to serve similar selfobject functions. Just as men and women find it difficult to tolerate flaws in the people they have idealized, psychoanalysts may have difficulty tolerating flaws in the theories they have idealized. When this intolerance is extreme, and when idealization becomes *over*idealization, it interferes with the acknowledgment of interdependency, a female concern. Reliance on overidealization enables one to maintain an illusion of self-sufficiency as long as identification can be maintained with the overidealized selfobject. Moreover, overidealization requires that boundaries be clearly maintained (a male concern) either between overidealized maleness and undervalued femaleness — by some men and women — or between one's overidealized theory and the others — by some psychoanalysts.

Men and women who are unable to value the female dimensions of themselves often rely, in different ways, on overidealized men (e.g., Superman) or on symbols of maleness, such as physical strength or objectivity. Psychoanalytic theory, a creation of contemporary Western men and women,[5] reflects the overidealization of maleness in

---

[5]Despite the facts that in Eastern cultures women are also the primary caregivers and men are also overvalued, there is evidence (Roland, 1980) that selves are organized differently.

both its structure and its content. Therefore, just as men and women are limited in their ability to value femaleness, psychoanalytic theory too is limited in its ability to form positive representations of women, the content and structure of female thought, and the feminine dimensions of the selves of men and women. The overvaluation of men and maleness represents an unconscious effort to promote security and self-esteem. *Maleness has become an unconscious talisman or selfobject.* Maleness is often used to cope with disappointments in the self and in both parents for being fallible, vulnerable, limited, and imperfect.

The psychological determinents and functions that contribute to a pervasive overvaluation of maleness and to the use of maleness as a selfobject are not adequately understood. In the remainder of this paper, several hypotheses are offered: (1) the feminine dimensions of the self are insufficiently valued by women and men because femaleness is unconsciously associated with fallibility; (2) maleness is defensively overvalued by both women and men in order to keep maleness "uncontaminated" by the fallibility that is associated with femaleness; (3) although this preserves maleness for use in promoting security and self-esteem, an overreliance on this form of self-restoration represents a developmental arrest that is related to the facts that women generally rear the children and that their gender is undervalued. Implications for psychoanalytic theory and treatment are briefly discussed.

There are relatively distinct qualities and perspectives associated with maleness and femaleness in contemporary western culture (Gilligan, 1982; Chodorow, 1978). People vary in their awareness of and ability to make use of both male and female frameworks, and in the degree to which each has contributed to their self-organization. *Qualities that are considered male or female occur to varying degrees in people of both sexes.* "Female" qualities have been undervalued and female perspectives have been neglected in the theories of human development (Erikson, 1950; Gilligan, 1982; Lachmann, 1985; Silverman, 1985), in world history (Thompson, 1981), and in the sciences (Capra, 1982).

The theories of the sciences and humanities, including psychoanalytic theory, are androcentric. Feminist scholars (Bleier, 1984; Fox Keller, 1985) have increasingly come to question whether many of the long-held sacred truths of their disciplines are indeed value neutral. Rather, many of those 'truths' increasingly seem laden with gender-associated biases.

"Objectivity, 'the ostensibly non-involved stance,' is the male epistemological stance," according to philosopher of science, Catherine MacKinnon (1982, p. 538). The ideals that pervade the sciences and humanities often represent "a radical rejection of any commingling of subject and object" (Fox Keller, 1985). Fox Keller suggests that what is radically rejected is any commingling of male with female.[6]

The radical separation of male and female is also evidenced in the traditional division of parental labor. While mother's traditional role as primary caretaker has involved a considerable "commingling" of boundaries between parent and young child, the father's traditional role has involved a much greater degree of separateness. Indeed, it is often father's "task" to promote individuation.

Among the qualities that are commonly regarded as "female" are encompassing, embracing, unifying, emotionality, warmth, caring, interconnectedness, intuition, expressiveness, maintaining attachments, contextuality, cooperation, interdependency, and the ability to enjoy temporary relinquishment of boundaries between self and other and to permit commingling of "male" and "female" dimensions of the personality. Gilligan (1982) has proposed that female moral concerns are more personal than abstract, centering on the maintenance of attachments rather than on cool, detached reasoning generally associated with masculinity.

In our culture, qualities commonly associated with maleness include aggression, instrumentality, rationality, activity, individuality, separation, linearity, division, dominance, hierarchical authority structure, and the tendencies both to value distinct boundaries in thought and in relationships and to value objectivity and detachment in approaching problems.

Whether these qualities are universally associated with a masculine or a feminine perspective is a question that may never be empirically determined. Central to the subject of this paper is that in promoting security and self-esteem persons of both sexes in our culture (including psychoanalysts) commonly unconsciously make extensive use of a perspective they *associate* with father and maleness, and make far less use of that associated with mother and femaleness.

Because the self is inherently limited and vulnerable, it always needs some way of promoting security and self-esteem. While all means of self-regulation require some compromise of personal freedom, androcentrism has two particularly serious limitations: (1) the

---

[6]Winnicott's (1953) concept of transitional phenomena and Kohut's (1971, 1984) concept of selfobject emphasize the importance of a psychological realm in which subjectivity and objectivity are in contact. Thus, the theories of these two *men* conceive of a self of unspecified gender that permits a commingling of boundaries.

pervasive undervaluation of femaleness with which androcentrism is often associated commonly interferes with one's access to a broad range of experiences, values, and qualities that one associates with the maternal legacy; (2) female undervaluation interferes with intimacy and opportunities for mutual admiration between the sexes, since femaleness is central to the organization of selves of both sexes.

Despite the fact that our child care pattern provides children with greater contact with women than with men, and with female more than male values and approaches to life, cultural gender patterns impede appreciation of women, femaleness, and those concerns that mothers commonly represent. An unfortunate result is that women and men often undervalue fundamental feminine aspects of themselves and one another and are unable to make full use of feminine approaches and concerns.

Many men reveal this inability when they cannot nurture, enjoy the experience of being nurtured, or value interdependency because they consider nurturance and interdependency irreconcilable with male gender identity. Such erroneous beliefs are often perpetuated when these men become fathers. Unless a man has been able comfortably to embrace his own maternal legacy — to find a way to assimilate his maternal identification rather than to sustain its repression — he is unlikely to be able to promote in his children a full appreciation of, and comfort with, "femaleness."

Women commonly reveal an undervaluation of their maternal legacy when they subordinate their own approaches and ways of thinking to those of men. When women do not promote their own qualities and perspectives and their generally greater ease with an intermingling of femaleness and maleness, they contribute to the perpetuation of cultural gender patterns that maintain artificial divisions between maleness and femaleness and between male and female roles, including the roles of mother and father. Often, women perpetuate androcentrism because it provides an illusion of closeness with an elusive father whom they unconsciously imagine protects them. In subordinating themselves, however, they cannot enjoy their share of adult responsibility.

Just as the female dimensions of the self must be more fully assimilated by individuals in contemporary western societies, female concerns and structures must be more fully reflected in psychoanalytic theory. Until this is accomplished, psychoanalytic treatment will have only limited effectiveness in restoring necessary idealization to the female dimensions of the selves of its patients.

In the next section, it is suggested that the fact that women rear the children contributes to a pattern in which women are undervalued. However, many other factors may also contribute to female undervaluation. Explanations of this phenomenon are widely divergent and include: a ubiquitous unconscious fantasy that women's genitals are inferior (Freud, 1931); a fear of the overpowering nature of female sexuality (Sherfey, 1973); the denied envy of women's nurturing and procreative capacities (Horney, 1932; Klein, 1957); the need to protect against the power of woman as mother (e.g., Dinnerstein, 1976); the association of mother with fallibility and mortality (Becker, 1973).

Indeed, the reasons men and women overvalue men and maleness and undervalue women and femaleness are complex and far from being understood. This paper identifies one important function of the maintenance of these distortions: *to preserve self-cohesion and self-esteem while one tries to cope with a difficult fact of life — that people are limited, flawed, and fallible.* When unable to embrace this reality (as most of us are), both men and women frequently invoke an unconscious selfobject connection to an overidealized man or to a male attribute, value, activity, or approach to life. It is as if we believe that this connection can insure our protection.

An action can be understood as a use of maleness as a selfobject to the extent that its function is self-restorative and that its value for the person lies in its association, conscious or unconscious, with maleness or its dissociation from femaleness. Maleness is most apt to be used for self-restoration when the self is especially vulnerable or endangered by experiences that one consciously or unconsciously attributes to mother or mother's limitations to one's own limitations, which are blamed on mother's failings. Since women are generally the primary providers of care for children, many diverse experiences are attributed to mother and her limitations.

GENDER ASYMMETRY[7] AND FEMALE UNDERVALUATION

The primary caregiver is generally that person with whom the child forms the initial and strongest attachment; but the caregiver is also liable to be experienced as the source of greatest disappointment.

---

[7]The fact that the female gender is generally more responsible than the male for the care of children will be referred to as "gender asymmetry of parenting." The impact on the phenomena discussed in this paper of the increasing participation of men in the care of children requires further study.

From the first weeks of life, the infant knows who its primary caregiver is and begins to form distinct expectancies of the two parents that contribute eventually to generalized expectancies about the two genders (Spieler, 1984). Four-week-old infants can discriminate between the inputs of mother and father (Yogman et al., 1976) and soon begin to turn to each of the parents seeking different responses. It is unlikely that infants understand that men are more highly valued than women, but it is likely that they understand that mother participates more in their care than does father. Thus, very early, infants are aware, in some rudimentary fashion, of the asymmetrical world of gender arrangements.

When the capacity for symbolic thinking emerges during the second year of life (Stern, 1983), previous expectancies about the parents are likely to become associated with their respective genders. If disappointments in the primary caregiver are significant, it is likely that they become associated with the caregiver's qualities, including his or her gender.

Most psychoanalysts agree that some disappointment in the primary caregiver is inevitable and even desirable if psychological growth is to proceed. Although there are differences in the extent to which oedipal or preoedipal factors are invoked to explain the sources of disappointment, these explanations have in common the fact that they consider the experience of disappointment a reflection, though perhaps a distorted one, of actual events. Thus, they imply that a prior state of perfection, and perhaps a maternal idealization, is lost.

Whether mother was initially experienced as idealized or a fantasy of maternal idealization was invoked retrospectively, compensation may be needed to cope with such an actual or fantasied loss. Freud (1931) believed that the primary disappointment was in mother and that it was focused on genital differences and related to oedipal concerns. He thought that girls believed they were missing a penis and that they concluded that the appropriate compensation was to replace the lost penis by obtaining a baby from father. He thought that the boy's "discovery" of this maternal "deficit" prompted repression of the earlier maternal identification and a secondary identification with father. Kohut (1971), on the other hand, suggested that when the child's disappointment in mother resulting from mother's early empathic failures taxes the child's psychic resources, the child may turn to the father to seek compensation.

While Freud and Kohut differ in their explanation of the initial source of disappointment in mother and in the way that compensation can be obtained, both agree that the disappointment is related to something real about the mother (e.g., either her lack of a penis or her empathic failures) and that father can provide suitable compensation. In so doing, both Freud and Kohut neglect several important considerations: defensive functions that might be served by maintaining a view of the mother as disappointing (such as that in promoting separation or in promoting paternal *over*idealization when father is insufficiently involved to promote his idealization); the fact that paternal *over*idealization may be needed to promote heterosexuality when paternal idealization has not been possible; the adverse impact of maternal undervaluation on heterosexuality and self-esteem; or the question of how father's image as compensator becomes transformed to a more realistic image of father.

In a family structure in which one parent is primary and the other is secondary, disappointment is likely to be associated with the primary caregiver; reassurance and compensation, with the one who is secondary. To some extent this is true irrespective of what the parents actually do. Since usually the primary caregiver is a woman, gender asymmetry of parenting contributes to initially differential attributions to the parents and, more specifically, to their respective genders.

As the child discovers that mother is not always able to provide protection from frustration, loss, physical pain, overstimulation, and understimulation, disappointment, and wounds to self-esteem, the child is less able to believe in mother's infallibility. Since a belief in and use of mother's omnipotence is an early "strategy" of the self for maintaining security and esteem, challenges to this belief are distressing. Although it is not inevitable that associations of disappointment with mother and compensation with father will endure, cultural factors engrave these associations more deeply into the child's representational world. Contributing further to the demise of the illusion of mother's omnipotence and often, unfortunately, to the ability to retain an idealized maternal imago as well, is the child's growing awareness of father's and of the culture's devaluation of mother and women.[8]

Gradually or suddenly, the child discovers the attitudes toward mother and femininity that the society holds. Probably, the child will discover too that mother and father hold these attitudes. Even if mother has provided highly attuned care, the discovery that she is less valued by the world because of her gender is likely to shake the child's security and self-esteem. The degree of prior attunement will

---

[8]There is growing evidence (e.g., Perlmutter, 1984) that the changing role of women is contributing to changes in the ways that mother is seen by her children.

attenuate the degree of disappointment and distress, but disappointment, distress, and perhaps even shock related to this discovery seem inevitable. The cultural undervaluation of women adds to the child's prior disappointments in mother, thereby interfering further with the child's ability to believe in the power of femaleness and to make needed use of mother as an idealized selfobject. Moreover, mothers in cultures that value men more than women are less likely than fathers to think of or to present themselves as worthy of idealization. Because of their lack of belief in their own importance they often interfere with the process of idealization, for example, by self-denigration or excessive humility. Increasingly unable to bask in the pure light of mother's former grandeur, the child loses an important source of safety and self-esteem and an illusion about omnipotence. The discovery of mother's fallibility often leads the child, all too aware of its dependence on a less-than-perfect world, to join father and the culture in the undervaluation of mother. This enables the child to draw a clear distinction between mother and her fallibility on the one hand and the fantasy of an infallible father on the other.

Although the construction of a clear distinction between mother and father serves a protective function, a price is paid. When the self is unable to retain adequate idealization of its feminine dimensions, it is deprived of an important source of self-esteem, of a previously experienced love for mother, and of the riches derived from her qualities and values. Blaming aspects of this legacy for our fallibility interferes with access to them and contributes to difficulty in providing for, or "mothering," the self. Psychologically, until mother is "pardoned" we are like orphans in need of care. Vulnerable in relying on an imperfect mother and vulnerable in turning away from her, the child anxiously "seeks" and, to some extent, constructs protection in a heroic father.

MALE OVERIDEALIZATION

Children need parents whom they can idealize. Children's knowledge that they are loved, admired by, and associated with idealizable people promotes a sense of the self as valuable and a sense of safety and well being. Ultimately, idealization also promotes internalization. Of course, idealization is different from *over*idealization. Many factors contribute to the need to *over*idealize fathers, men, and maleness. Overidealization is, by definition, compensatory. It suggests that the self had difficulty in coping and had to compensate to maintain a stable sense of self. Overidealization further taxes the psychic resources of an already taxed self. While idealization is needed under normal circumstances, *over*idealization is defensive, its function being to protect a vulnerable self.

Freud (1931, 1933) seems to have believed that maternal devaluation is an understandable response to the child's discovery that mother lacks a penis. He also seems to have viewed the phallic *over*-idealization that is associated with this "discovery" as equally understandable. In fact, both responses are understandable only when seen as childhood theories. While it is common in early development for the father's penis to be idealized as an expression of the child's love and admiration for the father, phallic *over*idealization represents an arrest in development and reveals a failure of other sources of self-regulation to provide what is needed.

When fathers are available and idealized, warmth and recognition from them can help to mitigate the pain of life's disappointments so that children can more readily assimilate difficult truths, such as those associated with discoveries about their own and mothers' vulnerability. Although fathers cannot protect against fallibility any more than mothers can, young children often need to believe *someone* can until they are ready to relinquish this illusion.

Aware of their own vulnerability, children need to know that their fathers are admirable (Kohut, 1971). When a father demonstrates that he can provide protection and reassurance, (e.g., through his reliability, gentle, attuned holding, demonstrations of physical and emotional strength, or evidences of success or social recognition), he communicates that the child has a father who is worthy of admiration.

Knowing one is valued and understood by an admirable person is far more reassuring than similar demonstrations of love from a person whom the child does not admire. Conversely, doubts that one is valued and understood by a person whom one admires are far more distressing than similar doubts about a person for whom one has little admiration. Thus, the impact of a father's minimal participation in a child's care will be influenced by the degree to which the father is esteemed by the child. Having an admirable father will enhance the child's self-esteem unless the quality or quantity of father's involvement leads the child to doubt his or her importance to him.

If father has promoted the child's appreciation of mother and femaleness, if mother has successfully remained idealized, and if father's participation in the child's care has been adequate, compensatory overidealization of maleness will probably be unnecessary. However, a child who has been unable to retain an idealized *maternal* imago will probably need an idealized *paternal* imago even more. If father is inaccessible, *over*idealized maleness will instead be used by the child for calming and self-restoration. Far more significant to the child than the nature of parental genitals (cf. Freud, 1931) in producing phallic overidealization, then, are unmitigated disappointment in mother for her failure to provide protection against fallibility on the one hand, and father's inaccessibility on the other.

> Both boys and girls succumb to the desire to flee the sex represented by the mother; they need little coaxing to identify with the father and his world. He seems more neutral physically, more cleanly powerful, less immersed in body determinisms; he seems more "symbolically free," represents the vast world outside of the home, the social world with its organized triumph over nature, the very escape from contingency that the child seeks (Becker, 1973, p. 40).

Belief that the "power of maleness" is extraordinary is fostered by the minimal participation of fathers in child care. When men do not participate in domestic life, they can more readily seem "uncontaminated and untarnished." Moreover, they become blank screens onto which the hero fantasies of women and children can be projected. Often men derive illusory benefits from such overidealization. Many men are driven to pursue their careers and are often encouraged to do so because of an unconscious fantasy shared by men and women that a "solution" to human limitation and vulnerability will be found in relentless pursuit of fame, fortune, physical strength, political or economic power, creative expression, or any other value they have endowed with restorative power.

Until it became common for women to pursue careers themselves, such overidealized fantasies about men and their careers could readily be maintained. Perhaps contemporary men and women have anachronistically maintained clearly differentiated sex roles because both unconsciously share the wish to retain "uncontaminated" the restorative properties of overidealized maleness. The mutual understanding that is possible when women and men share the parenting and breadwinning roles may interfere with the ability of both to maintain overidealizations that have long provided reassurance and restoration.

Even when the many practical issues that commonly interfere with a breadwinner's ability to participate in child care can be overcome, father's ability to nurture may be restricted by the limitations of his own self-organization. He too probably was reared in a gender-asymmetrical situation and lived in a world in which femaleness was undervalued and maleness was overvalued. His access is often restricted to his own maternal–feminine dimensions. This limits his ability to feel safe with nurturing and other experiences in which boundaries are temporarily blurred, and to feel at ease with the knowledge that nurturance and generativity are as much components of male gender identity as they are of female gender identity (Erikson, 1950; Ross, 1975).

Although little is known about the consequences of the minimal involvement in child care of a parent who is primarily a breadwinner, there is considerable evidence that when a parent of either sex is absent in early life, children often maintain overidealized fantasies of the missing parent (Neubauer, 1960). By maintaining an overidealization of the missing parent, children provide for their own needs as best they can. What these children need seems to be a real person with whom to identify, whatever the psychic functions they are unable to provide for themselves without the missing parent, and the good feelings about themselves that they might have if that parent were more available.

Although the absence of a parent due to death or divorce is apt to have different consequences than the parent's simply being out of the home most of the time and therefore minimally involved in the child-care, some similar issues apply. Young children cannot understand why this parent (traditionally, the father) must go to work; father's minimal involvement leads children to doubt their importance to him. This insecurity may seem to be mitigated by the creation of overidealized fantasies about the father. Providing themselves with an overidealized experience of father may soften the hurt associated with loving a person who appears to consider his work more important than they. There is a price to be paid, however — an *over*idealized paternal imago lacks the reality and substance that closeness with a real father can provide. Moreover, it interferes with the assimilation of an idealized *maternal* imago.

Needing overidealization in order to maintain self-esteem and a belief in father's infallibility, children may be unable to allow themselves to acknowledge that his emotional and physical absences tarnish his shining armor. Trying to preserve his perfection, children may devalue themselves instead or direct anger and blame intended for father against mother, who as primary care giver is most available to receive it. The child whose father participates minimally in his or her care is likely to fear that directing anger at him will drive him further away, since his lesser participation in child care may signify to the child that his commitment is more tenuous (Spieler, 1984).

Many parents unconsciously share with their children a fantasied hope that father can overcome mother's shortcomings; mothers often also embody human fallibility in the fantasies of adult men and women. While such fantasies may unconsciously fuel many great social, commercial, intellectual, and artistic enterprises, excessive demands by parents that their boy-children fulfill unrealistic hopes and dreams often interfere with the transformation of sons' archaic narcissism.[9] Such unrealistic demands often reveal limitations in the parents' ability to accept human limitation, leaving it to the next generation to make better peace with the issue. Sons often believe that they can and should accomplish heroic feats, an expectation that is unconsciously promoted by the culture. Also contributing to the persistence of male overidealization are men's difficulties in admitting limitations, even to themselves, because of the sense of failure and shame that such revelations might generate.

Unconsciously, both sexes collude to maintain an overidealization of men and of maleness. Women subordinate themselves to idealized men and endow maleness with greater power than femaleness. They experience this subordination as restorative in the protection it seems to afford against having to accept that all people are fallible. Men deny their own limitations, even to themselves, striving desperately to uphold the expectation of their parents, the culture, and the women and children in their lives that they must deliver everyone from fallibility. In fact, until male fallibility can be avowed by women and men, and until men's shame at being fallible can be addressed in psychoanalysis (O'Leary and Wright, 1985) men must hide their shortcomings and present themselves as images of manhood that lack reality and substance.

ANDROCENTRISM — A DEVELOPMENTAL ARREST

We cannot avoid coming to terms with the fact of our fallibility — even if coming to terms with it means simply to disavow it. A widespread pattern of male overvaluation represents a way that many people in our culture bolster their vulnerable selves in an attempt to face this difficult and inescapable fact.

---

[9] Often such untransformed narcissism remains unrecognized in the analyses of men because it has been accepted as "normal."

As noted earlier, male overvaluation, or androcentrism, even permeates the ways that people think, solve problems, and view life. In their inability to embrace the female perspective, people who are androcentric reveal a developmental arrest pervasive in this culture. Such an arrest is likely to occur when persons of one sex are primarily responsible for the rearing of children and when the caretaking sex is undervalued.

A woman's androcentrism is revealed when she makes choices whose unconscious motivation lies in their renunciation of her maternal legacy. It is not *what* she chooses that determines whether her choice is androcentric, but *why*. Thus, for example, although nurturance is not inherently feminine, and career success is not inherently masculine, some women betray their maternal legacies and their selves when they value career success more highly than motherhood. When the pursuit of her work is motivated by an unconscious belief (shared also by many men) that having a career provides a way of renouncing association with mother, her behavior is androcentric.

Curiously, the same betrayal and renunciation may also underlie the assumption of the more traditional female role of full-time mother and homemaker. The traditional role may appear to represent a woman's identification with a beloved mother and appreciation of her maternal heritage. Indeed it may sometimes be just that. On the other hand, the primary unconscious motivation in assuming this role may be to experience her self as subordinated to and thus protected by an overidealized man or maleness. When this is the case, it is likely to be a sign that something was missing in her psychological development (e.g., a close relationship with a present and participating father or an idealizable mother) something that is now missing in her representational world and her self-organization. A woman which subordinates herself to overidealized maleness, often is attempting unconsciously to cope with anxiety or conflict that interferes with her ability to assume more individual responsibility and to participate in a relationship as an equal partner. Her unconscious choice to assume the traditional female role is an attempt to provide her self with something that she has missed. Although it is often assumed, in a more classical framework, that what she feels she is missing is a penis (and indeed this is sometimes how she experiences it), often her choice is motivated primarily by her attempt to provide herself with the father she has missed (not specifically his sexual organ) or to compensate for her lost maternal idealization. Such a choice masks a developmental arrest.

A man's androcentrism is commonly revealed when he considers "female" values such as caring, tenderness, and the importance of interrelatedness naive. "Swaggering" masculinity denies its maternal roots and reveals a distorted notion of father's identity, perhaps due to father's elusiveness. A man whose "self-centered" demand to have his — and only his — perspective prevail disregards the significance of other perspectives and commonly reveals an inadequately idealized and assimilated maternal heritage and a compensatory exaggeration of the importance of what men have to say. A man who does not experience a conflict between his responsibility to his career and to his children and who feels certain that a commitment to his career is a clear priority has failed to assimilate the feminine dimensions of his self and exaggerates the importance of "what men do." The ability to experience conflict between these competing requirements suggests that he can emphathize both with the longings of his children and with those of the child-that-he-once-was. If the child-that-he-once-was "disidentified" from his preoedipal mother in acquiring a masculine identity, and if subsequently he was not able to assimilate her contributions, he is unlikely to appreciate the needs of his children because he will fear that such appreciation signifies a loss of self or of manhood. Such a man is likely to demand that his children also live without the sustaining bond to a valued maternal heritage that he, because of his own developmental arrest, must live without.

Although attachment is associated with a female framework and separation with a male framework, when mothers are unable to foster separation and when fathers are unable to foster attachment, both situations reflect deficits in self-organization. The need for clearly differentiated roles is often associated with an unconscious belief that their commingling might contaminate the power of maleness with female fallibility. A similar unconscious belief under lies the need to maintain separation in thought between subject and object and between male and female frameworks.[10]

Until mother's imperfect contributions can be appreciated, they cannot be assimilated, and sustenance cannot be found in other potential idealized female selfobjects. The person is, therefore, narcissistically vulnerable and necessarily dependent on the use of compensatory overidealization to bolster a vulnerable self. Androcent-

---

[10]Men's fear of women's unique subjectivity commonly interferes with their ability to empathize with women or to be used by them as mirroring selfobjects.

rism unconsciously aims to restore the self that is disappointed in
mother and the self that lacks adequate contact with father. It reveals
a compromised attempt to provide two missing ingredients necessary
for the progression of psychological development: an adequately
idealized maternal imago, and the kind of prior relationship with
father that would have provided sufficient real experiences, and not
primarily fantasies, for the shaping of the paternal imago. Male overidealization only partially succeeds in facilitating the forward movement of development and thus is symptomatic of developmental
arrest.

*Over*idealized maleness lacks reality and substance and cannot
compensate for idealized maleness. Present and participating fathers
are needed to provide the building blocks of a well-grounded psychological organization. Although the aim of androcentrism is to
facilitate coping with universal human concerns about vulnerability,
the masculinity and femininity that result are often caricatures of
what they can be when they are connected to their maternal roots.

Androcentrism betrays the very vulnerability that we strive to
disavow. Ironically, efforts to convince ourselves that we are not
vulnerable often leave us less secure and result in alienation from
those aspects of our selves and of each other from which we might
otherwise derive sustenance and recognition — aspects we associate
with our mothers and mothering. While representing an effort to
preserve security and self-esteem when the self is unable to assimilate
the meaning of human fallibility, androcentrism concurrently interferes with the experience of temporal continuity through the disavowal of association to something of the past — the significance of
the prior relationship with mother. Thus, the anachronistic persistence of initially adaptive protective efforts falls short of the original aim.

PSYCHOANALYSIS: A LOST MATERNAL LEGACY

New visions of the infant and of the person are emerging. Current
research (e.g., Stern, 1983) finds the infant alternating between
states of oneness and states of separateness. Current theory about
the self portrays it as in-relation to partially differentiated others
(i.e., selfobjects) that it uses to sustain itself and to foster the realization of its creative-productive potential. With few exceptions, previous psychoanalytic theory focused on the move from dependence
to independence and described the human striving to be separate and
autonomous, but it neglected both the human need to soften the

experience of separateness[11] through experiences of oneness and the self's need to reconcile the pursuit of its own fulfillment with the pleasure that is derived when one fosters the fulfillment of an other who is loved as separate from the self. In so doing, psychoanalytic theory has envisioned and perpetuated an unrealistic linearity and unnatural dichotomies between separateness and connectedness and between connectedness and self-fulfillment.

These dichotomies have been paralleled in artificial dichotomies between femaleness and maleness and between the role of mother and the role of father. With changes in the gender asymmetry of parenting, it is hoped that this need to keep male separated from female will be obviated. Mothers and femaleness have too exclusively come to represent attachment, while fathers and maleness have come too exclusively to represent separateness. Moreover, femaleness has become equated with self-abnegation and maleness with self-realization.

When separateness is overvalued in theories of human development and in people themselves, what is lost are healthy human strivings for connection — not as expressions of pathological regression, but as expressions of creative progression.

When separateness is radically pursued, it is achieved at the expense of normal human needs for interrelatedness. Also overlooked are the ability to fulfill one's creative/productive potential in and through relationships and the fact that loving another and helping another to find fulfillment can also bring fulfillment to the self.

The overvaluation of separateness is reflected in a theory that contrasts autonomy as a hallmark of mental health with dependence as a sign of developmental arrest. Since separateness has come to be associated with maleness, and oneness with femaleness, separateness and maleness have overidealized connotations, while femaleness and oneness have negative connotations. When interrelatedness is seen as endangering the self's ability to realize its goals, it is because femaleness has lost its value as a framework for self-realization. The overvaluation of the male promotes the radical pursuit of separateness in men (and now sometimes in women too) and hampers the ability to feel important, which women need if they are to promote the recognition of their own values, needs and visions.

---

[11]Mahler's (Mahler, Pine, and Bergman, 1975) concept of "rapprochement" does not do justice to the human need for connection since it portrays this need as one that is increasingly renounced as the ability to be separate is achieved.

As yet psychoanalysis does not have an encompassing theory that reflects a pluralism of metapsychologies (Wolstein, 1959) and of human strivings for both connection and autonomy and that allows for their creative synthesis in a healthy tension between the need for self-fulfillment and the love of others. At best, we have several distinct or inadequately integrated theories, each reflecting particular, limited visions of the person, human strivings, and the sources of dread in life.

Curiously, the difficulty in synthesis and integration among psychoanalytic models is paralleled in a difficulty of synthesis and integration in male identity as it is portrayed in prevailing psychoanalytic theory. According to this vision, male identity requires disidentification from mother (Greenson, 1968) and repression of feminine identifications (Freud, 1931). When the feminine dimensions of the self are repressed or disavowed, empathy with women's subjectivity is experienced as a dangerous commingling of male and female identifications caused by a return of the repressed maternal identification. When the pluralism of embracing another's perspective seems dangerous, important dimensions of experience are foreclosed. The tightly organized vision that is maintained is reassuring but limited. When psychoanalytic theory successfully reflects a pluralism of syncopated human strivings, it will also reflect and foster greater synthesis and integration of maleness and femaleness in human experience.

When psychoanalysis is experienced as helpful, it is often because it has extended the person's sense of pride, integration, temporal continuity, and vitality by attention to disavowed aspects of experience. Analytic attention is one of the factors that enables patients courageously to avow what is feared. Both women and men commonly enter treatment having failed to avow the fact that a fundamental and profound aspect of their psychological inheritance is derived from mothers who, like themselves, are simply fallible. Relying on androcentrism, many suffer a developmental arrest indicating an abortive attempt to face the painful fact that the self is inherently limited and vulnerable. Unable to "pardon" mothers, they often are cut off from the wellspring of their origins, and aspects of their selves remain undeveloped, alienated, depleted, and sterile. This contributes to a demand that men be infallible and interferes with men's ability to admit limitations. Because the androcentrism in psychoanalytic theory limits the success of psychoanalytic treatment, many terminate treatment with aspects of these same disabilities still in operation.

Although progress may ultimately require a change in the structure of parenting, when we more fully understand that the need to keep male "uncontaminated" by female is defensive, we will foster integration and enrichment of selves long deprived of access to a rich maternal legacy.

REFERENCES

Becker, E. (1973). *The Denial of Death*. New York: Free Press.

Beebe, B. (1985). *Mutual Influence in Mother-Infant Interaction*. Paper presented at Eighth Annual Conference on the Psychology of the Self, New York.

Bleier, R. (1984). *Science and Gender*. New York: Pergamon Press.

Blum, H., ed. (1977). *Female Psychology*. New York: International Universities Press.

Capra, F. (1982). *The Turning Point: Science, Society, and the Rising Culture*. New York: Bantam.

Chasseguet-Smirgel, J., ed. (1964). *Female Sexuality*. Ann Arbor: University of Michigan Press.

Chodorow, N. (1978). *The Reproduction of Mothering: Psychoanalysis and the Sociology of Gender*. Berkeley: University of California Press.

Dinnerstein, D. (1976). *The Mermaid and the Minotaur*. New York: Harper & Row.

Erikson, E. (1950). *Childhood and Society*. New York: Norton.

Fairbairn, W. (1946). Object-relationships and dynamic structure. In: *An Object-Relations Theory of the Personality*. New York: Basic Books, 1952.

Fox Keller, E.(1985). *Reflections on Gender and Science*. New Haven: Yale University Press.

Freud, S. (1905). Three essays on the theory of sexuality. *Standard Edition*, 17:135–143. London: Hogarth Press, 1961.

_____ (1923). The ego and the id. *Standard Edition*, 19:12–59. London: Hogarth Press, 1961.

_____ (1931). Female sexuality. *Standard Edition*, 21:64–145. London: Hogarth Press, 1961.

_____ (1933). New introductory lectures on psychoanalysis. *Standard Edition*, 22:5–182. London: Hogarth Press, 1961.

Gilligan, C. (1982). *In a Different Voice*. Cambridge, MA: Harvard University Press.

Greenson, R. (1968). Disidentifying from mother: Its special importance for the boy. *Internat. J. Psycho-Anal.*, 49:370–374.

Horney, D. (1932). The dread of women. In: *Feminine Psychology*. New York: Norton, 1967.

Klein, M. (1957). Envy and gratitude. In: *Envy and Gratitude & Other Works: 1946–1963*. New York: Delta, 1975.

Kohut, H. (1966). Forms and transformations of narcissism. *J. Amer. Psychoanal. Assn.*, 14:245–272.

_____ (1971). *The Analysis of the Self*. New York: International Universities Press.

_____ (1984). *How Does Analysis Cure?*, ed. A. Goldberg & P. Stepansky. Chicago: University of Chicago.

Lachmann, F. M. (1985). *On Ambition and Hubris—A Case Study*. Paper presented at Eighth Annual Conference on The Psychology of the Self, New York.

Lerner, L., ed. (1982). *Women and Individuation: Emerging Views. Psychoanal. Rev.*, 69, 1.

MacKinnon, C. (1982). Feminism, Marxism, method and the state: An agenda for theory. *Signs*, 7:515–544.

Mahler, M., Pine, F., & Bergman, A. (1975). *The Psychological Birth of the Human Infant.* New York: Basic Books.

Mendell, D. ed. (1982). *Early Female Development: Current Psychoanalytic Views.* New York: Spectrum.

Neubauer, P. (1960). The one-parent child and his oedipal development. The *Psychoanalytic Study of the Child*, 15:286–309. New York: International Universities Press.

O'Leary, J., & Wright, F. (1985). *Shame and Gender Issues in Pathological Narcissism.* Paper presented at American Psychological Association Convention, Los Angeles.

Perlmutter, B. (1984). *The Validation of a Measure of Masculinity, Femininity and Androgyny in Children.* Unpublished doctoral dissertation. New York University.

Rilke, R. M. (1903, 1904). *Letters to a Young Poet.* (trans. M. D. Herter Norton). New York: Norton, 1962.

Roland, A. (1980). Psychoanalytic perspectives on personality development in India. *Internat. Rev. Psycho-Anal.*, 73–87.

Ross, J. M. (1975). The development of paternal identity: A critical review of the literature on nurturance and generality in boys and men. *J. Amer. Psychoanal. Assn.*, 23:761–783.

Sherfey, M. J. (1973). *The Nature and Evolution of Female Sexuality.* New York: Random/Vintage.

Silverman, D. (1985). *What Are Little Girls Made Of?* Unpublished Manuscript.

Silverman, L., Lachmann, F., & Milich, R. (1982). *The Search for Oneness.* New York: International Universities Press.

Spieler, S. (1984). Preoedipal girls need fathers. *Psychoanal. Rev.*, 71:63–80.

Stern, D. (1983). The early development of schemas of self, other, and "self with other." In: *Reflections on Self Psychology*, eds. J. D. Lichtenberg & S. Kaplan. Hillsdale, NJ: The Analytic Press.

Stolorow, R., & Lachmann, F. (1980). *Psychoanalysis of Developmental Arrests.* New York: International Universities Press.

Thompson, W. I. (1981). *The Time Falling Bodies Take to Light: Mythology, Sexuality, and the Origins of Culture.* New York: St. Martins Press.

Winnicott, D. W. (1953). Transitional objects and transitional phenomena. *Internat. J. Psycho-Analysis*, 34:89–97.

Wolstein, B. (1959). *Countertransference.* New York: Grune & Stratton.

Yogman, M., Dixon, S., Tronick, E., Adamson, L., Als, H., & Brazelton, T. B. (1976). *Development of Infant Social Interaction with Fathers.* Paper presented at the meeting of the Eastern Psychological Association, New York.

3 Some Notes
on the Development
of Female Gender Role Identity
ADRIA E. SCHWARTZ

Just as Freud had difficulty in communicating his notion of an infinitely complex, polymorphously perverse sexuality that began in infancy to a Victorian world organized around discreetly understood categories of sexual behavior that occurred only after the fall of innocence, so there has been similar confusion about and resistance to refining our understanding of sex, gender, and sexuality. By now, the difference between sex and sexuality has become clearer: the former most often has to do with concrete, observable behaviors, whereas the latter usually refers to a much more comprehensive conundrum of feelings and behavior, internal and interpersonal, intrapsychic and object related, having to do with erotic life. The differences between sex as a biological category and gender, however, have remained obscure, coming to light only relatively recently.

In Simone de Beauvoir's (1953) revolutionary work on women, *The Second Sex*, she attempted to construct womanhood through biological, sociohistorical and sexual determinants, differentiating the biological female from the world of meanings in which she lives. Almost concurrently, in an entirely different context, Money, Hampson, and Hampson (1955), in their studies of sexual anomalies, were deconstructing our traditional understandings of biological sex and simultaneously introducing the idea of gender role.

As Person and Ovessey (1983) point out, Money et al. (1955) originated the term "gender role," and Money (1965, 1973) later attempted to differentiate it from what he termed "gender identity." Gender identity, an internal experience, refers to a continuity of feelings having to do with maleness or femaleness, whereas gender role has to do with the "public expression of gender identity" primarily through behavior. Unfortunately, this attempt at clarification reified a split between behavior and experience that Money had been attempting to obviate in his initial definition of gender role, a definition that had included references to dreams, fantasies, and the general phenomenology of gender and erotic life.

"Core gender identity," another widely used term of late, was introduced by Robert Stoller (1968) in his work on *Sex and Gender*. Core gender identity refers to that immutable sense that "I am a girl" or "I am a boy," which solidifies somewhere before the end of the second year. It is the recognition of belonging to a biological category, a categorical identification that, according to Kohlberg (1966), is the basic cognitive organizer upon which further identities rest.

In 1983, Person and Ovessey introduced the notion of "gender role identity," which had to do with one's psychological self-image of one's masculinity or femininity as measured against societal norms for masculine and feminine behavior. The definition offered by Person and Ovessey (1973), however, omits reference to internal psychic representations having to do with the bodily self, the phenomenology of being male or female.

Gender role identity refers here to a gendered sense of self, which is multiply determined by biological, sociological, and psychological facets. Gender role identity involves an internal self-evaluation of maleness or femaleness and is thus continuous rather than discrete, mutable in a way that core gender identity is not. A thorough understanding of gender role identity calls for an enriched developmental perspective detailing critical periods in the emergence of gender role identity, as they differ from and converge with other aspects of cognitive, affective, and intrapsychic development.

This chapter focuses on three developmental stages: the rapprochement subphase of the separation-individuation process, triangulation, and adolescence, in an attempt to understand their impact on female gender role identity. The chapter presents an overview of current psychoanalytic work (Fliegel, 1973) including the author's (Schwartz, 1984a, b, c), which reflects an explicit or, more commonly, implicit, acknowledgment of the longstanding feminist critique of traditional psychoanalytic models of female psychosexual development. Psychoanalysis as a heuristic tool has been particularly valuable for the study of gender role identity formation. The psychoanalytic reconstructions of early experience through dreams, fantasies, and anamnesis, in addition to more current explorations of conscious and unconscious conflicts around gender role identity, afford us a unique opportunity for observation. Gender role identity, however, is in large part a social construction as well, mediated through the family as the generic representative of society.

The heart of the feminist critique of psychoanalysis lies in what appears to have been a refusal to accept the internalization of social proscriptions as an appropriate arena for psychoanalytic inquiry. The social construction of gender was seen by many of Freud's disciples as the proper ground for sociology, not psychoanalysis. Attempts by Freudian revisionists (Horney, 1924, 1926, 1932, 1933; Thompson, 1964) to address issues of the cultural valuation of gender were largely dismissed by orthodox Freudians as irrelevant and not having to do with the real stuff of psychoanalysis, that is, instinct theory and the viscissitudes of the libido. In a similar but contrary way, Karen Horney's critique of Freud's theory of development was not embraced by feminists because it rested ultimately on a biological foundation of gender. With the increasing influence of object relations theory and self psychology, coupled with the heightened attention being paid to observational research on infants and toddlers, psychoanalytic thinkers have been more receptive to the complexities of gender and gender role.

Gender role identity, as it refers to the ongoing sense of being female or male, has to do with meanings — with being and the meaning of being in a male or female body. In this chapter, the section on Internal Representations highlights the importance of these unconscious representations in the emotional and cognitive life of the emerging female.

Gender role identity, as defined here, has to do with the integrative function of gender as the basic cognitive organizer and its alloplastic and autoplastic adaptations to a particular idiosyncratic historical milieu. The section on Asymmtery of Parenting, preceding the presentation of the Developmental Sequence, considers the impact of our particular social structure on the deepest roots of gender role identity formation.

THE DEVELOPMENT
OF INTERNAL REPRESENTATIONS

The task of developing a firmly boundaried image of self is complicated for the girl because of her difficulty in perceiving the limits of various internal feelings and locating and differentiating the sources of stimulation for feelings of pleasure and excitement. As Bernstein (1983) points out, touching the external genitals stimulates internal sensations, and these deeply internal sensations can stimulate anal feelings. Moreover, it is the particular nature of vaginal eroticism to provide pleasure that tends to spread out in waves of excitement throughout the body. Thus for young girls the internal psychic representations of pleasure and other various feelings of stimulation lack precise limits, laying the groundwork for confusion about insides and outsides at a time when ego boundaries are most permeable (Montgrain, 1983). This indeterminancy, this fundamental not knowing about beginnings and ends, is likely to have developmental sequelae, especially when the direct causal links between physical action and the perception of pleasure or pain are obfuscated by the fuzziness of internal proprioceptors. The experience of the internal is often diffuse, generalized, and fused with Mommy (Bernstein, 1983).

There is a tendency for writers in this area to pathologize or make problematic the female task of coming to understand the confluence of her physical and psychosexual selves, the implication being that males do not face such difficulties. The developmental tasks are different of course, but the external location of male genitals, with their consequent exposure and vulnerability, has enormous consequences for gender role identity — a fact obvious but seldom represented as a particular "problem" of male development. A more accurate understanding of the development of male gender role identity must begin similarly to account for the variations of internal psychic representations of the gendered self.

To return to the developing female, the normative lack of differentiation between the infant daughter and her mother is complemented by the mother's own blurring of boundaries — she cannot help but see herself in her infant daughter. The many ways in which these reverberations echo throughout the mother–daughter relationship have tremendous impact on the developing gender role identity and continue, with periods of greater and lesser decisiveness, through adolescence.

The girl's task is both to identify with and to separate from the omnipotent, boundless, and therefore frustrating mother, just as she must separate from and identify with the all-giving, tender, nurturing mother, source of all pleasure and comfort (Dinnerstein, 1977). This process entails a subtle interplay of the girl's constitutional appetites and rhythms, her particular history of pleasures and frustrations — Winnicott's (1965) "good enough mothering" — coupled with her mother's responses to her sameness/difference both with regard to her individuation and her own gender attitudes as they relate to that sameness/difference.

These internal psychic representations of a gendered self continue to be shaped and remolded like a living sculpture. They are immutable, fixed, as core gender identity appears to be. The process continues throughout separation-individuation and triangulation, with the finishing touches of the chisel applied at adolescence.

The mother's perceived omnipotence is certainly part of the common male experience of her as a great devouring hole incorporating oral, anal, and vaginal images seen as alternately limitless, engulfing, and insatiable (Dinnerstein, 1977). As mother is personified as a threat to autonomy and the struggle for individuation, the constant lure of regression is perceived as an external threat embodied in the frustrating, engulfing mother with whom the boy grows to disidentify (Greenson, 1968; Chodorow, 1978).

Because of the early presymbolic nature of these internal psychic representations, it is difficult to access them within the framework of psychoanalysis. Exploration here, as it tends to approach core gender identity, is often felt to be a threat to the integral sense of self.

The sociocultural tendency to mystify the female gender can undermine the young girl's attempts to solidify her gender role identity in an appropriately self-affirming fashion. Waites (1982) has determined that "there are systematic, culturally produced distortions in female ego development which often manifest themselves in specific uncertainties about reality" (p. 30). Because too often girls are socialized for dependence and passivity, their questions about their bodies and the specifics of how they work, and the feelings of helplessness and uncertainty that such questions can engender, have been viewed as ego-syntonic with the adults they are to become. Not knowing, not *really* understanding has been acceptable for females in a way that it has never been for males.

For a female child, how mother feels about her gendered self is of primary importance. Has mother internalized some version of role contempt and objectification, so that she too fears her sexual powers and the awesomeness of her reproductive capacities? Or is she able to express her femaleness with pleasure and creativity, which she offers to her daughter for incorporation and identification? Such a dichotomy of course does not exist, but rather there is a continual interweaving of intrapsychic, sociocultural, and idiosyncratic historical determinants that effect the ongoing development of both mother and daughter.

ON THE ASYMMETRY OF PARENTING

As Chodorow (1978) and Dinnerstein (1977) have so eloquently pointed out, women — and only women — mother. This asymmetry in parenting has a significant effect on the psychological development of both sexes and of course takes its toll as well on mothers, who too often are depressed or forced into a position of narcisstic relation to their offspring. It is well established within psychiatric epidemiology that women suffer from significantly higher rates of depressive disorders than do men (Lewis, 1976; Guttentag, Salasin, and Belle, 1980). Moreover, despite the seemingly liberating change in women's social roles, rates of depression for women are on the increase (Guttentag et al., 1980). Narcisstic disorders are too fine a diagnostic category to be scrutinized within the nonanalytic bounds of most epidemiological studies, but common clinical sense tells us that many of the problems that bring women and men into the consulting room have their roots partially in the limitations inherent in narcissistic mothering. Women who are devalued or otherwise inappropriately mirrored, partly because of their gender, are bound to transmit their narcissistic difficulties to their children. This is not to highlight the pathology of mothers, but to illustrate the sequelae of asymmetrical parenting within a cultural context of gender privilege.

Chodorow (1978) points out that the difference in relational versus positional identification helps to create stereotypic male denigration of women, which contributes to the culturally validated devaluation of females. The sins of the fathers are visited on their sons *and* daughters. The myths and stereotypes begin at birth. In an interesting study of 30 primaparous parents and their 30 female and male offspring (Rubin, Provenzano, and Luria, 1979), gender stereotyping was found to exist within the first 24 hours of infancy. Although the hospital data found no significant differences in birth weight, length, or Apgar scores of the 15 male and 15 female newborns, the girls were rated by both mothers and fathers to be significantly softer, finer featured, smaller, and more inattentive. Fathers tended to rate boys firmer, larger featured, better coordinated, more alert, stronger, and hardier than the softer, finer featured, more awkward, less attentive, weaker, more delicate girls. In general, fathers tended more toward stereotyping, which might have been related to the fact that they were not allowed to hold the baby during the first 24 hours, whereas the mothers were permitted some contact during feeding. Far from washing out the effect, however, this finding is in keeping with the general asymmetry of parenting that the culture continues to support.

As the infant girl turns to her father or other significant male figure between the ages of 8 and 18 months (Abelin, 1980), she must see herself through the mirror of his eyes; and as in the mirror of mother's eyes, the reflection will have a significant effect on gender role identity as well as ego development (Levinson, 1984). Thus, it is the earliest reception to her gender that is recorded, internalized, and integrated — mother's projections and identifications, superimposed and interpenetrated with that of a female as other. Thus, along with the cognitive organization and process of identification — her/like-me/female — there is a reflection in the eyes of the other: woman as other seen through the eyes of the male. This is the Other that Simone de Beauvoir was writing about in *The Second Sex* (1953) and the Other of concern to French feminists in the Lacanian tradition. The Other as absence, the Other as not . . . Other as less than.

We begin to understand, then, why the sexual arrangements generative of the human malaise that Dinnerstein (1977) refers to are so impervious to change, lying as they do within the deep structure of a gender role identity that is infantile in its origins and unconscious in habitat. It is universal that women mother and that they or their same-gendered surrogates are the primary child tenders and first models of identification. Consequently, girls will continue to have difficulties with boundaries and Otherness, the emergence of a true self that is differentiated and valued, while boys will have to contend with the violence of separation and repression of "female-identified" forms of relatedness that is too often laid as the cornerstone of their maleness.

Freud (1931) noted that male denigration and contempt for women was more or less a natural outcome of the oedipal conflict. He was presaging the work of feminist theorists who trace the psychological origins of patriarchy back to the earliest infantile roots of male bonding and identification. As part of the natural recognition of gender difference and the ensuing solidification of gender role identity, the young boy is faced with the task of deidentifying with mother, the primary significant Other. Because of the relative absence of the father in the day-to-day world of the infant/toddler, nascent male gender role identity is based on being not-like mother/female, rather than on an authentic, experience-filled, relational identity: like-daddy/male. In addition, as Dinnerstein (1977) argues, since mother is associated with the earliest and most regressed pleasures, infantile desires and the states of dependence they recall are most stringently and rigidly repressed by the growing male child, who learns painfully that boys don't have needs for nurturance and support. Boys are not weak like girls — they are not dependent like girls — they are not so fickle, so emotionally labile. The reward for this constriction of their humanity is to belong to the instrumentally empowered world of men. When this constriction of affect is so integral to male gender role identity, the despair that Freud (1937) described becomes more understandable.

> At no other point in one's analytic work does one suffer from an
> oppressive feeling that all one's repeated efforts have been in
> vain, than when one is . . . seeking to convince a man that a
> passive attitude to men does not always signify castration. . . .
> The rebellious overcompensation of the male produces one of
> the strongest transference resistances. The resistance prevents
> any change from taking place [p. 252].

For girls, issues of separation-individuation continue longer than for
boys. The infant girl's natural developmental attempt to differentiate
from the symbiotic dyad must encompass the mother's natural tendencies toward projective identification.

As long as women mother, they more than men will be open to and
preoccupied with those very relational issues that constitute mothering: feelings of primary identification, lack of separateness or differentiation, ego and body-ego boundary issues, and primary love not
under the sway of the reality principle. A girl does not simply identify with her mother or want to be like her. Rather, mother and
daughter maintain elements of their primary relationship, which
means that they feel alike in fundamental ways (Chodorow, 1978).
For those women who experience particular difficulty with the
emergence and differentiation of self from mother, there is a prolonged and sometimes damaging preoccupation with issues of
boundaries and separateness that can detract from successful autonomous functioning in the public arena and thus can effect achievement and integration into the wider, extrafamilial world. It is those
very relational concerns, however, which have consistently sought to
mitigate the effects of aggression and alienation, all too common
symptoms of the male model of competition and independence.

ON THE RECOGNITION OF SEX DIFFERENCES

The great debates of the twenties and thirties within psychoanalysis
had to do with the primary versus secondary nature of female sexuality and the derivative issues of penis envy, castration anxiety, and
their meaning or relevance within a viable theoretical model of
female development (Fliegel, 1982; Lacan, 1982).

It is not surprising that these debates began in the 1920s, a time of
heightened feminist consciousness, when women were claiming
equal rights in the arenas of work and suffrage. The debate was
raised most vociferously again in the 1960s and early 1970s, when
women began to protest their roles and demand a credible psycho-

logical subjectivity of their own. It has been argued that political correctness has little do with scientific reality. However, the apperception of that reality is, as Thomas Kuhn (1962) so eloquently elaborated, dependent on a particular cultural-historical milieu. Any investigation of sexual difference must see clearly through the mists of phallocentric mystification and take care to elude the illusory promise of a psychosexual androgyny, to compensate for the unfortunate human tendency to ascribe hierarchical values to difference.

A model of gender differentiation has been proposed by Irene Fast (1984) whereby a slow recognition of the limits of both gender categories (male and female) are met with a sense of loss and protest.

> The differentiation process is hypothesized to be patterned in ways similar to those of other major developmental differentiations (e.g., self-other, subjective and object reality, intention and physical causality): an initial narcissistic undifferentiated period; recognition of limits with a response of protest, sense of loss, denial and so on; a recategorization of experience in which one differentiation product is integrated as part of self, the other recognized to be independent of self, the two in productive relationship [p. 44].

This obviously is strikingly different from the traditional psychoanalytic models, based on Freud (1925, 1931), where it is the girl who must come to terms with *her* difference and *her* sense of loss and must learn to contain *her* sense of masculine protest. As Fast (1984) points out, the developmental model of gender differentiation is in some ways the obverse of Freud's. In Freud's model, the genitals are sex specific and determine the subjective definition of maleness and femaleness.

> Gender differentiation theory suggests that genital experience is objectively sex-specific, but subjective definition of genital organs and experience as male and female is learned. It suggests that before differentiation processes begin, children's genital experience is well established but children do not categorize it in gender terms, nor recognize limits imposed by their actual sex [p. 88].

For the little girl, a natural part of the gender differentiation process will be the recognition that she does not have a penis, and that boys stand up to urinate whereas she sits; just as boys will notice that women bear babies and men do not. The intensity and qualitative nature of that sense of limitation is idiosyncratic and largely dependent on the nature of the mother-child interaction (Mahler, Pine, and Bergman, 1975; Kaplan, 1978; Tyson, 1982; Schwartz, 1984b), the role of the father (Abelin, 1980) and the wider social-cultural milieu (Waites, 1982).

The feminist critique of Freud's model of female development as phallocentric, coming as it does from a patriarchal culture, does not negate the recognition of gender differentiation as primary in development (Chodorow, 1978; Schwartz, 1984a).

Accepting Fast's notion of a parallel developmental process of self and gender differentiation, one must look to situations of ongoing difficulty, for example, persistent penis envy or the development of a castration complex, for the determinants of pathological development of self. Grossman and Stewart (1976), in an interesting reframing of penis envy as a developmental metaphor, categorize the traditional ways of understanding this complicated set of feelings as those belonging to earlier narcisstic injury, and those resulting from a later disappointment in object relations—a regressive effort to resolve oedipal conflicts. In either case, they recognize the "necessity to consider penis envy as the manifest content of a symptom that needs analysis, rather than as 'bedrock' or ultimate conflict" (p. 211).

It is the author's experience that the castration complex, or rather the persistent and continuing belief or fear that the current female genitals are the result of a castration, occurs predominately in those situations where there has been a severe maternal failure. Severe maternal failure often entails undue rejection of the daughter due the mother's competitive or jealous feelings or wish for a male child. Such rejection may also be accompanied by multiple empathic failures throughout the early stages of separation-individuation, so that the daughter is in a constant state of rage, which is turned inward—the castration experienced as punishment for her murderous wishes and simultaneous failure as a satisfactory object for the rejecting mother.

DEVELOPMENTAL SEQUENCE

The sequence to be presented deals primarily with three developmental periods that are key in the formation of female gender role identity: the rapprochement subphase of separation-individuation; the phase of triangulation; and adolescence. A comprehensive treatment of the complexities of this developmental sequence would require a book to itself. Nonetheless, fundamental processes and constructs can be highlighted for further theoretical exploration, as well as clinical and developmental observation.

Rapprochement

The rapprochement subphase of the separation-individuation process extends from approximately 14–15 months to 24 months or beyond. This period is marked by growing recognition of separateness from mother and the consequent vulnerability that ensues from the toddlers's confrontation with the failure of her omnipotence in relation to mother and the world at large. During this period, too, comes the core gender identity, the fundamental knowledge that "I am a girl," which is accompanied by heightened awareness of the genitalia both in relation to gender difference and the potential for sensual pleasure.

According to Kaplan (1978),

> The girl discovers the sexual difference under the impetus of first discovering the pleasures of genital self-stimulation. The primarily exploratory and boundary seeking type of genital manipulation to the ten to twelve month old girl has by sixteen months been converted into focused pleasure seeking activity. Now with self/other awareness, the girl connects her frustrations as well as her delights with a person who might be contributing to them. As with the person-associated emotions of joy, anger and sadness, pleasure seeking genital arousal has the potential of becoming associated with other people. . . . The discovery of the pleasure possibilities of her own genitals at around fifteen or sixteen months impels the girl to become aware of the genitals of others and to ascribe meaning to the awareness [pp. 221–213].

By 18 to 19 months, the toddler is capable of making cognitive distinctions between genders and ascribe meaning to those distinctions.

Notice the timing here. At the same period that the toddler is dealing with the shame and frustrations of the failure of her omnipotence ("The world is not my oyster") and negotiating a new relationship of independence from Mother ("Mommy is not part of me. My wishes and needs do not control her. I am often helpless and alone"), she is also confronting the anatomical differences between the sexes and the social construction of gender. Quite a handful for a not-yet-two year old!

The critical issue in the emergence of gender role identity in this stage is that difficulties in negotiating the rapprochement crisis will become linked to gender. Penis envy is not inevitable, nor must it be. Mahler and her colleagues (1975) and Kaplan (1978) suggest that the loss of separation from mother and the fall from omnipotence is inevitably associated with the lack of a penis and that mother is held permanently accountable for the little girl's state in the world as damaged . . . less than . . . without. Such inferences are perilously close to Freud's original position that the girl holds her mother accountable for her narcissistic injury, an injury based on the obvious superiority of the male genital. As noted earlier, any ongoing sense of penis envy must be regarded as symptomatic on the one hand and as a cultural given on the other, insofar as culture is mediated through primary caretakers.

In keeping with the asymmetry of parenting, during the rapprochement crisis, the toddler tends to blame both herself and mother for her disappointments, her daily shames and humilations, her letdowns and frustrations. She will alternately seek out and reject mother as she struggles with yearnings for independence and mastery and contradictory desires for regression to an earlier, less complex state of merger. A depressed, unavailable mother, a narcissistic mother who is able to relate to her daughter only as a selfobject will present stumbling blocks for the child through her empathic failures.

Thus the possibility arises for the establishment of a destructive cycle where feelings of not-getting are confused with not-deserving-as-female, and aggressive wishes are confused with damaging effects, such as castration. When in certain circumstances this negative cycle is associated with gender, difficulties naturally arise in the firming of a positively valued and esteemed sense of self-as-female.

For both genders, however, a successful negotiation of this period is vital for the development of object constancy, for a boundaried, positive, ongoing sense of self in relation to others, for the ability to tolerate ambivalence, and for the integration of sexual and aggressive feelings.

Triangulation

Proceeding along classical lines, one might next expect an extended discussion of the oedipal stage and its relation to gender role identity in girls. However, for girls it is the phase of triangulation and not the oedipal phase that is the proximate critical developmental era. On phallocentric grounds alone, metaphorical reference to Oedipus' dilemma is a poor choice to speak to the female experience. More to the point, analysis of oedipal dynamics, if and where they are accentuated in little girls, does not help to apprehend accurately the development of gender role identity, which we now understand clearly

predates the emergence of the oedipal. Gender role ascriptions begin
at birth; core gender identity is formed by the age of 18 months.
Current theory and observation indicate that triangulation, too, predates the traditional phallic oedipal period (Stoller, 1968; Abelin,
1971, 1980; Kleeman, 1976).

The oedipal conflict more universally has to do with the mechanism by which the boy is able to effect his separation from the
omnipotent mother (Dinnerstein, 1977) and the boy's consequent
identification and entry into the world of men. As Gilligan (1982)
points out in her work in superego development, male models are not
applicable to the understanding of the female experience.

Traditionally, the oedipal phase has referred to a turning or a shift
in erotic object choice from the mother to the father with accompanying feelings of rivalry and jealousy. However, as these turnings
occur with greater and lesser frequency and intensity throughout the
triangulation period, as the girl turns towards the father or significant males outside the mother–daughter dyad, one must inquire not
only about the shifts in object choice, but also about the viscissitudes
in identification and internal psychic representations integral to
emerging gender role identity.

Moreover, in today's society, where there are so many single-
parent families, we must take into account not only the effects of
asymmetrical parenting (women as primary caretakers and nur-
turers) but also the ever growing incidence of "nontraditional" families, where there might be multiple significant male others or same-
sex parents. Psychoanalysis must have a model to incorporate these
"deviations" as the norms they are becoming.

It is interesting to note too that Freud's view of female heterosexuality is strangely in keeping with that of those more radical feminists who see women turning to men as a lesser compromise of self.
For Freud it is the "shock of recognition" of the anatomical differences between the sexes and the ensuing castration complex that
spurs the girl into the oedipal phase. According to Freud (1925),
there is no motivation for heterosexual object choice that does not
include a denigration of femininity. It is the wish for a penis as a
clearly superior organ that turns the little girl's eye towards her
father. "She gives up her wish for a penis and puts in place of it a
wish for a child; and it is with that purpose in view that she takes her
father as a love-object. Her mother becomes the object of her jealousy" (p. 256).

Parens, Pollack, Stern, and Kramer (1976) did observe a psychosexual shift in girls from a predominance of oral and anal concerns to
genital, in what they termed a shift into the protogenital phase.

According to their observations, this awakening of genital sensuality is most often an expression of the girl's "primary, constitutional feminine disposition" rather than a demonstration of phallic concerns (p. 83). They question Freud's criteria for marking the girl's entry into the oedipal era: evidence of the castration complex and further object-related differentiation followed by a wish to have a baby. In their view, both the phase of protogenitality and the observable heightened interest in "having a baby" that little girls demonstrate in play and verbal behavior are reflective expressions of inborn gender characteristics.

This position, of course, implies innate heterosexual object choice, which they refer to as "constitutional disposition to heterosexuality," as well as an innate "drive-derived" wish to have a baby, neither of which has been empirically demonstrated to be true. What is important here is the recognition of the girl's own genitality, which is *hers* and has to do with an expression of her self as subject rather than a flawed other, a poor relation of the male subjective.

Thus the oedipal phase will remain subsumed in the proposed model under the general heading of triangulation, a larger, more encompassing developmental period having to do with the incorporation of significant others into the object world of the child, blossoming genitality, the firming of erotic object choices, and the solidification of gender role identity.

Fathers and significant male others, in the positive affirmation of the girls's tentative sexual advances, help consolidate her sense of being both the subject and the object of desire. Moving out into the world, increasingly able to join and leave mother, the little girl has an other on whom to exercise her many creative skills and abilities. The quality of the mirroring of those abilities and skills, the reception or lack of it, their enhancement or denigration will inevitably be linked to gender and the apprehension of gender role.

It is during this period of triangulation, too, when issues of object choice come to the fore. Current theorists have increasingly linked issues of gender role identity with sexual orientation and Lesbian choice. Eisenbud (1982) has identified two paths to Lesbian choice, which relate to these issues of gender role identity as they heighten during the phase of triangulation. In what she terms "exclusion from identification with the mother," a double bind exists in which the daughter is forbidden to identify or compete with the mother and is often asked to replace the husband as confidant or to serve as the mother's "male self." That is, the girl must be active, strong, and independent in order to tend to the mother's needs, but she must not compete as a female.

The least stable of choices, according to Eisenbud, appears to be "escape from inclusion," which speaks implicitly to a failure of triangulation whereby individuation is sought by erotic domination of mother in lieu of identification with her.

Joyce McDougall (1970) outlines two paths of female gender role identity, which include a repudiation of any identification with the genital mother. She distinguishes those women who have a masculine ideal and thus disparage women and all things feminine (heterosexual women in McDougall's view) from those women who desire other women within a homosexual context.

In a later paper (1980) she states more explicitly that "female homosexuality is an attempt to resolve conflicts concerning the two poles of psychic identity: one's identity as a separate individual and one's sexual identity" (p. 87). She offers a variation of the resolution of the triangulation phase whereby the little girl gives up her father as a love object and identifies with him instead, while mother is sought in an idealized form in the homosexual relation. This traditional explanation of the negative-oedipal (Nagera, 1975) is interesting in that she relates this choice to the girl's need for a strong sense of subjective identity, which has been difficult within a family constellation where issues of separation-individuation have not been successfully negotiated. In these constellations, the father has been deemed unacceptable as an object choice, being perceived as bad, dirty, dangerous, unavailable, or rejecting.

Schwartz (1984b) has delineated a dynamic similar to McDougall's repudiation of identification with the genital mother. Schwartz refers to this dynamic as "deidentification with mother as female" — a process founded on the internalization of gender role stereotypes and confounded by difficulties with separation and individuation. Schwartz does not offer a model of etiology, but rather a developmental description of this path of deidentification with mother as female, which is common but not exclusive to nor universal among lesbians.

Where this type of deidentification occurs, mothers, because of their own difficulties, appear to have epitomized the negative female stereotypes of passivity and general inadequacy in worldly matters. In their family constellation, the asymmetry of privilege and esteem was initially mystified by a quasi-sadomasochistic dynamic where father represented activity and effectiveness, strength and excitement, while mother epitomized weakness and constriction, paralleling and reinforcing the cultural stereotype.

Little girls, like little boys, can identify with the family member who appears socially valued, competent, independent, and free from the risk of humilation and contempt. Like her archetypal "brother," the girl forms her identification on the basis of being "not like mother," an active dissociation from the female world. During this period of triangulation, this particular girl, conflicted in her gender role identity, attempts to gain father's respect and interest by proving that she is not like mother." She will become the "apple of Daddy's eye," not by accepting her feminity but by distancing from it.

This process of deidentification with mother involves the repression of nurturant needs, the precocious development of pseudoindependence, and the denial of relatedness. The narcissistic and depressed mothers of such children often collude in this development, seeing the premature emergence of independence as a lessening of nurturant demands they feel unable to meet. The process of deidentification is often accompanied by a project of "saving mother." This is accomplished by not needing or not wanting, by being strong, capable, and good. Moreover, the young girl is more able to retain "mommy" as a good object if she is successful in repressing much of her rage at the empathic failures of the rapprochement crisis. In the service of the project to save mommy, she assumes the role of caretaker, the idealized good parent, who is more often than not an angry, crying little girl inside.

Often in families where there has been a marked asymmetry in gender role privilege, as well as some perceived deficiency in "good-enough" mothering during the previous phases of separation-individuation, the young girl keeps her identification with the genital mother but adopts a characterological acquiescence to a prescribed stereotypic female role, which can include feigned passivity, denial of assertive sexuality, and low self-esteem.

Angry active resistance to perceived male privilege — resistance often pathologized as "unresolved penis envy" — has its root in this phase of triangulation as well. Such angry active resistance that does appear symptomatically as an overconcern with issues of power and excessive vulnerability to narcissistic injury develops when gender privilege is reflected within the nuclear constellation but the earlier phases of separation-individuation have been more successfully negotiated. Here, the young girl has a more positive, firmer sense of an autonomous gendered self, which recoils in hurt, anger, and dismay at her exclusion as independent subject from the instrumental world of male power.

The phase of triangulation marks the end of the safe but limited world of the maternal dyad and offers instead an arena for the further maturation of ego and interpersonal skills. Friendships and jealousies, challenge and competition, mastery and, alas, defeat become greater possibilities as the internal world of the self/other becomes more constant and the gendered world becomes more of a reality.

Adolescence

For the young girl, the onset of menarche is the clearest biological marker of her entrance into womanhood. It marks the onset of a normal developmental crisis that can enhance or impede the further blossoming of the adult woman in all her aspects (Ritvo, 1976). Yet, far from being a universally celebratory rite of passage, the counterpart of the coming of age for men, the beginning of menstruation is a reminder not only of the woman's unique potential to be the bearer of life, but of the cultural fear and defensive devaluation associated with such potential.

In many societies the onset of menstruation means seclusion or isolation from the family or tribe for periods of a few days to a few years; it can mean symbolic defloration or actual genital mutilation, including clitoridectomy (removal of the clitoris) and infibulation (the sewing up of the entrance to the vagina) (Delaney, Lupton, and Toth, 1977).

In the Judeo-Christian tradition, the Old Testament offers clear directions for the treatment of the menstruating woman (Leviticus 15:19–33).

> And if a woman have an issue, and her issue in her flesh be blood, she shall be put apart seven days: and whosoever toucheth her shall be unclean until the even. . . .
>
> And whosoever toucheth those things shall be unclean, and shall wash his clothes, and bathe himself in water and be unclean until the even. . . .
>
> . . . and the priest shall make an atonement for her before the Lord for the issue of her uncleanliness.

Lest we feel that our postmodern society has progressed beyond such primitive fear and superstition, Breit and Ferrandino (1979) point out that the euphemisms used to refer to menstruation — "falling off the roof," "on the rag," "sick time," "the curse" — reflect our attitudes of negativity, avoidance, and denial.

One might wonder how the sociocultural dimensions of the menstrual taboo influence our psychoanalytic understanding of the development of gender role identity. If adolescence is a time of developmental recapitulation (Blos, 1979; Ritvo, 1976), then cultural myths and stereotypes can reinforce earlier misconceptions and confusions in internal bodily repensentation and the imagined punishments of a harsh infantile superego. Some girls perceive the first menstruation as an excretory function, reviving old conflicts in that area. Feelings of passivity and helplessness can be accentuated as the pubescent girl feels herself to be bleeding from within, with a periodicity and intensity over which she has no control. While the development of breasts and other secondary sex characteristics is apt to bring her much positive attention, she must carry around this "friend" in private.

In Western culture, adolescence is an extended period of transition from childhood to adulthood that demands not only intrapsychic integration, but the working through of one's place in the social order. It is during this period that the gender role identity of the young girl is solidified, incorporating the cultural expectations of womanhood with her biological capabilities and limitations.

Erik Erikson (1950) termed this stage one of "Identity versus Role Confusion":

> The integration now taking place in the form of ego identity is, as pointed out, more that the sum of the childhood identifications. It is the accrued experience of the ego's ability to integrate all identifications with the vicissitudes of the libido, with the aptitudes developed out of endowment, and with the opportunities offered in social roles [p. 261].

He points out that adolescents must confront problems of ideology and aristocracy, which for Erikson means the "best people will come to rule and rule brings out the best in people" (p. 263). It is just this confrontation with ideology and aristocracy, better known in feminist circles as patriarchy, that is decisive for so many young women.

What is it, then, that the pubescent girl faces on the dawn of her womanhood? Bodily changes are accompanied by heightened sexual desires, dreams of love and romance. Too often, however, she experiences heightened desire at more or less the same time as she encounters increased sexual objectification by adolescent boys forced once again by cultural expectation and the revival of early conflicts in identification to "prove their manhood" by sexual conquest and renewed contempt for and denigration of women. Moreover, with the expansion of social and educational spheres, the young girl is reacquainted with the overvaluation of the male world in sports, the media, and the military.

It is during this time that many girls are forced by both parents into traditional roles of which they had been free during childhood. Mothers who had been content to let their daughters be "tomboys" or otherwise deviate from cultural norms can become frightened and guilty during their daughter's adolescence. Mothers can block their daughters' natural attempts at identification because of the threat of competition; they may resent their daughters' seeming rejection of their status as the "second sex" and thus squelch creative attempts to experiment with the variegations intrinsic to any social role. During their daughters' adolescence mothers invariably feel the resurgence of their own psychosexual and role conflicts as their gender role identity cones into question through the questioning of their daughters.

Adolescence is a time too when fathers unmistakenly recognize their daughters as sexual women, and it is a time when heretofore hidden or denied misogyny often comes to the surface. Father's view of women as objects worthy only of sexual desire or derision and his defense against his own sexual interests in his daughter can lead to a hypervaluing of the adolescent's sexuality, so that it engulfs her definition by its presence or absence. A positive affirmation of her burgeoning sexual interest, however, coupled with a genuine appreciation of the physical manifestations of her womanliness, is tremendously important in the solidification of a fertile, growth-enhancing gender role identity.

For all girls, adolescence is a time for fantasy and dreams. It is time of becoming and wishing to become. Feminist analyses and political action have resulted in expanded opportunities for the more privileged classes in European and North American societies. There is greater flexibility of social role for both genders as women are increasingly permitted to achieve in the world of work and men are permitted and encouraged to nurture. For these young women, as well as for women in the most rigidly structured societies where there is little possibility for conscious role conflict, adolescence can be a time when young women begin to realize the enormous potential for creative use of their abilities.

Where asymmetry of gender role privilege continues to exist in clearly dysfunctional ways, the normal confusions of identity can be heightened for the female adolescent. But contradictions can facilitate growth. Where the early internalizations of female gender role identity have been positively based on relational identification with mother and other significant females and reflected through the affirming eyes of the male other, such contradictions, when finally integrated, can lead to a richer, more fully textured subjective sense of the female self.

SUMMARY

Gender role identity, as it refers to the ongoing sense of being female, has to do with meanings. It has to do with the integrative function of gender as the basic cognitive organizer and its construction within a particular biological, psychological, and sociohistorical milieu.

The development of internal representations of the gendered self has a special importance for women in that the particular nature of female sexuality can lead to a certain amount of lability as to the boundaries of inside and out, as well as the extent of a felt internal locus of control.

The asymmetry of parenting, which is normative in our society, is, according to feminist theorists, a major cause of male denigration and contempt for women. This is in contrast to Freud's view, which was that male misogyny is an inevitable outcome of psychosexual development. For women, asymmetry of parenting allows for a relational identification with mother, which can serve as a solid foundation for an esteemed gendered role at the same time as it can contribute to increased difficulties in emerging from the mother–daughter dyad.

The gender differentiation model suggests a common sense of loss and protest on the part of both genders at the recognition of differences. Ongoing penis envy or castration fantasies in girls and women is suggestive of pathology and symptomatic of problems in gender role identity.

The rapprochement phase of the separation-individuation process, the advent of triangulation, and adolescence are especially significant in the development of gender role identity. The danger during the rapprochement subphase is that difficulties in negotiation will become linked to gender. In some situations, the fall from omnipotence is experienced as a gender-linked inadequacy, while in others the child's rage at empathic failures will be omnipotently experienced as having yielded a punishment of gender difference.

The entry of father or significant male figures contributes to the consolidation of the gendered self as subject and object of desire. During the triangulation period there is a firming of object choice and increased recognition of sex differences, both of which coincide with the apprehension of gender privilege. For young girls, the seeds of a characterological stance toward such perceived privilege are sown here, with acquiescence, resistance, or deidentification with the genital mother as a possible outcome.

Adolescence allows for an extended period of solidification of gender role identity within the social order. The onset of puberty ushers in a recapitulation of early conflicts and confusions about the gendered self with its limitations potentials.

Work and motherhood, production and reproduction are foreshadowed during adolescence, but it is generally not until adulthood that they are fully integrated into a women's gender role identity, and the understanding of that gender role is necessarily incomplete without them.

REFERENCES

Abelin, E. (1971). The role of the father in the separation-individuation process. In: *Separation-Individuation*, ed. J. B. McDevitt & C. F. Settlage. New York: International Universities Press, pp. 229–252.

———— (1980). Triangulation, the role of the father and the origins of core gender identity during the rapprochement subphase. In: *Rapprochement*, ed. R. F. Lax, S. Bach & J. A. Burland. New York: Aronson, pp. 151–170.

Beauvoir, S. de (1953). *The Second Sex*. New York: Knopf.

Bernstein, D. (1983). The female superego. *Internat. J. Psycho-Anal.*, 64:187–201.

Blos, P. (1979). *The Adolescent Passage*. New York: International Universities Press.

Breit, E. B., & Ferrandino, M. M. (1979). Social dimensions of the menstural taboo and the effects on female sexuality. In: *Psychology of Women*, ed. J. H. Williams. New York: Norton, pp. 241–254.

Chodorow, N. (1978). *The Reproduction of Mothering, Psychoanalysis and the Sociology of Gender*, Berkley: University of California Press.

Delaney, J., Lupton, M. J., & Toth, E. (1977). *The Curse*. New York: Mentor.

Dinnerstein, D. (1977). *The Mermaid and the Minotaur*. New York: Harper.

Eisenbud, R. J. (1982). Early and later determinants of Lesbian choice. *Psychoanal. Rev.*, 69:86–109.

Erikson, E. (1950). *Childhood and Society*. New York: Norton.

Fast, I. (1984). *Gender Identity*. Hillsdale, NJ: The Analytic Press.

Fliegel, Z. (1973). Feminine psychosexual development in Freudian theory. *Psychoanal. Quart.*, 42:385–409.

———— (1982). Current status of Freud's controversial views on women. *Psychoanal. Rev.*, 69:7–28.

Freud, S. (1925). Some physical consequences of the anatomical distinctions between the sexes. *Standard Edition*, 19:245–260. London: Hogarth Press, 1961.

———— (1931). Female sexuality. *Standard Edition*, 21:223–246. London: Hogarth Press, 1961.

———— (1937). Analysis terminable and interminable. *Standard Edition*, 23:209–245. London: Hogarth Press, 1966.

Gilligan, C. (1982). *In A Different Voice*. Cambridge, MA.: Harvard University Press.

Greenson, R. R. (1968). Dis-identifying from mother: Its special importance for the boy. *Internat. J. Psycho-Anal.*, 49:360–374.

Grossman, W., & Stewart, W. (1976). Penis envy: From childhood wish to developmental metaphor. *J. Amer. Psychoanal. Assn.*, 24(5):193–212.

Guttentag, M., Salasin, S., & Belle, D. (1980). *The Mental Health of Women.* New York: Academic Press.

Horney, K. (1924). On the genesis of the castration complex in women. *Internat. J. Psycho-Anal.*, 5:50–65.

―――― (1932). The dread of women: Observations on a specific difference in the dread felt by men and by women respectively for the opposite sex. *Internat. J. Psycho-Anal.*, 13:348–360.

―――― (1933). The denial of the vagina: A contribution to the problem of the genital anxieties specific to women. *Internat. J. Psycho-Anal.*, 14:57–70.

Kaplan, L. (1978). *Oneness and Separateness.* New York: Simon & Shuster.

Kleeman, J. (1976). Freud's views on early female sexuality in the light of direct child observation. *J. Amer. Psychoanal. Assn.*, 24(5):3–28.

Kohlberg, L. (1966). A cognitive-developmental analysis of children's sex-role concepts and attitudes. In: *The Development of Sex Differences*, ed. E. Maccoby. Palo Alto, CA: Stanford University Press.

Kuhn, T. (1962). *The Structure of Scientific Revolutions.* Chicago: University of Chicago Press.

Lacan, J. (1982). *Feminine Sexuality*, ed. J. Mitchell, J. Rose; trans. J. Rose. New York: Norton.

Levinson, R. (1984). Intimacy, autonomy and gender: Developmental differences and their reflection in adult relationships. *J. Amer. Acad. Psychoanal.*, 12:529–544.

Lewis, H. B. (1976). *Psychic War in Men and Women.* New York: New York University Press.

Mahler, M., Pine, F., & Bergman, A. (1975). *The Psychological Birth of the Human Infant.* New York: Basic Books.

McDougall, J. (1970). Homosexuality in women. In: *Female Sexuality*, ed. J. Chasseguet-Smirgal. Ann Arbor: University of Michigan Press.

―――― (1980). The homosexual dilemma. In: *Plea for a Measure of Abnormality.* New York: International Universities Press, pp. 87–141.

Money, J., Hampson, J. G., & Hampson, J. L. (1955). An examination of some basic sexual concepts: The evidence of human hermaphroditism. *Bull. Johns Hopkins Hosp.*, 97:301–310.

Money, J. (ed.) (1965). *Sex Research.* New York: Holt, Rinehart & Winston.

―――― (1973). Gender role, gender identity, core gender identity: Usage and definition of terms. *J. Amer. Acad. Psychoanal.*, 1:397–402.

Montgrain, N. (1983). On the vicissitudes of female sexuality: The difficult path from anatomical destiny to psychic representation. *Internat. J. Psycho-Anal.*, 64:169–186.

Parens, H., Pollack, L., Stern, J., & Kramer, S. (1976). On the girl's entry into the oedipal complex. *J. Amer. Psychoanal. Assn.*, 24(5):79–108.

Person, E., & Ovesey, L. (1983). Psychoanalytic theories of gender identity. *J. Amer. Psychoan.*, 11:203–226.

Ritvo, S. (1976). Adolescent to woman. *J. Amer. Psychoan. Assn.*, 24(5):127–138.

Rubin, J., Provenzano, F., & Luria, Z. (1979). The eye of the beholder: Parent's views on sex of newborns. In: *Psychology of Women*, ed. J. Williams. New York: Norton, pp. 134–141.

Schwartz, A. (1984a). Psychoanalysis and women: A rapprochement. *Women & Ther.*, 3(1):3–12.

_____ (1984b). *On choosing to be a lesbian: Conflicts in gender role identity and their clinical implications.* Presented at the Annual Meeting of Association for Women in Psychology, Boston, MA.

_____ (1984c). Earliest memories: Sex differences and the meaning of experience. *Imag., Cog. Personal.*, 4(1):43–52.

Stoller, R. (1968). *Sex and Gender,* New York: Science House.

Thompson, C. (1964). *On Women,* ed, M. Green. New York: Mentor.

Tyson, P. (1982). A developmental line of gender identity, gender role, and choice of love object. *J. Amer. Psychoanal. Assn.*, 30(1):61–86.

Waites, E. (1982). Females self-representation and the unconscious: A reply to Amy Galen. *Psychoanal. Rev.*, 69:29–41.

Winnicott, D. (1965). *Maturational Processes and the Facilitating Environment.* New York: International Universities Press.

|II| *Freudian Theory & Beyond*

4 Morality, Gender, and Analysis

JUDITH L. ALPERT
JODY BOGHOSSIAN SPENCER

Analysts consider material that patients bring and attempt to go beyond that material in order to enlarge the patient's life. In this chapter, the "patients" are four theorists, and the material they present concerns morality. The intent here is to go beyond this material on morality to enlarge psychoanalysis. Hence, the purpose of this chapter is broader than furthering theory about moral development and, it is hoped, this paper will raise some questions about psychoanalysis.

The first part of the chapter considers Freud, Horney, Kohlberg, and Gilligan's theories of moral development. For the most part, the theories of psychoanalysis and of related disciplines have run a parallel course, there has been little attempt to account for discrepancies and to further integration. It is for this reason that both analytic and nonanalytic positions are considered here. Freud and Horney were selected to represent the analytic positions. Although there has been theoretical and technical progression from Freud, modern psychoanalysis continues to be based on his assumptions and mode of thinking, and therefore this chapter begins with Freud. Because Horney was an early revisionist, her views are considered here. Kohlberg and Gilligan were selected to represent the nonanalytic positions. Kohlberg based his theory on Freud's and Piaget's work, and Gilligan responded to Kohlberg and based her theory on her own research as well as that of Chodorow's.

We gratefully acknowledge Dale Mendell for her helpful comments on a draft of this paper.

An abbreviated version of this paper was presented at the Annual Meeting of the American Psychological Association, Division 39, Los Angeles, 1985.

In the second part of the chapter, some implications from the previous analysis are considered. For ease in understanding, the words "therapy" and "analysis," as well as "sex" and "gender," are used interchangeably throughout the chapter.

The points to be made are:

1. There are differences in the study and conceptualization of morality across theorists, as well as within and across disciplines.

2. Some of the major differences between the male and female theorists are consistent with Gilligan's findings and support gender differences in orientation.

3. Given these tendencies towards gender differences in orientation, there needs to be consideration of (a) the analyst's gender and psychotherapeutic work, and (b) some selected aspects of traditional psychoanalysis.

FREUD'S CONTRIBUTION

While there is controversy over Frued's views on feminine psychology and, specifically, superego development, modern psychoanalysis continues to be based on his assumptions and mode of thinking. Consequently, it needs review. Freud demonstrated how little he understood about female development. Although many of Freud's early ideas derived from his work with female patients, he acknowledged that his formulations were based on the study of men, that his theory of superego development evolved out of his study of male children, and that there was more to learn about women. While Freud (1933) considered the influence of a girl's preoedipal attachment to her mother and suggested that female development might be different in the preoedipal years, his final conceptualization of female development did not retain this consideration (Freud, 1937, 1940). In his later works, Freud returned to an earlier and more patriarchical view, which considered female development as "both second best and second rate-second best in the experience of the girl and women and second rate in the judgment of patriarchal spokesmen of civilization at large" (Schafer, 1974, p. 461).

Freud's conceptualization of female superego development, which is tied to the phallic-oedipal phase and particularly to castration anxiety, is consistent with his view that female development is a variation of male development. He held that female superego development is weaker than the male's, because girls are already castrated and consequently have no motivation for superego formation. Freud (1925) stated:

> I cannot evade the notion that for women the level of what is ethically normal is different from what it is in men. Their super-ego is never so inexorable, so impersonal, so independent of its emotional origins as we require it to be in men. Character-traits which critics of every epoch have brought up against women — that they show less sense of justice than men, that they are less ready to submit to the great exigencies of life, that they are more often influenced in their judgements by feelings of affection or hostility — all these would be amply accounted for by the modification in the formation of their superego which we have inferred above [pp. 257–258].

To consider Freud's view of superego development, selected aspects of his preoedipal and oedipal formulations need review. Freud held that boy's and girl's sexuality was masculine in orientation until the phallic crisis (Freud, 1905), and he maintained this position in later writings (Freud, 1933). During the phallic stage, the interest of both sexes in external genitalia is intensified, and the girl is confronted with her penisless state. According to Freud, the little girl's observation that she is anatomically different from her male counterpart leads to a castration complex, which, in turn, provokes her penis envy. This chain of events leads to the "loosening of the girl's relation with her mother as a love-object" (Freud, 1925, p. 254). Feelings of inferiority ensue, as, in Freud's (1933) words the little girl "loses her enjoyment in her phallic sexuality. Her self-love is mortified by the comparison with the boy's far superior equipment . . ." (p. 126). She is left, according to Freud (1925), with a "wound to her narcissism and develops, "like a scar, a sense of inferiority" (p. 253),which can be rectified only by the girl's turning toward her father and the wish for a baby, especially a male baby, who could potentially be given to her by her father's penis.

Her Oedipus complex is described as incomplete and is attributed to the relative absence of castration anxiety. Freud states (1933), "In the absence of fear of castration the chief motive is lacking which leads boys to surmount the Oedipus complex. Girls remain in it for an indeterminate length of time; they demolish it late and, even so, incompletely. In these circumstances the formation of the superego must suffer; it cannot attain the strength and independence which gives it cultural significance . . ." (p. 129). Thus, according to Freud, because the boy's fear of castration and its severe superego heir is not present in the girl, she lacks the incentive to develop and rigidly maintain the moral stance that Freud considers to be characteristic of males. In short, Freud held that because the girl lacks the major impetus for superego formation — castration anxiety — she fails to develop as autonomous a superego as her male counterpart.

Freud (1925) maintained that the differences in male and female biology create fundamental differences in the boy's and girl's experience of the oedipal phase. While in the female the oedipal phase is initiated with a castration complex, for the male the oedipal complex precedes the castration complex. During the oedipal phase, the young boy wishes to place himself in his father's position and dreams of having intercourse with his mother. This oedipal dream is shattered by the boy's fear of castration. Thus, in boys, fear of potential castration is central. The threat results in the boy's moving away from mother and toward an identification with father. Not wishing to be castrated, like his female playmates, he represses his sexual wishes for his mother and identifies with his father.

Thus, there are differences in the chronologies of the castration complex and Oedipus complex in girls and boys. As Freud wrote, (1925), "Whereas in boys the Oedipus complex is destroyed by the castration complex, in girls it is made possible and led up to by the castration complex" (p. 256). The difference in sequence of the complexes leads to the formation of different superego structures. For boys, the fear of castration provokes the relinquishing of Oedipal objects and leads the boy to replace these objects with identification in the form of the authority of the father or parents. These identifications become introjected into the ego and eventually make up the nucleus of the superego or, as Freud (1924) states: "[the superego] takes over the severity of the father and perpetuates his prohibition against incest, and so secures the ego from the return of the libidinal object-cathexis" (pp. 176–177). For boys, paternal prohibitions are internalized under pressure of castration threat, and this results in a strong superego; in girls, since castration anxiety is not strong, internalized prohibitions do not result in as strong a superego.

DISCUSSION

Many of Freud's ideas about early female sexuality have been validated through direct observation of children. Among these are the universality of genital self-stimulation, the presence of infantile sexuality, and the significance of the preoedipal attachment to the mother (Stoller, 1964; Kleeman, 1977). However, Freud's position about the onset and nature of early feminine gender identity, which is basic to his formulation of superego development in females, is not supported. Research with young children (e.g., see Stoller, 1964; Galenson and Roiphe 1977; Kleeman, 1977) indicates the emergence of gender identity within the first year of life and its irreversibility by age 18 months. These studies uncover the need to modify Freud's views about the onset and impact of early female identity formation. The studies suggest that early biological and cultural manifestations may be more integral to femine gender identity than Freud realized, while later and more anatomically based factors, such as penis envy, may be of less universal significance in the development of femininity. An important component of Freud's psychology of women — the view that girls begin their development thinking they are like boys and develop feminine wishes only as a consequence of the castration complex — is not supported. Consequently, the basis on which Freud formulated his view of superego development is called into question. If the establishment of gender identity is less traumatic than Freud held, then the development of the superego in males and females might not be characterized as Freud states.

Freud's (1924, 1925) superego formulation has been challenged by theorists as well as by researchers. Four central points in Freud's theory of superego development are controversial: his conceptualization of the superego; his connecting superego development to the phallic-oedipal phase and particularly to castration anxiety; his relating superego with morality; and his contention that women have weaker superegos. His conceptualization of the superego is regarded as narrow by, for example, Schafer (1974) and Bernstein (1983). Schafer indicates that Freud was referring to a quality of moral rigidity that characterizes men more than women and is associated with the tendency for men to be less easily moved by emotional appeals or consequences in personal relationships and to follow more consistently seemingly objective and abstract principles. Further, he notes that Freud was a product of his time and was confusing values with observation: Freud valued holding to seemingly objective and abstract principles over emotional appeals and confused this value with his observation that men have a greater capacity for isolation of affect while women are more likely to demonstrate hysterical activity. In addition, Schafer (1974) objects on a psychoanalytic basis to Freud's judgment that obsessives are more moral than hysterics, explaining that the obsessive model is a poor model of morality.

Bernstein (1983) comments that Freud emphasized "firmness of superego structures," which is more characteristic of the male superego, and used it as the sole criterion for desirable superego while neglecting other criteria, such as strength, structure, and contents. She questions whether firm structure is more desirable than flexible structure, indicating that one can rigidly follow a commandment that may not necessarily lead to a moral decision. Within her critique she presents another way of conceptualizing superego and its development. Bernstein defines and traces the history of superego contents, strength, and structure to identify the differences between male and female superego. She defines superego contents as specific admonitions, some of which appear to be universal or culturally dependent. She defines superego strength as the efficiency with which the contents are regulated or the degree to which the contents are enforced; for example, one who appears obedient may be demonstrating great superego strengths by enforcing a directive. Bernstein defines superego structure as the organization or inter-relationship of the contents, with structure being more fixed in men and more flexible in women because of developmental factors. Women are likely to be flexible in choosing superego contents, with the final organization depending on the demands of a particular situation. However, this flexibility does not necessarily connote a less moral position. It is possible to have many contents, enforced with great strength, and a rigid structure, which result in immorality. While Freud assumed that the maintenance of a moral position demonstrated firmer morality, and that men surpass women in this regard, both Schafer and Bernstein point out that there are other ways of conceptualizing morality.

With regard to connecting superego development with the phallic-oedipal phase, Schafer (1974) emphasizes that this view places too much focus on the role of castration anxiety. Bernstein (1983) concurs, moreover, she holds, the core of the superego is formed much earlier than the phallic-oedipal phase and is revised throughout each stage of development. She traces three aspects of the superego to the child's earliest interaction with the parents. She concludes that boys and girls have different experiences in their relationships to the outer and inner world and that these experiences form the superego.

Freud (1925) held that the tendency of women to shift their standards to accommodate those of their loved ones indicates superego weakness. This accommodating style, Freud believed, was a consequence of women's great concern with loss of love. However, because Freud (1926) viewed this female fear as less narcissistically detached from its oedipal origins than the fear of castration anxiety in men, he believed that women have been provided with a less adequate foundation for the development of moral activity. In this regard, Schafer and Bernstein note that Freud did not appreciate the value of other factors that might be of significance in a young girl's moral development. For example, although he sometimes hinted (1931) at the importance the maternal object might have in the girl's moral development, in the final analysis Freud (1937, 1940) did not consider the maternal relationship in the evolution of a woman's superego. He also (1905, 1933) did not consider the potential role of other environmental factors in female moral development.

Freud's (1925) position regarding the relation of superego and morality is that the unconscious infantile superego is the foundation of individual morality and establishes its character. Schafer (1974) asserts that the superego and morality can not be equated and that before morality is established, there is considerable adjustment in the superego's contributions. Schafer maintains that the superego is characterized by unconscious vindictiveness against oneself. Rather than being the enforcer of respectful observance of fundamental personal, familial, and societal taboos associated with morality, the superego is a powerful set of primitive prohibitions and policies of self-punishment. Given this, Schafer (1974) suggests, Freud may have falsely concluded that boys have a stronger superego. In fact, given her inexorable superego, the female might be better suited to develop an enlightened, realistic, and civilized moral code.

Freud (1925) states that women are more often influenced in their judgments by feelings of affection or hostility, and he consider their responsiveness to emotional demands as a potential corruption of an abstract sense of fairness and justice. In response, Schafer (1974) argues that the rigid morality of men is a reaction formation against sadistic impulses and unconscious guilt. Further, he holds that women's morality may have different origins and may be derived from a fear of loss of love. However, this does not necessarily result in a weaker moral position. In fact, Schafer concludes that male morality may be a poor model, as he questions a system of morality detached from affects and experiences like loss of love. Furthermore, decades of clinical activity have not confirmed Freud's belief.

HORNEY'S CONTRIBUTION

In the 1920s there was controversy concerning Freud's theories of female sexuality. Karen Horney was a major critic, who objected to the phallus-centered nature of Freud's views of women's development and noted its congruence with the patriarchal thinking of the time. She noted that Freud's theorizing on female sexual development was based primarily on his observations of men. Horney objected to Freud's applying male standards to theorizing about women and viewed their use as "obvious [given that], psychoanalysis [had been] the creation of a male genius" (1926, p. 324) with primarily male followers.

Horney did not focus directly on Freud's conception of the superego or of the difference in superego development between males and females. She considered the role of penis envy in Freud's theory of female development to be overemphasized and focused on this rather than the circumstances (such as inadequate superego development in women) that follow from this phallus-centered formulation. Focus, on superego development is embedded in her consideration of Freud's conception of women's castration and penis envy. Horney (1924) objected to Freud's view that penis envy occurs in all women and that it may be a permanent condition. She (1926) suggested that his view might have more to do with male narcissism than with biological science. Further, Horney questioned Freud's view that penis envy leaves impenetrable scars on a woman's development and that a woman's most significant attitudes or wishes derive their energy from her penis wish. It appeared to Horney (1939) that Freud regarded most "feminine" character traits (such as vanity and envy) as rooted in penis envy and held that feminine inferiority feelings are an expression of a woman's contempt for her own castrated sex. Horney's position is that although little girls may express a wish for a penis, this wish is not more significant than the equally frequent desire for female breasts.

Horney (1926) recognized penis envy but held that it should be conceptualized as consisting of primary and secondary stages. In Horney's view, primary penis envy is based on early observation of sexual differences; secondary penis envy, a regression from the Oedipus complex, occurs later in development. Primary penis envy is regarded as but one component of a natural and universal curiosity of childhood, an expression of interest in the new and different, as typically a temporary state. Horney postulated that if a girl is allowed to be contented in her feminine role and encouraged to develop an appreciation of her femaleness, this condition will not be permanent; however, if her family does not provide adequate encouragement, she might want to flee into masculinity. Or if the young girl is experiencing profound guilt about wanting to replace her mother with her father or if she has had considerable anxiety about punishment, she may reject the female role and retreat to secondary penis envy. The wish to be a man, Horney (1926) held, is often more appropriately characterized as a flight from the dangers of womanhood — vaginal injury, mother's punishment, or the inability to satisfy men — rather than an envious desire to be masculine. Moulton (1975) elaborates on some of these ideas.

Horney (1926, 1932, 1935) contends that because women are defined only from the male vantage point, all female behavior has had to conform to masculine standards. This male-dominated, patriarchal reality often results in women's being completely unaware of their own value and, with society's reinforcement, may result in women's own adoption of the masculine disregard of women. Consequently, women may fantasize about masculine possibilities while ignoring female capabilities. Women may perceive the female organ as damaged and the male sexual organ as glorified. The inequities of society underscore such early childhood unconscious processes as rivalry with a brother or oedipal attachment to a father.

Horney takes issue with Freud's general formulation of the superego. She (1950) maintains that Freud ascribe to the superego a type of tyrannical power, which she saw as "counterfeiting morality and conscience" (p. 374). She points out that within a person there are "shoulds," inner dictates, which lack moral pretense and so do not lead to moral action. It is only by focusing on the entire range of inner dictates that one can get a proper perspective on the quality of these inner demands for moral perfection. Horney (1950) identifies another aspect of one's inner dictates (or superego) that makes them different from genuine moral standards and calls this "coercive character" (p. 73). Thus, like the Freudian critics who follow her, Horney (1939) disputes Freud's value of an inexorable superego, because ideals can have an obligating or coercive power over our lives, which can lead to extreme feelings of pain and disillusionment if one is unable to realize the ideals of the superego or "cruelties [are] committed in the name of moral demands" (p. 213).

Horney also holds that the inexorable strength of the superego leads to the impression of strivings towards ever-increasing perfection and independence but that these strivings often are rooted in pretense. They are strivings for the appearance of perfection, infallibility, independence rather than the reality of them. The desire is to appear perfect in one's own eyes as well as the eyes of others. Horney concludes that this desire is the result of dependence rather than independence. Thus, the inexorable quality of the superego, as defined by Freud, may not be concern with moral issues at all, but rather with the *appearance* of moral issues and the achievement of the egocentric goal of infallibility. It was Horney's belief that the inexorable superego can result in an individual's having no judgment and instead relying on the judgment of others. When viewed from this perspective, the superego cannot be conceptualized as a special agency within the ego but, instead, as an agent that takes on the special needs of the person. The superego, then, is not an advocate of moral perfection but a transmitter of the neurotic's need to keep up the appearances of perfection.

Horney does not view the superego as a natural phenomenon representing both conscience and morality, as Freud does. While Freud sees the superego as neurotic in character only if it is unusually cruel, Horney holds that inner dicates of any sort are a neurotic force that impede one from living one's life. To Horney, such inner dictates are an expression of one's unconscious drive to make oneself into something one is not. Thus, Horney's therapeutic aims also differ from Freud's. While Freud aims at reducing the severity of the superego, Horney's is to help the individual to rid of inner dictates altogether, which is an impossibility within Freudian theory.

Discussion

At the time of Horney's writing, there was within the psychoanalytic movement support of Freud's views and disparagement of contradictory views. Freud seemed to have a strongly adverse reaction to Horney's views. It is Fliegel's (1973) view that Freud's 1925 paper, in which he presented new formulations about women, was a reaction to Horney's work. Perhaps the strong reaction, as Fliegel suggests, was evoked because Horney's contrary view was voiced at a time when both Freud's life and the psychoanalytic movement were in jeopardy. Timing too may explain why Freud's followers were so willing to accept and advance his ideas about the feminine condition, as presented in his 1925 paper, and give little credence to Horney and others who disagreed. Horney's disagreement might have been perceived as less threatening at another time.

In "Female Sexuality," Freud (1931), discussing the preoedipal phase in little girls' development, writes: "Everything in the sphere of this first attachment to the mother seemed to me so difficult to grasp in analysis . . ." (p. 226). He went on to claim that female analysts "for instance Jeanne Lampl-de Groot and Helene Deutsch — have been able to perceive these facts more easily and clearly because they were helped in dealing with those under their treatment by the transference to a suitable mother-substitute" (p. 227). Of course, both these female analysts were supporters of Freud, In contrast, what Horney concluded, Freud dismissed. In fact, as Kelman (1950) suggests in his introduction to *Feminine Psychology*, it may have been Horney to whom Freud (1940) was alluding when, in discussing the lack of agreement among analysts, he said, "We shall not be so very surprised if a woman analyst who has not been sufficiently convinced of the intensity of her own wish for a penis also fails to attach proper importance to that factor in her patients" (p. 197). This is certainly one way to disarm the dissenting voices. Unfortunately for Horney, Freud, and the psychoanalytic movement, the strength of the adverse reaction to Horney's formulations caused her ideas to be disregarded or ascribed to others for many years.

KOHLBERG'S CONTRIBUTION

Freud focused on the development of the superego and differences in development between males and females. Like Horney, Kohlberg says relatively little about sex differences in morality. Rather, his interest is in cognitive development and moral reasoning, and his focus is on the identification and measurement of moral development stages. Whereas Freud's focus was on how the superego came to be, Kohlberg's is on what it is like at various stages of development; whereas Freud focused on its initial development, Kohlberg traces its development over time. What is similar about both Freud's and Kohlberg's theories is that both have been considered sex biased — Freud's, for advocating that the sexes are different in level of moral development; Kohlberg's, because his means of assessing moral reasoning appears to favor males and creates the impression of female deficiency in moral reasoning.

According to Nadelson (1983), Freud's view of moral reasoning and sense of justice has been translated into the moral development theory of Kohlberg, which is an extension of Piaget's (1965) work. Kohlberg (1981) believes that he has separated structure from content in morality. He describes a typology of stages involving an invariant developmental sequence through which all individuals pass, although at differential rates. Kohlberg's view is that the environment has considerable influence on moral development. Moral development does not evolve out of internalized rules but stems from social interaction involving moral dialogue, moral decision making, and moral interaction. Such interaction provides the developing individual with role taking opportunities that enable adopting the attitude of others, becoming aware of others thoughts and feelings, and putting oneself in their place (Kohlberg, 1984). Thus, moral development is influenced by the amount and variety of social experience and the opportunity to take roles and to encounter other perspectives.

According to Kohlberg (1969, 1981), cognition plays an important role in moral development also, as it influences the time when stages begin. Moral development involves the acquisition of new modes of thought, which are dependent on the reorganization and displacement of preceding modes through a self-constructive process.

Kohlberg has attempted to devise a taxonomy to track the developmental sequence and stages of moral reasoning in children and young adults. He has identified three levels, each containing two stages: the preconventional level (stages 1 and 2); the conventional level (stages 3 and 4); and the postconventional level (stages 5 and 6). Kohlberg describes the preconventional moral level as that of most children under the age of nine, some adolescents, and many adolescent and adult criminal offenders. The conventional level is the level of most adolescents and adults in our society. The postconventional level is reached by only a minority of adults and is seldom seen in individuals under the age of twenty-one.

Kohlberg (1984) suggests that one way of understanding these three levels is to think of them as three different types of relationship between the self and society's rules and expectations. Those at the preconventional level view the rules and regulations of society as external to themselves. Those at the conventional level identify and integrate themselves with the rules and regulations of the society; those at the postconventional level, having integrated and differentiated, define their values in terms of self-chosen principles. In order to differentiate the three levels further, Kohlberg considers the sociomoral perspective, which is the point of view taken by the individual in formulating moral judgments. Kohlberg holds that this perspective is intrinsically moral in nature rather than a logical or social-cognitive structure applied to a moral domain. The social perspective taken by the individual at the preconventional level is concrete — the individual obeys the rules because rules are meant to be obeyed. In contrast, the individual at the conventional level has a member-of-society perspective and is loyal to the group, is concerned about maintaining social approval, and is concerned about the welfare of others. The individual at the postconventional level is most highly evolved and is able to use his conventional knowledge of society in order to define an individual moral perspective.

Four general criteria are relevant to the stages (Colby and Kohlberg, 1984). First, the stages imply a distinction, or qualitative difference, in structures or modes of thinking. Second, these different structures form an invariant sequence in individual development. While cultural factors may speed up, slow down, or stop this development, they do not change its sequence. Third, a given stage response on a task does not represent simply a specific response determined by knowledge with the task but rather an underlying thought organization. Last, Kohlberg views the stages as hierarchical integrations. That is, stages form an order to increasingly differentiated and integrated structures for fulfilling a common function and, accordingly, higher stages are believed to integrate the structures found at lower stages.

Kohlberg's definition and means of measuring moral judgment has undergone a number of changes over the last 25 years (Colby and Kohlberg, 1984). The Standard Issue Scoring system, the most recent system, is a theory-based assessment procedure believed to measure one's moral development stage according to Kohlberg's theory. The Standard Issue Moral Judgment Interview consists of three hypothetical moral dilemmas. Each dilemma is followed by 9 to 12 standardized probe questions designed to elicit justification, elaboration, and clarification of the moral judgment. For example, in one dilemma one must respond to the question "Should the husband steal a drug to save his wife's life?" This dilemma concerns the conflict between life and law. The second and third dilemmas focus on the conflict between morality and conscience and between authority (obey one's parent) and contract (abide by or hold someone to an agreement) respectively. The scoring system is lengthy and involves scoring rules, stage criteria, and definitions of developmental sequences (Colby and Kohlberg, 1984). Kohlberg believes that he has created a standard scoring system in which interpretation is a science rather than an art.

Discussion

Kohlberg has been criticized for not explaining some real-life moral behavior. For example, in his lecture on psychoanalysis and moral development, Coles (1981) considers Ruby Bridges, 6 years old, black, Southern, of extremely poor background, and an unlikely candidate for the moral accolades she was to receive. She was in the middle of her Oedipus conflict and had cognitive limitation consistent with her age. Hardly a candidate for high level moral performance, it was 6-year-old Ruby, who in 1961 initiated school desegration in New Orleans. Ruby's moral behavior would not have been predicted on the basis of Kohlberg's major determinants of moral development — amount and variety of social experience — nor on the grounds that principled morality is the ability to reason logically and is represented by the stage of formal operations.

Kohlberg's theory has raised other questions. Some theorists have challenged Kohlberg's claims that stages are culturally universal and irreversible (e.g., Colby and Kohlberg, 1984; Kohlberg, 1984; Simpson, 1974). Others, notably Gilligan (1982), have charged that Kohlberg's theory and methodology is biased against women and consequently does not adequately describe moral development.

In discussing women's development, Gilligan (1982) notes that Kohlberg and his predecessors, Freud and Piaget, developed most of their conceptualizations from the study of men. The focus on men has resulted in a male-oriented view of moral development and a concentration on men's concerns. Gilligan notes that Kohlberg's six stages of moral development are empirically based on a study of 84 boys whose development Kohlberg followed for a period of over twenty years. She suggests that because the study was conducted on males, Kohlberg's means of conceptualizing and measuring moral development lacks representativeness, and as a result the generalizability of his stage sequence is questionable. Recently some attempts have been made to support the validity of the model on longitudinal samples of males and females (Simpson, 1974; Walker, 1984). However, it is difficult to determine whether the same stages and sequences would have been derived if females had been part of the original sample. Further, although Kohlberg claims his stage sequence is universally applicable, groups not used in the original sample rarely reach Kohlberg's higher stages of moral development (Simpson, 1974; Holstein, 1976).

Gilligan (1982) states that Kohlberg's conception of moral development is based on the evolution of autonomous rights rather than the evolution of care, concern, and responsibility, which are concerns of females. In Kohlberg's schema, such concerns are highly underrated and, in turn lead women to be underrated within the Kohlberg system. Gilligan suggests that morality includes two moral orientations. The first is the morality of justice, as stressed by Kohlberg, and the second is an ethic of care and responsibility, which has received relatively little attention. It is the second of these two moral orientations that Gilligan holds to be more central to the understanding of female moral judgment and action while the morality of justice is more central to the understanding of male moral development. Further, Kohlberg's original equation of morality with autonomy and justice places women at a severe disadvantage in his moral development typology and may result in his system being inappropriate for women. Typically, women are unable to exceed the third stage, which has an interpersonal focus and equates morality with helping and pleasing others. Kohlberg and Kramer suggest (1969) that, in fact, women might not be able to exceed this stage unless they leave their housewifery tasks and enter the arena of traditional male activities. This view is based on Kohlberg's belief that the experience of participating within society's complex work and educational institutions leads to further moral development.

Kohlberg (1984) has responded to Gilligan's concerns. He acknowledges that sex bias may exist, as a result of his reliance on an exclusively male sample, and agrees that there is a predominance of male protagonists in the moral dilemmas used as stimulus material, although he is not clear about the effects of this. He agrees too that the justice dimension does not pull for the care and responsibility orientation and that the scoring manual does not lead to a full assessment of the aspect of moral reasoning. He does not, however, agree that the justice reasoning dilemmas and stages lead to an unfair biased down-scoring of female reasoning. Rather, he holds that the moral dilemmas call for an integration of orientations.

Clearly, Kohlberg and Gilligan disagree on these issues. Dialogue between them and their followers has just begun, and more is needed. What Gilligan has done, however, is to raise the issue of women's morality as being different rather than deficient and suggested that any reported deficiency in women's morality may be a function of bias in moral reasoning theory and assessment.

GILLIGAN'S CONTRIBUTION

According to Gilligan (1977, 1982), women are oriented toward attachment and connectedness to others and men toward individuation and separateness from others. To explain the origin of different orientations, Gilligan (1982), citing Chodorow's (1974) work, notes that boys must individuate from mothers and deny such early feelings as dependency and relatedness, which they experience as having to do with this earliest relationship and therefore with femininity. Girls, in contrast, grow up with a greater sense of continuity with and similarity to mother and feel more at ease with relational connections.

It is Gilligan's (1982) contention that from these early distinctions of morality arise an orientation of care and concern, which focuses on an understanding of the responsibilities essential to relationships, and an orientation of justice, which focuses on issues of autonomous rights, equity, and fairness. According to Gilligan, care and concern is more central to women's morality, while justice and fairness are the central issues for men. Thus, women's deference to others and reluctance to judge may be indicative not of self-doubt but of the care and concern for others, which leads women to attend to others' voices and to consider other points of view.

Gilligan (1982) believes that women should tell their own stories of moral conflict, crisis, and decision so that a theory of female moral development can be grounded in their lives. Therefore, Gilligan studies women's moral decision making by considering women at different developmental points as they confront various moral dilemmas. It is from the structure, language, and content of these female narratives that Gilligan derives a theory of moral development that reflects women's actual experiences. Gilligan's data analysis indicates that from early on and extending throughout moral development, a woman views herself as evolving and growing in relationship to others. Thus, in contrast with her male counterpart, a woman does not see herself as an independent agent who can make autonomous decisions about her growth. Rather female developmental decisions are made with others in mind. As a result, woman's view of moral failure and success involves avoiding hurt and providing care, while woman's definition of a moral problem most often involves a conflict of responsibilities rather than rights. Additionally, it appears that women more frequently conceptualize moral problems in a contextual and narrative form rather than in the formal and abstract manner more common to men. In short it appears that women see moral dilemmas as existing between people in a particular social context and tend to conceptualize the resolution of these dilemmas as requiring care and responsibility.

Gilligan (1982) suggests that the catalyst for moral change in both men's and women's lives is usually a crisis. It appears, however, that the nature of the crisis that initiates moral growth is different for men and women. For men, the crisis involves an intimate interaction; for women, already comfortable and familiar with intimate relationships, the crisis involves confrontation and acknowledgement of their own needs and their potential conflict with those of another. An example of such a crisis situation is decision making around abortion. According to Gilligan, at such a moral juncture a women's early learned reliance on relationships creates conflict as she must make an important moral decision involving a conflict between her own needs and the needs of another.

Although Gilligan's (1977, 1982) focus is on gender differences, like Kohlberg, she traces moral development over time and identifies three moral stages. Initially "being good" consists of pleasing others and gaining approval. This conventional goodness is followed by a more authentic goodness, in which focus is on helping rather than merely pleasing others. Finally, there is the responsible, caring attitude, which is directed to both herself and others. At this level a woman can acknowledge the truth of feelings and the realities of moral life.

Discussion

Challenges to Gilligan's theory have centered on three points: (1) identification of bias against women in Kohlberg's theory; (2) the existence of distinct and mutually exclusive orientations; and (3) the existence of different orientations based on gender.

With regard to the first point, Kohlberg (1984) holds that his typology is not sex biased, because his stage sequence has been supported, on males and females, by both longitudinal (Holstein, 1976) and experimental (Walker, 1984) studies. While this countercharge suggests that Kohlberg's stage sequence may be applicable to both males and females, it does not address Gilligan's concern that the stage sequence was initially derived from interviews with an exclusively males sample. It is unclear whether Kohlberg's stage sequence would have been conceptualized differently if his initial sample had included women. Nor is it clear whether the use of mostly male protagonists in Kohlberg's hypothetical moral dilemmas had a differential effect on male and female responses. Studies have produced conflicting results here (e.g., Simpson, 1974; Holstein, 1976; Lyons, 1983).

Regarding two orientations, Kohlberg (1984) holds that the two orientations are not necessarily distinct, that both sexes utilize both orientations. Although emphasis is on defining morality from a justice perspective, Kohlberg stresses that use of the caring orientation does not result in deflated scores on his instrument. Although there may be sex differences in preferential orientation to framing moral dilemmas as Gilligan suggests, Kohlberg holds that this does not invalidate the justice reasoning test as an assessment of competence in justice reasoning. The problem with this reasoning, according to Gilligan (1982), is that Kohlberg equates justice reasoning with moral reasoning. In this way she questions the very foundation of his perspective.

Regarding the existence of moral orientation based on gender, Kohlberg (1984) claims that there is no empirical support for her statement that women are more likely than men to use spontaneously the caring orientation in their moral reasoning. Here, he focuses on empirical issues and accuracy of citation. He believes that women do not use one orientation more frequently than another but, rather, phrase their responses more personally. The thrust of Gilligan's contribution, however, is not in her empirical work. It is in her effort to develop a theory of moral development which is grounded in the life experience of women.

CONCLUSION

This brief consideration indicates a number of similarities and differences across the theorists as summarized as follows:

1. Accounting for Moral Behavior. Kohlberg's theory is limited in accounting for behavior. He indicates that when there are inconsistencies in moral behavior, there is a difference between performance and competence. In contrast, Gilligan holds that moral developmental theory should be grounded in people's experience. This focus on reality and context is also common to Horney, who considers women's experience and the patriarchal reality. Freud is closer to Kohlberg here. Although he attempted to explain his experiences, there were many inconsistencies between his theory and his own experience with female and male colleagues, patients, and family, as Speigel (1977) and Freeman and Strean (1981) indicate, which mitigates against a theory of lesser morality in women.

2. Conceptualization of Gender Differences. The work of Freud and Kohlberg has been identified as pointing to female deficiency. While Kohlberg denies that his theory points to female deficiency, he states that participation within society's complex work and educational institutions leads to further moral development and it follows that women who work at home are less likely to be morally developed. Both Freud and Kohlberg regard moral independence as more moral than emotional appeal. Freud holds that women are more likely to alter their moral positions; Horney and Gilligan acknowledge the masculine disregard of women and their assets and question the inexorable superego.

The work of Gilligan points to gender differences in valuing human experiences and morality. Gilligan holds that the female and the male orientations predispose women toward interest in human relations and men toward individual achievement, and that the two orientations are different rather than one's being inferior to the other. She seems more interested in describing than in ordering the different moral orientations. While Horney does not consider sex differences in morality, it follows from her theory that she too favors a different rather than a deficient model. Gilligan and Horney, focusing on culture, context, and society, place less emphasis on the vertical dimension (ranking and ordering) by means of scoring systems, typologies, or evaluation and more on the horizontal one.

3. Conceptualization of Morality. The two men — Freud and Kohlberg — share some assumptions and values, while the two women — Horney and Gilligan — share another set of assumptions and values. Specifically, Freud and Kohlberg assume that a developmentally more advanced moral position involves justice, fairness, and a perspective within which it is possible to rank order traits. In contrast, Horney and Gilligan stress a perspective within which flexibility is maintained and different perspectives are acknowledged as well as valued. In addition, they value the self-control needed to attain moral goals. Freud's and Kohlberg's conceptualizations of morality are more limited in scope and more evaluative. Freud's definition concerns structure and neglects other aspects of the superego, such as strength and contents (Bernstein, 1983). Moreover, he regards firmer structure as the criterion for desirable superego development. Freud's conceptualization may also be seen as harsh — Horney commented on Freud's harsh conception of the superego and indicated that Freud conceptualized the superego as an inner agency of a particularly forbidding character. She described the Freudian view of the superego as a secret and punitive police department with tyrannical power (Horney, 1939).

Although Kohlberg's conceptualization may take into account the structure and strength aspects of the superego, it is limited by its focus on a narrow content. His conception is based on the evolution of autonomous rights and, as he himself indicates, does not make a full assessment of the caring, concern, and responsibility aspect of moral reasoning. Further, Kohlberg's system centers on evaluation and precision: identification of stages, hierarchical levels, invariant sequences, cultural universality, and irreversibility (1969, 1981, 1984).

Like Freud's, Horney's and Gilligan's conceptualizations concern structure; however, they acknowledge both firm and flexible structures and do not herald an inexorable superego. Horney asserts that an inexorable superego can exist in an individual who has no judgment and instead relies on the judgment of others. Firm adherence to external standards may cover a weakness — one can depend on external standards for judging what one should want and still give the impression of strength of character.

In contrast to Freud and Kohlberg, Horney and Gilligan hold to a broader conceptualization of morality. Horney indicates that there should be focus on the entire range of inner dictates. Further, she indicates that there are shoulds within a person's inner dicates which lack any kind of moral pretense and, consequently, do not lead to morality. It would follow from Horney's theory that those who demonstrate an inexorable superego may be dependent, concerned with appearance, and relying on the judgments of others.

Gilligan acknowledges that males and females frequently have different moral understandings. Gilligan, like Bernstein, holds that there is no evidence that females are less efficient in enforcing directives but rather that they enforce different directives. In Gilligan's terms, men and women hold different moral orientations and they order human experiences in terms of different priorities.

Horney's and Gilligan's theories of feminine psychology support inclusion, harmony, flexibility and other-orientation. They focus more on describing, context, and narrative than on ordering, ranking, and abstraction.

Comment

As Schafer (1974) argues, Freud's generalizations about females are injurious to his psychoanalytic method and clinical findings. Freud's achievement is most impressive when considered within the context of his time. Although Kohlberg theorized later, his was still a time of patriarchal complacency. Given advances in the understanding of women, we are now better able to clarify the limitations of the theories of both Freud and Kohlberg.

IMPLICATIONS

Some of the major differences between the male and female theorists discussed in this paper are consistent both with Gilligan's finding of sex differences in orientation as well as the general public's perception that males and females are different. Although Maccoby and Jacklin's (1974) analysis and interpretation of existing research point to few sex differences, critiques of their work (e.g., Brooks, 1974; Bloch, 1976; Emmerich, 1975) point to a reconsideration.

The theorists discussed here were not selected to represent male and female orientations specifically. Clearly, some males have an orientation more characteristic of females, and some females have an orientation more characteristic of males. The point is that gender differences in orientation are indicated by a consideration of and comparison between the male and female theorists considered here.

Differences in Orientation

As indicated, there are similarities between Horney and Gilligan and between Freud and Kohlberg with respect to (1) accounting for moral behavior; (2) conceptualization of gender differences, and (3) conceptualization of morality. Freud and Kohlberg conceptualize vertically, employing ordering, deficiency, and evaluation, and, in the case of Kohlberg, a concern with invariance and precision with respect to methodology and typology. In contrast, Horney and Gilligan utilize the horizontal dimension, whose emphasis is on context and culture — inclusion, expressiveness, harmony, flexibility, and other-orientation. The horizontal–vertical dimension can also be conceptualized as an impersonal, or autonomous, orientation in males and an interpersonal, or related, orientation in women.

Chodorow (1978b) has attempted to explain these differences between male and female orientation. Chodorow's analysis is a feminist adaptation of object relations theory. Chodorow considers psychodynamic processes within their social and political context. She acknowledges the role of social learning, as well as differential ego development and structure, to account for differences between males and females. Chodorow's (1978a,b) psychoanalytic account concerning males and female's differing needs and capacities for intimacy are consistent with recent feminist psychoanalytic thinking (e.g., Miller, 1976; Dinnerstein, 1976) and organize and give coherence to a large body of psychological research on gender difference. This literature implicates, for example, gender difference in friendship patterns and values (Brenton, 1974; Bloch, 1980); empathy (Bem, 1978; Hoffman, 1977) responsiveness to the young (Berman, 1980); self-disclosure (Hacker, 1981); conversational interaction (Spender, 1980); cognitive style (Witkin and Goodenough, 1977); and behavior in groups (Aries, 1976; Eagly, 1978). A theme common to these findings is that women have an interpersonal orientation in which attachment to others is Central, whereas men have an impersonal orientation (Golden, 1982). These differences reflect enduring aspects of psychic structure, which are gender related.

Because females are parented by a person of their own gender, they experience themselves as less differentiated than boys and as more continuous with and related to the external world (Chodorow, 1978b). Chodorow believes men should be involved in the child rearing process to provide daughters with what women provide sons. That is a male would enable a boy to experience his earliest sense of connection to a person of the same gender. In this way, a boy could identify as a male without having to deny his earliest identification and sense of oneness with a woman and without repressing that part of his ego which has the potential to develop and express connectedness.

Masculine, or vertical, orientation is forward moving and goal directed. It promotes separation, impermeability, and distance, and mitigates horizontal connection with others or connections with context. Vertical orientation seems to be related to men's fears — of merging, loss of boundaries, dependency, exploitation by an omnipotent other (mother).

Feminine, or horizontal, orientation moves across, within a context. It promotes fludity, flexibility, connections, continuity, relations, and mergings. Horizontal orientation seems to be related to the nature of the preoedipal mother-daughter relationship. Girls from early on experience themselves as more continuous with and related to the external object world. Since their gender identity is not determined by differentiation from mothers, as it is in boys, they do not need to deny preoedipal relational modes to the same extent. Thus female ego boundaries remain more flexible and fluid which leads to greater capacity for close interpersonal relationships as well as empathy (Chodorow, 1978b).

Questions

A consideration of the approach of two male and two female theorists mirrors some of the gender differences discussed in the literature and seems consistent with general public opinion. A number of questions can be raised that have implications for psychoanalysis. Given space limitations, only two questions will be considered here briefly. Inasmuch as the questions are the same whether the consideration is of brief, goal-oriented therapy, long-term therapy, or classical psychoanalysis these terms are used interchangeably.

Analyst's Gender and Psychotherapeutic Work

How do male and female analysts deal with moral issues in analytic sessions? Put another way, how are male and female analysts different? (Related questions are considered in this volume. See chapters by Gornick and Schachtel.) There is in the literature support for the idea that male and female analysts are different. Although the classical analytic position and research do not indicate differences in treatment outcome based on analyst's gender, trends have emerged (Mogul, 1982). Although they do not apply equally to all males and females and although a gender effect is less apparent with experienced than with inexperienced therapists (Kirshner, Genak, and Hausser, 1978; Howard and Orlinsky, 1979), trends indicate greater patient satisfaction and benefit from psychotherapy with female therapists. Possibly the reason why the male therapist, particularly the inexperienced male therapist, tends to have more difficulty than his female counterpart is related to his having a more judgmental moral system. This is an area that needs investigation and has implication for analytic training.

Male and female analysts may deal with moral issues differently. Although the implicit assumption underlying analysis is that its dynamics transcend such reality issues as the gender of the patient or therapist (Seiden, 1976), male analysts, at least at the beginning of their training, may be less able to understand women's moral dilemmas, and priorities; inexperienced female analysts may be less able to understand the moral dilemmas of their male patients. Also, male and female patients may bring to sessions different moral dilemmas and may conceptualize moral resolutions differently. Further, patients may expect a male analyst to be more judgmental, a perception that may influence the selection of the analyst as well as some aspects of the treatment. Analysts should be trained around issues of gender and morality, so that they will understand perceptions based on gender, gender differences in conceptualizing and resolving moral issues, and issues relevant to moral growth in men and women.

Some Selected Aspects of Traditional Psychoanalysis

How does psychoanalysis — created by Freud, with followers, who are mostly male — reflect an orientation that is more characteristic of males? And, had psychoanalysis been created and nurtured by a female, how would it be different? This fascinating topic is the subject of a lengthy paper (Alpert, in preparation), and only brief consideration can be given to it here.

Aspects of traditional psychoanalysis, such as some values and parts of the patient–therapist relationship, reflect a masculine orientation. Regarding values, Kohut (1984) teaches that predominant values of psychoanalysis are independence and knowledge and that these values guide psychoanalytic work. Consistent with this view, Low (1984) writes that in psychoanalysis there is a devaluation of the mother-daughter relationship, and a frequent goal in a woman's analysis is independence from her mother. Consequently, practitioners are taught to encourage female patients to push for independence and separation from their mothers.

What might psychoanalysis' values be if analysis had been developed and nurtured by those with a more female orientation? Perhaps the values of healthy dependence, caring, relationships, and responsibility would be more prominent. Analyst's, for example, would work to enable patients to utilize existing resources and become more *effectively* dependent on mother and on others. Some of the works in progress published by the Stone Center for Developmental Studies throw light on the question of the values of psychoanalysis for those with a more feminine orientation. Stiver (1984), for example, defines dependency as "a process of counting on other people to provide help in coping physically and emotionally with experiences and tasks encountered in the world, when one has not sufficient skill, confidence, energy, and/or time" (p. 10). Her notion of dependency allows for one's being strengthened by being able to count on others for help; dependency can be thought of as normal and as facilitating development. As another example, Surrey (1984) indicates the need for a new model of development to account for the centrality and continuity of relationships throughout women's lives. Her "feminine orientation" results in her conceptualizing relationships as central to women's lives.

Regarding the structure of the patient–analyst relationship, the objective, impersonal neutrality characteristic of traditional psychoanalysis is, at least in our culture, more congenial to men than to women. One of the assumptions underlying this kind of relationship is that the analyst be nonemotional, relatively impersonal, and able to maintain distance in order to be helpful, again, a style more congenial to men than to women (Stiver, 1985). While warmth and kindness are seen as important assets, they must be carefully monitored. The present model of therapy, as Stiver points out, is essentially a masculine one, and the distancing between therapist and patient may be a countertransferential reaction. Obviously, analysts differ with respect to the amount of distance maintained. Kohut (1984), for example, who views many patients' difficulties as related to parental coldness and nonresponsiveness, attempts to provide a warm, empathic, and affirming environment and is concerned about using concepts that are experience relevant rather than those that are abstract, structural, or distant.

Comment

The 'male' orientation is more common in men, because there seems to be repression of the relational self in the process of becoming male-identified. However, both men and women analysts are concerned about the mother–daughter relationship and the maintenance of distance, and, clearly, these concerns cannot be linked simplistically to analyst's gender: some male analysts have a responsive, egalitarian, empathic, genuine, and flexible stance; some female analysts have an authoritarian and impersonal one.

The concern here is with the inexorable commitment to certain technical rules and traditions by some contemporary classical analysts and with what seems to be an inexorable commitment by feminist psychoanalysts to such theories as Object Relations Theory and Self Psychology, and what seems an inflexible disregard for other theories, such as Classical Theory. This is not a time to make an inexorable commitment to one theory, but, rather, is a time to reconsider and, as necessary, revise aspects of existing theories. Some analytic theories may throw little light on women's development or reflect only weakly a feminine orientation; other theories may have great relevance to the understanding of both men and women. We are suggesting that aspects of psychoanalysis, as well as the content of psychoanalytic theories relevant to women's development, be examined. We are suggesting, further, that there may be masculine ideologies inherent in psychoanalysis, as there seems to be in other sciences (e.g., Kuhn, 1962; Bleier, 1984; Keller, 1985). Psychoanalysis could be enlarged and enriched as a result of a consideration and analysis of such ideologies.

A goal of analysis is to enlarge analysis. We need to begin to consider aspect of psychoanalysis and look at the extent that these aspects reflect male models only and throw light on masculinity only. We need to enhance traditional psychoanalytic theory so that it is more consistent with practice by including feminist ways of thinking and greater understanding of women. While there has been some feminist influence on psychoanalytic theory, the potential remains enormous.

REFERENCES

Alpert, J. L. (in preparation), Psychoanalysis and the male orientation.
Aries, E. (1976), Interaction patterns and themes of male, female, and mixed groups. *Small Gp. Beh.*, 7:7–18.

Bem, S. (1978), Beyond androgyny: some presumptuous prescriptions for a liberated sexual identity. In: *The Psychology of Women,* ed. J. Sherman & F. Denmark. New York: Psychological Dimensions.

Berman, P. (1980), Are women more responsive than men to the young? A review of developmental and situational variables. *Psychol. Bull.,* 88:668–695.

Bernay, T. & Cantor, D. (Ed.) (1986), *The Psychology of Today's Woman.* Hillsdale, NJ: The Analytic Press.

Bernstein, A. E. & Warner, G. M. (1984), *Women Treating Women: Case Material from Women Treated By Female Psychoanalysts.* New York: International Universities Press.

Bernstein, D. (1983), The female superego: A different perspective. *Internat. J. Psycho-Anal.,* 64:187–201.

Bleier, R. (1984), *Science and Gender.* New York: Pergamon Press.

Bloch, J. (1980), *Friendship.* New York: MacMillan.

Block, J. (1976), Debatable conclusions about sex difference. *Contemp. Psychol.,* 21:517–522.

Blum, H. P., ed. (1977), *Female Psychology.* New York: International Universities Press.

Brenton, M. (1974), *Friendship.* New York: Stein & Day.

Brooks, J. (1974), Review of the psychology of sex differences. *Libr. J.,* 99:3204.

Chodorow, N. (1974), Family structure and feminine personality. In: *woman, Culture and Society,* ed. M. Z. Rosaldo & L. Lamphere. Stanford: Stanford University Press, 1974.

———— (1978a), Mothering, object-relations, and the female oedipal configuration. *Fem. Stud.,* 4:137–159.

———— (1978b), *The Reproduction of Mothering.* Berkeley: University of California Press.

Colby, A. & Kohlberg, L. (1984), *The Measurement of Moral Judgment.* New York: Cambridge University Press.

Coles, R. (1981), Psychoanalysis and moral development. *Amer. J. Psychoanal.,* 41:101–113.

Dinnerstein, D. (1976), *The Mermaid and the Minotaur.* New York: Harper & Row.

Eagly, A. (1978), Sex differences in influencability. *Psychol. Bull.,* 85:86–116.

Eichenbaum, L. & Orbach, S. (1983), *Understanding Women.* New York: Basic Books.

Emmerich, W. (1975), The complexities of human development. *Science,* 190:140–141.

Fast, I. (1984), *Gender Identity.* Hillsdale, NJ: Lawrence Erlbaum Associates.

Fliegel, Z. O. (1973), Feminine psychosexual development in Freudian theory. *Psychoanal. Quart.,* 42:385–409.

Freeman, L. & Strean, H. S. (1981), *Freud and Women.* New York: Ungar.

Freud, S. (1905), Three essays on the theory of sexuality. *Standard Edition*, 7:125–243. London: Hogarth Press, 1953.

––––––– (1923), The ego and the id. *Standard Edition*, 19:12–59. London: Hogarth Press, 1961.

––––––– (1924), The dissolution of the oedipus complex, *Standard Edition*, 19:171–179. London: Hogarth Press, 1961.

––––––– (1925), Some psychological consequences of the anatomical distinction between the sexes. *Standard Edition*, 19:243–258. London: Hogarth Press, 1961.

––––––– (1926), The question of lay analysis. *Standard Edition*, 20:179–258. London: Hogarth Press, 1959.

––––––– (1931), Female sexuality. *Standard Edition*, 21:223–243. London: Hogarth Press, 1961.

––––––– (1933), Femininity. *Standard Edition*, 22:112–185. London: Hogarth Press, 1964.

––––––– (1937), Analysis terminable and interminable. *Standard Edition*, 23:211–253. London: Hogarth Press, 1964.

––––––– (1940), An outline of psycho-analysis, *Standard Edition*, 23:141–207. London: Hogarth Press, 1964.

Galenson, E. & Roiphe, H. (1977), Some suggested revisions concerning early female development. In: *Female Psychology.* ed. H. Blum. New York: International Universities Press, pp. 29–57.

Gallop, J. (1982), *The Daughter's Seduction: Feminism and Psychoanalysis.* New York: Cornell University Press.

Gilligan, C. (1977), In a different voice: women's conception of self and morality. *Harvard Educ. Rev.*, 47:481–517.

––––––– (1982), *In a Different Voice.* Cambridge, MA: Harvard University Press.

Golden, C. (1982), *Feminist Psychoanalytic Theory: A Perspective Psychologists Can't Afford to Ignore.* Presentation at the Conference of the American Psychological Association, Washington, DC.

Hacker, H. (1981), Blabbermouths and clams: Sex differences in self disclosure in same-sex and cross-sex friendship dyads. *Psychol. Women Quart.*, 5:385–401.

Hoffman, M. (1977), Sex differences in empathy and related behaviors. *Psychol. Bull.*, 84:712–722.

Holstein, C. (1976), Development of moral judgement: A longitudinal study of males and females. *Child Devel.*, 47:51–61.

Horney, K. (1924), On the genesis of the castration complex in women. *Internat. J. Psycho-Anal.*, 5:50–65.

––––––– (1926), The flight from womanhood: The masculinity complex in women, as viewed by men and women. *Internat. J. Psycho-Anal.*, 7:324–339.

––––––– (1932), The dread of women: Observations on a specific difference in the dread felt by men and by women respectively for the opposite sex. *Internat. J. Psycho-Anal.*, 13:384–439.

_____ (1950), *Neurosis and Human Growth*. New York: Norton.

_____ (1967), *Feminine Psychology*. New York: Norton.

Howard, K. I. & Orlinsky, D. E. (1979), *What Effect Does Therapist Gender Have On Woman in Psychotherapy?* Presentation at the Conference of the American Psychological Association, New York City.

Keller, E. F. (1985), *Reflections on Gender and Science*. New Haven: Yale University Press.

Kelman, H. (1950, Introduction. In: *Feminine Psychology*, K. Horney. New York: Norton.

Kirshner, L. A., Genak, A., & Hauser, S. T. (1978), Effects of gender on short-term psychotherapy. *Psychother.: Theory, Res. Prac.*, 15:158–167.

Kleeman, J. (1977), Freud's views on early female sexuality in the light of direct child observation. In: *Female Sexuality: Contemporary Psychoanalytic Views*, ed. H. Blum, New York: International Universities Press, pp. 3–27.

Kohlberg, L. (1969), Stage and sequence: the cognitive-development approach to socialization. In: *Handbook of Socialization Theory and Research*, ed. D. A. Goslin. Chicago: Rand McNally.

_____ (1981), *Essays on Moral Development: Vol. 1. The Philosophy of Moral Development*. San Francisco: Harper & Row.

_____ (1984), *Essays on Moral Development: Vol. 2. The Psychology of Moral Development*. San Francisco: Harper & Row.

_____ & Kramer, R. (1969),Continuities and discontinuities in child and adult moral development. *Human Devel.*, 12:93–120.

Kohut, H. (1984), *How Does Analysis Cure*. Chicago: University of Chicago Press.

Kuhn, T. S. (1962), *The Structure of Scientific Revolutions*. Chicago: The University of Chiago Press.

Low, N. (1984), Mother-daughter relationships: The lasting ties. *Radcliffe Quart.*, December, 1–4.

Lyons, N. (1983), Two perspectives: On self, relationships, and morality. *Harvard Ed. Rev.* 53:125–145.

Maccoby, E. & Jacklin, C. (1974), *The Psychology of Sex Differences*. Stanford: Stanford University Press.

Menaker, E. (1982), Female identity in psychosocial perspective. *Psychoanal. Rev.*, 69:75–83.

Mendell, D. (Ed.) (1982), *Early Female Development*. New York: Spectrum.

Miller, J. B. (Ed.) (1973), *Psychoanalysis and Women*. New York: Brunner/Mazel, Inc.

Miller, J. B. (1976), *Toward A New Psychology of Women*. Boston: Beacon Press.

Mitchell, J. (1974), *Psychoanalysis and Feminism*. New York: Random House.

Mogul, K. (1982), Overview: The sex of the therapist. *Amer. J. Psychiat.*, 139:1–11.

Moulton, R. (1975), Early papers on women: Horney to Thompson. *Amer. J. Psychoanal.*, 35:207–223.

Nadelson, C. (1983), The psychology of women. *Can. J. Psychiat.*, 28:210–218.

Piaget, J. (1965), *The Moral Judgment of the Child.* New York: Free Press.

Schafer, R. (1974), Problems in Freud's psychology of women. *Amer. Psychoanal. Assn.*, 22:459–485.

Seiden, A. M. (1976), Overview: Research on the psychology of women II. Women in families, work and psychotherapy. *Amer. J. Psychiat.*, 133:1111–1123.

Simpson, E. (1974), Moral development research: A case study of scientific cultural bias. *Human Devel.*, 17:81–106.

Spender, D. (1980), *Man Made Language.* London: Rouledge & Kegan Paul.

Spiegel, R. (1977), Freud and the women in his world. *J. Amer. Acad. Psychoanal.*, 5:377–402.

Stiver, I. (1984), *The Meanings of "Dependency" in Female-Male Relationships.* Stone Center for Developmental Studies, Wellesley College, Wellesley, MA.

——— (1985), *The Meaning of Care: Reframing Treatment Models.* Stone Center for Developmental Studies, Wellesley College, Wellesley, MA.

Stoller, R. J. (1984), A contribution to the study of gender identity. *Internat. J. Psycho-Anal.*, 45:220–226.

Surrey, J. (1984), *Self-in-Relation: A Theory of Women's Development.* Stone Center for Developmental Studies, Wellesley College, Wellesley, MA.

Walker, L. (1984), Sex differences in the development of moral reasoning: a critical review. *Child Devel.*, 55:677–691.

Witkin, H. & Goodenough, D. (1977), Field dependence and interpersonal behavior. *Psychol. Bull.*, 84:661–689.

5 The Alienation of Desire
Women's Masochism and Ideal Love
JESSICA BENJAMIN

The growing consensus that girls achieve gender identity not by repudiating an initial masculine orientation toward the mother but by identifying with her maternal attributes appears finally to discredit many problematic assumptions in Freud's original ideas about women. The idea of core gender identity (Stoller, 1968) — the preoedipal assimilation of gender identity based primarily on identifications and object relations, mediated through parental assignment of gender — paves the way for a multifaceted reappraisal of female development (Chodorow, 1978; Fast, 1984). The problems that have aroused most controversy in regard to femininity, in this case masochism, can now be discussed without the rearguard arguments against notions of anatomy as destiny and feminine nature that so shaped earlier debates. On the other hand, we now require fresh explanations for the problems of femininity that do not have recourse to nature.

The theory of penis envy and the feminine Oedipus complex as Freud (1924b, 1925, 1931, 1933) bequeathed it provided compelling answers to the question of why women might have a propensity to masochistic fantasies, or why femininity might be associated with masochism. It may seem ungrateful to challenge a theory that has rescued femininity from its association with envy, narcissism, masochism, and passivity. But the new view of femininity based on maternal identification offers a less seamless explanation for the appearance of such phenomena. Rejecting Freud's view of penis envy as the organizer of femininity in favor of the theory of maternal identification, we may relinquish the idea that the little girl begins as a little boy, that femininity is characterized by the transformation from active to passive love. Yet we are still faced with a lacuna, an unsolved problem: the problem of *woman's desire.*

The problem begins with the fact that the mother is not articulated as a sexual subject; she is the woman without desire. That is to say, in culture and theory alike, she is always refracted through the lens

113

of the child's experience, in which passion, with all its implications of selfishness and independent subjectivity, is denied. Mother is there to serve the interests of the child; the image of her sexual power is too frightening for this denial to be challenged directly. The identification with her thus seems an ill-fated beginning for the developing sense of sexual agency. Whence, if not through the phallus, through masculine orientation, do women derive their sense of sexual agency? And what represents it? There is no equivalent symbol of female desire that, like the phallus, suggests activity and potency. And the actual evidence about the cultural representation of women's sexuality is disheartening: the sexy woman is object, not subject, able to attract and ignite the passion of others. Her desire is known as a function of her physical desirability.

The alternative to the female sex object is seemingly the active or "phallic" mother. But the mother is not regarded as a sexual subject even in psychoanalysis — her emblem of power is the borrowed phallus that she loses when she becomes the oedipal, castrated mother. Phenomenologically speaking, she is not someone who actively desires something for herself; her power consists not of the freedom to do as she wills, not of control over her own destiny, but at best control over others. By contrast, the power of the father, signified by the phallus and expressed as sexual agency and potency, is clearly the power of a sexual subject. Even without attributing the ultimate power of desire to the phallus, it appears nontheless associated with father and masculinity and so still at odds with the primary feminine identification.

The frequent occurrence of woman's submission confirms the old idea that women enter into love relationships with men in order to acquire vicariously something they have not got within themselves. That women often try to protect their autonomy by avoiding intense involvement with men implies the same predicament: woman's desire too often conflicts with her sense of agency and is bound up with the fantasy of submission to an ideal male figure. This search for ideal love, the eroticization of submission in fantasy or reality, points us back to the problem of masochism. Underlying the wish for submission to an idealized other can be seen the issues of separation-individuation and self-other recognition. These issues, I shall demonstrate, are intricately bound up with the establishment of early gender identity and the search for an object of identification. Masochism, especially the variant I call ideal love, can be seen as an alienated attempt to resolve the difficulty of representing female desire — a difficulty that arises out of the tension between identifying with and separating from a desexualized mother, between wishing and being unable to identify with a father who stands for desire. Unable to create a representation of desire based on maternal identification, a sense of sexual agency that is active and feminine, the girl turns to idealizing love for a male figure who represents desire.

THE CONCEPT OF FEMININE MASOCHISM

Let us first briefly review the history of the concept of feminine masochism in the early psychoanalytic movement. The association of femininity with masochism derived both from the inherent suppositions of Freud's view of feminine development (1924b, 1925, 1931, 1933) and from his explicit statements about feminine masochism (1919, 1924a). Masochism "as an expression of feminine nature" was the form "most accessible to our observation" (1924a, p. 161). What masochism expresses that is "natural" to women appears to be the passive sexual stance assumed toward the father in the Oedipus complex. Masochistic fantasies generally "place the subject in a characteristically female situation; they signify, that is, being castrated, or copulated with, or giving birth to a baby" (p. 162). Freud thought that both feminine masochism and moral masochism are derived from a primary erotogenic masochism that is defined as pleasure in pain. As it turns out, this understanding of pain and pleasure is as problematic as his construction of femininity.

Freud's exposition of feminine masochism was far less influential in promulgating the idea than the work of Helene Deutsch (1930, 1944) and Marie Bonaparte (1953). It was they, especially Deutsch, who elucidated the idea more fully in lengthy works on female sexuality. Deutsch has become notorious for her view that masochism, narcissism, and passivity are the decisive tendencies in women's sexual and psychic life. The acceptance of the notion of feminine masochism was of course influenced by the widely held fantasies of submission and rape these analysts found among their female patients. The problem, as Horney (1933) argued, lies not in this finding, but in an explanation that has primary recourse to nature. In turning to Freud's theory of femininity for an explanation of such fantasies, Deutsch found the logical psychoanalytic explanation in women's lack of a penis. In realizing that she has no penis, in relinquishing her active-aggressive sexual stance that was associated with the clitoris, the oedipal girl makes the decisive step toward masochism (Deutsch, 1930). It is now inevitable that she will turn her aggression against herself and transform her sexuality into the wish to be castrated by the father in the act of being penetrated by him

(Deutsch, 1930). Without a turn to an alternative view of femininity and female psychosexual development, an alternative explanation for these widespread fantasies could not emerge.

Deutsch's conception of masochism did not really comprehend the distinction between the reality of pain and the symbolic meaning of the fantasy of pain: extrapolating from erotic fantasy life, she generalized about pain in actual life. Deutsch (1945) argued that women's acceptance of pain, humiliation, and lack of gratification is not only crucial to sexual relations with men but also comprises an important part of mothering and childbirth. Thus, the idea of feminine masochism drew its force from two sources: first, the prevailing view of femininity as determined by the lack of the penis; second, the psychoanalytic postulate that a symbolic relation in fantasy (giving birth stands for painful castration) also represents an unconscious wish. It was a short step from the idea of the wish as the underlying motive of fantasy and reality alike to the conclusion that women derive masochistic pleasure from the pain of childbirth.

The idea of "pleasure in pain" has also misled Freud's critics. Most recently, Paula Caplan (1984) has contended that women continue to be seen as masochistic by clinicians and that this represents a mislabeling: what women do is not pleasureful but merely the performance of their assigned role. She correctly points out that the capacity to endure pain has been confused with the wish to undergo it and enjoyment of it. Altruism and nurturance have been confused with self-abnegation and martyrdom. As de Beauvoir (1952) and Blum (1977) have also pointed out, the classical view of masochism did not distinguish the willingness to bear pain in the service of a higher goal from perverse, self-destructive acquiescence to abuse. Having disputed that women enjoy pain, Caplan wrongly concludes that she has refuted women's proclivity to masochism. In any case, she must still explain women's acceptance of submission. Caplan proposes as explanation that what is "called masochistic has tended to be the very essence of trained femininity in western culture" (p. 137). This implies that social learning of a cultural myth about womanhood suffices to explain the presence of masochistic fantasies in women, or that the association of feminity with masochism is the result merely of a pejorative view of women's nurturance and altrusim. Undeniably, femininity and motherhood as we know them have been tainted with submission, self-abnegation, and helplessness (even if submission works to conceal or deny a certain kind of power that woman as mother exercises). But from a psychoanalytic point of view that is interested in unconscious motivation, it is unsatisfactory to attribute the pervasiveness of submission fantasies in erotic life merely to cultural labeling or to derogation of women and their attributes. The alternative to a biological explanation must be sought not only in culture, but in the interaction of culture with intrapsychic processes.

The Freudian theory of feminine masochism reflects, no doubt, both the ideology and some of the painful reality of female sacrifice and subordination. One important aspect of Freud's notion of masochism as dictated by the pleasure principle was that the original sexual drive is reversed into passivity and the original aggression is turned against the ego. Both phenomena, passivity and the internalization of aggression, are quite readily observable in people who display what Freud called moral masochism, what Horney simply summed up as the masochistic person. Horney (1933) synthesized the attitudes of erotic and moral masochism with a description of what we now see as narcissistic pathology — low self-esteem, difficulty in separation, helplessness, and passivity. In this sense, she was moving toward the more comprehensive understanding of masochism that has developed in the last twenty years. Horney contended that the girl's discovery that she does not have a penis does not suffice to explain her abdication of active pursuit of sexual pleasure. But Horney tried to replace Deutsch's (1930) theory of feminine masochism as feminine nature with an explanation derived directly from sociocultural factors, such as woman's dependency and inhibited aggression. In order to explain the origins of woman's condition, she then resorted to woman's biological vulnerability, winding up with a position she wished to refute. While Horney's perceptions of culture are accurate, her argument reveals the absence of both an alternative theory of female psychosexual development and of self or ego pathology that could compete with the Freud-Deutsch interpretation.

The confusions that arose from the concepts of erotogenic masochism as "pleasure in pain" could be dispelled only by the evolution of theories of object relations and ego development. The question now became: what does masochism do for the ego in its struggle to individuate from the primary object (Menaker, 1973)? The concept of erotogenic masochism pointed to a highly significant phenomena — in this case the apparently fascinating contradiction that people can derive pleasure from pain. I do not mean to dismiss Freud's suggestions about the eroticization of negative stimuli and the internalization of aggression. But the idea of "pleasure in pain" is misleading insofar as the crucial point in masochism is not the experience of pain, but of submission. Submission may involve eroticized pain, but more often pain is a symbol or metaphor for submission. Indeed, pain may be associated not with submission but with erotic frenzy or physical performance of a clearly triumphant nature — it is only masochistic when it is "wanted as proof of servitude" (de Beauvoir, 1952). As has been shown in regard to the original Masoch, the enjoyment of pain required the context of submitting to a woman he idolized (Smirnoff, 1969). The fantasy of pleasure in pain has less to do with enjoyment of pain than enjoyment of submission, the annihilation or loss of will under what appear to be conditions of control and safety.

The desire for submission — for release from, annihilation, and loss of self — directs us to the ego issue in masochism: the issue of sustaining separation from the object, independence of the self. The symbolic significance of pain is violation, a rupture of ego boundaries; its aim is the loss of self through submission to an idealized other (Benjamin, 1983). How much concrete pain a person seeks depends on the capacity for symbolization, whether the person tends to somatize, act out, fantasize, or sublimate symbolic meanings. But without the surrounding experience of the master's power, without the idolatry and ritual, without the sense of submission to a higher authority or purpose, the infliction of pain loses its meaning and becomes unsupportable or disgusting (Smirnoff, 1969; Khan, 1979). When the analysis of masochism shifts from the concept of pleasure in pain to submission, the focus moves to the ego or self. Contemporary discourse on masochism has therefore emphasized such issues as object loss and separation (Stoller, 1975, 1979; Khan, 1979), the idealization that results from inability to separate from the primary object (Menaker, 1973), and the attempt to ward off self-dissolution and supply missing self-structure through merger with an ideal object (Kohut, 1971; Stolorow and Lachmann, 1981). This perspective on masochism is essential to any reinterpretation of the association of femininity with masochism. It allows us to reformulate the problem by asking, what are the vicissitudes of feminine development that predispose women to seek out relationships of submission?

The question — what is woman's desire and how does it become a desire for submission? — is still valid and provoking even though we are not satisfied by the answer Freud gave. Freud (1924a) associated both moral masochism and feminine masochism ultimately with the wish to be beaten by the father, which stands for the wish to have a passive sexual relationship with him. He argued (1919) convincingly that the guilt experienced by the little girl at wishing to be her father's lover and the wish itself ("father loves only me") are satisfied by a regression to an anal-sadistic, punishing form of eroticism. But in thus unraveling the secret of masochism, Freud implied that submission and passivity are not the true oedipal stance of the little girl but a product of guilt. Why then should the little girl be more prone to guilt and disavowal of oedipal wishes, to passivity and punishment, than the little boy? Why should the fantasy that emerges for the little girl involve the beating of a boy, a fact that Freud (1919) attributes to the spurring of her "masculinity complex" by the regression? The challenge posed by Freud's analysis is to explain woman's greater guilt, that is to say, fear, in regard to active sexuality and her attempt to resolve that predicament by a masculine orientation, without simply attributing it to her lack of phallus, the emblem and entitlement to desire. The perversion of woman's sexual agency, the alienation of desire that is masochism, remains to be explained.

THE FATHER-LIBERATOR OF RAPPROCHEMENT

When an omnipotent mother perpetuates primary love and primary identification in relation to her daughter . . . a girl's father is likely to become a symbol of freedom from this dependence and merging [Chodorow, 1978, p. 121].

Paradoxically, the father seems to occupy a much more important place in the psychosexual development of the boy than of the girl, be it as a love object or as a rival [Chasseguet-Smirgel, 1970, p. 95].

The key to reinterpreting masochism as a feminine experience must be sought in the already worked out consequences of the theory of core gender identity (Stoller, 1968). Nancy Chodorow's book *The Reproduction of Mothering* (1978) is the most comprehensive analysis of how the fact that children of both sexes receive primary care from and find their first object in a woman influences the pattern of identifications and object relations that create individual and gender identity. I suggest that the patterns of gender identifications and separation-individuation that arise from female parenting creates a feminine proclivity to masochism. Masochism is here considered in its dimension of submission to an idealized other — ideal love. Ideal love can be seen as rooted in the relationship to the father during separation-individuation. While its occurrence in that phase is normal, its common frustration in girls can lead to a transformation in which the adult search for ideal love becomes the basic content of masochistic fantasy.

The father's role as a figure of separation from the preoedipal mother has been elucidated in reinterpretations of penis envy. In emphasizing the power of the preoedipal mother and early object relations, the French analysts Torok (1970) and Chasseguet-Smirgel (1970) and the American feminists Dinnerstein (1976) and Chodorow (1978) concur that the power of the father and his phallus derives from the role they play in separating from the mother. Standing for difference and separation, the phallus becomes the desired object for children of both sexes, who wish to possess it in order to have that power. The meaning of the penis as a symbol of revolt and separation derives from the nature of the child's struggle to separate from the original maternal power.

The psychological imperatives of early narcissism and separation-individuation conflicts invests the father and the phallus with idealized attributes. The father, not the phallus, is the starting point — but this means the father as he is internally represented and refracted through the child's psyche. The origins of ideal love and the problem of woman's desire lie in the relation to this father. The unconsicous conflicts from which the phallus derives its significance do not begin with oedipal difficulties and regression from the feminine stance, what Horney (1926) called "the flight from womanhood." The development being emphasized is that of the ego (or self), and the conflict is the preoedipal one of separation.

Before the theoretical delineation of preoedipal ego development, the discussion of the father's connection with the phallus was couched in terms of the oedipal phase and the girl's switch in love objects. But as it has become apparent that the issues of separation and of gender identification begin in the second year of life, the girl's early narcissistic interest in the penis must be seen in terms of the conflicts of that phase. Although psychoanalytic theory has not caught up with the observational research suggesting that fathers and infants become attached much as mothers and infants do (Spieler, 1984), psychoanalysis has accepted the idea that the father does not delay his appearance on the scene of male gender development until the oedipal phase. Probably the father's differences from the mother are actually first formulated by the child at the height of separation-individuation, the rapprochement phase (Abelin, 1980). It is here that the struggle to differentiate becomes fatefully intertwined with gender identity. The realization of gender identity — one's own and one's parents — evolves between the ages of 18 and 36 months. This means that the realization of gender identity coincides fatefully with rapprochement.

In the rapprochement phase, the child's awareness of its separate existence intensifies (Mahler, Pine, and Bergmann, 1975). Realizing for the first time that the parent's help is outside its magical control or omnipotence, the child now resents its dependency. A considerable tension now arises between the wish to be independent and the wish to restore magical dependency with the primary parent. Rapprochement can be seen as the great fall from grace, when the conflict between self-assertion and separation anxiety brings forth an essential tension. In rapprochement the child experiences its own activity and will as a counterpoint to a more powerful parent and to its own helplessness. The child's self-esteem can now be damaged by the realization that it does not control mother and that much of what mother does is not an extension of its own power. It must be repaired by the mother's confirmation that the child can do real things in the real world. Thus originates the need to be recognized as independent by the very person upon whom one once depended. This paradoxical need for recognition by the other is a source of the great conflict and tension of this period; it is entangled with the narcissistic vulnerability of recognizing one's own dependency.

But the struggle for recognition is not only a matter of compensation for lost magic. The child is also gaining something new; it is becoming conscious of will and agency in a new way. In becoming conscious of will, of desiring, the child advances a step toward being the subject of desire. The child now wants not simple satisfaction of need. Rather, in each of these wants lies the desire to be recognized as a subject — above and beyond whatever is wanted, the child wants recognition of its will, its desire, its act.[1] Rapprochement inaugurates the first in a long series of struggles to achieve a sense of agency, to be recognized in one's desire.

It is precisely in rapprochement that the awareness of gender identity emerges. The difference between mother and father begins to take hold symbolically in the psyche and to meld with the vital conflict between separation and connectedness, independence, and dependence. The struggle for recognition joins with the moment of differentiation between mother and father; differentiation between self and other, male and female, become structurally intertwined.

---

[1]My interpretation of rapprochement places more emphasis on desire and agency than on loss and abandonment as blows to omnipotence. Kohut's (1971) discussion of the child's need for an object that mirrors the grandiose self and an ideal object that allows the self to become cohesive in the image of that ideal is pertinent. Probably both functions contribute to the early representation of the father as an ideal object who can mirror the child's grandiose aspirations.

This conjunction ought to be thought of as the rapprochement complex. It is a nodal point that vies in theoretical importance with the Oedipus complex. In the rapprochement complex the father begins to assume the crucial role of standing for freedom, separation, and desire. Here begins the child's relationship to the father that has been adduced to explain the power of the phallus.

No matter whose theory you read, the father is always the way into the world. There is rather widespread agreement that the father is the "knight in shining armor" (Abelin, 1980). He appears as powerful, but not as all controlling, all giving, all perfect oneness (Dinnerstein, 1976). The asymmetry of the father's role for boys and girls, the fact that little girls cannot as readily utilize the father in their separation from the mother, has, with some important exceptions by women analysts (Clower, 1977; Lax, 1977; Bernstein, 1983; Levenson, 1983; Spieler, 1984), been uncritically accepted as inevitable in psychoanalytic literature. That little girls in rapprochement become more depressed, lose more of their practicing enthusiasm than boys, is noted as a natural occurrence (Mahler et al., 1975). The family organization and object relationships responsible for this occurrence are simply taken for granted. But once we do challenge a system in which women are always the primary parent, we may also investigate this apparent fact of female development. Similarly, we wonder about the fact that boys escape the depressive mood of rapprochement and deny the feeling of helplessness that comes with the realization of separateness. According to Mahler and her colleagues (1975), the boy succeeds in this denial by virtue of his "greater motor-mindedness," the buoyancy of his body ego feelings, his pleasure in active aggressive strivings. What accounts for this difference?

Ernest Abelin (1980) argues that in rapprochement the father plays the liberating role for the boy more than for the girl. The father was already tuned into his toddler's "wild exuberance" in practicing. He remains exciting, "a stable island of practicing reality," while the mother "becomes contaminated by feelings of intense longing and frustration" (p. 155). Essentially, the identification with the father offers the boy toddler his first model of desire, "the first symbolic representation of the object and the separate self, desperately yearning for that object" (p. 154). The boy now imagines himself to *be* the father, the subject of desire, in relation to the mother. (While Abelin attributes central importance to the wish, "I want Mommy," I suspect that the father's externality and representation of the subject who desires and acts in the world has a more general significance.)

Abelin (1980) suggests that the shift in the child's interest toward being the subject of desire coincides with the transition from the sensorimotor stage to a symbolic perception of the world. Earlier, the sensorimotor child experienced desire only as a property of the object, as in "It is desirable." Now the child can be a subject aware of desiring, as in "I desire it" — hence the importance of the father as a different kind of subject than the mother, a subject of desire. The other subject is not the object of gratification, the supplier of need, but the other who gives recognition. This means that the father's entry is a kind of *deus ex machina* that solves the quandary of rapprochement. Instead of having to get the confirmation of independence from the one he or she still belongs to depend on, the child can turn to the father for that recognition. The father is a vehicle not merely for enabling separation, but for avoiding conflict, denying helplessness and the loss of practicing grandiosity. In the boy's mind, the magical father with whom he identifies is still as omnipotent as he would like him to be. Recognition through identification is now substituted for the more conflictual need to be recognized by the primary parent with whom he feels his dependency. The boy can have the fantasy that he is being the father toward the mother rather than her helpless baby. The father of rapprochement is internalized as the ego ideal of separation and, like the oedipal superego, can be seen as a psychic agency that embodies a specific resolution of the rapprochement conflict.

The upshot of this analysis is that for boys separation-individuation becomes a gender issue: the issues of recognition and independence become organized within the frame of gender. Male gender formation revolves around the gradual replacement of an original, primary identification with the mother by a new identification with the father. This disidentification with mother (Greenson, 1968) is widely held to be crucial at this point for the fate of the boy's masculinity (Stoller, 1975). But the switch to the father, as we now see, is suffused with the rapprochement issues of wanting simultaneously to be independent of mother and yet be recognized as independent by her, of wanting to leave her and yet return to her. On one hand, the assumption of masculine identification allows a defensive resolution of the rapprochement paradox; on the other hand, the rapprochement ambivalence thrusts the child toward his father and shapes the nature of his masculinity. This reciprocal interaction between gender and identity formation within the context of the father-son relationship also contains the core experience of being the subject of desire. It appears that what is crucial to masculinity is not the phallus or the father, but the internal representation of a new relationship toward the mother that cancels the primary identification with her: separateness appears to be the essence of male identity. (Keller, 1978; Chodorow, 1979).

What is striking in psychoanalytic theory is how, in contrast to the boy's, the girl's relationship to the father hinges on the phallus more than on the identification with him. When we turn to the little girl's story, we find no coherent integration of the interlocking elements of gender, individuation, and paternal identification. The question of how successfully the paternal identification is offered by the father, confirmed by the mother, and integrated by the girl has not been endowed with structural meaning in psychoanalysis. Too often we still hear the argument that not having the penis suffices to determine identity. We are likely to find either a denial that the father is as important to the girl's identity (Abelin, 1980) or an assertion that she is really concerned with the penis (Roiphe and Galenson, 1981). In terms of the rapprochement complex, the girl's wish for a penis can be given a more precise meaning. Girls desire it for one of the main reasons that boys cherish it — because they are struggling to individuate. They are seeking what toddler boys recognize in their fathers and wish, through identification, to affirm in themselves — recognition of their own desire. But they find themselves in conflict about this wish to tear themselves from the attachment to mother — often greater than the conflict of boys because of the intense narcissistic bond between mother and daughter — and seek to find another *object* with whom to identify. This other object is the father, and his otherness is guaranteed and symbolized by his other genital.

The rapprochement complex is not simply an earlier version of the Oedipus complex. The early identification with the father includes, of course, the element of active desire toward the mother than Freud originally emphasized. But the meaning of the phallus and of desire here, especially for the girl, leans far more in the direction of separation from than reunion with the mother. This does not mean that the girl's love for her mother is not intense, but that it is not yet associated with the phallus. Possessing a penis with which to woo the mother is a later, genital, oedipal idea. In this phase the representational aspects of the phallus are shaped by the anal tendencies and have more to do with the difference between father and mother, with agency and independence (Torok, 1970). So the girl must make what is *not hers* represent her desire. Can the girl, through a more positive identification with the father, resolve this difficulty and come to feel that desire and agency are properly hers?

Too often, little girls cannot or may not use their connection with the father, in both its defensive and its constructive aspects, to deny helplessness and to forge a genuine sense of separate selfhood. The depressive response to the rapprochement complex may be attributed to the lack of the boy's manic defense. Because girls are more aware of gender and generational differences — less able to deny them as boys do — both the difficulty of separating from mother and their own helplessness confront girls more directly. This deflation of early omnipotence may be viewed positively as generating the ego's capacities for sociability and sublimation (Roiphe and Galenson, 1981; Gilligan, 1982) or the future capacity to be a parent (Abelin, 1980). But we also know that many girls are left with a lifelong admiration for those who get away with their sense of omnipotence intact; they express their admiration in relationships of overt or unconscious submission. They grow up to idealize the man who has what they can never possess, the emblem of power and desire. Putting the other in the place of their own ego ideal, they seek to incorporate him sexually, rather than striving to attain their own ideal.

Much of this problem in girls' development must be attributed to fathers themselves. Fathers often do prefer their boy infants, forming a more intense bond based on identification, which is followed by greater mutual attachment and mutual identification in toddlerhood (Lamb, 1977; Gunsberg, 1982). When the father is not available to the girl, it is can be argued that her helplessness and depression increase, turning inward her aspirations for independence and her anger at being denied recognition. Galenson and Roiphe (1982) sum up one little girl's position thus: she longed for "the missing excitement and erotic nature of their relationship, which had earlier been attached to the father in toto and now was identified as emanating from his phallus in particular" (p. 162). This transformation from excitement and desire in general to the symbol of the phallus in particular may indeed begin in rapprochement, especially enhanced when the father himself is "missing."

Long before the phallic representation is formed by the child, the father is experienced in his total kinesic and affective behavior as the exciting, stimulating, separate other — his play is more active (Lamb, 1977), more stimulating, discrepant, and novel (Yogman, 1982), more fostering of differentiation (Kestenberg, Marcus, Sossin, and Stevenson, 1982; Gunsberg, 1982). From the beginning, then, the father is the representative of excitement, outside, otherness. The rapprochement wish to be like the father, the identificatory impulse, is not only a defense, an alternate route for recognition that avoids the ambivalent mother. It also is rooted in an intrinsic need at this point in development to make desire one's own, to experience it as legitimate and self-originated. Now excitement begins to be felt not simply as the property of the object, but as one's own, *inner desire* (Abelin, 1980). Desire is now felt as emanating from within; it is a property of one's own will. While the child looks for recognition in both parents at this time, the exciting father is the one who recognizes in the child what the child recognizes in him, recognizes the child as *like* himself. Thus the multiple functions of the rapprochement complex evolve into multiple reasons for the father to become the symbolic figure of recognition — the need to separate, the need to avoid ambivalence, and the need to find a subject who represents desire and excitement.

What I am stressing here is the role of identification in love and desire. Peculiar to this phase of development is a kind of *identificatory love*. Identification — being like — is the chief mode in which a child in this phase can acknowledge the subjectivity of another person, as the well-noted fact of parallel play implies. The first loving of someone as a subject, as an agent not a source, is this kind of identificatory love. Structurally, then, a particular type of relationship of identification intervenes for the male child during his key period of struggle with independence. Inner desire and will are consolidated, the need for recognition is fixed on the paternal object, and masculine identity is established through separation. Identificatory love is the matrix in which these developments occur. The strong mutual attraction between father and son allows for recognition and identification, a special erotic relationship. The practicing toddler's "love affair with the world" turns into a homoerotic love affair with the father, who represents the world. The boy is in love with his ideal. This homoerotic, identificatory love is the boy's vehicle for establishing masculine identity. Through this ideal love he begins to see himself as subject of desire; in this relationship of recognition he finds his sense of self.

Ideal love can be understood through reference to this identificatory, homoerotic love between toddler son and father.[2] We can

---

[2]This interpretation obviously resonates with Freud's (1921) discussion of the ego ideal, which he saw as beginning in the boy's preoedipal identification and love for the father. This identificatory love did not conflict with but prepared for the Oedipus complex, Freud thought; but it could be lost sight of if, as in the case of girls and some boys (in the negative Oedipus complex), it were translated into object love for the father.

locate the origins of ideal love in the period when the child is beginning to confront his own helplessness but can still comfort himself
with the belief in parental omnipotence (Mahler et al., 1975). He
seeks to recognize in this parental power the power of his own
desire; he elaborates it in the internally constructed ideal. This love is
structurally important not only for masculinity, but for the search for
an ideal image of the self. I conclude, then, that this father-son love
affair is the model for ideal love; that the rapprochement conflict
between independence and helplessness is the model conflict that
ideal love is usually called on to solve; and that the wish, or desire,
that underlies ideal love is the desire for recognition.

IDEAL LOVE

All my foolish acts and all the good things I have done have the
same cause: an aspiration for a perfect and ideal love in which I
can give myself completely, entrust my being to another . . .
How I envy the ideal love of Mary Magdalene and Jesus: to be
the ardent disciple of an adored and worthy master; to live and
die for him, my idol . . . (Janet's patient, cited in de Beauvoir,
1952, p. 716–17).

The analysis I have offered to the roots of ideal love in the identification with the rapprochement father of separation affords the possibility of reconstructing and reintegrating theories of masochism
and femininity. The failure to appreciate the importance of ideal love
in the father–daughter tie and its parallelism with many aspects of
the father–son tie has led to many psychoanalytic misunderstandings
of women. The boy's early psychic structure is seen as derivative of
both mother and father bonds; the girl's psychic structure, whether
derived from the maternal identification or organized by penis envy
is seen as strangely detached from the father. The current emphasis
on maternal identification may ignore the problem that the mother is
not articulated as a sexual subject and the crucial role played by the
father as a figure of identification. In Freud's understanding of wom-
en, the gap in the girl's subjectivity left by the missing father appeared as "the lack" and the theory of penis envy emerged to fill it.
The conclusion was drawn that the girl's masculinity complex was an
obstacle to femininity and that feminine sexual self-esteem could be
drawn from the passive oedipal relation to the father. More recently,
Blum (1977) has argued that penis envy should be seen as the organizer not of femininity but of "female masculinity" which may actu-

ally impede the development of femininity. Here the danger of accepting the notion of primary feminine identity and rejecting
bisexuality becomes apparent. I believe, rather, that this envy represents a desire for important elements of selfhood associated with
masculinity: independence, self-esteem, excitement, and agency.
What is desirable is the integration of those elements through the
girl's integration of maternal and paternal identifications. It is the
failure to achieve this integration and the accompanying withdrawal
from autonomy and agency, especially sexual agency, that fosters
conflict with femininity and, ultimately, masochism.

A full delineation of the failure of this integration is still the gap in
our theory. "In this culture there may be a basic contradiction between sexual liberation and personal liberation (or autonomy) for
women isofar as sexuality as constructed expressed dependent or
masochistic trends," wrote Person (1980). The psychological beginnings of this contradiction may be seen in the girl's struggle at rapprochement — a struggle vastly complicated by the prevalent denial
of women's subjectivity. The frustration, or absence, of an ideal
identificatory love relationship with someone who represents desire
and excitement can be seen to damage any child's sense of agency.
But even with successful paternal identification in the early father-
daughter tie, conflict may arise between the preoedipal and oedipal
love for the father, that is, between identification with the object love
for him. Once genital love has entered the picture, in the oedipal
phase or in adolescence, the situation becomes more complicated and
conflictual for all parties. While these further developments demand
a great deal more exploration, some gross patterns deriving from the
gender division are obvious: difficulty in integrating agency and love
may arise both from the father's ultimate refusal to accept a feminine
equal to the mother's inability to model autonomy. A succinct statement of the problem was made by Doris Bernstein (1983):

> Analytic literature says little about the relationships of fathers
> and daughters: primarily the focus is on the father as libidinal
> object, as protector and rescuer from the mother. Fathers do
> not seem able to offer themselves as objects of identification to
> girls as they do to their sons — with few exceptions. To the
> extent that the father's individuation rests on the biological base
> of difference from mother, to the extent that he mobilized, or
> continues to mobilzie the "no, I am unlike" to maintain his
> autonomy, the more *unable* he is to permit or welcome his
> daughter's identification with him as he is his son's. Repeatedly,
> women have complained that their fathers encouraged intellec-

tual development and education but only up to a certain point
[p. 196].

The point is that paternal identification is not merely defensive,
but reflects positive strivings that must be fostered through identification and parental recognition. Although it is preferable, under the
present gender constellation, that fathers should be as available to
their daughters as to their sons, this solution is not without conflict
for the girl. In the girl's inner world, the obstacles to paternal identification are reflected in injury to the grandiose self, to narcissistic
self-esteem, and to the sense of agency, and in inability to separate
from the primary object. This means that loving the father will often
be associated either with one's own castration, since father's lover
must relinquish agency and competition, or with the guilt of castrating him (Chasseguet-Smirgel, 1970). As long as the sexual division
persists—the mother representing the primary attachment object,
who holds and soothes, and the father representing the separation
object identified with the outside world of freedom and excitement—
the father will be important to girls as well as to boys in the effort to
differentiate and recognize themselves in another subject of desire.
The difficulties that attend this paternal identification, as well as its
absence altogether, is the basis for adult versions of ideal love.

Ideal love may characterize a whole spectrum of relationships,
including those of covert submission and idealization, those featuring
persisting unrequited longings in the face of abandonment and rejection, and those that openly erupt into sadomasochistic practices.
Most of the issues of separation and recognition, the narcissistic
pathology associated with masochism, can be contextualized in terms
of rapprochement issues in general and difficulties in consolidating
father-daughter identification in particular. Women are often drawn
into relationships of submission because they seek a second chance
for ideal love, a chance to reconstitute father-daughter identification
in which their own desire and subjectivity can finally be recognized.
Even in those relationships that involve annihilation of the self, one
can often discern the fantasy of resolving the conflict between activity and passivity. As de Beauvoir (1952) wrote, "This dream of
annihilation is in fact an avid will to exist . . . when woman gives
herself completely to her idol, she hopes that he will give her at once
possession of herself and of the universe he represents" (p. 717).

Woman's ideal love, the submission to or adulation of the idealized
other in whom one hopes to recognize oneself, parallels the identificatory love of the boy's rapprochement complex. The masculine
orientation that Freud (1919) noted in women's beating fantasies—

the fact that they were the boy being beaten — may now be seen as modeled on the homoerotic, identificatory nature of the boy's love of the father in this phase. In fantasy, the girl is portraying herself as the boy that is in love with his father; but finally she is punished, castrated, denied that vital link of identity and equality with the father.

Although ideal love is often charged with oedipal fears and guilt and is combined with genital object love for the father, it can also exist by itself as the legacy of the girl's rapprochement complex. The replay of identificatory love for the father is best seen not as regression into masculinity but as a revival of unresolved conflicts and aspirations that attended this earlier phase. In the boy's ideal love he seeks to protect his omnipotence and grandiosity, to establish separateness through identification with someone who is already separate, to recognize his desire in the father's desire and be recognized in return. These aims can also be found as primary motives in woman's ideal love. Perhaps what most distinguishes our approach from Freud's is the notion that these aspirations are legitimate and may hold the key to active femininity, once they are disentangled from the helpless envy and disavowal of womanhood that have filled the lack of her own desire and agency.

By way of illustrating the roots of ideal love in the identificatory love of rapprochement, I shall briefly sketch a case. Elaine was a young woman writer who could not get over her preoccupation with a man who had left her. This man represented the idealized father with whom she wanted to identify in order to disidentify from her mother. Elaine explicity saw her lover as her ideal, a person like herself as she wished to be: he was magical, outrageous, creative, imaginative, unconventional. He alone understood her, her eccentricity, her outrageousness, her wild and free spirit, her refusal to be a conventional female. After his departure, she began work on a mystery novel in which he was the incestuously loved older brother and she was the tomboyish sidekick whom he took everywhere. She rejected the trappings of femininity, dressed as a boy, performed feats of physical courage and mechanical ingenuity. When her hero deserts her, the heroine struggles to carry on, still living in the shadow of her brother's charismatic abilities. She tries to prove herself to him, to live up to the independence she thinks he embodies, in the hope that he will finally acknowledge her. The story parallels Elaine's actual ideal love affair, which was largely fueled by the need to have a person highly different from her mother who would recognize her. it bore all the features of longing for a homoerotic, narcissistic love affair with the father and the world. Her lover was so vital and attractive to her because of "something to do with freedom." She often said he was "the only one who recognized my true self; he made me feel alive."

Elaine perceives her ambitions to have been thwarted by both parents in a sex-stereotypical way. Her mother, who had many children, was weak and ineffectual, wholly without aspirations for herself or her children, and especially paralyzed when it came to helping them with "anything we did *outside*." Her father had never given her the recognition she wanted. He had been too outside — distant, angry, judgmental, and impatient with his children and wife, involved in his own work and failure, and frequently critizing her for being stupid or timid when she did not meet his expectations. Elaine believes that her mother was valuable as a source of comfort and soothing to her babies and children when they were little, but that she was devoid and discouraging of any excitement or spark — all that is important in life. When Elaine identifies with her mother or sisters, she feels paralyzed, sick, weak. Moreover she is terrified of the depths of submission and self-annihilation her sister reached in her terrible desire to please her father. As a result Elaine refuses to invest the therapist with the power to help her and suffers because of what she terms her inability to have "faith," which she readily admits reflects her fear of devotion to an idol. At the same time, she expresses contempt for any soothing or comfort, although her agitation and inability to self-soothe is flagrant; fearing the debilitating sympathy her mother offered, she must remain separate from her at all costs.

Elaine's memories confirm that the mother withdrew the moment her children began to crawl away from her, returning when a child was injured and required her ministrations. The withdrawal of the holding environment in the face of the child's separation is the commonly cited environmental failure underlying ego pathology of this kind (e.g., Masterson, 1981). The crisis of separation has occurred in a context where all separation is experienced as a threat to attachment, and so the object is both inconstant and potentially engulfing. Elaine became one of the many children who, by rapprochement, are clinging and fearful in mood, making occasional dangerous and disastrous forays out of the mother's orbit. The masochistic ideal love is a simultaneous expression of this helplessness and separation anxiety even while it is an attempt to overcome it by borrowing the other's cohesiveness. On one hand, Elaine is seeking a heroic sadist, one who represents the liberating father rather than the engulfing mother. On the other hand, what she really needs is someone who supplies not only the missing excitement but also the holding environment. Such containment is acceptable only in its most masculine form because it would otherwise threaten to pull her back into the fusion with the helpless, engulfing mother.

The ideal love is chosen to solve the problem posed by frustration of desire and agency and the ensuing rage at nonrecognition — an avenue of escape through a figure of identification. In this sense, it is defensive. But the creation of this father figure, seen in terms of the normal splitting of the rapprochement also entails a wish. This wish should not become invisible to us merely because it appears in the more disturbed version fueled by rage and frustration. Successful treatment involves both aspects. In escaping her mother, Elaine hopes to escape her own tremendous rage at her for failing to withstand her daughter's attack. Unleashed activity and aggression would destroy whatever remains of the good mother within. Thus she regards her anger and desire as highly driven, even monstrous, and can unleash them safely only in the hands of a man who is more powerful, in control, and does not depend on her for his strength. Only when such destruction is permitted can she find her own creativity, she maintains. Here ideal love, sustaining the idealized phallic father image, combines two sets of needs: (1) to achieve what boys get from their fathers in the normal course of rapprochement, a vehicle of solving that conflict between separation and dependency that preserves grandiosity and omnipotence, salvaging self-esteem and independent will and desire; (2) to put her desire finally in another's hands, make him the manager of the highly disturbing and driven need for freedom and self-expression that is permeated with rage and so can be contained only by a figure of supreme independence and power. On one hand, the father's unavailability for identificatory love has led to the effort to recreate it in a masochistic relationship. On the other hand, the inadequacy of the mother as a figure for identification has intensified that longing for identificatory love and combined it with the search for an object that can withstand aggression and separation. The ideal love seeks the never attained synthesis by imbuing the loved man with features of both the ideal mother and the ideal father, containment and excitement.

The need for an object who is truly outside, who does survive destruction in Winnicott's (1971) sense, is crucial to the fantasy of the ideal love. The man who does not depend on her can be truly outside, and it is this fact — not merely the propensity for suffering — that so often makes only the unreliable abandoning figure a safe or attractive one. The ideal lover seems to offer the boundedness and limits within which one can experience abandonment and creativity. The analysis of masochistic fantasy repeatedly shows that in the control of the other, the masochist seeks the freedom of releasing her own desire, as well as the recognition of her deepest self (Benjamin, 1983). Elaine has also described such experience in reference to her teachers, saying that they provide you with the freedom to turn inward and explore, understanding when you have "got it." The element of containment and boundedness that informs this fantasy underscores the important role played by failure of the holding environment in the etiology of masochism. This is the failure of the ideal mother, the containing, holding mother who can support excitement and outside exploration, who can withstand and limit aggression, who can give permission to separate and can recognize the child's independent accomplishments. Her direct recognition is as crucial to the child as the indirect recognition achieved through identification with the ideal father.

In Elaine's history and treatment it is apparent that the need to escape a weak, engulfing mother is at war with the need to turn back to the mother and engage in the struggle for that recognition — the struggle to death for the life of the self. Simply, we are talking about the mother's ability to provide a structure for the child's aggression that makes it possible to integrate that aggression with its close relatives: activity, will, and desire. It is not merely the recognizing response of the exuberant father than ignites the child's own sense of activity and desire. As discussions of the psychoanalytic situation as a holding environment suggest, the function of containment is also important. Or, as Elaine described the good teacher, the need is for an other whose presence does not violate but permits and helps to recognize the experience of one's own *inner* desire.

Behind the ideal love we have seen the early father identification. But this identification is part of a whole complex that includes the ambivalence toward the mother, the struggle to reconcile independence and dependency, the need for recognition from a mother who survives that struggle. In the actual analysis of masochism, returning to the struggle with the mother is as crucial as reexperiencing the disappointment with the ideal father. The problem of woman's desire must finally be situated in the difficulties with mother and father in the rapprochement complex. These difficulties stem from the gender division: the mother is not the active subject of desire for the child, and the father is that subject. For the daughter, the constellation of a mother who is lacking subjectivity and a father who does possess it presents a difficult choice. Particularly if she fails to receive that recognition from her father, but even if she does so, her active subjectivity and her sense of femininity must be in conflict. A frustrated identification with the father is one primary motif in the masochistic relationship. But even a "successful" identification can create conflicts with feminine identity as long as the girl is confronted with the mother's own lack. Usually, this means that she will find herself faced with a conflict between her sexuality and her sense of autonomous self, because the longing for ideal love exerts the greatest pull on her sexuality, if not on her activity in the world. The sense that female sexuality is an active creative force ultimately depends as much, therefore, on the mother's actual realization of subjectivity as on the father.

While the ego and self pathology that underly masochism can readily be traced to failures in the holding environment and the internalization of a containing mother, the gender content of masochism, its association with femininity, involves the dynamic relationship of mother and father in our present gender system. The structural conditions of gender that now exist do not allow for reconciliation of agency and desire with femininity. Although they often fit the common reality of our gender arrangements, we have criticized the theoretical assumptions about early female development that make feminine submission seem inevitable: that mothers cannot be a figure of separation for both children, that fathers cannot offer their daughters what they offer their sons. We must challenge the structure of heterosexuality in which the father supplies the missing excitement and the way out of the dyad, functions defensively to "beat back the maternal power" (Chasseguet-Smirgel, 1976), and denies the mother's subjectivity as too threatening (Dinnerstein, 1976). The normative image of motherhood that psychoanalysis has long adumbrated must be revised: the ideal of a mother who provides symbiosis and then separation "on demand" must be replaced by the mother who also moves under her own steam. The mother's own integration of separateness and agency must be the profound source from which her recognition of the child's autonomy proceeds. Ideally, the adult woman's sense of agency and separateness should mitigate her sense of having to *be* the all-perfect mother of infantile fantasy, and so should help disconfirm the child's fantasy of maternal power and paternal defense.

The drawbacks of the constellation of idealized masculinity as a protection from primitive maternal power have been pointed out by many feminists: the defensive repudiation of the mother by the boy may further his separation but does not help him to resolve intimacy and independence (Miller, 1973; Gilligan, 1982; Chodorow, 1978, 1979). I believe that the idealization of the father resulting from the conventional gender role and parenting constellation is never fully counteracted. Even when reality contradicts this paternal ideal, it remains active inside as a longing, a fallback position whenever real agency and recognition fail. The father remains the figure who stands for subjectivity and desire, so that, culturally speaking, woman's desire must always contend with this monopoly. Both sexes can therefore continue to comply in ideal love the prevalent form of domination and submission in erotic life. The association of femininity with masochism, the submission to an idealized other, derives above all from the early idealization of the father, an idealization charged with the urgency of resolving the crisis of separation and establishing the self. The other side of this idealization is the derogation of femininity and motherhood and the consequent difficulty in reconciling maternal identification with an active sense of self, preventing the emergence of woman's desire.

In the analysis of ideal love an inverse relationship emerges between desire and recognition on one hand and submission on the other. To oversimplify: the more agency and recognition, the less submission. But this does not necessarily mean that the opportunity to exercise agency — as some feminists imply — will reverse the tendency toward submission once it is firmly in place as an internal object relationship that compensates and eroticizes the loss of self. Once the relationship of identification in which the child recognizes her own desire has been marked by failure with the appropriate parent at the appropriate phase, the search for a powerful ideal figure who represents the desiring self begins to replace it. Agency and recognition are achieved vicariously by submitting to this ideal lover, often in conventionally acceptable forms of wifely self-sacrifice. When identification such as that between toddler and father occurs at the appropriate phase with the pleasure of mutual recognition, then identification serves as a vehicle of development. But when identification emerges later in ideal love, it becomes an impediment, a vicarious substitute. Thus ideal love becomes a perversion of identification, an extension of early identificatory love into a substitute form of embodying one's own desire. Ultimately, we can agree with Freud that woman's masochism is linked to the retreat from active sexuality; however, this retreat begins not with resignation to anatomical imperatives but with failures in early individuation. And we see in masochism, especially the variant of ideal love, woman's alienated search for her own desire.

REFERENCES

Abelin, E. L. (1980). Triangulation, the role of the father and the origins of core gender identity during the rapprochement subphase. In: *Rapprochement*, ed. R. F. Lax, S. Bach, & J. A. Burland. New York: Aronson, pp. 151–170.
Beauvoir, S. de (1952). *The Second Sex*. New York: Knopf.

Benjamin, J. (1983). Master and slave: The fantasy of erotic domination. In: *Powers of Desire*, ed. A Snitow, C. Stansell, & S. Thompson. New York: Monthly Review Press, pp. 280–299.

Bernstein, D. (1983). The female superego: a different perspective. *Internat. J. Psycho-Anal.* 64:187–202.

Blum, H. (1977). Masochism, the ego ideal, and the psychology of women. In: *Female Psychology*, ed. H. Blum. New York: International Universities Press, pp. 157–192.

Bonaparte, M. (1953). *Female Sexuality.* New York: International Universities Press.

Caplan, P. J. (1984). The myth of women's masochism. *Amer. Psychol.*, 39:130–139.

Chasseguet-Smirgel, J. (1970). Feminine guilt and the Oedipus complex. In: *Female Sexuality*, ed. J. Chasseguet-Smirgel. Ann Arbor: Michigan University Press, pp. 94–134.

–––––– (1976). Freud and female sexuality. *Internat. J. Psycho-Anal.*, 57:275–286.

Chodorow, N. (1978). *The Reproduction of Mothering.* Berkeley: University of California Press.

–––––– (1979). Difference, relation and gender in psychoanalytic perspective. *Socialist Rev.* 9(4):51–70. Also published as: Gender, relation, and difference in psychoanalytic perspectives in *The Future of Difference*, ed. H. Eisenstein & A. Jardine. New Brunswick, NJ: Rutgers University Press, 1985.

Clower, V. L. (1977). Theoretical implications in current views of masturbation in latency girls. In: *Female Psychology*, ed. H. Blum. New York: International Universities Press, pp. 109–126.

Deutsch, H. (1930). The significance of masochism in the mental life of women. In: *The Psychoanalytic Reader*, ed. R. Fliess, New York: International Universities Press, 1969, pp. 195–207.

–––––– (1944, 1945). *The Psychology of Women*, Vols. 1 & 2. New York: Grune & Stratton.

Dinnerstein, D. (1976). *The Mermaid and the Minotaur.* New York: Harper & Row.

Fast, I. (1984). *Gender Identity.* Hillsdale, NJ: The Analytic Press.

Freud, S. (1919). A child is being beaten. *Standard Edition*, 17:179–204. London: Hogarth Press, 1955.

–––––– (1921). Group psychology and the analysis of the ego. *Standard Edition*, 18:67–144. London: Hogarth Press, 1955.

–––––– (1924a). The economic problem of masochism. *Standard Edition*, 19:159–172. London: Hogarth Press, 1961.

–––––– (1924b). The dissolution of the Oedipus complex. *Standard Edition*, 19:173–182. London: Hogarth Press, 1961.

–––––– (1925). Some psychical consequences of the anatomical distinction between the sexes. *Standard Edition*, 19:248–260. London: Hogarth Press, 1961.

–––––– (1931). Female sexuality. *Standard Edition*, 21:225–246. London: Hogarth Press, 1961.

_____ (1933). New introductory lectures on psychoanalysis: Femininity. *Standard Edition*, 22:112–135. London: Hogarth Press, 1961.

Galenson, E., & Roiphe, H. (1982). The preoedipal relationship of a father, mother, and daughter. In: *Father and Child*, ed. S. H. Cath, A. R. Gurwitt, & J. M. Ross. Boston: Little, Brown, pp. 151–162.

Gilligan, C. (1982). *In a Different Voice*. Cambridge, MA: Harvard University Press.

Greenson, R. (1968). Dis-identifying from mother: its special importance for the boy. *Internat. J. Psycho-Anal.* 49:370–374.

Gunsberg, L. (1982). Selected critical review of psychological investigations of the early father-infant relationship. In: *Father and Child*, ed. S. H. Cath, A. R. Gurwitt, & J. M. Ross. Boston: Little, Brown, and Company, pp. 65–82.

Horney, K. (1926). The flight from womanhood. In: *Feminine Psychology*. New York: Norton, 1967, pp. 54–70.

_____ (1933). The problem of feminine masochism. In: *Feminine Psychology*. New York: Norton, 1967, 214–233.

Keller, E. F. (1978). Gender and science. *Psycho-Anal. Contemp. Thought.* 3:409–453.

Kestenberg, J., Marcus, J. H., Sossin, K. M., & Stevenson, R. (1982). The development of paternal attitudes. In *Father and Child*, ed. S. H. Cath, A. R. Gurwitt, & J. M. Ross. Boston: Little, Brown, pp. 205–218.

Khan, M. (1979). *Alienation in Perversions*. New York: International Universities Press.

Kohut, H. (1971). *The Analysis of the Self*. New York: International Universities Press.

Lamb, M. E. (1977). The development of parental preferences in the first two years of life. *Sex Roles*, 3:495–497.

Lax, R. (1977). The role of internatization in the development of certain aspects of female masochism: ego psychological considerations. *Internat. J. Psycho-Anal.*, 58:289–300.

Levenson, R. (1984). Intimacy, autonomy and gender: developmental differences and their reflection in adult relationships. *J. Amer. Acad. Psychoanal.*, 12:529–544.

Mahler, M., Pine, F., & Bergman, A. (1975). *The Psychological Birth of the Human Infant*. New York: Basic Books.

Masterson, J. F. (1981). *The Narcissistic and Borderline Disorders*. New York: Brunner/Mazel.

Menaker, E. (1973). *Masochism and the Emerging Ego*. New York: Human Sciences Press.

Miller, J. B. (1973). New issues, new approaches. In: *Psychoanalysis and Women*, ed. J. B. Miller. Baltimore: Penguin, pp. 375–406.

Person, E. S. (1980). Sexuality as the mainstay of identity: Psychoanalytic perspectives. *Signs*, 5:605–630.

Roiphe, H., & Galenson, E. (1981). *Infantile Origins of Sexual Identity*. New York: International Universities Press.

Smirnoff, V. (1969). The masochistic contract. *Internat. J. Psycho-Anal.* 50:665–671.

Spieler, S. (1984). Preoedipal girls need fathers. *Psychoanal. Rev.*, 71:63–80.

Stoller, R. J. (1968). *Sex and Gender.* New York: Aronson.

———— (1975). *Perversion,* New York: Pantheon Press.

———— (1979). *Sexual Excitement,* New York: Simon & Schuster, 1980.

Stolorow, R. D., & Lachmann, F. M. (1980). *Psychoanalysis of Developmental Arrests.* New York: International Universities Press.

Torok, M. (1970). The significance of penis envy in women. In: *Female Sexuality,* ed. J. Chasseguet-Smirgel. Ann Arbor: Michigan University Press, pp. 137–170.

Winnicott, D. W. (1971). The use of an object and relating through identifications. In: *Playing and Reality.* Harmondsworth, Middlesex, Eng: Penguin, pp. 101–111.

Yogman, M. W. (1982). Observations on the father-infant relationship. In: *Father and Child,* ed. S. H. Cath, A. R. Gurwitt, & J. M. Ross. Boston: Little, Brown, pp. 101–122.

6 Learning the Lines
Women's Aging and Self-Esteem
_____RUTH FORMANEK

> *You cannot always keep that unfakable young surface. You must*
> *learn your lines.*
> — Philip Larkin (1965)

This paper demonstrates how pejorative societal views of aging women contribute to women's negative feelings about themselves. To counteract their negative feelings, women employ narcissistic operations that earlier in their lives were successful in raising self-esteem. With increasing age, however, these narcissistic operations no longer work and become inappropriate. More phase-appropriate attempts to raise self-esteem include, both for older women and for older men, a relation to things reminiscent of people, depersonified abstract ideals and interests, and, for women at any age, intimate relationships to family and friends.

In the course of this paper we shall embark on a number of excursions — into developmental theories of aging, societal perceptions of women and their effect on women's self esteem, differential experiences of aging according to gender, and narcissistic operations designed to maintain high self-esteem in old age. We explore those areas to compensate for the dearth of literature specific to gender differences in aging and for the historical neglect of experiential differences in social class and age periods. One gains the impression of a homogenization of post-middle-aged women. They are pictured

I am grateful to Miriam Formanek for a critical reading of this chapter.

as all alike — whether in their seventies or eighties, rich or poor, physically healthy or ill. It is hoped that future research will focus on differentiations according to gender, age period, and social class, both by means of empirical studies and by the accumulation of data from older women in psychoanalysis or from psychoanalysts themselves.

THEORIES OF AGING

Observations on aging may be as old as the process of aging itself. The Bible refers to the association of aging with a withering of strength, a lack of vigor, on the one hand, and with wisdom, respect, reverence on the other. Shakespeare's (1936) account of old age is part of a theory of life span development: the Seven Ages, from *As You Like It:* "The sixth age shifts into the lean and slipper'd pantaloon, with spectacles on nose and pouch on side, his youthful hose, well saved, a world too wide for his shrunk shank; and his big manly voice, turning again toward childish treble, pipes and whistles in his sound. Last scene of all, that ends this strange eventful history, is second childishness and mere oblivion, sans teeth, sans eyes, sans taste, sans every thing" (p. 677).

In our times, Erikson's theory of the Eight Ages of Man has been most influential. According to Erikson (1968) those who have adapted to the triumphs and disappointments of being and who have been capable of generativity will experience "ego integrity." Erikson's account of the last stage of his life cycle theory refers to the acceptance of one's life and of the people significant in it. Acceptance includes "a new and different love of one's parents, free of the wish that they should have been different, and an acceptance of the fact that one's life is one's own responsibility. . . ." Lack of integration is signified "by disgust and by despair: fate is not accepted as the frame of life, death not as its finite boundary. . . ." (p. 139).

The need to resolve earlier envy and rivalry, according to Melanie Klein (1963), is a requirement for adjustment to adulthood and old age. Adults who can resolve their destructive feelings will be able to identify with and share the pleasures of their own children. Yet, despite the resolution of earlier conflicts, loneliness can persist because of pain from earlier and internal sources, which, Klein argues, remain powerful throughout life. Jacques (1970), influenced by Melanie Klein, speaks of the inevitability of facing death and of the existence within oneself of hate and destructive impulses. Such recognition leads to a depressive reaction, and the early "depressive position" must again be worked through. The successful outcome of mature creative work is based on "constructive resignation" to one's imperfections as well as to the shortcomings in one's work.

Kernberg (1980), who combines some of the ideas of Erikson and Klein, lists "life tasks" in middle age (i.e., between thirty and sixty years). One of these tasks is the need to understand one's past and be aware of one's future, as middle age demands a coming to terms with one's past self- and parental images. During this period, earlier conflicts reawaken, and oedipal issues and separation anxiety again become salient. Past and present dyadic object relations, especially the oedipal situation, contribute to the contents of the middle-aged person's fantasy, behavior and conflicts. The major tasks of middle age are "to accept the inherent conflicts in love and marriage and to contain them in a stable object relation" (p. 128); to come to terms with external aggression, sadism, corruption and envy; to accept one's final responsibility to oneself; to face increasing losses and the physical manifestations of aging without denial or pathological anxiety; and to accept the limits of one's creativity.

While these theorists outline the quandaries and tasks of middle and old age, their generalized accounts seem insufficiently tailored to the lives of individuals. Self psychology offers another perspective, one not based on the conflicts of early childhood, which, for some theorists, pose almost irreconcilable problems with aging. Kohut (1984) has suggested that we know little of the selfobject needs during our later years, or when we have to deal with debilitating illness, or when we confront death. This more positive view of the creation of selfobjects throughout life, as well as the changes, with maturation, in the types of selfobjects needed and created, permits the charting of a developmental line. Wolf (1980) has begun to chart this line.

Like all attempts to describe life-span development, Wolf's account devotes most of its pages to youth. From birth to the emergence of the self, the child's primary need is for selfobject relations that lend organization to the emerging self. Once the self has emerged, self boundaries need securing within the context of selfobject relations, with the aid of the confirming selfobject and, simultaneously, through confronting the selfobject. The confrontation serves the development of healthy aggression, which promotes the cohesive strength of the self. The contradictory need for selfobjects to be both allies and antagonists accounts for the inevitable ambivalence of this early phase of development and colors all subsequent relations. With the oedipal period, selfobject relations advance, and selfobject needs can now be satisfied not only by the primary caretaker but by other family members as well. Increasingly, selfobject needs can be met by others such as peers, and dependence on any one selfobject is decreased. With maturation, selfobject needs and relations become less intense, and symbols may be substituted for persons. Individuals are unaware of their selfobject needs as long as the social matrix satisfies them by providing mirroring responses and idealizable values. However, should individuals lose their benevolent social context and find themselves in an alien or hostile environment, even strong selves may fragment. Such adversity could describe the experience of the elderly.

In sum, each account emphasizes a different aspect of aging consistent with each author's theory. Erikson contrasts the acceptance of aging with its rejection and attendant despair. Klein and Jacques identify the need to resolve feelings of envy and rivalry, to accept within oneself the presence of destructive impulses. All of them stress the need for resignation to one's shortcomings. While Kernberg addresses his comments to the middle-aged, the tasks of those beyond this period may be presumed to be similar: the need to accept one's limitations, the awareness of destructive impulses within oneself and within others, one's aging, and the experience of losses. The quality of internalized object relations is all important — the aging individual must come to terms with earlier conflicts deriving from relationships to parents. In contrast to these theories, based on the presence of destructive impulses and conflict, Kohut and Wolf stress the development of selfobjects over the life span, the possibility of substituting symbols for persons as gratifying selfobject needs.

Despite these developmentalists' theories about middle-aged and older individuals, most psychoanalysts have continued to neglect issues of old age, particularly of older people's feelings about themselves and their aging. This neglect may be due partially to a denial of aging and death, which fosters our societal and clinical emphasis on youth. Our clinical knowledge of the experiences of older people is sparse, since our tendency to deny old age and death leads us to avoid treating older patients. This paucity of information is only inadequately overcome by empirical studies such as that conducted by Lieberman and Tobin (1983), who investigated adaptation to stress in old age. They explored the extent to which nearness to death represents a crisis and how it functions as an organizer in the minds of the elderly. The authors describe the critical issues during the last two decades of life: how one maintains a consistent self-concept despite the obvious, externally induced changes that are part of being old. This maintenance of a consistent self-concept is a task of the elderly, some of whom meet it successfully and others do not.

While some elderly people engage in potentially self-destructive mechanisms, others invoke life-enhancing strategies. For example, how well is the "historical self," or one's relationship to one's past, integrated into the elderly person's current life? And to what degree does this integration determine response to stress? Similarly, hope, or the extension of the self into the future, acts as a life-enhancing mechanism. Since the elderly person's time is limited, facing the future realistically and positively is a crucial but possible task.

Strategies for resolving stress in old age, however, are likely to differ between men and women, who experience the process of aging with separate agendas. None of those who have researched middle or old age have differentiated according to gender. Theorists have exaggerated the differences between boys and girls but have overlooked them in older men and women.

How can we study the experience of the aging woman? While little information is available on aging beyond demographic data, a study of the experience of aging women could be conceptualized as a study of self-esteem. We shall next turn to women's self-esteem in the course of their adult development and explore self-esteem as it is subject to internal and external influences.

SELF-ESTEEM

According to Jacobson (1964), self-esteem depends on what we aspire to be — the ego ideal — measured against our sense of our actual self — the self-representation. Jacobson refers to self-esteem as the discrepancy or harmony between the ego ideal and the self-representation.

Stolorow and Lachman (1980) provide another description of self-esteem, one derived from self psychology: "Mental activity is narcissistic to the degree that its function is to maintain the structural cohesiveness, temporal stability and positive affective coloring of the self representation" (p. 10). Self-esteem may be defined as that "positive affective coloring of the self representation." In other words, almost any mental activity might be useful as a defense against low self-esteem, but some activities are more successful than others. Success or failure of an activity depends to some extent on whether it is "phase appropriate." For example, failure may result when attempts to maintain self-esteem through narcissistic ties to an idealized object (e.g., the mother) are used beyond the appropriate phase — childhood. Similarly, narcissistic ties to an idealized object in adulthood (e.g., submissiveness to a lover) may be unsuccessful to maintain self-esteem. Self-esteem in such relationships may vacillate with the fate of the frequently unstable relationship. On the other hand, self-esteem may successfully stabilize with depersonified, abstract, and internalized values or with enduring and mature relationships with persons.

Strategies for maintaining self-esteem may, moreover, depend on gender differences, although few authors have explored this issue. Annie Reich (1953) argues that extreme submissiveness in women maintains and stabilizes the woman's self-representation and aids in defensively mastering injuries to her self-esteem. Certain women who are submissive to men form narcissistic object ties to aggrandized phallic ideals. The woman's male partner represents her external ego ideal, and her submissiveness counteracts the trauma of her imagined castration and her resulting sense of inferiority. According to Reich, the woman's idealization of her partner and her fusion with him is a particular type of narcissistic object choice available to women.

External Influences on Women's Self-Esteem

In addition to those internal influences, which exert a force on the self and on the maintenance of self-esteem, there are external influences. Parental influences are directly transmitted to the child; societal ideals are more indirectly transmitted. Societal ideals are nevertheless pervasive, although frequently hidden and implied. Myths, for example, transmit universal, but covert, meanings. For example, the stories of Demeter and Persephone and of Echo provide female ideals.

The main theme of the story of Demeter and Persephone is attachment, maternal devotion and the use of power to restore the mother–daughter relationship after a disruption. According to Robert Graves's (1955) account, Demeter, the goddess of the cornfield (or of fertility), was inconsolable when her daughter Persephone was taken from her. Hades, the god of the underworld, having fallen in love with Persephone, had asked her father Zeus for permission to marry her. When Zeus would neither give nor withhold his consent, Hades abducted the girl. To no avail, Demeter sought Persephone without food or rest for nine days and nights. When she learned who had abducted her daughter, she was so angry that she wandered about the earth, forbidding the trees to yield fruits and the herbs to grow, until all humans stood in danger of extinction. She swore that the earth must remain barren until her daughter was returned. Zeus now brought pressure on Hades to return Persephone to her mother. But Persephone had tasted seven pomegranate seeds from a tree in Hades's garden — she had eaten of the food of the dead — and Hades now had a hold over her. A compromise was finally reached: Persephone would spend three months of the year (winter) in Hades's company and the remaining nine with her mother.

According to Robert May (1980), this myth shows "caring confirmed and endurance rewarded" (p. 13). Attachment and loss are necessarily intertwined, and genuine caring requires a willingness to suffer the loss of what we care for. In the myth, sorrow, loss, and suffering are followed by an ecstatic return to fullness and growth. This myth finds expression in children's stories (e.g., *The Runaway Bunny*) and provides a model to females; but, like most other myths, it also reaffirms traditional power relationships.

Another female model derives from the myth of Echo, the nymph in love with Narcissus. Echo, whose existence is obscured by the tragedy of Narcissus, embodies several stereotypically feminine qualities. She is Narcissus's vocal reflection, paralleling the river, which provides his visual reflection. Echo loves Narcissus but, as a woman punished by the Gods, she is not permitted to act, only to react; cannot initiate speaking, but must "echo" what another has spoken. An enduring role model, she is dependent, powerless, and mute until spoken to.

More overt than mythic models, but still subtle, are historical influences on woman's development of the self, influences that until recently were virtually ignored. The present explosion of information in women's history, however, now permits the study of how society has viewed women at different epochs and how such views have changed over time. Eighteenth-century American women, for example, remained relatively insulated from their changing environment. With time, however, the patriarchal family began to be replaced by a new type of family — more private, more affectionate, and less authoritarian. Women and children began to assume enhanced roles as distinctive individuals. By 1800, woman was "no longer considered morally suspect, mentally dim, or potentially dangerous to those around her. She was no longer . . . viewed as a loudmouthed shrew, a meddling interloper, or a devil's accomplice, whose only salvation lay in silence, industry, and obedience" (Woloch, 1984, p. 67). Woman was considered more rational and quasi-autonomous within the family, became the custodian of values — capable of transmitting ideas, exerting a positive influence on her children, and, hence, playing a role in society.

Another shift in the perceptions of women and the family occurred between 1800 and 1860. The home began to be seen as an emotional space, a refuge from the competitive world, a source of stability and order in an unstable society. Women were viewed as presiding over an insulated, privatized, feminized shrine — the home. Magazines articulated the canon of domesticity and motherhood, featuring scenes of mothers at home, surrounded by children, in affectionate poses. The female character began to be newly assessed, and character traits, like social roles, were now divided between men and women. Men were characterized as competitive, assertive, individualistic and materialistic; women, as domestic, dependent, affectionate, pious, pure, gentle, nurturant, benevolent, and self-sacrificing. While these 'softer' virtues had been filtering in throughout the 18th century in advice tracts destined for the upwardly mobile, during the early 19th century, "the 'softer' virtues became accepted as innate" (Woloch, 1984, p. 119). Moreover, they have continued to be accepted as 'innate.'

Women internalize mythic, historical, and prevailing images of themselves. Irigaray (cited in Schor and Grandet, 1985), a French feminist and critic of Lacan's emphasis on the mirror as the beginning of the symbolic stage, has suggested that the little girl does not view the essence of her own image in the mirror, but rather her reflections from others, a patriarchal image. The little girl internalizes the dominant view of herself — a masculine view. One can only speculate on the particular distillations taking place in the process of internalization and the degree to which older perceptions merge with newer ones. In general, although the position of women has changed since 1776, there is continuity with the view of women as inferior to men. It is their internalization of this masculine view of women's inferiority that renders women prone to low self-esteem.

To bolster their self-esteem and for their own security, women have had to be sensitive not only to those in their care, but to the perceptions of those in power. These power relationships, internalized, produce and reproduce certain personality types, such as the helpless, eager-to-please "little woman." When she objects that her needs for affection and protection are not being met, her behavior is described in the most negative terms. This negative perception of women by men seems to have several sources. Stiver (1985) has suggested that men deny their own empathic qualities in order to defend against the strong, but prohibited and devalued, connection with their mother, a point earlier made by Dinnerstein (1976). Anger in men may be due to their sense of having been abandoned early in life, as well as from their envy of women's freedom to express feelings more openly. According to Stiver, men's anger has found its way into the professional literature through their descriptions of female patients. For example, "hysteroid dysphorics" are described as follows by Donald Klein in *Psychopathy and Psychopharmacology:*

> They are fickle, emotionally labile, irresponsible, shallow, love intoxicated, giddy and short-sighted. They tend to be egocentric, narcissistic, exhibitionistic, vain and clothes-crazy. They are seductive, manipulative, exploitive, sexually provocative, and think emotionally and illogically. They are easy prey to flattery and compliments.
>
> Their general manner is histrionic, attention-seeking and may be flamboyant. In their sex relations, they are possessive, grasping, demanding, romantic and foreplay-centered. When frustrated and disappointed they become reproachful, yearnful, abusive and vindictive and often resort to alcohol [quoted by Stiver, p. 9].

WOMEN'S SOCIALIZATION: DEPENDENCY AND CONNECTEDNESS

Freud (1933) believed that women experience shame arising from their need to conceal their castrated state, but Lewis (1978) has suggested that shame is due in part to women's sensitivity to others. Women are more easily embarrassed, humiliated, and shamed when they fail in their other-directed tasks. Thus, women's self-esteem can be expected to show wider fluctuations in response to the reactions of others than would be the case for men's self-esteem. Men are not socialized to be sensitive to others critical evaluations of their interpersonal functioning. And assertiveness, which is stressed in boys' socialization, is the equivalent of caring less for the opinion of others. May (1980) has suggested that caring, giving and altruism are at the center of women's lives. The bond between mother and daughter "stands out as a special example of the general concern for human ties in the female pattern" (p. 65). Evidence has accrued from many sources that girls develop in intimate relationships they seek to maintain in adulthood (see Dinnerstein, 1977; Landsberg, 1982; Smith-Rosenberg, 1975).

Yet, women's dependency has more often than not been viewed as pathological. Annie Reich (1973), for example, in describing "estreme submissiveness," focuses on the "special dependency of one adult upon another: the impossibility of living without the partner, the willingness to comply with all the partner's wishes, thereby sacrificing all interests of one's own, all independence and self-reliance . . . a perversion" (p. 85). We have accepted dependency as a negative trait, a judgment no doubt deriving from men's fears of becoming dependent again as well as from its feminine connotations. For women, however, caring and attachment seem to be requirements for high self-esteem as the loss of these attributes is correlated with low self-esteem and depression. Drawing from a large-scale epidemiological study of depression in women, Brown and Harris (1978) list the following factors as among those predisposing women to depression: loss of the mother before the age of 11 years, a lack of intimacy with the husband, the experience of loss or disappointment, the threat of an actual separation from a key figure, an unpleasant revelation about someone close, or a life-threatening illness to a close relative (p. 274).

Self-in-relation theory (Kaplan, 1984) postulates that the loss of a relationship represents a loss of confirmation of women's relational self-structure. Women experience the absence of intimacy due to a loss as a failure of the self and feel responsible for failed relationships. Their self-worth rests on their ability to build relationships. With loss, women experience a sense of inadequacy and low self-esteem, especially when they measure themselves against culturally valued and internalized masculine norms. Our society denigrates relational qualities as it denigrates 'woman's work' — knitting, embroidery, weaving, cooking, cleaning, and child rearing.

Self-in-relation theory asserts that women's connectedness to one another is positive. Girls' psychological development is based on mutual understandings and reciprocity of affect: "It is the flow of empathic communication and mutual attentiveness from one to the other that not only permits the child to feel cared for, but begins to develop in a child a sense of herself as a caring being, as one who derives strength and competence from her own relational capacities. . ." (p. 6).

THE CRISES OF WOMEN'S REPRODUCTIVE LIFE

Reproductive functioning exerts a complex influence on women's self-esteem. The complexity derives in part from societal connotations, which are internalized and have an impact on woman's bodily experience. Puberty, menstruation and menopause are socially defined crisis points, markers of age periods, and are attended by taboos.

The first book on menstruation published in English, a compendium of ancient and current views on women's reproductive functioning, begins with the lament:

> Wretched surely and unequal seems the condition of the female sex, that they who are by nature destined to be the preservers of the human race, should at the same time be most liable to so many diseases. . . . If they enter into a wedded state, even from that source of pleasures something bitter arises, and pregnancy brings with it at least a length of loathing, if nothing more calamitous; if they make a vow of celibacy . . . they will hardly be able to avoid labouring under some distemper . . . because they are strangers to a mother's pangs. . . . [Freind, 1729].

Pejorative statements from 19th physicians continued to be negative and portrayed woman as frail, sickly, vulnerable to illness and madness, especially in connection with her reproductive life. One of the dangers of puberty and of menopause, according to Napheys (1871), was the 'green sickness,' or chlorosis: "Hardly any one has watched women closely without having observed the peculiar tint of skin, the debility, the dislike of society, the change of temper, the fitful appetite, the paleness of the eye, and the other traits that show the presence of such a condition of the nervous system in those about renouncing their powers of reproduction. . ." (p. 296).

Our own era is not without the residue of the last century's pejorative view of women's biological cycle. Helene Deutsch (1945) believed that "woman's biologic fate manifests itself in the disappearance of her individual feminine qualities at the same time that her service to the species ceases. . . . Everything she acquired during puberty is now lost piece by piece; with the lapse of the reproductive service, her beauty vanishes, and usually the warm vital flow of feminine emotional life as well. The physiologic decline is felt as the proximity of death, life begins to seem pale and purposeless" (p. 461).

And according to popular writer David Reuben, with the onset of menopause "The vagina begins to shrivel, the breasts atrophy, sexual desire disappears. . . . increased facial hair, deepening voice, obesity . . . coarsened features, enlargement of the clitoris, and gradual baldness complete the tragic picture. . ." (quoted by Fausto-Sterling, 1985, p. 107).

The association of menopause to depression was, and for some writers still is, believed to be a strong one. "Involutional melancholia" was still to be found in DSM II (American Psychiatric Association, 1968) and, more recently, Lax (1982) described the "expectable depressive climacteric reaction." According to Lax, this reaction manifests itself in "sadness, in a sense of loss, and in mourning for the youthful self of one's past" (p. 164). But, according to Greene (1984), the view "that there exists a specific and distinct involutional syndrome is no longer tenable." When psychiatric disorders occur during the climacteric, Greene states, on the basis of his survey of research, they are coincidental, or there is often a previous history of psychiatric breakdown in women of vulnerable disposition.

What, then, are the social, personal and symbolic meanings of the menopause? Does it portend a "change of life," the beginnings of old age — an end to sexual desire and its gratifications, physical beauty, and feminine traits?

Taboos and a lack of interest in women and their 'female troubles' have helped maintain ignorance about the menopause and other female states. It was not until 1975 that a study was launched to interview women on the nature of the menopausal hot flush (Voda, Dinnerstein, and O'Donnell, 1982). Other syndromes have been similarly neglected, for example, the premenstrual tension state. The psychological consequences of such neglect include women's embarrassment with their 'symptoms,' their feeling ashamed of experiences that are not permitted to surface in 'polite' society. Women experience a general disparagement of themselves and their biological functioning — what they feel is not to be shared and must remain unspoken. These feelings lead to a sense of peculiarity and inferiority, and ultimately to a lowering of self-esteem.

GENDER DIFFERENCES IN AGING

Susan Sontag (1972) has suggested that women's concerns about aging reflect an accurate perception of the double standard of aging that distinguishes men from women. As their youth fades, women are considered less attractive and therefore less worthwhile. Because men are judged more on achievements than on their looks, aging men tend to be viewed as "distinguished.' Researchers have suggested that both young and old men and women judge old women as less attractive than old men — another instance of women adopting a masculine standard!

Attractiveness is important to self-esteem, according to several studies. Lerner and Karabenich (1974) suggest, moreover, that attractiveness and body attitudes are a more important component of self-concept for females than for males. Simmons and Rosenberg (1975) found that adolescent girls tended to be more concerned with their looks than were their male peers and also perceived themselves as less attractive than did boys. Those girls who perceived themselves as unattractive had lower self-esteem scores than girls who were satisfied with their appearance. Fallon and Rozin (1985) report that men and women both distort the perceptions of their bodies, with women distorting their body perceptions negatively, whereas men distort the perceptions of their bodies in a positive, self-aggrandizing way.

Women have been socialized to beautify themselves in order to please men. Cosmetics, which play a major role in present day beautification, were known in ancient Egypt. But they were not available to the middle and lower classes in the Western world until early in this century, when they began to be mass produced. Until that time it was more difficult to find what Elaine T. May (1980) has called "purchasable solutions to personal problems." And the personal problem is to attract a man. The man will offer a traditional identity: wife and mother of his children. Many young women fear that unless they are beautiful or have learned to beautify themselves, they may not find husbands. Thus women's concern with beautification is not necessarily primary, not always a devotion to the body for its own sake. Rather it is a means to an end: to satisfy her traditional role as a woman-in-a-relation.

What appears to be an unusual concern with physical appearance may also be a defense against understandable anxiety. For example, one young woman, who had internalized the ideals of her family and society to marry, expected every eligible man to fall in love with her — instantly. Her efforts to make herself attractive and the admiration she expected were only a first step in approximating her goal — to find a spouse who could provide her with the role and status she was expected to achieve. Her concern with her body, then, defended against the anxiety that she might not find a husband.

Focusing on the body may not only defend against anxiety, but also raise self-esteem. Sports activities, for example, produce highs, perhaps as a consequence of the release of endorphins, and lend a sense of control and power over one's body. A recent trend in "body building" corrects or redesigns certain body parts by developing muscle groups. Hence, disguising of what one finds unattractive by artifice or by cosmetic surgery is no longer the only solution.

Dieting and dietary concerns also add to a sense of control over one's body and the aging process, if not over one's destiny. On the other hand, Brownmiller (1984) has suggested that dieting resembles foot-binding and corseting, restrictions that represent a mutilation of women's bodies for the sake of beauty. While being thin is important to current standards of health and attractiveness, an overemphasis on dieting implies that the female body is deficient and in need of reshaping.

Implied in the effort to develop the body and make it more attractive is an orientation to the future. With age, the orientations and strategies for changing one's body become more illusory. More realistic views of the brevity of the life span, of living on borrowed time, are bound to emerge and force themselves into the consciousness of the aging woman.

AGING AND GENDER DIFFERENCES
IN NARCISSISTIC OPERATIONS:
PEOPLE AND THINGS

Older women are doubly hit by prevailing attitudes, which may lower self-esteem. On the one hand, women may experience physical changes and a simultaneous loss of social status as a result of aging and the ending of their reproductive capacity. On the other hand, the use of narcissistic operations, which earlier raised self-esteem, becomes inappropriate with increasing age: submissiveness to a powerful man or devotion to the beautification of the body no longer work. When older women continue to use such strategies, when they follow a "phase-inappropriate" dress code or makeup, the results are viewed as pitiable, grotesque, even bizarre.

To the aged, potential external supplies to bolster their self-esteem fade away. The aged lose their parents, sometimes their children, friends and colleagues, heroines and idols, a way of life, a job, an income. They become progressively more powerless as their losses also include bodily and psychological functions: hearing, eyesight, mobility, short-term memory, reaction time, and so forth. The aged fear illness, further losses, the inability to care for themselves, being sent to a nursing home, death.

When external supplies that earlier raised self-esteem fade, what happens to the relationship between ego ideal and self-representation? Does the nearness of death temper our wishes to approach our ideals? Do we settle for a cohesive self-representation and let go of the possibility of its positive affective coloring? And do gender differences in self-esteem remain as they were in younger days?

Old age begins a leveling process through which some male–female role differences appear to vanish. But it is unclear what changes occur in self-representations. Role changes are visible ones: aging women, especially with adequate incomes, begin to resemble men in caring less for the views of others and becoming more assertive than they were when younger and more dependent. Aging men, when they retire, begin to resemble women: they lose the power base derived from their success as wage earners. Subjective reactions to these changes in role may differ. While men may become despondent over their lack of status and power, women may return to earlier activities. Women may devote themselves to their close relationships with children, other relatives, and friends, or find new projects and, with them, new independence. Most women have always had two power bases, their household work and their families. While retiring men may find the transition to being at home difficult, retiring women's domestic and social skills and their network of children and friends provide support.

As suggested by Wolf (1980), the originally personal, concrete, and focused relation to the selfobjects of childhood needs transforming with increasing age. Substitution of persons, depersonal diffusion, and symbolization create new selfobject relations. A major change begins early and continues lifelong: the substitution of friends for family members. Due to their socialization, women, at any time of their life span, appear to be particularly capable of forming close friendships.

Researchers have consistently described the friendships of girls even as young as preschoolers, and women to be intimate, dyadic, supportive and maternal. Olesker (1985), for example, found little girls to be more involved with their mothers than were little boys, and to engage in peer play with a special friend. The boys seemed to prefer toys to people and, in fact, barely discriminated among people. Gender differences in friendship have been reported at almost any age, with girls forming few and close dyadic relationships, and boys becoming members of teams, gangs, or groups (Formanek, 1984; Whiteside, 1976).

No doubt the ideal and the reality of friendships have helped to maintain women's self-esteem. Friendship seems to be of particular importance to women, especially since their longer life expectancy has resulted in a much larger proportion of widows to widowers. Women's capacity to form close friendships may help compensate for the loss of a spouse and fight off feelings of isolation and depression. "All my old friends are in the graveyard, and if I hadn't made some new ones, where would I be?" said a 92 year old widow (Blythe, 1979, p. 266).

In addition to friendships, involvement with things may compensate for the loss of people, role, or status. Self-esteem can be maintained through an attachment to things reminiscent of people that they replace. Csikszentmihalyi and Rochberg-Halton (1981) found that women and older people valued things of contemplation, such as books, pictures, or photos that reminded them of former attachments.

Another attempt at substituting things for people is shopping. Women, especially of the middle class, spend many hours shopping, either alone or with companions. Shopping, while also a social activity, represents a particular relation to things: shopping for acquisitions may replenish the self, provide the possibility of changing one's appearance or the appearance of one's home, and may provide contact with new people. Whatever its individual and idiosyncratic meanings, shopping seems to bolster women's self-esteem.

Collecting, a special type of attachment to things, may also serve to defend against low self-esteem in both women and men and bring on a more optimistic mood. Freud, the antiquities collector, described it in a letter to Fliess: "On the next rainy day I shall walk down to my beloved Salzburg; the last time I was there I picked up a few old Egyptian things. Those things cheer me and remind me of distant times and countries. . ." (p. 291). The interest of adult collectors in things from the past — antiques, toys, children's books, pictures — suggests restitution. One wishes to repair a loss, to substitute for something meaningful that was lost. We acquire things as consolation for the loss; we hold onto a thing as an emotional link to a person, a community, an age period. We continue to need contact with selfobjects, with the past, with people, and with a style of life never to return. We also want to retain a connection with ourselves as we were then — as children.

In both old women and men, information and its recording aids in maintaining a sense of self: "There is no reality now except what I can sustain inside me. My memory is failing. I have to hang on to every scrap of information I have to keep my sanity, and it is for that purpose that I am keeping a journal. . ." (Sarton, 1973, p. 4).

Dwelling on early memories by both old women and men may also be viewed as a defense against low self-esteem. Life review among the elderly is a universal mental process, characterized by the progressive return to consciousness of past experiences and particularly the resurgence of unresolved conflict. With their return to consciousness, these experiences and conflicts can be surveyed and reintegrated. Review offers the possibility of gaining a sense of integrity if conflicts can be successfully resolved. Life review has also been suggested as a useful procedure in the context of family therapy (Walsh, 1980; Lewis & Butler, 1974).

Similar to recording information and life review in their self-esteem function are ideals. Eagle (1982) speaks of those survivors of concentration camps who lived not for the sake of life itself, but for some ideal that transcended it. Devotion to a cultural, humanist, political, or religious view of life, to spiritual values such as morality, helped them to resist the horror of the concentration camps. Paradoxically, life in the concentration camps held — for the aging — some slight hope of freedom and continued life. Old age does not. No doubt the fear of death, the knowledge of finiteness, the lack of a future affect one's spiritual values and ideals. What becomes more salient than the maintenance of ideals is the maintenance of one's self-cohesiveness and stability over time. To retain the "positive coloring of the self-representation" becomes more difficult. Thomas Bernhard (1970) has suggested that when we think of death, everything becomes ridiculous.

What women ask of the mirror changes over the life span. Early in life we want to know if we are the fairest of them all. Later, our questions become more modest: How do I compare to others my age and to myself at an earlier time? Is my memory, hearing, eyesight still functioning? What about my arthritis, osteoporosis, shortness of breath? In the absence of reliable external supplies we need to replenish self-esteem by ourselves: "'I love you, I love you, I love you, I love you,' whispered old Mrs. Tannenbaum to herself in the mirror. The whole day went much better after that, she thought" (Dellis, 1984).

REFERENCES

American Psychiatric Association (1968). *Diagnostic and Statistical Manual of Mental Disorders (DSM II)*. Washington, DC: American Psychiatric Assn.

Bernhard, T. (1970). speech. In: *Ueber Thomas Bernhard*, ed. A. Botond. Frankfurt am Main, Suhrkamp. ". . . es ist alles laecherlich, wenn man an den *Tod* denkt."

Blythe, R. (1979). *The View in Winter*. New York: Harcourt, Brace, Jovanovich.

Brown, G. W., & Harris, T. (1978). *Social Origins of Depression*. New York: Free Press.

Brownmiller, S. (1984). *Femininity*. New York: Simon & Schuster.

Csikszentmihalyi, M. & Rochberg-Halton, R. (1981). *The Meaning of Things*. New York: Cambridge University Press.

Dellis, Nick (1984). from *Poem* by Alice Howe, read at meeting of Adelphi University Society for Psychoanalysis and Psychotherapy.

Deutsch, H. (1945). *The Psychology of Women*. New York: Grune & Stratton.

Dinnerstein, D. (1976). *The Mermaid and the Minotaur*. New York: Harper & Row.

Eagle, M. (1982). Interests as object relations. In: *Empirical Studies of Psychoanalytic Theory*, ed. J. Masling. Hillsdale, NJ: The Analytic Press.

Erikson, E. H. (1968). *Identity, Youth and Crisis*. New York: Norton.

Fallon, A. E. & Rozin, P. (1985). Sex differences in perceptions of desirable body shape. *J. Abn. Psychol.* 94:102–105.

Fausto-Sterling, A. (1985). *Myths of Gender*. New York: Basic Books.

Formanek, R. (1984). *The Female World of Friendship*. Paper presented at the Second International Congress of Women. Groningen, Holland.

Freind, J. (1729). *Emmenologia*. London: T. Cox, Preface.

Freud, S. (1933). New introductory lectures on psychoanalysis. *Standard Edition*, 22:5–182. London: Hogarth Press, 1964.

———— (1954). *The Origins of Psychoanalysis*. New York: Basic Books.

Graves, R. (1955). *The Greek Myths*. Baltimore: Penguin Books.

Greene, J. G. (1984). *Social and Psychological Origins of the Climacteric Syndrome*. Brookfield, Vt: Gower.

Jacobson, E. (1964). *The Self and the Object World*. New York: International Universities Press.

Jacques, E. (1965). Death and the mid-life crisis, *Internat. J. Psycho-Anal. 46*, 502–514.

Kaplan, A. (1984). *The Self-in-Relation: Implications for Depression in Women*. Work in Progress, Stone Center for Developmental Services and Studies, Wellesley College, Wellesley, MA.

Klein, M. (1963). *Our Adult World and Other Essays*. New York: Basic Books.

Kernberg, O. (1980). Normal narcissism in middle age. In: *Internal World and External Reality*. New York: Aronson.

Kohut, H. (1984). *How Does Analysis Cure?* Chicago: University of Chicago Press.

Landsberg, M. (1982). A Study of Adolescents' Friendships. Hofstra University Dissertation.

Larkin, P. (1965). Skin. In: *The Less Deceived*. New York: St. Martin's Press.

Lax, R. (1982). The expectable depressive climacteric reaction. *Bull. Menn. Clin.*, 46:151–167.

Lerner, R. M. & Karabenick, S. A. (1974). Physical attractiveness, body attitudes, and self concept in late adolescents. *J. Youth & Adol.*, 3:307–316.

Lewis, H. B. (1978). Sex differences in superego mode as related to sex differences in psychiatric illness. *Soc. Sci. Med.*, 12:199–205.

Lewis, M. E. & Butler, R. N. (1974). Life review therapy. *Geriatrics,* 29:165–173.

Lieberman, M. A. & Tobin, S. S. (1983). *The Experience of Old Age*. New York: Basic Books.

May, E. T. (1980). *Great Expectations*. Chicago: University of Chicago Press.

May, R. (1980). *Sex and Fantasy*. New York: Norton.

Napheys, E. H. (1871). *Physical Life of Woman: Advice to the Maiden, Wife, and Mother*. Philadelphia: G. Maclean.

Olesker, W. (1985). Sex differences in 2– and 3–year olds: Mother–child relations, peer relations, and peer play. *Psychoanal. Psychol.* 1:269–288.

Reich, A. (1973). *Psychoanalytic Contributions*. New York: International Universities Press.

Sarton, M. (1973). *As We Are Now*. New York: Norton.

Schor, N. (1985). Eugénie Grandet: Mirrors and Melancholia. In: *The (M)other Tongue*, ed. S. N. Garner, C. Kahane, & M. Sprengnether. Ithaca, NY: Cornell University Press.

Shakespeare, W. (1936). *The Complete Works of Shakespeare*. Garden City, NY: Garden City Publishing.

Simmons, R. G. & Rosenberg, F. (1975). Sex, sex roles, & self image. *J. Youth & Adol.*, 4:229–258.

Smith-Rosenberg, C. (1985). The female world of love and ritual: Relations between women in nineteenth-century America. In: *Disorderly Conduct*, ed. C. Smith-Rosenberg. New York: Knopf.

Sontag, S. (1972). The double standard of aging. *Sat. Rev. Lit.*, 54(Sept. 23):29–38.

Stiver, I. (1985). *The Meaning of Care: Reframing Treatment Models*. Work in Progress, Stone Center for Developmental Services and Studies. Wellesley College, Wellesley, MA.

Stolorow, R. D., & Lachmann, F. M. (1980). *Psychoanalysis of Developmental Arrests*. New York: International Universities Press.

Voda, A. M., Dinnerstein, M., & O'Donnell, S. R. ed. (1982). *Changing Perspectives on Menopause*. Austin: University of Texas Press.

Walsh, F. (1980). The family in later life. In: *The Family Life Cycle*, ed. E. A. Carter & M. McGoldrick. New York: Gardner Press.

Whiteside, J., Busch, R., & Horner, T. (1976). From egocentric to cooperative play in young children; a normative study. *J. Amer. Acad. Child Psychiat.*, 15:294–313.

Wolf, E. S. (1980). On the developmental line of selfobject relations. In: *Advances in Self Psychology*, ed. A. Goldberg. New York: International Universities Press.

Woloch, N. (1984). *Women and the American Experience*. New York: Knopf.

|III| *Female Patient*

7 Professional Success
A Conflict for Women

_____RUTH MOULTON

Success has always presented a problem for both men and women due to the universal conflict between the drive for mastery and self-assertion on one hand and the wish for security and protection on the other. The drive for mastery is associated with inherent capacities for growth and achievement, curiosity and self-expression. These lead to activities in the _outer_ world that facilitate the development of autonomy, independence, and ego strength. These same activities are experienced as threats to the opposing needs for security in the _inner_ world — being in a safe, protected place, secure from the dangers and uncertainties of the outer world, being taken care of by those who can be trusted. These needs lead to dependence on approval and a willingness to surrender autonomy in order to please others, with resultant ego-weakness. Clearly, success and achievement are sources of anxiety because they threaten to disrupt the fulfillment of hidden dependence needs.

To be secure, a child needs the approval of parents, peers, and significant adults in the immediate environment. Later, the adult must contend with the expectations of the entire culture. To win approval, the woman must not threaten others; it is dangerous to surpass them; the woman will be hated, excluded, punished for it. The basic reason for this reaction is to be found in the depth and extent of human envy. It seems to be safer to be the only one, the best one — or the failed one, who will be protected. During the state of infantile omnipotence, there may be fantasies of total conquest in which all competitors are subdued in a violent struggle. Fears of retaliation follow, and an inhibition of self-assertion develops because it is confused with hostile aggression. Success appears to be always at the expense of others, who may become hostile. The degree of intimidation or restriction of activity varies with the degree of permission and encouragement for individual growth and exploration of the outer world. Competitive pressures within the family or culture enlarge the conflict between needs for security and dependence and needs for growth and independence. These are factors that influence both sexes in the same way. However, there is a basic difference between the sexes: professional success usually enhances the sexual identity of men, whereas it threatens the sense of femininity of women.

In the past, success phobias were thought to occur more frequently in men than in women because men were more subject to the competitive pressures of the culture (Ovesey, 1956). Now that women are freer to compete in the outside world, much attention has been paid to their fears of success. Even when they have achieved, they often cannot enjoy their success; they find themselves denying or sabotaging it, falling prey to self-defeating masochism or depression (Fleigel, 1973; Symonds, 1976; Schecter, 1979). They have anxiety about using the new opportunities, which violate traditional sex role expectations, and disapproval may come from parents, peers, or the culture at large (Moulton, 1977). Modern women are still influenced unconsciously by old assumptions that masculinity implies strength, dominance, superiority and *success*, whereas femininity is linked with weakness, submission, inferiority and *failure*. Thus, for many women to be successful means that they are unfeminine and unlovable. Without male support, their success is experienced as being either empty or dangerous.

In a patriarchal culture, women are expected to be nourishing facilitators who serve the needs of others, especially of men and, children for whom they should gladly sacrifice their autonomy. A particular kind of guilt haunts women who forge ahead and glory in their own achievement. They may forget their traditional obligation to put others first. This is reflected in a familiar theme in folklore and literature, namely, that the ambitious woman who pushes ahead will be punished by having harm come to her child, who will be taken away by death or illness as punishment for her neglect. Retaliation will be directed toward her unique function of childbearing. This parallels man's fear that punishment will be directed toward his unique organ, the penis. He will be castrated. The woman, already castrated, will be made infertile or frigid.

In the Freudian view, success phobias derived only from rivalry with men, as vocational success was seen as a male prerogative. Competition in women was seen as a way to gain male attention or to become a man (penis envy). The significant competitive object from whom retaliation was expected was usually thought to be a male (Ovesey, 1962). This is in line with Freud's overemphasis on the role of the father and his early insistence that the Oedipus complex was the core of all neurosis. Freud (1916), writing about "those wrecked by success" gave examples of two women who were unable to accept and enjoy marriage, for which they had waited and planned many years, because it represented the fulfillment of unacceptable wishes to replace the mother in the father's affections. When the *external* frustration, the presence of the first wife (the mother), was removed, the *internal* obstacle of guilt prevented the woman from achieving her unconscious goal of marital happiness. She was literally made ill by her apparent success. It is interesting that in the case of the women Freud mentions, the success is achieved through marriage or through the position of the husband, as in Lady Macbeth. Freud, also refers to a man whose goal was to replace his revered academic teacher, who had retired. The obstacle was the feeling of being unworthy rather than guilty and afraid to compete with a father image. Freud appears to have felt that guilty oedipal wishes were much more of a problem for women than for men. His emphasis was chiefly on the value of fathers and men than on the value of mothers and women. Women crave, need men (who are seen as strong) more than men crave, need women (who are seen as weak).

In contrast, Jones (1935) felt that there was much more envy and jealousy of the mother than of the father due to early dependency on mother. The importance of the preoedipal struggle for mother's unconditional love and acceptance was largely overlooked until the observations by female analysts such as Horney (1924), Lampl-de Groot (1927), and M. Klein (1928), who saw that the primary yearning was for *mother*, not for father, for a nipple not a breast (Moulton, 1970). A sense of maternal deprivation and rage resulting from unresolved deep dependency needs may lead to a negative, hostile identification with mother (Moulton, 1977). Melanie Klein (1928) observed that the girl who is guilty about her rage at or competition with mother often expects punishment from mother by way of injury to her sexual organs — she will be ugly, sexually unattractive, infertile, or struck down by cancer of her uterus or breast. Retaliation will be aimed at the very core of her femininity.

This fear is evident in many professional women, who adopt new and unconventional life styles that are seen as defiance of mother. They may live alone, have casual affairs with men, live with men without intent to marry, and decide not to have children (Moulton, 1979). These lifestyles are much more acceptable to society now than in the past, but they nevertheless may lead to self-doubt at a point of stress. A typical example follows.

An unmarried woman of forty had undertaken an ambitious extension of her career. She enjoyed sex and good companionship with men but decided against marriage and family. Her contribution to society would be to write, teach, be politically active. She would "make words, not babies." At this transitional point, she was found to have an early cancer of the cervix, easily removed and pronounced cured. She took it as a sign of punishment for hating and abandoning her mother, for having had an abortion earlier in her life and, for deciding never to be a mother. In making her sex life fit into her professional wishes, she felt she was controlling it too consciously, being too independent, "like a man would." The return of the sense of pressure from her mother to be a "normal woman" caused her to revert to the Catholic ways of thinking that her mother had taught her. It was as though she made a pact with God: "Spare me from cancer and I will give up evil, uncommitted sex and only do good works." She was not aware of this unconscious bargain until she entered therapy for depression a year later. There was a buried wish that her mother rather than she would die of cancer. Her positive reaction to me was as a more appropriate mother, who would accept and understand her wish for a professional life. In her negative transference she feared my disapproval and assumed that I had had a mastectomy and would desert her by dying of cancer. Thus cancer of the sexual organs — breast, uterus or cervix — was perceived by her as punishment for hatred of mother or of woman's role as presented to her in the past.

Mothers play a very sepcial role in the psychology of women (Moulton, 1985). They are not only the original source of nourishment but the later source of sexual identification, positive or negative. Mothers hold baby girls closer than boy babies (Maccoby, 1966) and later allow them much less freedom to roam or be physically active. Women grow up to be more prone than men to separation anxiety. If the mother is overprotective and cannot tolerate the daughter's need for individuation, she may continue to make demands for homage and acknowledgment, for example, phone calls and visits. Her jealousy may be dominant so that the girl comes to see her growth as an act of hostile aggression toward the mother and to see her own success as being achieved at the mother's expense. If her mother has led a traditionally domestic life, the daughter is apt to feel guilty about being a professional, feeling that she has surpassed or defeated her mother (Schecter, 1979). Success may be felt as a threat to the early symbiotic bond with the preoedipal mother.

If the mother is seen as overtly rejecting, cold, and critical of her daughter, the daughter may turn to the father in a premature effort at independence that covers up her sense of maternal deprivation. If the father is accepting, she may use his support to move ahead, developing a facade of self-sufficiency and pseudoindependence. If the mother is not accepting of this growth, the daughter is liable to feel great guilt at her oedipal triumph and continue to be very vulnerable to female disapproval, to the envy and scorn of female bosses and peers. She may feel that her later success is fraudulent, is undeserved, will be taken away from her; that it has been achieved at the expense of her mother, with the collusion of her father, and is not rightfully hers to enjoy. She may also have the unfortunate experience of having her father withdraw his support when she enters adolescence, begins her own heterosexual life, and leaves home for college or graduate school. He may resent her autonomy, his loss of control over her, her using her education to enter a new world rather than to return to enrich his (Moulton, 1977).

An example of such a case is a girl whose mother valued only her beauty and popularity in high school and constantly measured her social success, numbers of dates, prestige of boyfriends, and so forth. Her father was proud of her good grades in college but increasingly afraid of her losing her virginity, smoking marijuana, or in any way jeopardizing her marriageability — as he construed it. She did very well on law boards, but he ridiculed her wanting to go to law school, saying "What a silly idea. Isn't that cute? Come be a hostess in my restaurant; you'll meet lots of eligible men there." She did manage one of his restaurants for a while but hated it and was so depressed that she did poorly on an entrance exam for law school. Too demoralized to reapply, she instead went into market research, which she found unchallenging. Eventually she married a young lawyer in the hope that she could fulfill her parents' expectations, give them grandchildren, and thus vindicate their way of life. She tried to break the engagement twice because the young man was too conventional, but her parents were very eager for her to marry soon and safely. That she felt she was entering a trap is shown by an episode of panic and claustrophobia that occurred when her family and fiance met to "seal the deal." The panic spread to include anxiety in small, hot, enclosed spaces like buses and reminded her of her mother's having locked her in a closet as a small child because she had ventured too far from home. She will be a good candidate to develop phobias after marriage (Symonds, 1971), when her resentment about accepting a restricted life space causes increasing restlessness and frustration. A career was renounced before it began because both parents opposed it, and the young woman lacked the drive and ego strength to pursue it on her own. She was also too dependent on parents to adopt a mentor or find a new role model for encouragement.

The fear of success in women can result from an unresolved pre-oedipal need for mother or guilt about oedipal strivings toward the father. Sibling rivalry and competition with peers is added to this basic matrix. Recently, emphasis has been placed on the preoedipal role of the father (Spieler, 1984). Freud (1933) felt that the pre-oedipal father was merely a rival, who interfered with the girl's close relationship with the mother, whereas Spieler suggests that the father plays an important role beginning in early infancy. "The father is not a stranger and the infant becomes aware of, interested in, and evolves mental representations of both parents concurrently and sequentially (p. 64)." The girl needs acceptance and secure attachments to both parents to serve as models for her future relations with men and women. If the father is absent or distant, the girl is more apt to cling symbiotically to mother and have trouble individuating from her. Or, if she turns to her father and is hurt or disappointed, she may feel unable to love, respect, or trust a man. She may become deferential to or hostile to men, which interfers with good working relations with them. Intrapsychic conflict may undermine a woman's ability to make use of new options that are theoretically available. One can legislate changes in institutions and overt social practices, but real change occurs slowly. Prejudice goes underground. The unconscious lags behind.

REVIEW OF CURRENT LITERATURE

Early studies of "women's liberation" were more optimistic but foresaw difficulties (Moulton, 1973), which have since been reevaluated (Moulton, 1977, 1979, 1980, 1985). Much of the psychological research on fear of success in women followed from Horner's (1968) observations that women anticipate negative social consequences for their achievement in competition with men, who expect that success will lead to further positive growth and cultural rewards. Horner's original findings led to more observations reinforcing the phenomenon (Horner and Walsh, 1974). The history of women's conflicts about achievement have been traced by Kanefield (1985) from Freud's early writings up to the present. It is useful to mention a few of the most recent contributions made by female analysts who have worked with new concepts, such as object relations and gender identity, and have used new language for clarification of familiar issues.

Applegarth (1976) emphasized that the female's fear and guilt about surpassing mother added to her fear of loss of a male sexual partner, thus increasing her underlying fear of loneliness. Males fear castration; women fear loss of love, reflecting their tendency to rely more on affiliation. Female identity in the past has so often been built on the need to please men that women deny their own interests and doubt their own abilities and competence (Stiver, 1983). It is difficult for them to intergrate work as an important source of identity, which deprives them of an essential source of self-esteem. Ambition is likely to be denied, obscured by pseudopassivity, which makes it difficult to pursue clearcut goals (Person, 1982). There often is more focus on social skills than work skills; women are not socialized to mastery of competitive tasks, so it is hard for them to work toward self-fulfillment, away from adherence to duty. Person feels that the fear of *deviance*, behavior that contradicts the traditional female role, is a special problem for women, whereas the fear of success is a catchword for all work inhibitions, affecting both sexes.

The development of women's sense of self is a subject of recent interest (Chodorow, 1978; Gilligan, 1982; J. B. Miller, 1985). The concept of self seems to be based on male development, which is tied to males' need to separate from mother, the primary caretaker. This often cuts off capacities for tenderness, empathy, and intimacy and leads to a more limited sense of self for which a more linear model is used. Infants of both sexes develop their sense of self as separate from others by means of a dynamic interaction with significant others. The nature of the internal, mental representations of one's self depends on the quality of this relatedness — how adequate, consistent, and appropriate it is to the innate resources and temperamental tendencies of the individual infant (A. Miller, 1981). Boys are encouraged to "grow up and be independent"; responsiveness is not encouraged as it is in girls. The female self is more encompassing, oscillating, more responsive to others. There is more separation anxiety, at first from mother, later from friends and men; husbands are often expected to take the place of mother. In contrast, men can more easily replace mother through the wife without their dependency needs being made obvious — those needs can be covered in this culture by male bravado or chauvinism.

Not only is autonomy more difficult for women to achieve, but it takes more ego strength to support it: criticism may come from parents and male partners; envy may come from friends as well as competitors. There is often a vicious cycle, as the successful woman may protect her femininity by denying its authenticity, thus depriving herself of much needed confidence. Success, rather than being internalized, is denied or attributed to outside forces. Contributing to fear of failure and undermining the need to work harder against prejudice, low self-esteem may result from a negative identification with mother as a person of low status, a figure who has been devalued by the men in her world, or who never developed herself. The mother may then openly resent the girl's growth and try to discourage her by emphasizing the need for family togetherness or her unmarriageable status, the specter of the renegade or the spinster. Boys should lead; girls should follow and stay in familiar relationships.

One traditional girl's school taught the generation of girls in the thirties that they should be quiet, sedate, attract no attention, be "seen and not heard," like obedient, passive children. A "lady" should not speak up or speak back, never be angry, never flirt or be sexual. Taped conversations between present-day teenage boys and girls revealed that girls asked questions, let the boys direct the flow of conversation, and withheld voicing their opinions if there was any possibility of disagreement. No wonder women are often less sure of what they believe; if they speak their minds, they fear being called controlling, castrating bitches. Again, assertion is confused with hostile aggression more in women than in men. Men tend to be more agentic and women more communal, although both characteristics could be accepted and validated within each man and woman (Kaplan and Yasinski, 1984). Self-promotion is more rewarded in a patriarchal culture.

Another result of these gender biases is that they interfere with creative productivity in women. In her study of women analysts, Schuker (1985) cites the "accumulation of disadvantages": women may be denied equal access to resources, are less encouraged to do creative work, hold fewer high-ranking positions in academic psychiatry, and thus get less outside stimulation while they actually need more positive reinforcement because less seems to be expected of them. She found that women publishing in mainstream psychoanalytic journals "were exceptional women who have accepted their deviant, role-breaking position" (p. 60). Those who still seek approval, rely too heavily on female role models, or have difficulties surpassing their male mentors may hide their ambition behind an ingratiating mask, denying the authenticity of their success. They may fear exposure because they feel fraudulent, with an internalized "little girl" self image, which further limits professional autonomy. A woman elevated to an executive position equal to men who were formerly her bosses may panic, feeling there is no strong man to rely on; she now has total responsibility for her own work and may tend to sabotage it or refuse the new position. This recreates the self-fulfilling prophecy that administrative competence, like scientific research, are basically male contributions. Harriet Lerner (unpublished research from the Menninger Foundation); using the Bowne Family Systems Level Interventions, is studying work and success inhibitions in women. A recent book by a man (Krueger, 1984) focuses entirely on work inhibitions in women. Krueger believes women's work inhibitions have been relatively neglected compared to those in men. By using ego psychological principles, developmental data, biological and social variables, and concepts of gender and sexual identity, he underlines issues unique to women.

CASES

An example of early preoedipal conflict was seen in Annie, a bright, attractive girl from a ghetto background. Her mother was a driving, manipulative woman of many skills, who abandoned her for her first five years, leaving her to be raised by an aunt who was warner and more caring than the mother. When the mother felt financially more secure, she took Annie in but cut her off totally from the aunt. The mother was jealous and possessive, controlling and intrusive, giving Annie no privacy, not even her own bed or a dresser drawer to call her own. Mother demanded love and attention. It was important to her to placate authorities and people with power and money. She placed great emphasis on appearances — a clean, neatly pressed dress every day. She objected to Annie's love of books, seeing it as abnormal and a waste of time, but she liked the idea that her daughter wanted to go to college, as that would be impressive. Her jealousy of Annie's achievements was so great that she did not go to the high school graduation, although she had promised to do so since her daughter was valedictorian.

Annie chose a college out of town to get away from mother and went to live with another aunt, who taught her how to cook, sew, and handle reality problems like an adult, whereas the mother had kept her unskilled and feeling dependent and inadequate. The mother was enraged at the "loss of her daughter" and withdrew financial support after one year of college. Annie got a job to support herself. Mother said, "You can't possibly work and study too." Annie was challenged, felt defiant, and went ahead to success, but labored under constant fear of her mother's malevolence. Each step ahead — her Ph.D., her new, sunny apartment, her new boyfriend — were experienced as blows to her mother. Her mother criticized or scoffed at each, so that Annie was unable to enjoy them. She feared being evicted from her apartment, unable to pay the rent. She could not let her mother visit her apartment because it was too nicely decorated and had a fine view, while the mother's apartment was dark, on an alley.

Marriage was the one thing the mother had that Annie did not, and the mother constantly made comments lamenting Annie's bad luck and extolling her own. It was as though she was saying, "You don't really threaten me as long as you are single and lonely." As a result, Annie dreaded that if she did marry — and she had many opportunities — her mother literally would die. This apparently irrational fear had a history. Annie had long been aware that her mother had a huge investment in her, lived vicariously through her, pressured her into areas of achievement that the mother felt were important, and would then take credit for any success Annie had. Or, she would take over a project of Annie's if Annie was slow or uncertain. Annie's response to this double bind was either to give up and withdraw into depression or else to flee to a safe place and hide her work from her mother. She tried to cut herself off from the past entirely, especially when she came to the East Coast. But then she thought, "If I get free, my mother will die" (both a wish and a fear). The mother colluded in this, saying , in effect, "You are killing me by not letting me hear about your life, not phoning me, not sharing you new ways with me."

Annie dreamed of being in a cattlecar stuffed of holocaust victims. She felt survival guilt not only about surpassing her mother in comfort, education, prestige, but also about rising above the socioeconomic level of her whole family, even though that had presumably been one of their aspirations. To leave the ghetto made her feel like a renegade. Her success seemed to be a burden, which she carried by withdrawing, hiding from her own people, feeling lonely and anxious in an alien world. She was safe only in her learned, professional role. At home she was depressed and sometimes suicidal on weekends, isolated in a beautiful new apartment she dared not share. In childhood, she had used isolation, hiding in corners and closets, to avoid her mother's intrusiveness. As a result she had been able to become her own person, whereas her sister, who had desperately tried to win mother's approval, ended up unhappily married like the mother, unable to be productive and hiding her sense of failure in alcohol.

To flee from her mother's attention was life-saving for this patient. But the mother continued to haunt the mind of the daughter who had escaped. The basic conflict was preoedipal. Annie never forgave her mother for the early abandonment; mother never forgave Annie for being unappreciative of her return and her misguided efforts at restitution. Malevolent transformation resulted. The great need for tenderness turned into an equal drive for revenge against the rebellious daughter.

Susan, another successful professional woman, also thought of herself as an ungrateful and resentful daughter. She came to treatment because she found herself sabotaging her executive position by not answering important mail, failing to explore new developments, lacking in leadership, suffering from an increasing dread of using the telephone. Her fear of making phone calls began with her mother's pressure on her to make social calls. Mother was uneasy about using the phone herself but screamed at Susan when she hesitated or made a mistake. The mother had married right after high school and was very insecure in a snobbish, upper-class environment where everyone had at least been to college. She pushed Susan to get good grades but punished her for any disobedience by trying to keep her at home on school days. This not only expressed her jealousy but was a way to torture Susan, who loved to learn and felt home to be a prison. Mother later sent a protesting Susan to a fancy finishing school. The father rescued Susan, seeing to it that she went to a good college of her own choice. After his divorce from her mother and remarriage, however, he abandoned her and never even acknowledged her Ph.D. She wondered how she could possibly be successful with neither parent behind her. In spite of her hatred for her mother, she felt drawn to her, yearning for a support she never felt. Her punishment for hating her mother was to become like her, and she dreamed that they would reunite in death. She had never been able to stand up to her mother, as her sister had, was more vulnerable to mother's criticism, less able to affirm her own identity, and was thus drawn into a malevolent identification with her mother. She felt herself to be a failure in the midst of success.

The overwhelming role of the maternal object in the psychic lives of these two women was determined partly by the absence of a consistent father figure. In both instances, the biological father was separated from the family. Although he was felt as kinder, more accepting, and less critical than mother, he eventually left due to the difficulty of living with the mother, whose desperate needs were then focused on the unfortunate daughter. Since mother was the only predictable, available parent, who 'sacrificed' for her daughter, the daughter felt excessive guilt about her anger at mother. This guilty anger interfered with the development of the younger woman's autonomy. She chose a career to be financially independent of both mother and husband and then felt her career to be at the expense of mother. This, in turn, reinforced the guilt and deepened the sense of separation, resulting in an increased need to return to find a good mother or to propitiate the bad mother, who felt abandoned by the dauther (Friedman, 1980). The character of the mothers was quite different: Annie's mother was effective and malevolent; Susan's mother was ineffective, a recluse. But the effects of their blaming accusations on the pseudoindependent daughters were very similar.

A third case illustrates the operation of oedipal dynamics. Sonia was a lawyer in her late twenties, the first woman to be hired by a large, prestigious law firm. She came to treatment because of ulcerative colitis, which first occurred when she decided to marry a successful Wall Street broker who earned twice what her father did and was much more knowledgeable. Her family was a tightly knit clan who ran their own business and suspected all outsiders. The father was dogmatic, the mother controlling. Both demanded loyalty to the family first. Both wanted Sonia to go to law school but expected her to return and work in the family business. When she married a powerful man and followed him into a new world, the parents were threatened and withdrew into disapproving silence. Sonia had been safe in her symbiotic bond with her mother, a martyr who was protective and nonthreatening but who warned her not to trust other women. Nourishing contact had been maintained by daily phone calls until Sonia's marriage; after marriage distance and silence developed and provoked separation anxiety in both mother and daughter. Sonia dreamed that her mother had cancer; her mother was also suffering. Both relented and phone contact was soon reestablished. With time, mother was able to accept Sonia's success and vicariously enjoyed it.

Separation from father and establishing a new equilibrium with him was more difficult. Sonia had been her father's favorite, a "good girl," who followed his lead, got excellent grades but often attributed them to her father's coaching and felt insecure about her own intelligence. Mother was submissive to men and taught the patient to be deferential to them, which interfered with her taking initiative at work. Unable to stand up to her father, she tended to be placating and would tremble before authoritarian male law partners when they wanted her to take responsibility. When she got a good work evaluation, she feared it was due to charm and sex appeal, not competence.

In treatment she began to realize that she had feared growing up and becoming successful professionally because it meant competition with her father and loss of family protection. She could please male bosses by working overtime but then dreaded the envy of women coworkers. The one woman who was superior to her was obese. In her anxiety, Sonia began to overeat. Being fat was a protection against female envy. Less would be expected of her if she were fat. To be thin was to be powerful. Power was both exciting and dangerous. It was safer to keep a low profile at the bottom of the ladder, where she could be liked by everyone and not be drawn into the competitive struggle.

There was a crisis when Sonia reached an apex of success. She had a flawless review, was given a special award for completing a very difficult job, and was put in charge of a new work section. It made her very anxious to be called "boss," and she feared sabotage by those she had surpassed. Many of her problems at work were typical of the female "executive" in a man's world as described by Hennig and Jardim (1976). With her perfectionism, she dreaded the new expectations placed on her. The firm knew she needed time to learn. She alone had omnipotent goals, expecting all superiors to be as judgmental as her father. At the height of her glory, she was sent to an important foreign conference in the executive jet. This was "too much," and she began to expect punishment, as shown by the following three dreams. First, she was singing on stage. The curtains opened, and she saw her father in the audience, feeling awkward and embarrassed. She could no longer sing and feared that she was becoming like him. In another dream, she was discovered by male lawyers while she was hiding in a bathroom with an exacerbation of colitis. She felt she was being punished by illness for showing off her power. In the third dream, she was in a car going to the airport to take the corporate jet to Europe. Her father was driving. The pilot was beside him, bleeding but unaware of it. Her thought was that her father was surreptitiously killing the pilot so that he could not take her on the plane. It was painfully clear that she felt that her father could not bear to see her taken care of by another man more powerful than he. The following week she did have a return of colitis and bleeding, which disappeared with further therapy.

Sonia is an example of a girl who used her father's encouragement to enter a "male" profession. As an oedipal daughter, she worked well with men as long as the "good girl" pattern was appropriate. When she moved up to a position of some power and authority, her adjustment broke down. The ruling men in her law firm faulted her for not being strong enough, for not taking initiative, for waiting for approval; they would reward her for assertion not compliance. The rules had changed. The qualities necessary for progress in a hierarchy, such as steadiness, reliability, willingness to follow orders, and be "easy to work with," often require much more flexibility and less assertiveness than are required when a top level of responsibility has been reached. At the top, much more creativity and aggressiveness are needed (Allen, 1979). Instead of *following* or pleasing an authority, the person aspiring to a higher position must *become* an authority. This change is apt to be more difficult for women than for men. Women, in a previously male profession, began training under male leadership and have had little experience in having men work *under* them or *for* them.

THE PROFESSIONAL WOMAN
AND MOTHERHOOD

Professional women face a special set of problems if they want children. Many women have trained as professionals to avoid the monotony of housework; they do not want to be trapped at home as they feel their mothers were. At the same, time, they want to be mothers. Many are able to perform their dual role very well.

One successful physician-mother tells of her youth, when, as the eldest child, she had major responsibility for helping her mother, who was housebound with a clinical phobia. The woman had helped her mother to raise the family and face the world and had assisted her father with his business as well. Later, the mother was so jealous of the interesting medical world her daughter was enjoying that she got a clerical job in the same hospital, hoping her daughter would have lunch with her daily and share this new world. She was angry when the daughter became pregnant and eventually had more children than she had had and raised them without mother's help. This was possible in part because of a very supportive husband, who thoroughly enjoyed fathering. Some men resent doing this, seeing it as "woman's work," and object to having less time alone with and getting less attention and service from their wives.

Less successful professional women may have children to compensate for their sense of failure or to do the one thing their husbands cannot. These unconscious reasons for undertaking motherhood make the dual task even more difficult. Having children to compete with mother or in defiance of her may lead either to overload — the "super-mom" complex — or to postponing pregnancy past age 35, when infertility problems increase. The rationale here is first to establish the profession firmly, to be self-supporting, and mature enough to raise a child well, better than mother did. Such delaying tactics do not necessarily resolve the anxiety about being a "good enough" mother, especially if the women had great conflict and rage toward their own mothers.

Many women in their late thirties and mid-forties come to therapy bitter because they have not conceived despite thorough fertility studies. This may be seen as punishment for putting career first and may interfere with enjoyment of it, and the ensuing sense of failure may lead to depression and disrupt established work patterns. These women may fear to let their wish for immortality rest solely on their careers. To have a child is seen as their final validation of being feminine, as security against loneliness, emptiness, and disappointment in old age. This reaction is often unexpected, the new focus being on zero population growth and the recognition that some women may contribute *more* to the world if they do *not* have children.

Other women have a third or fourth child even though it interrupts or prevents a career and is likely later to be regretted (Moulton, 1979). Elizabeth is an energetic, ambitious woman, rebelling against her Victorian mother, thinking that she could "have it all" — career, husband, and children — but unaware of the price to be paid for her omnipotence.

Like Annie, Elizabeth found her mother to be jealous but she had a special relationship with her father. Both parents supported her education; both were teachers who overvalued scholarship and considered social contacts unimportant, if not irrelevant. Her father was a scientist who had wished to go to medical school; her mother was an artist with many traditional feminine accomplishments, music, cooking, needlework. Elizabeth was the first born, much preferred her father to her mother, had a scientific mind and limited artistic talents, although she enjoyed the arts. A younger sister became a pianist and was the mother's favorite. When Elizabeth decided to go to medical school, her mother was appalled, fearing it would make her unmarriageable and unable to be a "good mother." Her father, on the other hand, had remarked when she was an adolescent struggling with issues of feminine identity that men envied women's ability to have children, so she should look forward to the enjoyment of being a mother (Moulton, 1977).

Caught between these two different messages, Elizabeth experienced motherhood with much anxiety. Like many women who do not have to work but choose professions, she put too much emphasis on mothering and trying hard to be with her children, even when it was difficult to do so, and suffering excessive guilt when she was away from them. Although her father's backing had been a major factor in her decision to go to medical school (he had wished to become a doctor himself, but his father had refused to support him), he had become dubious about it because he had never known a woman doctor and felt uncertain of her future. Elizabeth felt deserted and vacillated between over conscientious work and depression. She was Now alienated from her mother as well as her sister: she mistrusted women, remained a "loner," avoided joining women's organizations and devoted herself to patients. A good doctor, she had become an overburdened woman. As her relationships with men were better than those with women, she found herself overly dependent emotionally on her husband for encouragement and admiration. This, and her obsessive mothering, put a strain on her marriage.

The awareness of such stress is causing professional women to have fewer children or none at all, with less sense of guilt than in former generations. They are also better prepared to plan ahead and find new alternatives in the form of child care, maternity leave, part-time work, and so on.

THERAPY

Anxiety about success can be minimized if it is seen as an extension of parental and personal ambitions rather than as a competitive out-doing of them. Success may then be an acceptable achievement that is not at another's expense. Sonia's mother enjoyed her success; thus Sonia was much freer from guilt about surpassing her mother than were Annie and Susan, whose mothers were jealous and guilt provoking. The real nature of the parent plays an enormous role in the outcome of the daughter's struggle for autonomy. The mother who experiences her daughter as rival for the father's affection can make the daughter feel that she has no right to be competent. She can dare to succeed only in areas not valued or explored by her mother.

Parental sanction for achievement is even more important to girls than to boys because girls receive less cultural sanction for success in the outer world. Sonia had the sanction of both parents for law school and was able to do well there. Parental approval diminished at the time of Sonia's marriage, as that represented separation from the family.

The choice of career and success versus marriage is often unconsciously determined by parental attitudes even in girls who consciously feel free and independent. If parents are supportive, the career oriented woman is more able to withstand cultural disapproval. Many parents are very ambivalent about the success of their children; they consciously encourage achievement but unconsciously envy it, feeling humiliation and loss of self-esteem when the children surpass them in knowledge; they feel "left out" or "put down," no longer in control or worthy of respect. They may boast about the success of offspring in their absence but cannot admire them in their presence. It is useful in therapy if this conflict of the parent is pointed out to the younger generation, who may then be able to accept and forgive the evidence of stifled envy and relate instead to the modicum of parental pride that may also be present. If victory can be seen as extending parental ambitions, vindicating rather than outdoing them, success may be a shared gratification between generations. A nourishing inner other, like an approving parent or sibling, can help overcome guilt (Allen, 1979). If achievement can be seen as an interesting challenge, as problem solving, with enjoyment of the process of using oneself, rather than as a way to defeat another person, there is less anxiety. The goal does not become an end in itself. If success is sought to fill an unfillable emptiness, to cure neurotic self-doubt, to vindicate the fact of being a woman, then it is doomed to failure.

Treatment of today's enlightened women who are struggling for success in the outer world as well as in the home does not require any major breaks from sound, basic therapeutic principles. One must explore current patterns of behavior as they operate in the present social context and trace their origins back through the unique paths of individual development to early childhood influences, biological, interpersonal, and cultural. However, recent information about the role of these factors leads to new working hypotheses and undermines many old assumptions. For instance, the study of newborns shows some interesting statistical differences between the sexes — boys are slightly more physically active, more aggressive.

But there is much more difference between individuals than between sexes. The effect of parental and social expectations about sexual behavior soon overrides biological factors, so we must reexamine our assumptions about what is unalterably "masculine" and "feminine." Women's anxieties as they try to enter a man's world are not the result of their "going against their true nature"; all role-breakers are under stress, having no established patterns to follow, no tradition to support them as they try new roles. Sex role stereotypes and sex discrimination determine the atmosphere, set the stage on which the individual woman acts out her inner drives, needs, ambitions, and goals. The resulting behavior depends on the interaction between inner and outer forces. This may seem obvious, but it can be very difficult to assess the true functional effect of various factors, and any prejudice the therapist has will influence this evaluation. Some women may be born more passive, placid, reflective, than others, but the therapist must be curious about pressures that may have discouraged activity, the multiple defeats that may have inhibited assertiveness.

Human beings may search untiringly to find the truth about something that interests them, but at other times they have a need to hide from the truth when it is painful. In order to excuse or deny his antifeminine bias, a male authority may blame the aspiring woman for a lack of intelligence or poor motivation when this can be shown to be untrue. On the other hand, a woman who lacks the necessary resources for success (intelligence, drive, ego strength) may erroneously blame an institutions or a male in power, labeling them prejudiced when they fail to promote her. Such a projection, an inaccurate evaluation of the external situation, may be more comfortable than admitting an internal deficit. The deficit may be relatively unalterable, as in the case of limited intelligence or talent, or it may be modified only after great struggle, possibly intensive therapy, as in the case where crippling dependency or phobic avoidance of risks and challenges curtails the use of potential ability.

There is a continuing need to measure the relative importance of external, environmental forces versus internal, intrapsychic ones. How much real power does the parent, competitor, boss, actually have; or does the woman assume or delegate power to the man because of her own fear of assuming responsibility, being disliked, or not taken care of? Unfortunate experiences with parents or hostile authority may leave a woman so fearful of authority that she cannot assess its strength or direction. The boss may be angry at the aspiring woman not because of her aspirations but because she cannot speak up, lacks the courage of her convictions, needs constant praise or reassurance. On the other hand, these may be false accusations used by the boss who cannot accept the reality of the woman's dilemma of underprivilege or the real nature of her strengths. There is no formula for deciding such issues; each must be evaluated on its own merits. Previous experience with certain institutions or authorities and with particular, individual women, who may be patients, alerts one to certain possibilities that may be repetitive. An open, flexible, curious mind is needed to check the validity of hypotheses.

An example of this problem was seen in the therapy of a successful woman, Lorna, who had a dual-career marriage. She was more assertive, more popular, had a wider reputation than her husband, who was a socially inhibited, mildly depressive, very obsessional man. Early in her marriage she had given up the opportunity for an ideal, prestigious position in a top-ranked university in order to stay with him in a small women's college. Many years later when she had another similar opportunity, she came to therapy and realized how her rage at his need for her, the inhibiting effect of his fear of losing her, made decision making almost impossible. As long as she blamed him alone for her stalemente, clarification of more obscure issues was impossible. When she finally realized her fear of leaving the security of the small college, her "mother institution," and "alma mater," she was free to make realistic plans. Much to her surprise, her husband was encouraging her to move and was willing to help her with the household and commuting problems. She then recalled that he had warned her not to turn down the earlier opportunity but she did not believe he had meant it. He was probably ambivalent about it but willing to try to work it out. It was her preoccupation about the nature of marriage, judged by her mother's life, that stood in her way more than her husband's attitude. Her wish to have her husband replace her mother in taking care of her made her assume that he was much more traditional (like her mother) than he really was. Lorna and Sonia both overate to recreate early closeness to mother and worked on this issue in treatment. There are other situations where the husband *has* threatened to divorce a wife who had inconvenient professional needs that interfered with his comfort. It would have been easy for the therapist to assume that the husband had sabotaged his wife's career, expecially since the woman complained so bitterly that marriage had trapped and restricted her. It had to a degree, and the husband *was* obsessional; but these were not the crucial factors in the long run. The woman had to come to terms with *her* attitude to marriage and to herself.

In summary, three special considerations in the treatment of aspiring women should be kept in mind:

1) Inner, *intrapsychic barriers* to success must be explored as well as outer, environmental barriers. Our new awareness of the far-reaching effects of sexual prejudice, sex discrimination, and narrow sex role expectations may cause one to overlook the role of unconscious dependency needs, phobias about performance, and the like. Some of these are magnified by social pressures, but once they become embedded in the psychic structure, mere removal of external barriers is not enough to free the person to be effective in the outer world.

2) Women's problems with other women may be just as important as their problems with men. Recent emphasis on the role of men (father, lover, husband, boss) in holding women down may result in overlooking the regressive pull that can be traced to the deep need for mother's approval or rage related to the sense of deprivation from her. The identification with her, the need to return to her even in failure or death, undermines independent strivings for growth and

freedom. Half the women described in this paper either overate (obesity) or overdrank (alcoholism) to recreate an early sense of closeness to mother.

3) *Anxiety about success* can be diminished if its positive aspects are stressed, namely, the healthy sense of self-fulfillment, as opposed to the negative, hostile use of it to kill or defeat one's enemies. Doing a good job and enjoying the constructive uses of power diminish the guilt about competitiveness and the fear of aggression and retaliation. One can then be proud of success rather than anxious about it.

None of these considerations is peculiar to therapy with women, but at this point in time they need a renewed emphasis because of changes in our picture of women's role in current society.

REFERENCES

Allen, D. W. (1979). Hidden stresses in success. *Psychiat.* 42:171–176.

Applegarth, A. (1976). Some observations on work inhibitions in women. *J. Amer. Psychoan. Assn.*, 24:251–268.

Chodorow, N. (1978). *The Reproduction of Mothering.* Berkeley: University of California Press.

Fleigel, Z. (1973). Feminine psychosexual development in Freudian theory. *J. Amer. Acad. Psychoan.*, 42:385–408.

Freud, S. (1916). Those wrecked by success. *Standard Edition*, 14:316–331. London: Hogarth Press, 1957.

———— (1933). *Femininity. Standard Edition*, 22:112–135. London: Hogarth Press, 1964.

Friedman, G. (1980). The mother-daughter bond. *Contemp. Psychoan.*, 16:90–98.

Gilligan, C. (1982). *In a Different Voice.* Cambridge, MA: Harvard University Press.

Hennig, M., & Jardim, A. (1976). *The Managerial Woman.* New York: Simon & Schuster.

Horner, M. (1968). *Sex Differences in Achievement Motivation.* Unpublished doctoral dissertation, University of Michigan.

———— & Walsh, M. (1974). Psychological barriers to success in women. In: *Women and Success*, ed. R. B. Knudsin. New York: William Morrow, pp. 138–145.

Horney, K. (1924). The genesis of the castration complex in women. *Internat. J. Psycho-Anal.*, 5:50–75.

Jones, E. (1935). Early female sexuality. In: *Papers on Psychoanalysis.* Boston: Beacon Press, 1961, pp. 438–451.

Kanefield, L. (1985). Psychoanalytic constructions of female development and women's conflicts about achievement. Part I. *J. Amer. Acad. Psychoan.*, 13:229–247.

Kaplan, A. G., & Yasinski, L. D. (1984). Conflict and conflict inhibitions in women. *J. Amer. Acad. Psychoan.*, 12:13–30.

Klein, M. (1928). Early stages of oedipal conflict. *Internat. J. Psycho-Anal.*, 9:167ff.

Krueger, D. W. (1984). *Success and the Fear of Success in Women.* New York: Free Press.

Lampl-de Groot, J. (1927). The evaluation of the oedipal complex in women. *Internat. J. Psycho-Anal.*, 9:332–345.

Maccoby, E. E. (1966). *The Development of Sex Differences.* Stanford, CA: Stanford University Press.

Miller, A. (1981). *Prisoners of Childhood.* New York: Basic Books.

Miller, J. B. (1982). *Women and Power.* Work in Progress, Stone Center for Developmental Services and Studies, Wellesley College, Wellesley, MA, No. 82-01.

_____ (1984). *The Development of Woman's Sense of Self.* Work in Progress, Stone Center for Developmental Services and Studies, Wellesley College, Wellesley, MA.

Moulton, R. (1970). Re-evaluation of penis envy. *Contemp. Psychoan.*, 7:84–104.

_____ (1977). Women with double lives. *Contemp. Psychoan.*, 13:64–84.

_____ (1979). Ambivalence about motherhood in career women. *J. Acad. Psychoan.* 7:241–257.

_____ (1973). Psychoanalytic reflections on women's liberation. *Contemp. Psychoan.* 8:197–228.

_____ (1980). Divorce in the middle years: The lonely woman and the reluctant man. *J. Amer. Acad. Psychoan.*, 8:235–250.

_____ (1985). The effect of the mother on the success of the daughter. *Contemp. Psychoan.*, 21:266–283.

Ovesey, L. (1956). Masculine aspirations in women. *Psychiat.* 19:341–351.

_____ (1962). Fear of vocational success: a phobic extension of paranoid reaction. *Arch. Gen. Psychiat.*, 7:82–92.

Person, E. S. (1982). Women working: Fears and failure, deviance and success. *J. Amer. Acad. Psychoan.*, 10:67–84.

Schecter, D. E. (1979). Fear of success in women: A psychodynamic reconstruction. *J. Amer. Acad. Psychoan.*, 7:33–45.

Schuker, E. (1985). Creative productivity in women analysts. *J. Amer. Acad. Psychoan.*, 13:51–75.

Spieler, S. (1984). Preoedipal girls need fathers. *Psychoan. Rev.*, 71:63–80.

Stiver, I. P. (1983). *Work Inhibitions in Women,* Work in Progress, Stone Center for Developmental Services and Studies, Wellesly College, Wellesly, MA. No. 82-03.

Symonds, A. (1971). Phobias after marriage. *Amer. J. Psychoan.*, 31:144–152.

_____ (1976). Neurotic dependency in successful women. *J. Amer. Acad. Psychoan.* 4:95–103.

Thompson, C. (1942). Cultural pressures in the psychology of women. *Psychiatry.* 5:331–339.

8 Autonomy
A Conflict For Women

_____DOROTHY LITWIN

In most theoretical frameworks, separation and individuation are usually regarded as an important turning point in development. Some feel this stage is crucial for the child to become an emotionally healthy, mature adult. Many think that the degree to which the child and mother are able to separate successfully will influence the child's functioning as an autonomous adult with a minimal residue of separation anxiety. In contrast, some contemporary theorists stress the necessity for attachment and relationships rather than separation and autonomy (Menaker, 1973, 1982; Dinnerstein, 1977; Chodorow, 1978; Gilligan, 1982; Miller, 1984; Surrey, 1985). Affiliation and involvement with others appear to be essential for women; in contrast, detachment, independence and uninvolvement appear to be characteristic of male development. In addition, it is thought that Western society devalues women's affiliative inclinications and reinforces men's autonomy and power as the standard for success and acceptable behavior. Current thinking supports women's striving for relationships as progressive and worthwhile and emphasizes that the reason this effort has always been derogated is because women and their values have been continuously derogated. Relationships, interdependence, and intimacy are emerging as laudatory goals, worthy of emulation.

The focus of this chapter is on autonomy as a conflict for women. Caught in the quandary created by society's push for the traditional female role of caretaker and custodian of relationships, on the one hand, and the pull of autonomy on the other, the female in our society is in conflict concerning her identity. Born female, she acquires from her mother attitudes, reinforced by society, that can lay the groundwork for these conflicts. Not only are her nurturing proclivities an outgrowth of her relationship with her mother, but she may also reflect attitudes toward her gender role that are directly connected to her mother's conflicts in this area. Guilt over departures from this nurturing image is a current problem for women, and is discussed in the following pages.

REVIEW OF THE LITERATURE

Classical Freudian theory was an important milestone in understanding people. Toward the end of his life, Freud began to consider the psychology of women and the preoedipal relationship between mother and daughter. Object relations theory carried on the study of the preoedipal relationship between mother and child. Most object relations theorists continued to include the Oedipus complex and penis envy as core concepts. Bowlby and Sullivan, although not considered object relations theorists, are included in this survey because they recognize the importance of the mother child relationship and feel this is crucial to human development.

Classical Psychoanalytic Theory

While Freud was not unaware of the importance of relationships in a person's life, his main focus was on innate drives; people are merely the conduits through which drives are expressed. In his discussion of the relationship with the mother during the preoedipal period, Freud's thinking began to change regarding the meaning of relationships in development. In two important papers (1931, 1933), Freud discusses females and aspects of their development which distinguishes them from males. Though clearly using males as a standard of comparison and castration as a crucial developmental concept, lamenting that he does not really understand women and that this is better left to female psychoanalysts, he describes how he thinks the girl's personality develops in connection with her parents, but most particularly in relationship with her mother.

Freud states that the relationship between mother and daughter is marked by ambivalence and develops in two stages. The preoeidpal stage, almost exclusively a relationship between the child and the mother, is of greater importance than he originally thought and lasts longer for women. The "strong attachment and exclusive love" that characterizes this stage comes to an end with the discovery by the girl that she was born castrated, that is, without a penis. This ushers in the second stage: the girl feels injured, blames her mother, and rejects her in favor of the father, who becomes the new love object. One of the results of these attachments is that ambivalence is always present in the relationship with the mother.

Character formation and future relationships are based on early relationships with both parents. The girl turns away from her mother because she has been born a girl. Freud adds parenthetically that such an intense attachment to the mother has to end because of inevitable disappointments and resultant anger over expectations and unfulfilled needs. The preoedipal attachment to the mother and the later oedipal feelings toward both parents are never entirely surmounted and play a significant part in later relationships.

The course of the female's marriage, according to Freud, is based on her relationship with her parents and the manner in which she resolves her Oedipus complex. Her relationship with her husband can be interlaced with hostility left over from her relationship with her mother, straining her marriage with ambivalence. Another point of stress may be with the birth of her child. The female may use this as a way of reestablishing or reenacting her relationship with her mother and may repeat with her child earlier attachment patterns of behavior, thereby excluding her husband. In addition, the mother relates differently to her children of either gender; "a mother is only brought unlimited satisfaction by her relation to a son; this is altogether the most perfect, the most free from ambivalence of all human relationships" (1933, p. 133).

Thus, women do not surmount their conflicts entirely but, instead, absorb them into their character formation and personality development to influence their lives. Implied in this paradigm is that emotional separation between parent and child never is completed. The repetition of patterns through the generations comes about because of the early child–parent attachment, which directly influences the female's choice of a husband, her behavior towards him, and her attitudes toward her children.

Object Relations Theories

A major modification in classical psychoanalytic drive gratification theory has been the inclusion of and the emphasis placed on the early preoedipal relationship between mother and child. Drive gratification, psychosexual development, and the oedipal castration conflicts were left intact by some object relations theorists, while others departed considerably from these concepts. All seem to agree, however, that an early, essential, and significant relationship between mother and child precedes and influences all other developmental phases. Each theorist's imprint has been put on these descriptions of the early interactions between mother and child, generically called object relations.

Michael and Alice Balint

The Balints, early object relations theorists, try to bridge the gap between classical psychoanalysis and their views regarding the preoedipal attachment between the child and the mother (Greenberg and Mitchell, 1983). M. Balint maintaining his loyalty to both Ferenzi and Freud kept the erotogenous zones in his theory but emphasized that the relationship between mother and child is based on mutual emotional satisfaction. Initially, the relationship is maintained on a biological basis, but later the emotional satisfaction of "primary object love" is important. He states that if either mother or infant is not satisfied in this dyad, the relationship becomes imbalanced, with possible neurotic consequences for the child, the mother, or both.

Although the Balints (1937, 1939) find a reciprocal, instinctual relationship between infant and mother based on biological needs, they feel these are separate and distinct from erotogenic zones and psychosexual development. They do not abandon drive theory altogether but suggest that early object relations form the basis for character development and relationships. A. Balint (1937) expands on the idea of reciprocal mother–child attachment, stating that for the mother, the offspring is always a child, for to grow up means to separate. The mutual gratification that exists begins to give way to reality, with mutual regard for one another replacing pure instinctual mutual gratification. This is how the ability for loving is learned. The child grows, matures, and, by adapting to the mother, learns how to maintain relationships.

Melanie Klein

Melanie Klein (1963) has also been a link between the drive theorists and the object relations theorists. Although she has modified her theory many times, she retains drive within her theoretical framework, namely, aggression and the libidinal instincts. She emphasizes also the importance of the early, preoedipal relationship between mother and child. According to Klein, at birth the infant is a mass of physical needs. In satisfying these needs, an object relation is formed between the mother and child before the development of the Oedipus complex. Mother represents external forces, symbolized by her breast, which impinge on and frustrate the infant; the mother, that is, the breast, interacts with the child's discomfort, rage, and consequent projection of internal conditions. There is a continuous flow between the internal and external world of the infant that persists throughout life; the child not only projects onto the external world, but also introjects good and bad feelings derived from good and bad experiences with the mother. Between mother and child there exists a reciprocal relationship where the mother's relationship to the child is influenced by the child's reaction to her. Internalization of a good breast is the foundation for the future personality development of the child. The influence of both parents is important later on in accepting the child's aggression and helping the child to learn to deal with hostile, destructive impulses. However, the initial, important, indelible relationship is with the mother.

David W. Winnicott

Winnicott (1945a) uses the expression "good enough mothering" to describe the mother's adaptation to the infant's needs from birth onward. Until the reality of separateness from the mother is established, the infant ruthlessly exploits the mother as a resource; the breast is given to the infant at the right time in the right place, and "the infant perceives the breast only insofar as a breast could be created just there and then" (1945a, p. 239). The mother must give herself, for a short time, entirely to the care of the infant so that, in existential terms, the infant can continue "going on being" with the least amount of interference. This lays the foundation for future mental health. Gradually, the mother can provide the infant with a basis for objectivity in the relationship with her, as she resumes her life in conjunction with the infant's developing abilities (1963). For Winnicott (1945b), as for other object relations theorists, this early relationship is of utmost importance; he attributes failure in later adaptation to reality to failures during this stage of complete and absolute dependence.

Margaret Mahler

Mahler's (1968) views are based on natural observation of very young children. She states that the separation-individuation process that begins at about five months and normally ends at around 30 to 36 months is basic to all other developmental processes. Not only are psychosocial factors operating during this crucial developmental phase, but psychomotor, perceptual, cognitive, and physical processes are developing at the same time. All are interrelated and play a significant part in the unfolding of the young child's maturational processes of separation and individuation.

From birth until about two months, the infant is an undifferentiated mass of needs, totally unaware of the mothering one. Following this stage of "normal autism" is a period of "symbiosis," during which the infant and mother are merged; the infant is simply aware of needs' being satisfied within this dyad.

The ego begins to develop out of this matrix when the infant can wait for and expect gratification. This is the "hatching" period, when the perceptual motor development advances to greater locomotor activity. By actively leaving and returning to the mother, Mahler believes, the child is "practicing" to become a separate and autonomous person. The child not only is delighted with newly found physical capacities, but also is "elated to escape from fusion with the mother" (Mahler, Pine and Bergman, 1975).

Emerging as a separate and autonomous person is a source of great anxiety to the toddler, who has to harness feelings of omnipotence and integrate them with the reality of separateness from the mother; a strong pull in the direction of individuation is counteracted by real limitations. This is called the "rapprochement" phase, and it is in this intensely conflictful period that personality development is based.

The resolution of conflicts during the rapprochement phase foreshadows the manner in which future conflicts, namely, the Oedipus conflict, will be resolved. It is during this phase that problems and defenses are set into motion that are never resolved completely throughout the entire life cycle. Ideally, the mother will help the child to grow in the direction of independence. Premature locomotor development or an infantilizing or emotionally unavailable mother can affect the toddler's separation-individuation achievements. It is clear that Mahler believes that the child's well-being is closely tied to the relationship with the mother.

W. R. D. Fairbairn

Fairbairn (1952) sees the mother-child relationship as an integral part of the development of good libidinal object relationships. In fact, he sees anxiety around separation from the mother as a basic trauma giving rise to ambivalence and splitting in important interpersonal relationships.

The infant, initially totally helpless, dependent, and undifferentiated from the mother is, in reality, merged with her. The child must go through a transitional phase whereby total dependence is renounced and a separate, fully differentiated person who forms relationships based on mutuality and interdependence must emerge. This is a crucial stage because the child, in making the transition, is giving up primary attachments and the security of these object relations. This encompasses actual attachments as well as those fantasized and internalized to compensate for disappointments suffered in reality. Fairbairn suggests that this transition is never completely made because of the fear of separation and object loss (Greenberg and Mitchell, 1984). The child would have to be extremely secure in order to renounce these early attachments completely and establish personal autonomy as well as autonomy in interpersonal relationships.

For Fairbairn, as for others, the earliest and most crucial object relation is with the mother, with whom the child learns self-acceptance and self-love. Separation from this earliest intense attachment is too fraught with anxiety for the child to function as a separate, autonomous, cohesive, whole human being. Whether or not this stage is successfully negotiated, there is no doubt that the fundamental relationship between mother and child leaves a permanent imprint throughout life.

Others espousing different psychoanalytic points of view, namely H. S. Sullivan and J. Bowlby are not, strictly speaking, considered to be object relations theorists. They reject the concepts of the Oedipus complex and castration anxiety and are often described as interpersonal relationship theorists. However, because they emphasize the importance of the mother-child relationship, there is considerable overlap with object relations theory, and they have been included in this survey.

John Bowlby

Bowlby believes attachment to the mother is critical (1969, 1973) for the infant. Changing his early opinion (1958) that attachment behavior derives from a number of instincts, he now thinks in terms of dynamic forces rather than physiological needs. From observation of children in nursery school settings and an extensive review of the literature on attachment behavior Bowlby (1969), concludes that the child's experiences with separation from the mother have enduring significance. Because of the nature of the attachment to the mother, the child's reaction to her leaving is one of distress or anxiety. A typical sequence is enacted. At first, there is a vigorous protest followed by despair and preoccupation with her return. The child then seems to lose interest, becomes detached, and, provided the period of separation is not prolonged, renews the attachment after the mother's return. The child may insist on staying close to the mother for days or weeks thereafter, becoming anxious at the prospect of her leaving once again. Because the child's experience with separation can be difficult, "the behavior of a person's present interpersonal relationships may be explicable in terms of his experiences many years earlier" (Bowlby, 1973, p. 256).

The availability of a trusted attachment figure in physical as well as emotionally responsive ways is important. The degree to which this figure is available for the infant, child, or adolescent will determine the degree to which the person will develop confidence and trust in interpersonal relationships. The most sensitive period is between six months and five years, and the effect diminishes thereafter. The expectations based on actual experiences with significant people, particularly the mother, persist relatively unchanged throughout life.

Harry S. Sullivan

Sullivan (1953), similar to Bowlby in many ways, also does not include drive gratification as part of the developmental process. Though the two theorists share the view that interpersonal relationships are the common denominator for personality development, Bowlby stresses separation anxiety and its derivatives as the basic problem of the human condition, while Sullivan does not restrict himself to that conflict. Rather, Sullivan describes the relationship between infant and mother, and the resultant anxiety or euphoria, as crucial for emotional adjustment and personality development. For Sullivan, personality develops in ongoing relationships as a result of security operations in which the individual is involved in order to minimize the experience of anxiety.

According to Sullivan, the foundation for relationships rests on the initial one between mother and child. The empathic relationship between mother and infant is so close that the mother's emotional state is experienced by the infant as a feeling of tension or euphoria. With repeated experience of this kind with the mothering one, the infant soon develops sensations or images called "prehends" of a "good mother" or a "bad mother," and these, in turn, have implications for the manner in which the "self" comes to be perceived.

Certain patterns of interaction are learned, influence subsequent experiences with people, and reinforce feelings about people and the self. Each stage of development brings with it characteristic needs and always involves other people in seeking satisfaction. When anxiety and dissatisfaction are the outcome of interpersonal interactions, security operations develop. There is always a chance that corrective experiences can take place through interactions with people as the child matures and leaves the home; however, the basic, integral, important experiences that lay the foundation for personality development are with the mother.

Summary

Object relations theory extended classical psychoanalytic theory to include the early, preoedipal relationship between mother and child.

These theorists regard this as crucial to the development of self-acceptance and self-love. Because the attachment between mother and child is so intense and expectations of fulfillment so unrealistic, separation is fraught with anxiety. Although, initially, the relationship is based on fulfilling biological needs, emotional satisfactions for both soon become paramount. Though most object relations theorists include castration anxiety and the Oedipus complex as pivotal concepts in character formation, they stress that the relationship between mother and child is fundamental and leaves a permanent imprint on the individual throughout life.

CONTEMPORARY PSYCHOANALYTIC PERSPECTIVE ON THE MOTHER-DAUGHTER RELATIONSHIP AND ITS EFFECT ON AUTONOMY

Recently, classical psychoanalysts have begun to formulate ideas that female development is different from male development. Using object relations theory as a base, they emphasize the importance of the early preoedipal relationship with the girl's mother and the influence this has on shaping female attitudes toward her gender role. Not only are separation-individuation issues considered to be crucial, but superego conflicts centering around motherhood, ego ideal, and identity are considered important for the female.

Blum (1977) states that the contemporary perspective by psychoanalysts is on object relations formed in the preoedipal period and its effects on personality development. He regards the mother-daughter relationship in the context of the resolution of the Oedipus complex. It is ambivalent and encompasses negative attitudes toward the devalued, castrated mother as well as warmth, love, and admiration; in addition, the mother is regarded as a rival and an aggressor. Both superego development and the ego ideal are based mostly on identification with the mother and to a much lesser extent on the father. Blum equates "full female development" with motherhood, which, in turn, is based on the maternal ego ideal the girl has incorporated. Other interests and characteristics, such as "humanitarian concerns and caring responsibility, and the development of discipline and ethics" (1977, p. 176), are also byproducts of the feminine superego and the ego ideal.

In criticizing Freud's concepts, Blum retains the classical psychoanalytic structural theoretical orientation overlaid with a narrow interpretation, of current trends in thinking. He does not agree with

Freud's view that the female superego is weaker or deficient in comparison with the male's but concludes rather simplistically that the female has incorporated society's expectations of what femaleness should be. If she is passive and compliant, it is because these are behaviors expected of her and not because her superego is deficient in offering love. He also described female superego development in terms of motherhood, as though this were the only identifying characteristic of the ego ideal to which all women aspire. Even though he mentions early object relations, he regards this as crucial only in the development of attitudes toward mothering and motherhood.

In a much quoted study, Galenson and Riophe (1977) discovered through observation that a normal genital period occurs between 16 and 19 months of age, much earlier than that postulated by Freud. While they emphasize the importance of the early interactions between mother and child, they feel the pivotal point around which interaction with the mother takes place is the sexual drive and that this is the basis for later sexual responsiveness in interpersonal relationships. They feel that the discovery of genital differences at this early age has a profound effect on the development of gender identification, object relations, ego functioning, fantasy in girls, and, depending on early object relations, the castration reaction. Thus, they basically agree with object relations theory that pregenital relationships are important; but this phase shapes the direction the Oedipus complex will take.

Barglow and Schaefer (1977) incorporate ego relationships with classical psychoanalytic theory. While they also recognize the importance of the early infant-mother relationship and the effect on personality development, the Oedipus complex and penis envy are treated as central concepts in personality development. For example, the boy and girl interact with the mother in different ways. During the separation individuation phase, the little girl may have a closer attachment to the mother because of her smaller size and lower activity level, which is easier to handle. The boy, in contrast, may suffer a narcissistic injury because the mother may find him bigger, more active, and more difficult. Therefore, during this period the little girl may have a stronger ego. The boy's narcissistic injury, however, is reparable because he has a penis, whereas the girl's narcissistic injury, resulting from lack of a penis, is not. Barglow and Schaefer feel that parental attitudes and interactions are influential in gender identification; for females, it is defined in terms of motherhood and mothering based on penis envy, biological givens and identification with the mother's gender traits and secondarily with those of her father.

Childbearing and mothering functions, reinforced by parental attitudes, establish gender-related attitudes toward the self that "coincide with or even precedes castration anxiety and penis envy" (p. 432). They conclude that the way in which the Oedipus complex plays itself out depends on what has preceded this stage of development. They seem to separate this from other aspects of living for females and base female gender attitudes on acceptance of their roles for motherhood and mothering, which are based on parental attitudes.

Bergman (1982) elaborates on Mahler's (1968) stages of separation-individuation. For the woman, according to Bergman, there are special problems formed in childhood that influence the formation of her autonomy: the discovery of sexual differences and the girl child's reaction to castration; the rapprochement crisis, which girls seem to have greater difficulty resolving than boys; the dual process of having to identify and disidentify with the mother in establishing her individuality and separateness (rapprochement crises); the mother's attitudes toward her own gender as well as toward her girl child, which are evident from the moment of the dauther's birth. Basic to the girl's autonomy is a sense of self, which is greatly influenced by her mother's expectations of her as a girl. In turn, the mother's expectations of her daughter are based on her own female experiences and expectations defined by her psychodynamics and separation from her own mother.

All these factors interact and effect each other in influencing the girl's identity and ability to separate and individuate. The characteristic manner in which this evolves is rooted in the girl's relationship with her parents, most particularly with the mother.

Lebe (1982) distinguishes between the separation-individuation process of childhood, as described by Mahler (1968), and that which occurs between ages thirty and forty, when separation is completed. It is at this point that the Oedipus complex is resolved; the woman is able to accept her femininity by positively identifying with the mother and becomes autonomous.

During the normal course of psychosexual development, the boy, because he possesses a penis, can more easily turn from the omnipotent, powerful mother to identify with the father. The female child never completes the separation from her mother; she splits her feelings, turns to the father, assigns all his short comings to the mother, idealizes him, and remains for a long time dependent upon men.

By the time she is 30, the woman has had numerous opportunities to achieve her ego ideal, strengthen her ego, and counteract her narcissistic injury. She has had many occasions to know her mother more realistically, and she has had time to achieve in career, school, marriage, community. She sees men as human, not as all powerful, and she has dealt with her castration guilt.

An omnipotent, domineering mother, marriage to a man similar to her father, or a relationship in which the woman feels she has castrated her mate are determinants that can stand in the way of normal psychosexual development and the achievement of autonomy.

Lebe seems to be saying that psychosocial success experiences can help resolve the Oedipus complex for women, but she is pessimistic about seeing this come about, apparently because of anatomical differences between the sexes.

Bernstein (1979) describes parental conflicts that can get in the way of the daughter's establishing her autonomy. For the mother, it can mean losing a daughter through separation who is rejecting the traditional intergenerational female role and who in the process is also rejecting her mother's values. In addition, the daughter's striving for independence can be personally threatening to the mother, whose own conflicts regarding repressed desires to be autonomous may be reawakened. On the other hand, the father who can help his daughter to accept her desires for independence if his own needs regarding his domain and boundaries are not threatened can be supportive and help ease her struggle in identifying with him.

Applegarth (1977), theorizing about women's work inhibitions in career choices, points out that narcissism can play a major part in the development of autonomy. Not only is the narcissistic woman afraid of failure and unable to continue to try beyond a certain point, but goals set may be so high that they interfere with accomplishment. Likewise, women with low self-esteem, or those who are vehicles for parental achievement and reflected glory, may fail in career choices.

Further narcissistic disturbances in the achievement of autonomy can come about through penis envy. Attitudes regarding self-esteem and self-worth are heavily influenced by being born female and lacking something that is esteemed by family, society, and culture. Curiosity, exploration, originality, and aggression, necessary characteristics in striving toward autonomy, are blunted. Some women seek traditional female occupations; some may merge with a man through whom they can feel a measure of success and completeness; or others may have a baby as another adaptive mechanism.

Different standards apply to men and women regarding competition and aggression. For women, these traits are discouraged; in fact, appearing weak and seeming to be fearful are characteristics that are encouraged to support the masculine ego, or they may actually be experienced as the result of feeling a narcissistic injury.

Attitudes toward accomplishment on her own reflect an earlier relationship with the mother, who is seen as inadequate, Applegarth asserts, and in which the man is imbued with the image of protector, competence and power. The woman's range of activity is narrowed because she feels incapable of striking out on her own. Applegarth concludes that narcissistic dependency needs are fulfilled in some women by being taken care of and being protected; passive oral needs are gratified by other women, who feel as though they have been narcissistically injured and that they are entitled to be taken care of and protected. Complicating matters, conflicts revolving around career versus motherhood can come about by activating separation anxiety or by evoking earlier idealized images of proper mother love.

In an article written in 1942, Thompson (cited in Miller, 1973), responding to classical psychoanalytic theorizing about women's psychodynamics and resultant behavior (seen as penis envy) expressed an alternative explanation that seems as relevant today as it was then. Thompson proposed that women attempt to achieve independence by emulating men in becoming aggressive, decisive, and daring, rather than assuming their customary roles of gentleness and submissiveness. This does not mean that women are becoming masculine, but that these are necessary traits to compete in the world of business. Men do not have an exclusive right to these traits; however, the culture creates the conflict in labeling women who behave in this fashion as masculine. If a woman does reject being a woman, Thompson asserts, assuming that she wants to be a man is simplistic: "Being a woman may mean the negation of her feeling of self and a denial of a chance to be an independent person" (cited in Miller, 1973, p. 82). Rather than chance the loss of her identity in an intimate relationship, she may be trying to assert herself as an independent person. This need for independence may have its roots in early relationships, particularly with the mother, and the daughter may be reluctant to become dependent on any person. Marriage is a prime circumstance for autonomy conflicts to be reactivated, based on early experiences with mother. The spector of the mother influences later development.

Summary

Freud began focusing on the preoedipal relationship between mother and daughter in his attempt to understand the psychology of women. The object relations theorists extended his study in depth to the mother and the child. They recognized the importance of this relationship to the well being of both and knew it to be a powerful, enduring relationship that has lifetime consequences for the female.

They understood that emotional satisfaction replaced biological grat-ification in the maturational sequence, but they continued to view the Oedipus complex and castration anxiety as core concepts in under-standing psychological development.

This point of view has colored the understanding of female devel-opment and was to limit the appreciation of woman's full psychologi-cal nature. In spite of sociocultural changes and insights that have emerged in recent years, contemporary classical psychoanalytic the-ory concerning women continues to remain static and basically un-changed. Female ego ideals and superego development unfold along the lines of mothering and nurturing; conflicts regarding this ego ideal and society's expectations that independence and autonomy are the equivalent of maturity and success are either overlooked or ex-plained as penis envy. The clash between the superego and ego ideal is not an intrapsychic problem, but a conflict many women have to contend with in contemporary society.

The next section considers the conflicts created for women in our society between her propensity toward nurturing and the social val-ue placed on autonomy. Involved are not only ego issues of identity but also superego issues of guilt over the expression of indepen-dence.

AUTONOMY: A CONFLICT FOR WOMEN

The female is caught in a double bind. On the one side are expecta-tions that come from society's respect for autonomy as a goal to achieve and, on the other, is the role in which she is cast as caretaker and involved other person. There is a great deal of anxiety, casting about, progression and regression in attempting to arrive at a con-sistent role and acceptable self-image.

Autonomy, in the context of this chapter, is descriptive of a way of life, conceptualized by Maslow (1970), rather than a developmental term, used by Mahler (1968) as an outcome of separation-individua-tion or by Erikson (1968) as a measure of the child's control over the environment. Maslow's conception of the autonomous person, and its influence on our society, in which it has been adopted as an ego ideal, is described below.

The Autonomous Person

Maslow (1970) writing as early as the 1950s about self-actualization, and then revising and restating his views in 1970, defined the auton-omous person. From his study of self-actualization, autonomy emerged as an important characteristic, and Maslow seems to use the two terms interchangeably. His "autonomous" subjects like solitude and privacy; they find it easy to be aloof, reserved, calm, serene. They do not rely on other people's feelings or opinions but have their own interpretations. They have a quality of detachment about them that can be thought of as reserve, remoteness, or austerity. Self-actualizing people do not need others in the ordinary sense; their detachment can be interpreted easily as "coldness, snobbishness, lack of affection, unfriendliness or even hostility" (1970, p. 161). In terms of making decisions, autonomous people are self-starters, entirely independent of the influence of others; they are self-disciplined and strong, and they have more free will than others.

Self-actualization begins for autonomous people when their basic needs, as determined by Maslow, are gratified and they can become relatively independent of their environment. They stand alone and need little if any nurturance from outside sources for the continued growth and development of their potential. Least of all do they need people as a source of gratification and in fact "growth motivated people may actually be *hampered* by others" (1970, p. 162, italics added). Maslow goes on to say that inner growth and self-development are more important than loving and interacting with other people. In addition, these people are ruled basically by internal laws rather than the rules of society.

Changes in Ego Ideal

Maslow's writings provided impetus to the human potential movement, which endorsed these characteristics as virtues and goals to which to aspire. Menaker (1973) sees the drawbacks to this point of view: "There is hidden in the exaggerated valuing of a seeming autonomy and purity of purpose, an omnipotent self-conception and a denial of the interdependence of people and their interrelationships" (p. 139). She discusses the development of autonomy as having the potential to alienate people from one another; she goes on to describe how these values can be internalized as changed ego ideals. Neither society nor people is a static entity, but both are subject to change by circumstances, sometimes in reciprocal interaction and sometimes unilaterally. Manaker states that this process is brought about usually through changes in society that effect the individual or, less frequently, by a strong individual's impact on society when the time is ripe to receive such change, supported by historical factors. In turn, the individual introjects these new values, and they become part of the ego ideal or superego formation.

For some, the need for autonomy is so important that adopting it as an ego ideal is imposed on their children as a desirable way of life, and, according to Menaker (1973), results in sacrificing interpersonal relationships. In reaction to an earlier, more authoritarian society, modern parents raise their children with more permissive standards and with a great emphasis on self-actualization and autonomy in relation to goals and in relation to the influence of other people. Menaker feels that to be self-contained has become such an important value for some that there is now a narcissistic focus on the self to the detriment of relating to others. In addition, becoming autonomous very often is a command to children rather than a process that is allowed to develop naturally — it is a classical double bind. Imposing autonomy is a contradiction. Interference stifles growth, so that the end result must be an inevitable question in the mind of the child regarding the genuineness of autonomy in decision making. This may, in turn, contribute to greater intrapsychic conflicts regarding autonomy in the development of a sense of self.

Ehrenreich (1984) describes just such a transformation in ego ideal values, which she explains as an outgrowth of the demise of the male domination of the wage earning system in our society. She attributes the contemporary desire of women for more freedom in the "second wave of liberation" in part to a reaction of antecedent irresponsibility by men, which has been described as men's search for greater autonomy and called "men's liberation" (p. 117).

As a reaction to the conformity of the 1950s, after World War II, when the level of aspiration was for marriage, children, a home in the suburbs complete with car and pets, men were being lured away from these goals by the enticement of Playboy magazine toward a glamorous world of hedonism. Added to these allurements, according to Ehrenreich, was the attraction of the "Beat" life style, represented by Jack Kerouac, Allen Ginsberg, and Neal Cassady, who seemed to be living life to the fullest by indulging themselves in every way and by eliminating from their lives any vestige of responsibility. The "hippie" movement of the 1960s, combined with the human potential credo of self-actualization, reinforced the individual's 'inalienable' right to be responsible solely to one's self and to disregard future planning or goals beyond the moment of self-fulfillment. These temptations could be responded to by men in particular because of their relatively independent roles granted by society.

Because men opted out of family life for the lure of singleness, women were forced to become more independent. As a result, the pattern of society based on the male breadwinner has broken down so that the family wage system no longer exists. This has caused a major upheaval in an important balance between the sexes and has had a great psychological impact, creating pressure and conflict for women. According to Ehrenreich, the changed ego ideal is for women to assume greater autonomy and self-reliance as wage earners.

In this regard, Bernstein (1979) discusses the upheaval in our society's customs and values, which is creating chaos in traditional gender role assignments for women. She points out that the female's overly strict superego constrains her achieving autonomy, because female self-assertion is frowned upon unless it is in the interest of serving others. Contrary to the classical psychoanalytic portrayal of the female as having a weak superego, Bernstein feels it is the strength of the superego that interferes with the female's becoming more independent and following her own inclinations. Bernstein points out that the analyst and assertiveness training groups are replacing the customary superego ideals in supporting female autonomy. Even in situations of economic survival, becoming autonomous can be heavily interlaced with guilt because of the superego imperative to be a nurturing mother.

In summary, it is suggested that the ego ideal of the autonomous person is a source of conflict for women. This comes in part from the male point of view that autonomy is desirable, held to be the goal to strive toward, and from society's endorsement of autonomy as maturity, the equivalent of self-reliance — as though autonomy proves the ability to stand on one's own.

Because autonomy is an acknowledged and esteemed value, some females adopt it as a worthwhile way of life and make it their standard for what is right and desirable regardless of whether it is appropriate for them. For the female, the conflict comes from the expectations that being autonomous brings in opposition to being female and being available in interpersonal relationships. The external conflict of adopting masculine values as the way to be not only is imposed on the female as an expectation regarding issues of self support, but is adopted by her as an ego ideal, emulating men in accepting masculine codes as desirable and good. Man's world becomes woman's standard; the conflict includes expectations of herself, without regard to her gender, and judgment of herself as an acceptable person in light of these expectations and the expectations of others. It is as though the unique, solid existing and potential talents that women own as part of being born and raised female are not thought of as good enough nor respected as much as traits that men display.

Before detailed discussion of the special qualities inherent in the mother-daughter relationship related to gender identity and conflicts over autonomy, some brief remarks reflecting contemporary ideas about the mother-infant relationship follow.

Mother-Infant Attachment

Reviewing the literature on bonding, Sluckin, Herbert and Sluckin (1983) did not find any evidence that skin contact between mother and child immediately after birth bonds an intense lifelong relationship. Instead, they feel that the bonding that develops takes place gradually over weeks and months; they suggest that perhaps the bonding theory arose because "the relationship between mother and child and the kind of 'bonding contract' between them that is capable of lasting a lifetime requires an explanatory theory (or metaphor) that matches it in dramatic impact" (p. 22).

Rossi (1977) believes there is a physiological link between mother and child that does not exist between father and child. In fact, she is convinced that fathers will need compensatory child care training to make up for the missing hormonal factor that provides the innate predisposition to attachment between mother and child.

Infant research conducted by Beebe (1982) and Stern (1977), using microanalysis of 16 mm film, has demonstrated early interaction between mother and infant. The interaction between this dyad is mutual and reciprocal. Rather than a merging between the two in a symbiotic relationship, the infant is seen to be busily engaged in the relationship, creating and reacting to patterns of activity between them. Contrary to object relations theory, Stern (1983) envisions the infant as a separate person at birth who gradually, through reciprocal interaction, forms a relationship with the mother.

Menaker (1961), discussing infant-mother relationships, suggests that the earliest developmental process is attachment rather than frustration or gratification of a biological need. A reciprocal relationship evolves out of the memories of the mother's childhood, which the mother integrates with her own experiences in living, thereby leading to empathic responses toward her child. Menaker calls this a "social matrix" and feels that this experience is crucial to the future well being of the individual and "is basic to the formation of personality, be it normal or neurotic" (p. 165).

Cultural or social background of the mother, the mother's experiences in having been parented, her personality, her previous experiences with babies, sex and temperament of the baby, age of the mother, the ordinal position of the baby are all factors that are important in the relationship between mother and child (Sluckin et al, 1983).

While there is much in common in the maternal attachment to babies of either sex, because the mother and daughter are female, a qualitatively different kind of relationship develops between them than between the mother and son. Special personality characteristics are approved of in females that encourage different patterns in interpersonal relationships repeated through the generations.

Mother-Daughter Relationship

Bernstein (1979) suggests that the anatomy of the female aids in her gender identity with her mother but also hinders separation and individuation. Because she is like her mother, it is easy enough to identify with the physical sameness of the mother; however, because her sexual organs are not easily seen, her sexual experiences are diffuse and generalized. Bernstein likens this to the female's undifferentiated experience of herself in early infancy, which may intensify the blurring of boundaries between herself and her mother.

Chodorow (1978) and Dinnerstein (1977) discuss separation-individuation and autonomy as developmental issues, particularly in relation to gender differences. Involved in these developmental issues is the manner in which nurturing came to be an almost exclusively female function and is perpetuated as a gender role assignment in Western society. Both theorists agree that the sex of the daughter and mother being the same creates special problems of separation and autonomy. They begin by stating that the earliest and most important relationship for the infant is with the mothering one and that it is this relationship which has an enormous impact on the person for the remainder of life.

Combining psychoanalytic theory with a sociological point of view, Chodorow (1978) has analyzed the "asymmetrical" relationship between gender roles and the manner in which this is reinforced by society. She feels that because women are the caretakers, certain qualities in the relationship between mother and child are perpetuated and reinforced by society because it is in the interest of society to maintain this type of mothering pattern. Using psychoanalytic insights with object relations theory, she focuses on the mother-child dyad as a nuclear relationship and describes how this linkage is perpetuated from one generation to the next.

The mother comes into the relationship with her child with her own character formation based largely on being female and having been nurtured by a female; she treats the girl child differently from the boy child. Because they are of the same sex, the mother and daughter more readily feel as though they are the same person than can the mother and son. For the female, the preoedipal attachment to the mother is prolonged and, in fact, is the basis for the manner in which the Oedipal conflict is formed and resolved. The father does not supplant the mother, because the father is never involved enough in the parenting role to be an emotionally satisfying replacement. Instead, Chodorow feels, the father is added to the mother-daughter dyad, out of which a triangle is formed, and this becomes the paradigm for familial attachments for the female and subsequent heterosexual relationships.

One consequence for the female is that she never completely separates from the mother. In having a female child, the mother reconstructs the oedipal triangle in which she, her mother, and her father were the participants. The mother and daughter remain invested in one another, without a clear separation between them or complete autonomy for either. Though cognitively the female knows she is separate and different from her mother, there is a constant inner struggle for autonomy and separateness. While mother represents regression and lack of autonomy for both genders and children of both sexes are caught in the conflict of trying to break away from the mother, the boy is far more successful in this respect. The nuclear relationship is with the mother, from whom he is helped to detach himself by both parents in identifying with the father and all that is masculine. In contrast, the daughter is always involved in a reciprocal attachment with the mother, from whom she can never break free because her mother also has an investment in maintaining the relationship.

Another consequence of the attachment to the mother is the manner in which both sexes relate to people. The male, because he is expected to repress his early attachment and feelings toward the mother, does not develop his full capacity to relate to people. The mother-daughter relationship, in contrast, allows the female to be available to fuller, more involved relationships. Because the female sees herself as an extension of the mother and, in this way, is inherently related to another person, it is natural for her to want to continue in relationships with others; according to Chodorow, women define themselves relationally.

On a more philosophical plane, Dinnerstein (1977) writes that because of her power to give and take away life, to comfort or create distress, to merge with and potentially to be separate, the female is awesome and must relinquish her autonomy in order for Western civilization to survive in its present form. In the earliest, most primitive relationship, the quality of reciprocal need between the helpless infant and the mother's need to nurture forms the basis for later interpersonal relations and responses to the environment. As adults, both men and women seek to recapture this earliest, comforting, accepting, secure relationship with mother. The male, according to Dinnerstein, is always afraid he will merge with the female, wife or mother; therefore, he is ambivalent and regards such a relationship as threatening. The female, on the other hand, is more secure and comfortable in relationships, because she knows she will always be needed as a life sustaining force and, therefore, will be connected with people. However, Dinnerstein feels that ultimately the female must subordinate herself to the male because he fears her independence or spontaneity as a reflection of her power. Thus, the female assumes a passive submissive role but, at the same time, is a threat. The structure of Western civilization encourages and reinforces these respective complementary roles; for both sexes, there is a pretense that men have power because women's potential power is too threatening and must be suppressed.

Further, Dinnerstein sees women's role as a tradeoff. Men's interest in world affairs is empty and trivial and not at all enviable or advantageous. She feels that women are tacitly expressing this opinion by not becoming involved with the meaninglessness of men's "history making." By having babies and relating to people, women are alive, vital, and involved with important aspects of life.

Both Dinnerstein and Chodorow feel that as long as one gender is assigned the caregiver role, an asymmetrical character formation will inevitably emerge. Not only will the female remain the nuclear attachment figure for the child, but the development of autonomy and the capacity for relationships will continue along gender lines.

To summarize these points of view, these writers are suggesting that character traits are formed early in the mother-daughter relationship. Females tend to affiliate with others largely because of their early experiences and identification with the mother. More than anything else, this enables the female to generate future relationships. That women develop conflicts about how they are expected to mature and what they are expected to be like are restrictions imposed on their inclinations to be connected to people. Because maturation is equated with separation and autonomy, attachment becomes a failure in development. Gender differences in the need for affiliations seem to carry a judgment of right or wrong; differences are not seen as different, but better or worse, mature or infantile, dependent or autonomous. Separation, detachment, and independence are the criteria for acceptable relationships, with masculine values as the baseline for comparisons.

Surrey (1985) points our that those who advocate separation as a goal of maturation ultimately have to reconcile how people do relate to one another and the manner in which they form long-term relationships.

Relationships, particularly with the mother, have been the subject of criticism and ridicule by analysts, comedians, writers, and others in our society. Perhaps because clinical considerations have overshadowed the lifelong benefits to be derived from a loving, close affiliation, the latter has been overlooked. The following section highlights some current thinking concerning affiliation as a basic need for females.

Gilligan (1982) feels that relationships take precedence over moral reasoning and logic for women. Because women are empathic and feel compassion, they take into account human dilemmas in considering issues of right and wrong, whereas men tend to apply rules of logic and law. These disparities, according to Gilligan, do not come about as classical psychoanalytic theory would have it because of differences in the oedipal resolution that reflect a deficiency, weakness, or lack of moral judgment in women, but rather from the capacity to relate to people.

For Gilligan, the ability to relate to people is a strength rather than a weakness; but because it is not a masculine value, it is not respected in our society. In addition, interdependence is an ideal goal in which the female can participate only if she regards herself as an equal and is less concerned with taking care of others than with what is right for her. This requires feeling it is safe to assert herself without jeopardizing a relationship. She feels that when women are able to temper their capacity for nurturance with a measure of self-respect, genuine empathy will be attained. Gilligan observes that unilaterally taking care of another's needs is often based on the need for approval rather than a desire to help; caretaking, therefore, does not always promote wholesome attachments and can often cover resentment. Surrey (1985) points out that a relationship of mutuality requires mutual empathy.

Miller (1984) says that our society values separation rather than maintaining and enriching relationships as a way of life. Involvement in relationships does not necessarily mean the fulfillment of dependency needs but, rather, encompasses a desire to be understood, intimate, and valued. She sees the stage of separation-individuation and the establishment of autonomy not necessarily as a dissolution of attachments, but rather as a psychological reorganization, with the manner in which the person relates acquiring new and different meanings. Mother and daughter do not sever their relationships. To the contrary, in the evolution of the emerging ego, this is an important relationship that is and must be maintained; the interactions between mother and daughter must continue to be supportive, nurturing, and caring while they allow for individuality of expression and growth of the self. Menaker (1975), who basically agrees with Miller, suggests that there is a counteridentification with the mother rather than, as is commonly believed, a negative identification.

For Miller (1984) preserving and improving intimacies is of utmost importance. This does not contradict the development of a sense of self. In fact, it enhances the sense of self for a female, because she is brought up with a sense of herself in the context of understanding, being empathic, and feeling close to other people.

Surrey (1985) feels that the relationship between mother and daughter is based on mutuality and is always evolving. As they interact, they change as their needs change. She feels that this is learned by the daughter beginning in infancy, as mother and daughter develop a profound interest in one another which promotes caring and a sense of self-worth. The daughter therefore is raised in the context of a mutually empathic relationship, which not only enhances self-esteem, but lays the foundation for further growth, self-knowledge and affiliation as a way of life.

RELATIONSHIPS: A CONFLICT FOR WOMEN

Since men seem to be successful, their world has a great appeal for those women who feel they can achieve equality and success by identifying with and emulating men. Aspiring toward autonomy as a way of achieving maturity is one of the problems that adopting men's values has created for women. Being self-contained, independent, and responsible to oneself only has become a desirable way to be for some women. These are external standards sanctioned by society empahsizing self to the exclusion of others.

A separate but interwoven issue is the propensity toward relationships, which females learn very early in life. Separation from the mother is a masculine characteristic that is an accepted standard applied indiscriminately to both sexes. Because it is unmanly to be like the mother, males learn to identify with masculine characteristics; hence, separation from the mother is right and good. On the basis of that standard, the mother-daughter dyad has been largely condemned as destructive to female individuation and emergence of self. A value judgment is made that unless separation from the mother takes place, the daughter is doomed to a life of dependency and undefined boundaries as a person.

Because this issue does not remain only a mother-daughter issue of separation but is generalized to all interpersonal relationships, questions of intimacy become confused, contradictory, and laden with anxiety. Separation-individuation and autonomy are lumped together as characteristics desirable and necessary for emotionally healthy adulthood. Unspoken is that autonomy can also result in isolation and separation, concealing that relationships are being loosened or lost because closeness is equated with dependency. Intimacy is the most conflict-ridden characteristic of relationships in contemporary society.

Confusion about *what to be* is an issue for women. Since being separate and autonomous is good and being involved with and relating to people is not good, women are two-time losers. By extension, to become autonomous, to be free and independent, means giving up relationships. Not only is this position contrary to the role imposed on women by our society, but it is a goal impossible to achieve when discomfort and anxiety are created in the attempt to do so.

Kohut (1984) states that children do not separate from their mothers when they take their first steps. Instead they look to their mothers to share in their joy of accomplishment. The mother-child dyad changes as the child matures and becomes more self-reliant. He states, "Relationships form the essence of psychological life from birth to death, . . . a move from dependence (symbiosis) to independence (autonomy) in the psychological sphere is no more dependent on oxygen to a life independent of it in the biological sphere" (p. 47). He states further that people do not give up seeking important relationships; the people may change, but the essence of relationships they seek remains the same.

Kohut adds that psychotherapy enables people to be appropriately selective in choosing relationships that are supportive, sustaining, and enhancing. It is important for a person to have the support of others, particularly in times of stress, because it is a good feeling to know that there is a person to depend on for the same kind of warmth and security obtained in the earliest, most comforting, and most secure relationship with the mother.

For some, this is a direct contradiction to independence and autonomy, as though affiliation and autonomy cannot coexist. For women, particularly, passivity and subordination are generally encouraged, while self-assertion can be risky.

The theme of the next section is the recognition of the importance of relationships, which must be reconciled with the issue of autonomy in the psychic life of the female.

THERAPEUTIC ISSUES
OF AUTONOMY AND RELATIONSHIPS

According to Miller (1976), the female role is laid out for the child from the moment of birth. She is brought up to nurture and serve others and therefore learns to see herself through the eyes of others and as being in the service of others. A natural merging takes place with significant other people, and the loss of a significant relationship "is perceived not as just a loss of an interpersonal relationship, but closer to total loss of self" (p. 83). Autonomy can be threatening to women because it is often the equivalent of giving up affiliations in order to become self-directed and separate. This need not be an either/or proposition; but, for some women, achieving "authenticity" or being honest about their marital relationship and themselves might displease the mate and result in abandonment. Along with autonomy comes the anxiety of being separate and alone (Menaker, 1982).

Miller (1976) recognizes that relationships are vital to women but believes a restructuring of the nature of relationships is necessary in order for women to develop and grow. Menaker (1982) believes that ideally the daughter would achieve emotional stability by identifying with both the desirable characteristics of the mother and the new values that society has permitted the female to assume. Menaker believes that the success of the transition depends on the initial relationship between mother and daughter, the daughter's ego strength, and other sources of support. She concludes that people are "object seeking" and that therefore psychotherapy can be helpful in integrating conflicting values and roles. This would be possible only if the therapist were empathic, flexible, and open to recognizing changing roles and values in society and not invested in a particular theory or point of view.

Symonds (1973) describes the woman who after marriage changes from an autonomous, self-reliant, strong person to one who is dependent and helpless. Symonds calls this a "declaration of dependence" and describes the feelings as a loss of freedom and as a "symbolic expression of how the individual closes herself in, keeps down her impulses and imprisons herself" (p. 301).[1] Symonds states that in the interest of maintaining a relationship with a man, the independent, assertive behavior earlier observed becomes suppressed. Once involved in a relationship, "they tenaciously refuse to accept the concept of separateness" (p. 300).

As long as the wife is willing to maintain her subordinate position in the marriage, and the husband is willing to be in the traditional masculine role, the marriage can work, according to Symonds. In order to continue the relationship, constant vigilance and denial on the part of the wife are required so that no contradictory feeling can surface. The husband's lack of awareness of the spouse's needs rein-

---

[1]Symonds relates this syndrome specifically to the development of phobias. In my experience, this syndrome is not phobia specific, but cuts across symptomatic pictures, where many fears are manifested.

forces feelings of inadequacy; and rather than assert herself in the interest of greater understanding, the wife prefers not to recognize her own feelings for fear of the consequences.

For these women, the need for a relationship is so profound that it is valued more highly than the recognition of their other needs. The emotional extension of this paradigm for some would mean that greater self-expression would lead to autonomy, which, in turn, would result in aloneness, the equivalent of having no relationship or being abandoned. In this vein, Sullivan (1953) talks about loneliness as a condition so terrifying as to be beyond description, too frightening to reexperience and talk about. He says that people will do almost anything to avoid loneliness, and they even put themselves in anxiety-provoking situations because it is less painful than experiencing loneliness. Some women are so threatened by the prospect of loneliness that they make many compromises to avoid being alone.

A patient whose husband stubbornly refused to hand over the family finances to her, even though their financial situation indicated that this was definitely not his area of expertise, did not open her own checking account because it would be tantamount to establishing her separateness. She felt so threatened by this autonomous act that even this one small part of her life portended being alone.

On the other hand, a 52-year-old woman separated from her husband after 26 years of marriage is ashamed because she is feeling abandoned and alone. She is experiencing a great deal of conflict in admitting to herself that she misses the relationship, because she is supposed to be mature, strong, and self-reliant.

A female patient described an argument she had had with her husband because he had neglected her needs in taking care of his own. She became angry, accusing him of this misdeed. Part of her effort in relentlessly pursuing him was that she needed confirmation of her sense of what had happened. In addition, although she was able to recognize her anger, she was not able to tell him she felt he was making up excuses for himself because he could not admit a mistake. To have her own opinion about his behavior was "isolating," which, on further analysis, meant separation from him and being alone. It is so important for her to be connected that while she can venture her opinion in "helping" others, expressing her own independent thoughts about her husband is to her divisive and threatening.

Another patient complains bitterly that she needs two solid weeks by herself to complete her research for a novel which she is writing. She is spending a lot of time trying to find an appropriate school for her youngest child, who needs special placement, and she is driving her oldest child to school during the time period, early in the morning, when she works best. One of the reasons she is doing this is that she wants to spend time with her son, and this is when he is available. Her husband also wants to spend time with her and wants her attention. This patient is being pulled into two directions by forces of equal strength; she has not yet learned to combine both powerful needs. This conflict results in eruptions at her family, at times, and feelings of inadequacy and self-blame because she is not being as productive as she would like to be.

INTEGRATION OF AFFILIATIVE
NEEDS AND AUTONOMY

The therapeutic issues in treating women revolve around the dichotomy between autonomy and nurturing. It is important for women to recognize that it is possible to have ideas, opinions, and interests of their own — even contrary to those of a significant other person — to be autonomous and still remain connected. A woman is not negating a relationship by becoming a person with her own thoughts and feelings, even though it is important to be aware that independence for her may change the balance of the relationship. It is also important to understand that once issues are made clear, a rupture is not always inevitable; in fact, choices can emerge that may lead to compromises and can improve the relationship significantly.

Some women may want the right to be independent and prefer no lasting affiliations. Others have to accept their need for relationships *and* autonomy; they will have to learn to live with this conflict. To do so, women must feel good about themselves as people whose ideas are unique and valid. Menaker (1982) points out that incorporation of and identification with the mother is crucial for the development of the female. The mother who denigrates herself because of a lack of value placed on women by society passes these values on to her daughter, who cannot grow up feeling self-respect and self-love. This kind of personal history, plus society's reinforcement of those feelings, can only result in self-devaluation. With changes in society and new ego ideals, it is now possible for women to identify with and incorporate more acceptable standards of self-regard.

Finally, in our society choices have to be made regarding raising children and women's participation as caretaker and nurturer. While changes are slowly taking place and more men are being permitted to become involved as an interested parent, the Utopian androgynous society in which male and female share equally in child care does not yet exist. Realistically, until society changes, a therapeutic goal for women is to enable them to deal with the conflict of relationships while remaining authentic in thought and action. Until these conflicts are resolved, children of mothers who are caught in the double bind of autonomy versus nurturing will continue to be the visible symbols of their mothers' conflicts.

SUMMARY

In the 1930s, Freud wrote about the importance of preoeidpal relations, with particular emphasis on the significance of the mother-daughter dyad. Around the same time, following the lead of Ferenczi, the Balints published on the same subject. Klein and others followed, each interpreting the mother-child dyad according to their own orientation, but emphasizing the importance of this preoeidpal relationship. Object relations became incorporated into psychological theorizing and a part of the psychoanalytic framework. While castration anxiety, penis envy and the Oedipus complex remain intact as the crucial conflicts around which personality and character develop, most theorists accept that these psychic struggles can be influenced by the quality of early object relations. It is to be noted that very little in the way of social or cultural change has affected the manner in which these constructs are understood, and the male continues to be the standard by which female behavior is interpreted.

By examining the conflict of autonomy for women, it is seen that this is a uniquely female conflict in Western civilization. Beginning with the close relationship between mother and daughter, the female develops inclinations toward affiliations with people and falls easily into the role of nurturer. However, autonomy promoted as highly valued evidence of maturity and self actualization, is in opposition to the cultural expectations of the female as caregiver. The female is once again caught in the classical double bind of opposing expectations and denigration of her role in whichever direction she turns.

Current thinking is turning toward the direction of viewing women as unique and distinct from men with a psycho-social-sexual development of their own. Affiliation and attachment are regarded as progressive rather than regressive and maternal ties are considered to be positive and supportive rather than symptomatic of dependency and separation anxiety. Women are being encouraged to develop according to their own potential.

The level of self awareness which has come about in the last two decades is encouraging. More choices are open to women in terms of motherhood and/or career, but the Zeitgeist has not yet made it possible for women to pursue either course without superego constraints or identity conflicts. In whichever direction they choose to go, psychoanalysts can help resolve some of the conflict by enabling women to accept the necessity and the rewards of relationships.

REFERENCES

Applegarth, A. (1977). Some observations on work inhibitions in women. In: *Female Psychology*, ed. H. P. Blum. New York: International Universities Press, pp. 251–268.

Balint, A. (1937). Love for mother and mother love. In: *Primary Love and Psycho-Analytic Technique*. New York: Liveright, 1965, pp. 91–108.

Balint, M. (1939). Early developmental states of the ego. In: *Primary Love and Psycho-Analytic Technique*. New York: Liveright, 1965, pp. 74–90.

Barglow, P., & Shaefer, M. (1977). A new female psychology? In: *Female Psychology*, ed. H. P. Blum. New York: International Universities Press, pp. 393–438.

Beebe, B. (1982). Micro-timing in mother-infant communication. In: *Nonverbal Communication Today*, ed. M. R. Kay. The Hague: Mouton, pp. 169–195.

Bergman, A. (1982). Considerations about the development of the girl during the separation-individuation process. In: *Early Female Development*, ed. D. Mendell. Jamaica, NY: Spectrum, pp. 61–79.

Bernstein, D. (1979). Female identity synthesis. In: *Career and Motherhood*, ed. A. Roland & B. Harris. New York: Human Science Press, pp. 104–123.

Blum, H. P. (1977). Masochism, the ego ideal and the psychology of women. In: *Female Psychology*, ed. H. P. Blum. New York: International Universities Press, pp. 157–191.

Bowlby, J. (1958). The nature of the child's tie to the mother. *Internat. J. Psycho-Anal.*, 39:350–373.

_____ (1969). *Attachment*. New York: Basic Books.

_____ (1973). *Separation: Anxiety and Anger*. New York: Basic Books.

Chodorow, N. (1978). *The Reproduction of Mothering*. Berkeley: University of California Press.

Dinnerstein, D. (1977). *The Mermaid and the Minotaur*. New York: Harper.

Ehrenreich, B. (1984). *Hearts of Men*. Garden City, NY: Anchor Books.

Erikson, E. H. (1968). *Identity, Youth and Crises*. New York: Norton & Co.

Fairbairn, W. R. D. (1952). *An Object Relations Theory of the Personality*. New York: Basic Books.

Freud, S. (1931). Female sexuality. *Standard Edition*, 21:225–243. London: Hogarth Press, 1961.

_____ (1933). Feminity. *Standard Edition*, 22:112–135. London: Hogarth Press, 1964.

Galenson, E., & Roiphe, H. (1977). Some suggested revisions concerning early female development. In: *Female Psychology,* ed. H. P. Blum. New York: International Universities Press, pp. 29–57.

Gilligan, C. (1982). *In a Different Voice.* Cambridge, MA: Harvard University Press.

Greenberg, J. R., & Mitchell, S. A. (1983). *Object Relations in Psychoanalytic Theory.* Cambridge, MA: Harvard University Press.

Klein, M. (1963). On the sense of loneliness. In: *Envy and Gratitude and Other Works 1946–1963.* London: Hogarth Press.

Kohut, H. (1984). *How Does Analysis Cure?* ed. A. Goldberg & P. E. Stepansky. Chicago: University of Chicago Press.

Lebe, D. (1982). Individuation of women. *Psychoanal. Rev.,* 69:63–73.

Mahler, M. (1968). On human symbiosis and their vicissitudes of individuation. In: *Annual Progress in Child Psychiatry,* ed. S. Chess & A. Thomas. New York: Brunner-Mazel, pp. 109–129.

———, Pine, F., & Bergman, A. (1975). *The Psychological Birth of the Human Infant.* New York: Basic Books.

Maslow, A. H. (1970). *Motivation and Personality* (2nd. ed.). New York: Harper & Row.

Menaker, E. (1961). Idealization and ego. In: *Masochism and the Emergent Ego. Selected Papers of E. Menaker,* ed. L. Lerner. New York: Human Sciences Press, pp. 121–131.

——— (1973). The social matrix: Mother and child. *Masochism and the Emergent Ego. Selected Papers of E. Menaker,* ed. L. Lerner. New York: Human Sciences Press, pp. 151–166.

——— (1973). The influence of changing values on intrapsychic processes. In: *Masochism and the Emergent Ego. Selected Papers of E. Menaker,* ed. L. Lerner. New York: Human Sciences Press, pp. 132–166.

——— (1975). The effects of counter-identification. In: *Masochism and the Emergent Ego. Selected Papers of E. Menaker,* ed. L. Lerner. New York: Human Sciences Press, pp. 214–224.

——— (1982). Female identity in psychosocial perspective. *Psychoanal. Rev.,* 69:78–83.

Miller, J. B. (1976). *Toward a New Psychology of Women.* Boston, MA: Beacon Press.

——— (1984). *The Development of Women's Sense of Self.* Work in Progress, Stone Center for Developmental Services and Studies, Wellesley College, Wellesley, MA.

Rossi, A. S. (1977). A biosocial perspective on parenting. *Daedalus,* 6:1–31.

Sluckin, W., Herbert, M., & Sluckin, A. (1983). *Maternal Bonding.* London: Blackwell.

Stern, D. N. (1977). *The First Relationship: Infant and Mother.* Cambridge, MA: Harvard University Press.

——— (1983). The early development of schemas of self, other, and "self with other." In: *Reflections of Self Psychology,* ed. J. D. Lichtenberg & S. Kaplan. Hillsdale, NJ: The Analytic Press, pp. 49–84.

Sullivan, H. S. (1953). *The Interpersonal Theory of Psychiatry*, ed. H. S. Perry & M. L. Gamel. New York: Norton.

Surrey, J. L. (1985). *Self-in-Relation: A Theory of Women's Development.* Work in Progress, Stone Center for Developmental Services and Studies, Wellesley College, Wellesley, MA.

Symonds, A. (1973). Phobias after marriage. In: *Psychoanalysis of Women*, ed. J. B. Miller. New York: Penguin Books, pp. 288–303.

Thompson, C. (1973). Cultural pressures in the psychology of women. In: *Psychoanalysis of Women*, ed. J. B. Miller. New York: Penguin Books, pp. 69–84.

Winnicott, D. W. (1945a). Transitional objects and transitional phenomena. In: *Collected Papers.* New York: Basic Books, pp. 229–242, 1958.

_____ (1945b). Primitive emotional development. In: *Collected Papers.* New York: Basic Books, pp. 145–156, 1958.

_____ (1963). From dependence towards independence in the development of the individual. In: *The Maturational Processes and the Facilitating Environment.* New York: International Universities Press, pp. 83–92, 1965.

9 Lesbian Choice:
Transferences to Theory
RUTH-JEAN EISENBUD

TRANSFERENCE TO CLASSIC THEORY

Lesbian choices provide a touchstone for understanding the impact of new feminist thinking on classic psychoanalytic theory and treatment. In the 1982 *Annual of Psychoanalysis*, Leo Rangell discussed the effect of "transference to theory" incurred in the analyst's training. A transference, a lag between theory and practice, is reflected in psychoanalytic treatment of Lesbian choice. When I compare my essays of 1969 and 1982, my own writing also reflects this "transference to theory."

True, my positive transference to the theoretical framework of my early training and my own psychoanalysis had reinforced my feelings as a feminist and a humanist, but some theoretical assumptions inherited from classical psychoanalysis and patriarchal dogma were still unquestioned. The liberal Freudian framework within which I was treated and then studied and worked, from graduate school on to teaching and writing, had proven to be nourishing, enabling, and instrumental. The effect of transference to classic theory proved both positive and negative.

Much of the conceptual framework of my analysis and training still informs my work: the importance of ego development, the relationship of personality and symptoms to both outer and inner reality, the devout attention owed to both the present and to the personal historical past alive in the unconscious, in dreams and in the present. The purposeful nature of unconscious thinking, the many options of developmental choice in fulfillment of sexual needs, the important defensive nature of the ego's struggles, specific imprints of infancy and childhood traumas, early struggles for individuation, and adolescent conflict over autonomy are all still sources of understanding.

Revision: 1969 and 1982

In relationship to homosexual choice, a perseverative loyalty to a definition of homosexuality as anxiety over heterosexuality came out of my transference to theory and professional commitments. This explanation was embedded at an oedipal level as in both classic Freudian and patriarchal thinking. This "liberal" explanation of Lesbian choice as entirely a defense against oedipal inhibition, as an escape from the prison of its unfulfilled affectional and sexual longing, was dramatized in my essay in 1969. The theory then seemed to me entirely compatible with the respect, attention, and empathy with which I related to the Lesbian woman patient, a member of the persecuted minority.

Although a revisionist in my work as an analyst, already well aware of the Freudian phallic-centered account of female penis envy and aware too of the effect of patriarchal bias on the developing female personality, I had remained oblivious to the chauvinistic nature of application of certain classic dynamics to explain primary Lesbian choice. I was held back from reappraisal both by the positive transference I felt towards my generative home of psychoanalytic theory and because I had not yet integrated the new conceptualizations of "internalized objects."

Specifically, theoretical reliance on the concept of "regression" embedded in the old energy theory obscured clear observation and new understanding. Paradoxically, in 1969, my theoretical focus on the mother-infant diad as a fixation point itself led to neglect of preoedipal experiences of the little girl with her mother and the importance to her of individuation from mother. Other preoedipal libidinal experiences with mother and other people in the environment were also discounted (Loewald 1980).

There was a third explanation besides the oedipally based regression one and the one of inherited highly specific genetic determination of object choice. This was the belief that human sexual response is a learned behavior dictated by society and culture and not at all determined genetically or by innate drive in its timing. This third, "cultural," hypothesis, in view of the programmed sexual behavior of the rest of the animal kingdom, seemed even less tenable than the others. It involves a lofty denial, avowing that the urgent nature of sexual love, the overevaluation of the love object, the whole cycle of animal procreation behavior clearly integral to mating is in no way genetically, biologically programmed. In 1969, as reductionist as the regression fixation hypothesis itself might be, Lesbian love seemed best described as a regression under stress to an oral fixation in infancy.

Comparison of my "backward" paper on female homosexuality in 1969 and my recent extensive article in 1982 reflects the considerable revision and new understanding of most psychoanalytic thinking. In 1969, however, certain theoretical assumptions inherited from classical psychoanalysis were generally unquestioned in psychoanalytic theory and were still lagging far behind general practice.

From a feminist point of view we can define such perseveration as phallic centered. Female sexuality from a patriarchal point of view is defined as a response to the male. In Victorian days, in theory, female sexual arousal "normally" awaited male seduction or was awakened on the wedding night. Psychoanalytic observation took notice of male and female early libidinal feelings and inner fantasy but centered all early female genital desire on the wish to possess a penis. Penis envy was appointed the forerunner of oedipal arousal. Mother had a *lack*. Her fate, alas, was masochistic, so the little girl turned to father for a prized alliance. If she could not be a boy (of course, her primary wish), she could have a boy!

Nonetheless, oedipal feelings are predictable enough to allow us to infer an innate, genetically programmed tendency to mate; the "selfish" gene programs reproduction of our species. Certainly sexual romantic behavior is choreographed according to social prescription and example, to outward seduction, to fantasy, and, we must now admit, to ego aspiration as well. In fact, sexual genital response is quite diversely available to the ego in a search of pleasure in its struggle for survival or for self-destruction, and, we conclude, in primary Lesbian choice.

In 1982, I could hypothesize that sexual romantic object choice could be achieved as a precocious convergence of sexual impulses and same sex turn-on during preoedipal years. I could further posit that a precocious turn-on of sexual attraction to mother was the result, not the cause, of the little girl's yearning for a secure bond. This progressive, not regressive, turn-on, is a truly primary datum for sexual Lesbian preference. It is this first and enduring preoedipal internalization of romantic, sexual yearning for relationship that results in the programming operative in later life.

Use of the concept of regression in this context has precluded new thought of a primary Lesbian choice at the preoedipal level. Mechanical dependence on the male egocentric perception of classic theory and its energy view of dynamics led to the conclusion that the Lesbian ego was in a state of "regression." Therefore, one might predict the presence of an unresolved neurotic conflict, the sure result of repression of higher natural wishes and natural forward path of development. Both the choice and adaptation, therefore, were, predictably, "neurotic."

There were useful feminist aspects of the 1969 article on "The Sweet Enfranchisement of Lesbian Choice." There was respect for courageous new values, attention to feelings and life style, and empathy and appreciation for the experience of the Lesbian woman. My approach in that article was contextual and developmental. Following Frued, I could view the adaptive homosexual choices of the ego as a positive struggle for fulfillment.

In 1969, my treatment of Lesbian fantasy and role playing was particularly feminist in outlook: I thought of the oppression of a patriarchal society as its cause. Sex and gender had been little differentiated in the literature at that time (Stoller, 1975). In conventional heterosexual society and in analytic theory, gender role played by the male and gender role played by the female seemed to many an intergral, even biologically based part of sexual relationship. I pointed out that much Lesbian fantasy and role playing were built on acceptance of the dominant patriarchal decision that specific object choice was inherent in biology — anatomy was destiny. To obtain her sexual fulfillment without literal possession of male procreative anatomy, the Lesbian lover felt she must retreat in discontent to a fantasy world for the assigned gender roles.

I wrote in 1969:

Critical study must be prefaced with recognition of negative social pressure, both in reinforcement of regression and in the genesis of anguish, shame and anger. Because the neurotic conditions for satisfaction impose a narrow world, escape is sought in many ways, in fantasy and pretense [p. 247–48]. . . . One of the most striking and central characteristics of Lesbian life is the extent to which fantasy, illusion and make-believe are practiced. Being a boy is a fantasy, and sharing the belief with at least one other person that one possesses a penis is a double fantasy. One surrenders to the pretended boy partner while playing the baby and pretending the partner is the self, and thus one pretends that one is oneself a boy. One partner is the beautiful woman for both, and one the man for both, each very afraid to be insufficient to the other's projections. . . . The action in the homosexual dramatic script, is much less directed by biology and much more available to projection than heterosexual love [p. 259].

Where women in a Lesbian orientation in 1969 turned to enacting fantasies of male and female gender roles in order to find "a place" for romance and sexuality, today women with Lesbian orientation have new sanctions from their own group for their sexual orientation and, from the feminist cultural revolution, an escape from a narrowly prescribed gender role. Today there is less identification with the aggressor, much less make-believe drama of courtship and role differentiation. The chosen roles are far less stereotyped. We also note that "regressive play" and make-believe are indeed part of relaxation, transformation to early years, and sportive inclinations of homosexual and heterosexual lovemaking alike.

It must be admitted that the regression theory and classic approach as I accepted it was seriously misleading. Value judgment and distortion entered as a prejudgment. This was particularly true of my reductionist approach to the "compulsive" nature of Lesbian love and romance. I discussed these strong primitive feelings when present in nonconforming choice as an addiction, a repeat of infant fixation rather than as an attribute of minority living. My theoretical assumption of regression was further used to "explain" Lesbian ambivalence towards self and self-hate. In turn, such ambivalence toward the self seemed, in circular fashion, to validate classic theory.

The assumption of a set biological script of object choice and biological programming of sexual roles leads to serious errors. I quote from my paper of 1969: "Again, ambivalence is built into the Lesbian relationship and its narrow confines, because of all the ego has surrendered in the flight from womanhood. . ." (p. 260).

In that article, the concept of addiction brought forth intellectualized musings on built-in inferiority. "Perhaps the same ego weakness that determines an addiction to drugs or alcohol enters in the decision of whether or not, once seduced, the woman will continue with Lesbianism as a way of life" (p. 253).

In 1982, I hasten to add, I readdressed the question of why one woman adopts one solution as basic, while another avoids or rejects it, but this time in terms of the strength of preoedipal strivings. At that time recognition of the child's early strength in intellectual and emotional striving, her power to transform, the independence of mind needed for a nonconformist stance could even be recognized as determinants in a primary Lesbian choice.

In "The Sweet Enfranchisement" (Eisenbud, 1969), however, somehow I was sure that "the hypothesis that homosexuality is a defense and that its true definition is anxiety over heterosexuality, is insufficient. Homosexuality is rather enfranchisement from frustration and neurotic deprivation" (p. 251). I was still unable to go into

the choice as being earlier than oedipal or even as nonmale centered!
In the 1982 article, enfranchisement from frustration and neurotic
deprivation in preoedipal days and ego initiative provided the key to
the primary nature of basic choice.

Two discussants had been invited to comment on the 1969 article,
and both hated it (Eisenbud, 1969). Max Deutscher faulted it for its
dependence on the concept of regression. He reminded the reader of
the (to him essential) point, of mother-child interference with autonomy and the little girl's need to break with such a mother and be
Lesbian, in a sense to want to be a boy and not-mother. But
Deutscher chose a determinant related only to the vicissitudes of
socialization, common to both sexes and found in all human neurosis.
Possibly his own transference to an interpersonal theory of sexuality
entailed the disparagement and belittling of the romantic and specific
female sexual aspect of the same-sex choice. In contrast, the discussion by Bernard F. Reese faulted the paper primarily for its emphasis on neurotic addiction. He found its most grievous fault to
be its generalization of Lesbian adjustment as neurotic rather than
"natural."

Deutscher was angry at any distinction between primary and later
Lesbian explorations. He dismissed bisexuality as a ridiculous mis-
conception. Reese's transference to the theory of inherited biological
preference at that time seemed to make him seek and find my "male
point of view" in the article, nor would he admit any specific choice
particular to the Lesbian woman. Woman was not to be differentiated from man except for choice of object. In 1969 I could see
Deutscher's and Reese's transferences to their social and genetic
hypotheses respectively, but I did not realize how pervasive were my
own transferences to theory, clearly noticeable to them.

A Lesbian patient with whom I was working at the time was
shown the earlier article by a mutual colleague. The patient and her
partner had previously decided that I must be gay myself or I could
not show such empathy and understanding. They now shared the
1969 article and hurt and angry, strongly disagreed. In the end, my
patient (and her lover) decided to forgive my failure of taste and
enlightenment, and we continued our work together. In effect, they
forgave my prejudiced "straight" thinking and treated it as a temporary regression to an early fixation.

After twelve more years of experience with intensive psychoanalytic psychotherapy, and discussion with feminist thinkers and
Lesbian thinkers, I was encouraged to make a try at explaining basic
Lesbian choice as a primary positive sexual turn-on imprinted in
preoedipal years. Finding its origin in the little girl's early years

without a disclaimer or reduction attested to the Lesbian woman's own sense of the primary reality of her durable preference. Protest in poetry, in story, in personal statement, avowed the primacy of their choice. At hand was the conceptualization of the "object relations" school, which suggested a pluralistic dynamic storehouse in the unconscious, rather then the classic Freudian energy model. Moreover, new feminist thinking sponsored reappraisal and a female psychology. Without vilification by the culture, thinking about genesis of Lesbian choice was not confined to a dichotomy between a biological genesis and a neurotic flight or reduced to a learned social orientation.

In graduate school Robert W. White had been an important influence in resolving my transference to theory. He provided not only sponsorship of my own exploration of feminine psychology, but also profound feminist understanding and a model for quiet, clear, nonselfreferential reassessment. His work on "effectiveness" showed remarkable liberation from both positive and negative transferences to theory (White, 1963).

Much of my own work as a professor in postdoctoral training programs has centered on dreams and unconscious fantasy. The great importance of the context of personal lives in understanding dreams has reinforced my contextual thinking. Description of the "D state" of dreaming, and of the ego's use of the D state for diverse purposes in dreams (Jones, 1970) was an important stimulus to my new theory of early determinants. My suggestion that the ego in the preoedipal time could use sexual feelings in its struggles for relatedness and autonomy followed the dynamic of the ego's use of the D state, as Jones had described it, for conflict resolution in dreams. I was able to suggest that the little girl's ego could transform her cry for mother's care and mother's inclusion into a precocious sexual yearning and courtship of mother. Or, by an active stance of courtship in the interest of individuation, she might transform her passive surrender to mother's incorporation into its reversal. I quote Jones:

> In speaking of dream formation, therefore, we are on more solid ground if we accustom ourselves to thinking of the dream work as more transformative than distortive. The resulting transformations may subsequently be understood by the waking psyche in ways that make them classifiable as disguises, but they may be understood by the waking psyche in ways that make them classifiable as revelations, or expressions or inspirations or compensations, or creative insights, or what have you [p. 124].

Feminist thinking insisted on a reappraisal of the phallic-centered descriptions of women in classic psychoanalysis. My own reassessment of transference to a theory and discussion with feminist thinkers and Lesbian thinkers have supplied validation of an early basic female choice.

In writing and in personal statement, Lesbian women avowed the primacy of their choice. With less vilification by the culture and a new place won by their own social movement, thinking about origins was less confined to a political dichotomy between genetic predetermination and a free social decision. Finding the genesis in the little girl's early years provides a foundation for that sense of primary reality and durable preference.

CONFRONTING THE NEGATIVE

Men created the image of dread Lillith, the phallic, castrating woman, and images of Lesbian women still reflect this dread stereotype. The Lesbian woman is often selectively perceived as revengeful, competitive with a male, possessive and sadistic with a woman victim. The analyst with a feminist outlook both refuses the classic reductionist understanding of Lesbian choice as one of regression and fixation and also shuns any "vilification" that might give aid and comfort to the bigot. Sometimes the liberal analyst, in order to deny any negative, turns to theories of moral exoneration. Difficulty in dealing with Lesbian destructive hate or fear or insecurity create a strong preference for elevating benign theories. This kind of protective analysis is especially defensive, because by the new rules of mental health land, if you are not elevated and transcendent, then you are sick, borderline, impaired, or, worse "empty."

We have discussed a positive choice of same sex. What part do early internalizations of negative objects play? We need to confront distrust, claustrophobic fear, flight, competition, overevaluation, disgust — feelings toward the male and his approaches, toward the self, and toward other women. We must also admit the frequency of ambivalence in sexual orientation. Preoedipal fondness and delight in the male or ongoing strong oedipal attraction, masochistic or not, are stored internally.

A fashionable diagnosis today is to "explain" both these negative feelings and bisexual conflict as "fear of intimacy." To do so is to describe these feelings as an entirely defensive maneuver. Even if every choice of a same-sex love object were properly described as anxiety over heterosexuality, the catchall diagnosis "fear of intimacy" would still evade recognition of very real, intimate, and even wild negative feelings. The label "fear of intimacy" not only supports a diagnosis of a deficit in the ego's ability to experience object love, but suggests an assumption that there is a genetically "natural" specific object choice for the woman. Were Lesbian choice "unnatural," then we must choose among the burnt child hypothesis, genetic specific predetermination, or our new diagnosis of an impaired ego, inability to experience consistent choice or real object love. A primary, positive, early forward choice is itself precluded when we preclude traumatic negative feelings and defense against them.

Within the wider context of exclusion from mother as a determinant of Lesbian romantic choice, we reconstructed three specific etiologies somewhere between the ages of 18 months and 4 years (Eisenbud, 1982). The first is exclusion from being mothered, a struggle for a way in by turning on. The second is exclusion from identification with mother; for instance, the double bind when the child is "supposed to be a little girl, her gender is feminine, but she is supposed to be active, independent, self-reliant, nondemanding, and a support to her mother" (p. 101). In this second etiology, "punished for her activity, her independence, and her lack of affectionate behavior, the daughter becomes reserved and tough. Finally she suffers a sense of burning injustice and a need for flight or fight" (p. 101). The third etiology is a question of individuation. Her ego is threatened by engulfment by mother. The little girl seizes the intiative and reverses their positions by her own sexually aggressive courtship.

In all three of these briefly reviewed etiologies, the father must come into conscious focus at a very early age for urgent purposes. What kind of an object will he be? How will turning towards him for care or seeking him for a rescue be internalized? Will he be eligible for nurturance, needed when the little girl is excluded from mother? Will he be eligible for identification when she is put in a double bind? Will he be eligible for a rescuing presence when she is engulfed? An abusive father does not afford nurturance; an exploitative or dissolute or pitiful father does not provide the ego ideal that is needed to break symbiosis with mother, or truth and justice to sanction such resolution. A compromised father does not provide rescue or support or sponsor individuation. These fathers, and experience with fathers as bad objects, result in an internalized bad relationship to the male and the self. Internalization of ineligible fathers, of bad images of father, reinforce sadism, masochism, and dependence on the primary love of mother, as does internalization of a cruel mother.

Negative internalizations of men are reflected in many Lesbian dream images. In one, a group of women refuse to go on a trip on an

old plane because it stinks of vomit. In another, the dream of a
Lesbian woman who throws back the bedcovers so she and her
woman partner can climb into bed, there is the image of a dirty pair
of man's underwear beneath the bedclothes. The dream of father as a
somber enemy, formally dressed, going in a taxi to a funeral, speaks
of a formidable superego rejection. In another, a large boat pulling
out of a narrow channel to disappear out to sea, leaving a weeping
crowd, presents an ineligible abandoning father. In another, a group
of cruel, sadistic young men victimize a woman who walks out of a
house; it is not safe to leave mother. In another, men are marching,
but only their regimented, compromised feet show in the dream, as
they submissively surrender initiative and individuation. These
males provide no example of emancipation and are a hated threat. If
the mature Lesbian woman can find the place she seeks and a sexual
and emotional bonding with a loving woman, she can counteract the
internalized exclusion of bad mothering. But what can mitigate her
internalized anger at an internalized ineligible father, his abandonment, her disappointment, even his sexual abuse?

The stress of such internalization of father is intensified in the little
girl by the defeat of her various strategies to find someone eligible to
turn to. Her strategies may include dedication to unselfishness, the
role of a perfect femme, a maternal role, or the role of a she-devil.
Feared or idealized as father may have been, or seduced as she may
have been by father, she has repeatedly sought to earn his sponsorship. Repeatedly defeated, she will have identified with the aggressor and hated herself. Without even the fantasy of a future script
of romance and marriage and procreation with a father-man, she is
seriously discontented.

How can she reconcile her discontent and positively accept civilization? Even if she is strengthened by other good love, what will be
the vicissitudes of her internalized hate (Werman, 1985)?

With yet so real a persecution of her Lesbian choice as our society
affords, what transformation on her part can support her acceptance
of a patriarchal society and save her golden energy for positive goals
(Freud, 1930)? We must confront and study the negative and its
processes. When it comes to "the waning of her oedipal" rivalry, her
love, or her idealization of father, how will her "emancipatory
murder of father" take place without masochism or sadism (Loewald, 1980)? Denial of inner sadism and masochism by her or us
does not lead to emancipation. It even can lead to acting out of
sadism and masochism.

She herself, without denial, can achieve something. Within the
sanction and protection of a new cultural revolution, she calls others
to her, into her own community, a separate country. No longer in

search of a place "just for two," more and more she creates an "enclave," an extended second choice family and support circle, away from murder and protected from suicide. These new enclaves require a fair degree of civilization in order to emerge and survive as a positive resolution. Within them the Lesbian is committed to the preservation of personal sexual freedom, privacy, and caring responsiveness. The civilized enclave aspires to fulfill some of the basic needs that marriage offers: a constancy of object love, generative investment in the nourishment of life, allies in maintaining autonomy in the face of outer dangerous invasion or inner interchange of state.

Gilligan (1982) describes the gender difference of woman's morality in general as "a different voice," a belief in an instrumental, helpful web of nurturance and protection. She contrasts it with man's gender concern with individuated achievement and status. Her adult perceptive pen describes the kind of web of loving responsive care that the new Lesbian Enclave observably seeks to create. Gilligan's sponsorship of an elevated, different woman's voice speaks of dedication to a socialized, almost utopian level of relationship. Its utopian nature gives us pause — how can we get there from here?

A kind of negative transference to theory takes place in us as Gilligan sponsors women's devotion to the net of responsible caring. Although she clearly includes developmental variations, her moral vision can be heard as a familiar assignment of woman's place. She seems, in transference, to negate by association women's fight to overcome (selfishly) in the name of law and justice. Must equality wait upon the "withering away" of the patriarchal state?

As we read Gilligan, it also gives us pause that the patriarchal world has long devoutly acclaimed the caring value system for women as highly desirable, if morally inferior. It too willingly celebrates the mirroring little girl, the mother angel in the house, the unselfish and doting grandmother. The patriarchal world has quick positive transference to a reassertion of this "different voice."

Such morality as Gilligan delineates in women undoubtedly exists, and, in the balance, there is real creative satisfaction and a satisfyingly crucial role in civilization to reward her. Perhaps if we listen with positive transference to this responsible, loving voice, we might even stop what Virginia Woolf, in *A Room of One's Own*, calls "the glorious wars of history" and save us all from annihiliation! But negative transference warns the feminist clinician that there is a trap to such idealization and serious danger in group suppression of individuation and militant appeal to justice.

From a feminist point of view, from a Lesbian point of view, from a psychoanalyst's point of view, what are the vicissitudes of this benign projection of sisterhood and of the aspiration to a Lesbian

Enclave that exemplifies it? Denial of sadism and masochism, of rage and self-hate, may obscure or decry or tranquilize feelings that need recognition and resolution. We must acknowledge two separate value systems within woman, two disparate values. There is inner conflict between her own values as well as between hers and those of the patriarchal world that she has internalized. She needs to integrate desire for being female and caring with a fight for individuation.

The Lesbian woman's power, status, possessive sex, and greed must all be reckoned with somehow. Conflictual destructive feelings must be allowed room, if a creative enclave is to survive. In the twenties, discovery, that "the little lady wants to be bad" (as Eddie Cantor sang) admitted sexual and aggressive needs within the woman. Now we acknowledge that woman wants to be effective, be part of the hierarchy, even be president. We must also realize that often in conflict with competition for power and freedom, there are feminist and Lesbian needs to be maternal, caring, and responsive. The Lesbian woman has long had to cope with such anxious conflict in the cause of her special counteractive struggles.

When Gilligan (1982) evokes the myths of Demeter, goddess of fruitfulness, and of Eve in the Garden of Eden, she uses these metaphors to illustrate the natural rhythm between nature's nurturant summer and the cold, competitive winter of individualistic striving. However natural these systems, in both stories that Gilligan invokes — where Eve bites the apple of knowledge and where Persephone tastes the juicy pomegranate seeds — there are dire consequences to lust. Ceres (or Demeter) rages when her daughter, Persephone, is taken away by Pluto to the underworld, and Ceres' raging discontent makes winter. Eve is expelled with Adam forever from the Garden of Eden, and a sword guards against return. Gilligan's insightful summoning of the different moral voice of women from its exile by men calls us to her round table, in some sense like King Arthur's call for chivalry. Lesbian aspiration in creative, loving enclaves and new alliances encounters conflictual experiences of disruptive, "unwanted oedipal" murderous feelings, disturbing bisexuality, preoedipal struggles for individuation and flight from oppressive intimacy.

Stoller (1975) asks, in a chapter entitled, "Sex as Sin," is sex sin? He suggests that sex is declared to be sin not only as a power maneuver of economic class or church or patriarchal rule, but in the interests of civilization. Sex, he suggests, does represent individualistic antisocial striving. He reminds us that the most impassioned love is antisocial and of the thrill of release of woman or man's assertion of self in defiance of civilization.

Women and men are symbolic animals when it comes to aggression and sex. Unlike other animals, we are able to kill within the species because we can symbolically declare an individual or group the enemy and experience them, in effect, as a different species. We can deny any empathy and understanding to another point of view. In the struggle against identification with the aggressor, women and men continue to sanctify aggression by selective perception. Lesbian dreams, like all our dreams, reflect these complexities, this clash of egotistical and social aspirations, this bloody anger. The dreams also reveal profound commitment to rescue and mutual protection. Lesbian dreams reflect the ongoing danger of engulfment and surrender in life and, in transference, surrender to outer forces.

Myers' (1977) analysis of dreams and of transference reflects our modern emphasis on a relativistic cultural point of view, the reality of outer stress, and on the "contribution from all elements of the psychic apparatus" (p. 217). Although he reports working with dreams about interracial experience between the black patient and the white world, and the interracial positions of analyst and patient, he contributes to our understanding of Lesbian dreams and straight therapists as well. The position of the black minority, on the basis of color, has much in common with the Lesbian minority position on the basis of sexual orientation. Myers discusses (1) how the significance of black and white colors in dreams differentiates analyst from the original object; and (2) how the dreams reflect parental structuring of early family and social conflicts along color lines. Perhaps most important of all, Myers establishes that an ego that splits into good and bad self-images, as reflected in the use of color, need not be called "borderline" but does provide a mirror of a culturally degraded self-image. These insights relate to two dreams of a Lesbian patient.

Kim is in her early thirties at the time of these dreams. She has been in psychoanalytic psychotherapy for a year at home in Philadelphia and has now moved to Manhattan. She is a successful professional woman, a stock broker and market analyst, and Lesbian in sexual orientation. Kim is slender, youthful, informal, trim, delicate, with softly massed light brown hair and a quiet, responsive, equable expression. She is controlled, coordinated, and deliberate in movement. She might have been a picture in *Mademoiselle* magazine.

Kim has come into treatment because she becomes acutely anxious when alone and because she hopes to find a sexual and emotional commitment with another woman but fears that she may never attain and enjoy such intimacy. She can be passionate and romantic with a woman if she doesn't feel closed into a locked space and on trial.

She has enjoyed occasional uncommitted sex with handsome, muscular men in her own metier. She can't even imagine being married to a man and coming home in the evening to him, because she wouldn't want to live with someone who wasn't her best friend, and she could never be best friends with a man. When it comes to heterosexual love, she experiences a complete split between sex and romance.

Kim describes her mother as narcissistic, ineffectual, passive, and dependent. Her mother refused Kim maternal care, and Kim can remember her romantic yearning for and adoration of her glittering, attractive mother. As a little girl she wooed mother in vain. After seven, she was the virtual property of her father and in his care and rule. Her father was a handsome, vain, even squeamish lady's man, an entrepreneurial salesman who sang as cantor in the synogogue in West Philadelphia and lived for his performances. Until he deserted the family when Kim was in her teens, he dominated her physically and morally. She remembers telling a cousin how her father would lock the door and warn her about the dangers of men and expose himself to her to explain what dreadful, disgusting things men would require of her. She cannot remember now what happened inside the room, and she wonders if he really could have done it. When she asked her mother about it, her mother replied, with *belle indifference*, that yes, he had taken her into the room and locked the door, and she had often wondered what they could be doing in there.

Kim remembers wakeful nights and crying at the age of seven and after, wondering if she had been selfish that day, and how to be a good girl. Her father demanded perfect success at school, obedience, and unselfish female concern for his feelings. When she told him of her intention to obtain higher education and get a Ph.D. in economics at Penn State, he said no, she should be a teacher, that it was a better profession for a female. She took that to mean that although she must be a credit to him like a boy, she must not compete with him. Nonetheless, she went on to study and obtain her degree; with lonely, intense effort she fought her way up.

Kim remembers being frightened and intimidated by her parents' discipline of her older brother's unregenerate, impulsive conduct and by her mother's frantic attacks on him. Intense pity for her desperate brother led to further unselfishness on her part in relationship to sibling abuse and again closed her off from mother as a court of appeals. She is still protective and maternal towards him.

Her mother called her "stonehead" because she was perfectionistic and insisted on the literal truth and careful responsibility. When she entered her teens, her father left her mother and joined the woman with whom he had been secretly living for years. Kim was in shock. He had claimed to be a saint; she had worshiped him, and now she despised him. He was a liar and a hypocrite, and she was determined to rescue her mother from him. She yelled at her mother and told her to fight him and demand financial help and refuse him funds. When her mother took her father back, Kim raged. How could she allow him to fool her again? Nevertheless, Kim continued to talk with him, confide in him, get his advice.

When she had completed her degree, she began a career as a broker and market analyst. She had always been gifted in math and fascinated with gambling. Now in her profession as an analyst she could woo Lady Luck successfully, although she had wooed her mother unsuccessfully. Now she competed with men within the law and according to the rules. She was allowed to protect herself and stand up for fair play in her work if not elsewhere. She had discovered love in college and a Lesbian Enclave of good friends, who helped her and shared new insights and a new philosophy with her.

Since college, mother had become a kind of girlfriend, and they had developed a confidential relationship. She "came out" to her family. Mother was tolerant and curious about Lesbian friendship and love. Her father drew her aside and warned her against Lesbian love, because she would stretch her vagina and forfeit admiration from men. He disgusted her, and she began to feel seriously judgmental of the way he had dealt with her, his distorted view of life and hypocritical intrusion.

After a heartbreaking romantic fling with a straight married woman, who returned to her husband, Kim discovered a new kind of loving, a close commitment with a Lesbian woman, eligible and caring. Kim began to feel what she considered to be a kind of homophobic revulsion for making a permanent commitment with a woman. Slowly she felt the same revulsion about sex of any kind. She loved her friend deeply and began to wish to live with her and establish a home, but grieved that she failed to turn on and could not giver her lover what her lover needed. She feared the loss of her friend but was conflicted. She wanted to be in the mainstream of life and be somebody, not be treated as a child and be excluded from the arena, and not to let her father win.

Kim had advanced in her work. She spent long hours at it and was frequently exhausted and profoundly absorbed. She overcame her anxiety when alone and no longer ran to the telephone for a net of tender loving care and communication.

She herself became indifferent and impatient with some of the small talk, the personal details, the who had said what that the network of friends communicated to each other. She felt remorse at not caring every minute, not serving their needs in turn. She expressed guilt that she had even fallen asleep late one night in the middle of an intense discussion with her lover over somebody's personal predicament! She had in a sense outgrown the missed infant care she had been seeking so desperately before. She was in a moral crisis over providing for another's similar necessity, but she found herself unmoved, weaned from symbiosis. She tried to explain her new lack of interest, always caring, shamed, and remorseful. Finally, the feeling emerged in her that she had a right to an individual stance to a qualifield symbiosis. She began to experience her claustrophia, both physically and socially, as a kind of symptom of development and growth rather than as an inability to love or fear of intimacy.

These were the problems that provided a context for the two dreams that follow. We had worked with much concern over her identity dilemma and her helpless feeling of doom. She believed that she might never find a better, more loving and enjoyable person than her present best friend but had such "performance anxiety" over sex and such narcissistic shame over failure to turn on to her friend that at times she didn't want anyone to "sex at her" at all. Just before the occasion of this first dream, she made a passionate request that I help her kill father off; she did not want to be homophobic; she did not want to lead a split life; she wanted to go ahead and declare her love and be what she was without conflict.

We could call the first dream "A Revisit Home." We see in it the old submissive self-hate. In the second dream we see a new mobilization and intention. We might call it "A Writing Alliance." Even in the first dream, one can sense the transition that is taking place. The first dream has a childish air about it, but she is without father, even though he apologizes for having left her. It serves as a kind of farewell to childish "unselfishness."

Subsequent to the second dream, there was a visit home, which ended in a dreadful fight, with Kim sobbing and shouting but defying her father and even her mother's warning to hush. Father all but hit her and screamed at her and denigrated her, and she told him she would not allow him ever to do that again. Her strongest message was "Don't tell me what I think — I know what I think."

Kim's First Dream

"I was on my way to Sissy's apartment [her sister-in-law's apartment]. I was going to a reception for my brother. On the way, I looked into a mirror and saw my face. It was malformed and ugly — I looked like a mental case. I looked down at myself and I was wearing inappropriate shorts, like a child. I went inside, and there were all guys in there, and no women. My father was apologetic; he did not come with me. In the next scene, I was in a session with you. Sissy was sitting there, listening to us. It made me uncomfortable that she was sitting there."

Associations to the dream: "I have more in common with Bob [her brother] than with Sissy. I am filled with shame at being a Lesbian. I have more in common with the guys, but I look like a malformed girl in my own eyes." We talked about her father's concern about "malformed genitals" and her own concern about unselfishness. She cried, and we spoke of her identity crisis. All the children on the block where she had grown up were boys. She now worked with men and thought like a man. She hated it when the men treated her like a child or a "mere woman" at work. "Even in graduate school, there were mostly men, no girls in the class," and the wives were not like her. They were more like JAPs, and she had little in common with them. Only with her Lesbian friends had she found "friendship and caring, and fun and activity."

In the dream Father doesn't come with me. "He didn't go with me or support me during my teen years. Unlike father, my analyst "came with me" when I moved from Philadelphia!

Sissy was sitting there listening "when I went into a session with you. I had an uncomfortable feeling about her being there and listening to what I was telling you. She was a part of me; I'm like Sissy, like my brother's wife." Kim wants to be married, perhaps like Sissy, and be part of the big world. It makes her uncomfortable with me that she has such a jealous and backward wish. She wants to get rid of the Sissy in her and go on with her own life; she is bad and ashamed to envy Sissy.

At our next session, Kim presented a second dream.

Kim's Second Dream

"You were with someone else, and I was waiting for you and took a nap. In my nap I had a dream, and I was writing it down in my dream. The dream had something to do with writing a man's name down on a nail polish bottle. To remember it, in my dream I got up out of my nap and wrote it down."

Associations to the second dream: "The man's name was a three letter name, Jim or Kim, or something. Jim is the name for a penis. I make believe now, even, that I am a boy. When I have a sex fantasy, I am the abuser, I take advantage of a girl. I had to force the name down over a nail polish bottle. Nail polish reminds me of mother. She wishes that I would polish my nails, but when I work on my worksheets, I need to keep my nails short." I asked her about her feeling that I was with somebody else. Had she been napping because she was alone and neglected by me, perhaps, as she had been by mother and by father, who "had not come with her"? No, she had wanted to nap, so that she could give me a dream. (I had asked her permission at the end of the last session to use her dream in my writing.) She felt "that if you cared enough about us to write about us, I wanted to show my appreciation and give you another dream. You must think that we are of value [meaning Lesbians] if you write about us. I pulled myself out of my nap to get up and write my dream down."

We spoke of her wish to emerge from the hypnotic events of her relationship with her father and her inferiority feelings in relationship to mother's exclusion. We spoke of the aliveness of her feeling in the enclave of Lesbian friendship. She needed to pull herself out of her silly dream and write it down, share it with me, study her life, so that she could kill off her father, so that she could escape from "unselfishness and caring" into a different kind of autonomous identity. Antisocial or not, she wanted to have sexual fulfillment with her friend for her own sake. Kim was breaking through her character armor of unselfishness, determined to find a new self and an integration of her work and love and lifestyle. She would break with her transference to the moral elevation that her father's exploitation had impressed upon her.

One would have to tell a great deal more to convey Kim's strengths, her humor, her quick, logical, conceptual mind, her real importance to her clients and family, and her mutual support and loving concern with friends. All along, in a panic or no, she had been able to think of others with sincere empathy and of herself with sportsmanship.

What had really been lacking for Kim was an internalized moral law stronger than her parents'. She had needed a moral base, a "higher" psychological frame for security and individuation. As for father, she needed to win in that "male hierarchial struggle" of which Gilligan (1982) speaks to counteract him as a still internalized exploitative ruler, to break with her identification with the aggressor. She had been subverted by female empathy. She needed me, as her therapist, to value her as an individual and decry exploitation and "write" articulately about her to herself, that is, to become her honest mirror and internalized sponsor (Eisenbud (1985)). She needed to emerge from oedipal surrender into a place in hierarchical striving and her own free early choice to love a woman.

Lesbian women, like other women, sometimes find themselves lonely and isolated in spite of friendly enclaves, strong feminine values of loving and caring, and considerable ego strength. We need to give recognition in theory and practice, to internal negative images, to oppositional anger, to new "selfish" goals, and to individualistic ambition in order to help the struggle against locked doors and inner and outer demons.

Conflict between primary investment in caring and a counteractive hate of injustice mobilizes creative solutions. For emancipation, the Lesbian woman needs to be neither sadistic nor masochistic, but on the way she needs to confront the negative.

REFERENCES

Eisenbud, R-J (1969). Female homosexuality: A sweet enfranchisement. In: *The Modern Women*, ed. G. D. Goldman & D. S. Milman. Springfield, IL: Charles C. Thomas, pp. 247–271.

———— (1982). Early and later determinanants of Lesbian choice. *Psychoanal. Rev., 69:* 85–109.

———— (1985). Women feminist patients and a feminist woman analyst. In: The *Psychology of Today's Woman*, ed. T. Bernay & D. Cantor. Hillsdale, NJ: The Analytic Press, pp. 273–290.

Freud, S. (1930). Civilization and its discontents. *Standard Edition*, 21:59–145. London: Hogarth Press, 1961.

Gilligan, C. (1982). *A Different Voice*. Cambridge, MA: Harvard University Press.

Jones, R. M. (1970). *The New Psychology of Dreaming*. New York: Viking, 1974.

Loewald, H. W. (1980). The waning of the Oedipus complex. In: *Papers on Psychoanalysis*. New Haven: Yale University Press, pp. 384–405.

Myers, W. A. (1977). The significance of colors, black and white, in the dreams of black and white patients. *J. Amer. Psychoanal. Assn.*, 25:163–181.

Rangell, L. (1982). Transference to theory. *Annual of Psychoanalysis*, 10:29–56.

Stoller, R. J. (1975). *Perversion, the Erotic Form of Hatred*. New York: Dell.

Werman, D. S. (1985). Freud's "Civilization and Its discontents" — A reappraisal. *Psychoanal. Rev.* 72:239–254.

White, R. W. (1963). Ego and reality in psychoanalytic theory. *Psychological Issues*, Monogr. 11, New York: International Universities Press.

|IV| *Female Analyst*

10 The "Impossible Profession" Considered from a Gender Perspective

_____ZEBORAH SCHACHTEL

Do gender role differences affect how we, as men and women analysts, experience our work role? My assumption is that they must. Both males and females have been socialized to carry out different functions. As Gilligan's (1982) recent work suggests, female development emphasizes empathic attachment to others, whereas male development leads to separation from the modes of feeling and experience and to a focus on objective values and aims. The work of Chodorow (1978) and others (Gornick, 1984; Schlachet, 1984; Kaplan, 1985) supports this finding. Inherent in this distinction are profound implications for the management of personal feelings. To be in empathic relatedness means being open to one's own experience and having the ability to identify "from inside" with the internal state of the other person. As compared to male development, female development inevitably entails a more permeable boundary between oneself and the other person and may also entail a less rigid boundary internally between subjective and objective states.

Males, on the other hand, must learn to control and manage feelings in order to maintain separateness and to focus on the world of ideas, things, objectives. In terms of boundaries, the male must develop a less permeable boundary (than the female) both between his

The ideas offered in this paper have been developed over time in shared work and discussion with friends, colleagues, and supervisees. I want in particular to acknowledge my appreciation for the valuable comments given me by Carol Beauvais, Susan Coates, Alice Cottingham, Barbara and Kenneth Eisold, Marie Broudy Goldstein, Laurence Gould, Florine Katz, and Fern Schwartz.

An earlier version of this paper was presented to the Psychoanalytic Society of the New York University Postdoctoral Program in February, 1984.

internal feeling state and his aims and thoughts, and between himself and his awareness of, experience of, and availability to the feelings of others.

Thus, in carrying out gender role demands, we, male and female, must learn to manage the emotional aspects of ourselves very differently. The boundary around our *person* — the vulnerable, the feeling part — must be at a different place and of a different degree of thickness, as it were, for each gender. The concept I am drawing on and to which I shall return is *role/person boundary.*[1]

This polarity, or split, in how males and females deal with feelings is partially a function of the different tasks society assigns to each gender. The system within which these roles are learned and modeled is the family system, which is the training ground for gender role development. We learn who we are to become in a gender sense in the family, and gender roles become internalized, through the family, as a lifelong and primary identity.

Although of course there is a range of definition, it is also true that gender roles are consistent for the society as a whole. For any given culture, there is very powerful agreement about "who" one is as a female, and "who" one is as a male, including the "right" ways to behave in each case. Thus, one's internal sense of gender, learned in growing up, is also reinforced at all times by others' expectations of how one should behave as a male or as a female.

Gender has been referred to as *total role.* It represents a primary role identity and supersedes work role.

> Men and women are socialized in a culture which both explicitly and implicitly defines sex roles as *total roles* and which trains individuals in these roles. A total role is one which defines a sense of self and a set of appropriate behavior, including level and kind of authoritativeness; it permeates all aspects of life, and takes precedence over other more situation-specific work or social roles if they are incompatible. Dominance and

---

[1] I am following Rice (1969) in his use of this term. When an individual takes up a role, he must create a task system that will allow him to select from the totality available to him relevant skills, experience, feelings, and attitudes that will make for role effectiveness. This is an ego function which ". . . has to locate boundaries precisely across the individual/environment boundary and between role and person. If it fails to do so, confusion is inevitable . . . in roles and in the authorities exercised in them. Authority and responsibility appropriate in one role are used inappropriately in other roles. . ." (p. 44).

independence are linked with the masculine role, while submissiveness, passivity, and nurturance are linked with the feminine. The sex-linked role conceptions are learned through socialization, primarily within the nuclear family [Bayes and
Newton, 1978, p. 8].

What is the analytic work role and what impact does gender role
have on it? I shall be examining the analytic work system, focusing
on its tasks and considering the *role requirements* for carrying out the
tasks of that system, and reviewing those in relation to gender tasks.

The perspective I shall be using in this exploration follows Miller
and Rice (1967) and Rice (1969), in which *role* is conceptualized as
being part of a task or work system, the role carrying particular
delegation or authorization to perform certain work. Within the system, roles exist in hierarchical relation to each other, carrying different levels of authority and responsibility for the task. The work is
done through a division of labor, assigned by those authorized to
manage the system. Roles and tasks have boundaries that must be
managed and monitored if necessary work is to be carried out.

Any work system places people in a *role relationship* to one another.
Roles carry *requirements* based on the task of the system, which are,
in effect, constraints on personal wishes or needs, some of which may
conflict with task achievement. Each of us bears a responsibility to
manage our person, to deal with those conflicting or inappropriate-
to-task parts of ourselves in such a way so as not to compromise the
task. One can think of this management as involving a boundary
between ourselves as persons, and the parts of ourselves that must be
used in particular ways in specific roles, what W. G. Lawrence
(1979) calls "management of oneself in role."

Since gender role socialization leads to a different role/person
boundary for males and for females, it makes for a difference in the
experience of the analytic work role for males and females. I shall be
considering some of the forces, conscious and unconscious, that are
present for the analyst, who is simultaneously a member of at least
two systems: a gender system that is lifelong and permeates deeply
into who one is, from one's own standpoint as well as that of others,
who expect one to fulfill their expectations of who one should be;
and also a work system — that of psychoanalytic therapy — which has
to draw on this gender system through transference and countertransference (in fact, could not work without it), but which has a
very different purpose and goal from the gender task system. And
not only are these complex and contradictory forces present for the
analyst, but certainly also for the patient. Thus, as Gornick (1984)
says, for a woman to become a psychoanalyst has a different meaning

than for a man to become one; and for a man to become a patient has a different meaning than for a woman.

It is perhaps worth mentioning at this point that the issue being posed in the present paper and the viewpoints cited above seem thus far to be raised exclusively by women; that the meaning and significance of gender may represent an issue which poses conscious tensions for women that are not true for men who are practicing analytic therapists. This issue will be examined further in a later section of this paper.

Among the matters being raised by women therapists are: Do women come to the role already prepared to be empathic, whereas men have to learn to do this? (Schlachet, 1984; Kaplan, 1985). Are women "credible" authorities in the role? They may not experience themselves as "credible" nor may they be regarded as such by patients of either gender (Kaplan, 1979). The issue of women evoking more regressive, preoedipal transference has been raised, though the implications of this for the level and intensity of the countertransference thereby mobilized has barely been discussed. Gornick (1984), one of the few to talk about the countertransference issues for women treating male patients, reports that in a group of four female therapists in supervision with male supervisors, these countertransferential issues were not addressed.

A common theme that various viewpoints of the writers seem to be reflecting is the profound difference in the role/person boundary for each gender as we have been socialized to perform our gender roles in the culture. To put the matter briefly at this point, women's socialization is such that much more of their *person* and personal experience is available to them; the impact of the feelings of others is taken in with more weight. Men's socialization, allowing for more separateness, leads to a greater emphasis on *role* and less on *person*. This may also mean that women experience and are given greater authority in the use of their feelings than are men, but that may at the same time leave them feeling "not in role," but rather acting only as persons. I believe that these differences may account for the fact that women rather than men are beginning to address issues of how it *feels* to take the role of analyst.[2]

----

[2]In making this broad generalization, it is important to indicate that women do not have access to *all* feelings, and men are not cut off from *all* feelings; but that each gender has greater access to certain feelings than to others. For example, women may tend to deny or overlook aggressive and hostile feelings more than men do. There is a splitting of female-associated and male-associated feelings. Thus, feelings are differentially available to each gender. Men are "allowed" to fight and be angry; women may have to deny those feelings in order to carry out nurturing roles.

For me, one further realm of experiential data has led to a power-ful awareness of the impact of gender on the authority role. In Tavistock Group Relations Conferences (Rice, 1965), designed to study gender differences in relation to authority, underlying, fre-quently dissociated attitudes toward authority become apparent. Studying the impact of gender in these conferences, one readily perceives that both males and females in groups experience male leadership very differently from female leadership. I and other wom-en who have taken on major authority roles have often felt de-skilled, incompetent, isolated, ignored; and valued only for supposed mater-nal qualities rather than for competence. The work of Beauvais (1976), Wright and Gould (1977), Bayes and Newton (1978), Mayes (1979), and Kahn (1984) corroborates my own experiences that females in nonnurturant roles are experienced more negatively than males in the same roles.

This phenomenon may be explained by reviewing the issue of *authorization*. The female gender role authorizes empathy and nur-turance. Therefore, a woman behaving in a nonnurturant role may be consistent with her work role but not her gender role.

In the following sections I will explore the tensions and contradic-tions between gender role and tasks and analytic role and tasks more fully. I shall first explore gender role and tasks and next will examine the analytic task, the role requirements necessary to carry out the task, and the system as a whole, the dyad of analyst and patient, considering issues of authorization, power, status, and levels of re-sponsibility within the system.

The final section will put together gender tasks and role and analytic tasks and role, examining and contrasting the dilemmas and congruencies for each gender.

Throughout this discussion, I shall be considering the person/role relationship for each gender in carrying out specific work roles.

Although the present paper focuses on the experience of male and female persons in the role of analyst, I have chosen to avoid the clumsiness of "his/her" formulations and shall use "he" and "his" to mean *both*.

GENDER ROLE AND TASK AUTHORIZATION

For the purpose of the present exploration I shall be looking at gender role in terms of who, as males and females, we are to become in order to carry out the tasks assigned to us, since each society assigns different roles, tasks, and also status and power to each gender. Basically, these tasks have to do with the preservation of the culture (or the management of certain basic contradictions and quandaries within it) and the teaching, through parental role modeling, of the gender configuration for the children. In societies where the family is the basic social unit, as in our own, each parent has gender-associated responsibilities for maintaining that unit. There is a division of labor, but also a division of *spheres* within the system for which each parent has primary responsibility. These spheres become *gender linked*, as will be discussed later. In any work system, the management of the internal system has less status in the hierarchy than does the role that manages the system in relation to other systems.

Gender role is related to *tasks*, which refer to the family system and its importance as a vehicle or sphere in which psychosexual and psychosocial development occurs and where the attendant conflicts can be worked on and achieve some resolution. Within any given society what one has to work through in order to achieve the "right" form of maleness and femaleness will tend to have a specific and consistent configuration. Hence, each family, despite having a different "cast of characters," must also be sufficiently consistent with other families in terms of values and role modeling to produce children able to become appropriately functional adults of either gender and ultimately to carry on the process by performing parental roles themselves.

In this sense, we may say that we all share a common set of assumptions regarding parental roles and responsibilities, based on our histories of growing up in our families. From the same (family) sources, we also derive common conceptions regarding the roles of adult (parent) and of child. These common assumptions are reinforced by other social institutions, which become significant training grounds at different developmental stages. The result is a fairly strongly defined and agreed on idea of "who" one is to be as a female and "who" one is to be as a male, what is appropriate and inappropriate to each gender. There is a reciprocal understanding as well of who or how the person of the opposite gender is to be; we constantly monitor and keep ourselves and others in role through our expectations and responses to each other's behavior. One might think of this as a process through which we feel authorized in our roles to behave in certain ways and not in others, and in which we also authorize others to do likewise. If the behavior does not accord with the expectations, the experience of incongruence is likely to mobilize tensions, perhaps anxiety, perhaps conflict, depending on what it represents or triggers in oneself. On some level this would lead to "deauthorization" to allow someone to continue to act in ways that threaten one's own idea of what is right. We shall return to this at a later point to consider the forms in which this deauthorization takes place.

What are these role and task attributes in our culture for males and for females? What are we socialized to deal with? There is general consensus about some of the main differences and fair agreement regarding the age — about three years — at which these have become so "set" as to allow the term "irreversible" to be used (see Lewis, 1976; Chodorow, 1978; Gilligan, 1982). For girls, what has then begun is the process of an identity formation based on *attachment* and awareness of others' feelings as a central aspect of consciousness and concern, leading to the formation and reinforced development of *empathy;* whereas males separate from mother, curtailing the sense of empathic tie with her, becoming more individuated in the process, with their ego boundaries, as a result, more firmed defensively (see e.g. Gilligan, 1982). Masculine identity is defined by *separation* and is threatened by intimacy, while female identity is threatened by separation. Males tend to have difficulty with relationships; females with individuation.

Females accordingly develop a concern with a morality of responsibility; males, with the morality of "rights". Women's vulnerability to adverse judgments by others keeps them from taking a stand; there is a moral injunction against *hurting;* responsibility is for *caring* (for others). Taking a stand that might "hurt" would be counter to the gender demand.

In the course of development, gender roles are associated with different stages and represent the significant aspects of the role relationship existing between parents and child in that period. The role of the mother is internalized as the primary object in the preoedipal phase and is associated with developmentally earlier needs, highlighting the mother's *expressive* functions such as that of nurturer and the one who mediates tensions and feelings in the group. The father is associated with the postoedipal stage and comes to be associated with developmentally later aspects. The male role has been characterized as representing *instrumental* functions: rational, objective, goal-oriented aspects, as opposed to feelings (Chodorow, 1978). These attributes might be conceived in terms of representing internalized authorizations for each gender, what is expected as gender-appropriate responses.

These differences in development lead to marked differences in role/person boundary for each gender. For the female, gender role is more total and primary and takes precedence over other roles, because the girl does not separate but remains in a bonded and fused relationship with the mother, identifying with and assuming aspects of the maternal role. In terms of where this places the role/person boundary, there is likely to be a blurring between personal feelings and role, since the role *is* to be available in one's person to other persons: to know *through feelings* what is going on. Males, through separation and individuation, may have to suppress or repress feelings, particularly those associated with dependency and vulnerability, in order to achieve separateness and a sense of sufficient strength to be separate. This implies that in relation to their *person*, males may be less authorized to be accessible, both to themselves and to the feeling experience of others. At the same time, they would be much more able to manage role boundaries around different tasks and to move from one role to another, which in fact is what they are trained to do as a way of managing the external rather than the internal boundary of the small group of the family. The internal management — the nurturing, caretaking, knowing-what's-going-on-in-others role — is the jurisdiction of the mother, and the role for which the girl is socialized and trained.

It is worth pointing out that the female is associated with earlier "lower," more childlike needs, wishes and feelings; whereas the male, who "leaves" this through separation, is connected with "later," "more adult," needs and certainly with the world of things, aims, objectives. Women, therefore, represent and evoke early self-object internalizations for persons of both genders. This is part of the significance of "total role," especially for the woman, who cannot escape from this definition of who she is.

Another aspect is that the gender role differentiation which has been described reflects a high degree of polarization of attributes, really a process of splitting. One might consider what this means from the standpoint of what it allows us to defend against. Through splitting and projection, perhaps we deal with the loss of what we have to give up in the process of development. In this connection, Fast's (1984) gender differentiation hypothesis is relevant.[3]

I shall not attempt here to deal further with the issue of the *why* of gender differentiation, since my primary focus is on the *that* of it, and the *how* of it, and how that affects the taking of the analytic role.

---

[3]Fast (1984) has proposed a hypothesis that gender identity formation follows the same process of differentiation as other aspects, for example, "self" and "other." She argues that initially there is an undifferentiated, narcissistic stage; then, as sex differences are recognized, a sense of one's limits, and the loss of unlimited possibility must be experienced and dealt with. This is followed by a coming to terms with the sense of loss and a recategorization of experience, an integration of what belongs to self, what to other (p. 44).

ANALYTIC ROLE AND TASK AUTHORIZATION

In this section I shall first be considering psychoanalysis as a work system having tasks, roles, boundaries, and a technology and structure for carrying out specified goals. Next, I shall take up some of the underpinnings of this system, in an attempt to understand how and why psychoanalysis achieves its end and through what means. Then, I shall consider certain differences and similarities between psychoanalysis and psychotherapy, focusing on role and task issues, in order to elucidate critical dimensions distinguishing psychoanalysis from psychotherapy. Finally, I shall explore both of these work systems with respect to role/person implications for the analyst/therapist.

Psychoanalysis is a work system having as its task the resolution of unconscious conflicts that influence one's behavior. This resolution is a process of defining, deepening, interpreting, and working through over and over again the forms that these conflicts take in the transference and in the patient's present and past life experience in interacting with others.

How is the system structured to facilitate access to these data? The structure includes the role of analyst, who is hired by the patient and thereby is authorized to manage and design the plan for the work. The analyst first and foremost becomes available as a transference object, which is crucial to the system. As such, the analyst will receive the impact of the patient's attributions of transferential meaning, both directly and indirectly, in the form of the patient's conscious and more especially unconscious attitudes, through dreams, the pattern of free associations, and the interaction between patient and analyst as they work; in each transaction and communication, there is transference.

The analyst establishes the parameters of the work system; managing and determining external boundaries such as frequency of sessions, length of sessions, fees for sessions, and the manner in which the work will proceed within the sessions. As Newton (1973) put it, the analyst institutes the role of *patient* in the system. The responsibility for the work plan and for its monitoring rests with the analyst, who manages, supervises, evaluates and in an ongoing way sustains the process of the work with the patient. The analyst, in collaboration with the patient, "hears" the unconscious themes that link the patient's dreams and free associations, which connect present manifestations with historical origins. The analyst thereby also teaches the patient *how* to work within the system.

Again following a social system model (see Miller and Rice, 1967), we can say that the *import* into the system is a person wanting help in relation to how he feels or acts in his life; the *conversion* process (which enables the *import* to produce an *export*) includes roles and the technologies provided by the system for carrying out the *primary task,* namely, an alteration in the relation of the patient/client to his internal processes; the *export* is an analyzed person, who is now aware of and independently managing his own boundary between conscious and unconscious levels of experience.

While this describes certain aspects of the structure and the role relationship, what is central is that the patient, with certain conscious ideas and hopes, is entering into a system and a relationship that will be focusing deeply on unconscious wishes, fears, and their sequelae. Through the analysis of the transference, he is about to enter into a relation to himself that will greatly expand his understanding of who he is. Thus, he is actually authorizing the analyst to carry out work that will intensify and bring into awareness feelings that may be very painful and uncomfortable, to alter the boundaries that defend against anxiety, to sanction the increase of anxiety. He is, in effect, selecting in the analyst the person to carry the transferential feelings, to be the object and eliciter, as well as the interpreter, of what the patient attributes to him or her.

In this system, while the analyst has primary responsibility throughout for the task and manages both the external boundary aspects and the internal boundary — the task of interpretation to the patient of the meaning of unconscious processes — the patient does and must come to assume increasingly greater responsibility for this work of understanding and interpretation. As Newton (1973) put it, the analytic role relationship must become an increasingly collaborative one. From the standpoint of authority and delegation, the patient authorizes the analyst to conduct the analysis, and the analyst delegates and authorizes the patient to take responsibility for recognizing and dealing with the manifestations of his resistance to the analytic process itself.

Why should this work at all? Speaking of psychotherapy, Newton (1973) argues that there is an underlying parallel between this system and the family system. I believe this model applies equally to psychoanalysis.

Psychoanalysis aims to allow the patient to reexperience early aspects of his conscious and unconscious experience of self-and-other. The analyst serves as transference object through his authority in the role and through the patient's readiness to make use of an authority figure for transference. In analysis, the patient gives up conscious control and allows fantasies and wishes to have full sway. In a sense, what allows for the transference is the difference between the fantasied relationship and the "real" relationship, to use Stone's phrase (Langs and Stone, 1980).

There is no profession I know of that places more stress on the person/role boundary than psychoanalysis. The structure of the system is such as to maximize the transference, that is, to mobilize early childhood experience and fantasy, which is fostered by the withholding of the *real* person of the analyst. Thus, frustration is mobilized and it becomes possible to focus on the unconscious processes that motivate the patient's perceptions, drives, and impulses. The analyst has to tolerate the anxiety and pressure that will be aroused both in the patient and in himself — has to be able to stand back from the experience and process it to understand and to interpret the underlying meaning to the patient of what determines his experience and behavior.

In doing so, the analyst has to hold task and role clearly in mind. The analyst must be in touch with feelings empathically but also able to maintain sufficient separateness to be an effective "observing ego." To achieve this state, the analyst himself must constantly monitor "self in role"; no supervisor in or out of the room can do that for him.

To what extent are there meaningful differences in this if the task is psychoanalysis as opposed to psychotherapy? I think the principle and the monitoring issue probably are the same; the source for either kind of work is the same. For the purposes of the present paper, some speculations are offered regarding role/person boundary issues in the analytic role as compared with the analytically oriented psychotherapy role. In the analytic setting, role predominates and person is more hidden. The analyst is, of course, working from and through his person; the experience of transferential and countertransferential material could be processed only inside the person of the analyst, but he is "protected" by stringent role boundaries. The rule of *abstinence* describes a parameter of his boundary. The task and role boundary facilitates the processing of data and presumably reduces both the internal pressure of the transference on the analyst's person and the countertransferential reactions.

The analytic role can be considered to be the more stringent in terms of rules for managing the role, although it must be noted that the different analytic "schools" reflect considerable range with respect to those rules, not to speak of the individual styles and variations particular analysts may practice in their work. In the realm of analytically oriented psychotherapy there is even greater latitude, very much depending on the way the therapeutic task is conceptualized and the treatment structured. To the extent that a psychoanalytic, psychodynamic orientation prevails, the therapist is always working with the transference and countertransference but may engage the patient in more personal ways, through person more than through role. To the extent that greater flexibility exists in role definition, which would be truer of psychotherapy than of psychoanalysis, the individual therapist has less "protection" from the rule and must make his own decisions about how and when more personal material would be expressed.

INTERACTION OF GENDER ROLE
AND ANALYTIC ROLE

In this section I consider some of the dimensions of analytic task and role I believe are affected by gender role socialization and history. I shall focus primarily on the analyst and how the analyst's gender might affect certain aspects of the management of the task. Gender itself will be powerfully meaningful and evocative for the patient and analyst, not just in terms of specific transferential meanings, but in the larger sense of being engaged in the task of analysis with a woman or with a man. I will consider some of these wider issues; then aspects of the internal task structure from a gender standpoint, particularly access to transference and countertransference; and management of the boundaries of the system, considering gender differences. I shall include examples from supervisees of both genders. At this stage of professional development, as the analyst-in-training tries to internalize the role, there is heightened awareness of person/role quandaries.

For a woman to be in the analytic role means to evoke for herself and for her patient all that is associated with female gender role — preoedipal experience, the gender expectation of maternal or female caretaking, female sexuality, conception, "having mother to oneself" — with the result that the level of experience evoked is inherently more regressed when the analyst is female.[4] The press, in other words, for both analyst and patient will be on the gender role, which means that the female analyst and her patient will be traversing a transferential/countertransferential terrain of working through differences between gender and analytic role. This is likely to be a very tense place. Women have been trained to respond by doing something to and for the other person that is different from the analytic

---

[4]Gornick's discussion of this issue in this volume is particularly relevant.

role. The female analyst, therefore, is faced with a need to monitor a lifelong gender role if she is to carry a particular other role. This makes it unavoidable that women analysts would experience countertransferential issues in a more ongoing and pressured way than male analysts would. The woman analyst is faced with the pressure to "make it better" — when the task is not that. While this is true for the woman in any work role, the particular one of analyst, pulling as it does at so many old roots and parts, requires very special differentiation and monitoring. For example, the patient's anger and resistance in the face of non-nurturance may evoke in the female analyst feelings of being "bad" and of not understanding. These feelings may lead her to collude with the patient's view of her as depriving. An example follows:

A female supervisee is working with a male patient who deals with his anger at feelings of maternal deprivation by seductiveness and sexual manipulation. The patient "misses" a session before he is to leave for vacation. The therapist offers him a make-up session; feeling guilty, the therapist wonders, "What did I do wrong?" She feels at times drawn in by the patient's seductions and comes to realize that her underlying attitude is, "I'm supposed to give him everything he needs without letting him know that." This example was given by a supervisee who shared a common ethnic background with her patient. The issue of this shared background in the experience of gender roles within the family, by patient and analyst, is one that merits further attention (Mottola and Schachtel, 1984).

In terms of her socialization history, the female analyst will also be closer experientially to preoedipal aspects in herself and in the other (and will evoke those aspects more than will the male). This also implies that the woman's greater closeness to "early" feelings leaves her feeling more exposed and vulnerable. The gender-role requirement to know and respond to the feelings of others involves for the woman a total use of her person, which may cause her to feel exposed and unbounded within the professional therapeutic role. Women can be made to feel "bad" if they don't meet the needs of the other. So the female therapist may experience greater blurring of analytic and total female gender roles. The female also, by gender and by her own history, faces the transferential (and countertransferential) conflict of "good" and "bad" mother. The female analyst may be particularly vulnerable to the patient's feelings of anger, disappointment; she may experience herself as "bad mother," as "not giving," and feel the guilt associated with those experiences on a gender level. She may feel helpless and blocked in her analytic role, isolated and alone.

While the male analyst also gets to be the "bad mother," I contend that it will *feel* different and he will feel less "bad" inside.

For women analysts, abstinence in the role refers, I believe, to withholding their almost innate drive to provide nurturance and to relieve pain, in gender-role fashion as opposed to analytic working through. The resulting tension and pressure associated with containing these tendencies is clearly stressful for women and does not come up for men in this way. A related factor concerns the tendency for women analysts to elicit or evoke dependency needs in others and therefore to be experienced both by others and by themselves as more withholding than men in their therapeutic role. This may come up particularly in the management of the external boundary issues.

Male supervisees seem less stressed by boundary issues, such as management of fees and absences, probably because they feel less pulled by the gender experience of "giving and providing" than does the female, though each gender may also try to fight the pull. It is difficult to exclude from this discussion the experience of the patient's expectation: the ending of the session may feel very different when "she" does it than when "he" does it; also "he" and "she" who are doing it may experience that expectation differently. My impression from discussion with colleagues and from supervision is that the management of the external boundary issues is particularly difficult and stressful for women and that those issues often are not managed well. It would be useful to have some basic information from analysts of both genders about this issue, as well as data for fee comparison.

In working with transferential and countertransferential data toward integrative interpretation, the female analyst will be more in touch with and more evoking of preoedipal feelings, but she may become suffused by them and pulled into a place where gender role holds sway and where separateness is difficult. She may become the container of feelings, become filled up with and absorb them, and find it difficult to be clear about transferential and countertransferential boundaries. One of the differences between male and female supervisees is that females are often concerned about what to "do" with their feelings; they talk about them, feel overwhelmed by them, are often embarrassed by them. Under the pressure of the patient's needs and feelings, they may feel pulled into expressing them and find it difficult to *think about* them (moving from feelings into formulation).

By contrast, the male analyst is likely to be experienced and to experience himself as giving, since the expectations in relation to gender do not include a relationship based on concern for feelings. Also, the impact of the patient's transferential issues and the mobilizing of countertransference would be different for the male analyst in that the distance from the feeling level of it would be greater. The male analyst, feeling more separate from the patient's demands and needs, might find it easier to see them without having to feel the same pressure to respond to them, as a female would. For the patient too there may be stronger boundaries around feelings with the male analyst, since by his gender he evokes separateness.

Still, there is inherent for the man a more conflicted position on the use and the expression of feelings, particularly preoedipal ones, which may lead to a surface that is more contained but with more "rumblings" underneath. The male analyst is in a role which asks that he be in touch with the feelings of the other and of himself. In terms of gender-role socialization, which has stressed separateness and which has demanded of him that he break the tie with mother, it means being authorized to reenter the world of feelings. But he does so having had to manage the task of repression and separation from early feelings. The impact of the other's feelings on himself, and possibly also the impact of his own needs, is filtered or perhaps blocked. At the same time, through the analytic task he may be able to rejoin the parts of himself that he has had to suppress.

Male supervisees do not usually talk about their feelings, experience less pressure to respond, but may also feel out of touch, especially when confronted with "early" dependency needs. Attempts may be made to bind the patient's powerful feelings. At times, supervisees may become confrontative or engage in premature interpretations, without grounding in the actual experience of the patient. "Talking about" may be used to defend against their affective experience. In short, the female analyst-in-training may absorb and become the receptor for the feelings, while the male analyst-in-training may be "stonewalling" the feeling, perhaps defending against the possibility of losing control.

A male supervisee treating a depressed, superficially dependent man had great difficulty allowing himself to feel the shame and neediness in his patient. He would rely on *having to have a formulation.* "I feel very mean with him when I'm with him . . . want him to be more straightforward, which puts him on the spot; he's afraid of being humiliated." This supervisee had difficulty dealing with his patient's feelings about an unpaid bill, reiterating the formal requirement as a defense against exploring his patient's feelings. The patient at one point brought the following dream: "I was a private individual, not a newspaper man, attending a pageant, writing out my comments on a computer, which was very strange. I found myself viewing things as if I were a reporter, but I wasn't. I was with a friend — a male — on a camel, a bumpy ride. He asked, 'What are you riding?' I said, 'It's a camel, I think.' The camel knew when I leaned forward I wanted 'off,' so he got down, but my foot got stuck, so the camel had to get up." He associated: "The camel is a dumb animal, but we communicated in such a way I got everything I wanted. The world ignores you unless you know the right command. . . ." The supervisee in this case would frequently find himself silent for long periods of time and out of touch with his patient's experience.

The patient of either gender working with a male analyst, and also the analyst himself, may experience the fantasy of having the man for oneself, of the intimacy of a relationship based on feelings, which for the man in the socialized gender role is more problematic. For the male analyst, there may be in the analytic role a marriage of power aspects and of feeling/task aspects that can provide particular gratification. But the opening up of the defenses that have been forged to deal particularly with preoedipal feelings may need a degree of person/role redefinition.

This may lead the male analyst to take refuge in the *role* as a way of maintaining distance from the upsurge of feelings in himself and in the patient. In this connection I find pertinent Kernberg's (1965) comment on how countertransference regression can undermine the analyst's identity in role. As already indicated, for female analysts I think this is a constant factor. For male analysts, it represents the danger of feelings breaking through the boundary of control.[5]

Related to this is another difference I have found, which I feel is gender associated: the extent to which the analyst is aware of and is talking about what he feels in the room with the patient. This is very apparent in supervision, but I have been aware of it also in case presentations made by analysts of both genders. It is not surprising that female analysts are accustomed to speaking about and focusing on the state of feelings and that male analysts are not. This is not to say that males are not aware of their own and of their patient's feelings, but that they don't find a ready voice to express it. In this connection, I have the impression that there may be a significant

---

[5]Kernberg's (1965) discussion of countertransference does not consider the gender of the analyst. In reading his paper with that dimension in mind, it seemed to me that such issues as "the loss of analytic objectivity," which he discusses in terms of work with regressed patients, might be quite commonly or chronically felt by woman analysts whose gender would evoke greater regression even in neurotic patients and who would be dealing with more intense feelings. It seems to me that exploring gender differences in countertransference would be very illuminating.

difference in the extent to which countertransferential issues come into focus in supervision, depending on the gender composition of the supervisory dyad. Note, for example, Gornick's (1984) point that male supervisors did not pick up on eroticized transferential and countertransferential issues between male patients and female analysts.

The issue of which gender is experienced as the "right" one for the analytic role is of course influenced by the power relationship between the analyst and the patient, which reflects the status and power differential for the genders in the society as a whole. In this regard I take exception to the idea that the analytic relationship can be a *peer* relationship, because the role difference between patient and analyst implies differences in authority and responsibility for the task and both real and imagined differences in power: hence, the transference. These differences in level of authority and competence evoke earlier conflicts transferentially and will be triggered by the gender composition of the patient-analyst dyad. The following example reflects the way these issues were expressed in a female patient-female analyst dyad:

A female patient presented an "adoring," gift-giving attitude toward her female analyst. The analyst initially accepted the gifts and felt valued and important to her patient. Her patient at the same time watched her like a hawk, commenting and questioning each time the analyst looked away. The patient talked about her analyst as "being a patient too" and in various ways denigrated her analyst by *reducing* her, bringing her "down to the level of being a person (i.e., patient), too." The analyst had difficulty thinking in the room during the sessions and felt deflected from interpreting the patient's communications or from exploring the dynamics of the patient's interpersonal behavior. She felt uncomfortable and "controlled" by her patient but was unable to use this experience with the patient. It was as if there were a shared feeling that she must not denigrate the patient, which would be the case were she acknowledged as analyst, a role with greater status and power.

CONCLUSION

Gender-role socialization for males and females results in different *primary role identities,* involving marked differences in dealing with one's own and others' feelings, based on gender *tasks.* This clearly has powerful implications for how males and females work at the tasks of the analytic role. Yet this issue has received very little attention in the literature until very recently, and then primarily by female writers. That lack and other issues raised in this paper suggest that the dimension of how gender might impact on analytic role has been curiously neglected in the field.

This paper has focused on certain ways these differences are reflected. Examples have been given from supervisees of both genders since "person/role" problems are less resolved in this stage of internalizing the analytic role. This represents a beginning discussion of relevant dimensions needing study and validation. I hope it will stimulate further work in this area.

REFERENCES

Bayes, M., & Newton, P. (1978). Women in authority: a sociopsychological analysis. *J. App. Beh. Sci.*, 14:7–20.

Beauvais, C. (1976). *The Family and the Work Group: Dilemmas for Women in Authority.* Unpublished doctoral dissertation, The City University of New York.

Chodorow, N. (1978). *The Reproduction of Mothering: Psychoanalysis and the Sociology of Gender.* Berkeley: University of California Press.

Fast, I. (1984). *Gender Identity: A Differentiation Model.* Hillsdale, NJ: The Analytic Press.

Gilligan, C. (1982). *In A Different Voice.* Cambridge, MA: Harvard University Press.

Gornick, L. K. (1984). *Turning the Tables: The Woman Therapist and the Man Patient.* Unpublished paper.

Kahn, L. (1984). Group processes and sex differences. *Psychol. Women Quart.*, 8:261–281.

Kaplan, A. G. (1979). Toward an analysis of sex-role-related issues in the therapeutic relationship. *Psychiat.*, 42:112–120.

——— (1985). Female or male therapists for women patients. *Psychiat.*, 48:111–121.

Kernberg, O. (1965). Notes on countertransference. *J. Amer. Psychoanal. Assn.*, 13:38–56.

Langs, R., & Stone, L. (1980). *The Therapeutic Experience and its Setting.* New York: Aronson.

Lawrence, W. G. (1979). *Exploring Individual and Organizational Boundaries.* New York: Wiley.

Lewis, H. B. (1976). *Psychic War in Men and Women.* New York: New York University Press.

Mayes, S. S. (1979). Women in positions of authority. In: *The Gender Gap in Psychotherapy*, ed. P. P. Rieker & E. Carmen. New York: Plenum Press, 1984, pp. 91–110.

Miller, E. J., & Rice, A. K. (1967). *Systems of Organization.* London: Tavistock.

Mottola, M., & Schachtel, Z. (1984). *Shared Ethnicity Between Female Analyst and Male Patient: Views from the Analyst and the Supervisor.* Unpublished paper.

Newton, P. (1973). Social structure and process in psychotherapy. A sociopsychological analysis of transference, resistance, and change. *Internat. J. Psychiat.,* 11:480–512.

Rice, A. K. (1965). *Learning for Leadership.* London: Tavistock.

———— (1969). Individual, group and intergroup processes. In: *Task and Organization,* ed. E. J. Miller. New York: Wiley, 1976, pp. 25–46.

Schlachet, B. C. (1984). Female role socialization: The analyst and the analysis. In: *Women Therapists Working with Women,* ed. C. M. Brody. New York: Springer, pp. 56–65.

Wright, F., & Gould, L. J. (1977). Recent research on sex-linked aspects of group behavior: Implications for group psychotherapy. In: *Group Therapy 1977: An Overview,* ed. L. R. Wolberg & M. L. Aronson. New York: Stratton, pp. 209–217.

11 Developing A New Narrative: The Woman Therapist and the Male Patient

_____LISA K. GORNICK

During a summertime of the early 1890s, Freud set out on a journey to reach the summit of a mountain in the Eastern Alps reknowned for its spectacular view. Upon reaching the peak, he stopped for refreshment at a beautiful inn, where, after dining, he sat lost in his thoughts, enjoying the view, until he was reluctantly interrupted by Katharina, "the rather sulky-looking girl of perhaps eighteen who had served my meal" (Breuer and Freud, 1893–1895, p. 125). Katharina inquired if the gentleman was a doctor and then promptly told Freud of her nervous condition. His curiosity piqued by the possible occurrence of neurosis so high in the mountains, Freud embarked upon questioning and then interpreting the tale told by the young girl. The one-session treatment concluded when Freud reached a point about which he stated, "I could not penetrate further" (p. 132).

In 1895, Breuer and Freud published the case of Katharina along with the cases of Anna O, Emmy von N, Lucy R, and Elisabeth von R in _Studies on Hysteria_. With this volume, the critical concepts of conflict and defense were introduced, and, it is generally agreed, the psychoanalytic enterprise was launched. At the same time, the dominant narrative of a male doctor treating a younger woman patient was set. Furthermore, the theoretical account of the mutative factors of the treatment — in which Freud argued that the essence of the treatment consisted of pitting his will against the repressive force within his women patients, at times literally pressing his hands

I would like to express my appreciation to Judith Alpert, Sidney Blatt, Faye Crosby, Terry Eicher, Jesse Geller, Ruth Gruenthal, William Kessen, Helen Block Lewis, Michael Ryan, and Jerome L. Singer for their helpful suggestions on earlier drafts of this paper. An abbreviated version of this paper was presented at the Annual Meeting of the American Psychological Association, Division 39, Toronto, 1984 against their foreheads to fight the defense mechanisms — drew heavily upon the power disparities between the doctor and his young women patients.

Imagine, however, that it had been a woman who had climbed to a peak in the Eastern Alps and had then treated the young man who served her afternoon repast. What might have happened, and what sort of theoretical account might have been developed to conceptualize the treatment process? In posing this question, my aim is not to resuscitate the now familiar arguments that Freud was a sexist or that his accounts are valid only in the context of Victorian Vienna, but, rather, to attempt to locate the ways in which male authority is assumed in both the method and the theoretical metaphors of psychoanalytic treatment. In this paper, I will suggest that when the tables are turned so that a woman looks at, interprets, and (to borrow Freud's metaphor) "penetrates" a man, the treatment will differ in significant ways from the treatment of women patients by male therapists, and that, in order to capture this difference, it will be necessary to develop a new narrative line[1] that specifically addresses the relationships of boys to their mothers and the quite different meanings of power and sexuality for men and women in our culture.

Because the dominant narrative of a male doctor treating a woman patient maintains the normative structure of men occupying positions of authority over women, the importance of the gender of the participants in the therapeutic dialogue is obscured. When one turns, however, to the work of women therapists[2] with male patients, a

---

[1]Because the concept of "narrative" will be used throughout this essay, a few preliminary comments are due. First, to speak of narratives does not imply that an account is a "made-up" story but, rather, that "what we call reality can only be presented from one or another point of view, and on this account it is necessarily a reality of a certain kind in a certain context which has been established and told for certain purposes" (Schafer, 1983). In other words, there will always be a multitude of narratives that could be constructed about an event; what is challenged is the hope of ultimately finding a final, rock bottom truth. Second, adopting this postpositivist epistemology does *not* imply that what really happened does not matter, or (to plunge into the recent stir by Masson, 1984, and Malcolm, 1983) that a childhood seduction fantasy is equivalent to an incest experience. Rather, in adapting the critique of positivism to the subject of psychoanalysis, such writers as Schafer (1983), Spence (1982), and Schimek (1983) have challenged the notion that we will ever be able to have an account of the patient's inner world that can be disentangled from the theoretical propositions that describe, evoke, and transform it.

[2]Unless otherwise specified, I am using the word "therapist" to include both psychotherapists and psychoanalysts.

relationship that reverses many of the assumed orderings between men and women, the impact of the gender of the participants on the therapeutic dialogue becomes more salient. Due to the virtual absence of attention in the literature to the work of women therapists/analysts with male patients, those aspects of the therapeutic interaction that are distinctive to this dyad have been inadequately conceptualized.[3] Consequently, the woman analyst or therapist faced with a male patient works in an environment of theoretical impoverishment in which she must either transpose from other dyads or conceptualize her work without the benefit of a rich set of hypotheses. This matters in that, as Schafer (1983), Spence (1982), Schimek (1983) and others of the "narrativist" school have argued, what happens between analyst and patient is in part structured by the theoretical apparatus of the analyst/therapist.

Nor, in examining the gender related meanings of the different positions of the therapeutic dialogue, is my aim to challenge the essentially (and, I would argue, rightfully) ideographic nature of the clinical endeavor. Individual histories undoubtedly matter more than gender, or, to put this in more social-scientific language, there is more variance within the sexes than there is between them. Rather, in turning to the case of the woman therapist and the male patient, my aim is primarily "practical": to locate the ways in which the gender of the participants in the therapeutic dialogue influences both the dialogue itself and the theoretical constructs that are invoked in order to understand how this dialogue works.

Methodology. Research in the area of gender usually begins with the question: Are women different from men? Because, as Gove (1972) states, gender is a "master variable," the answer to this question is predictably affirmative. The interesting question then be-

---

[3]What happens when a woman treats a man seems to be one of those questions that has in some subterranean fashion been ready to emerge. Since this chapter was completed there has been a notable change in the previously barren terrain, with several papers related to the topic of the woman therapist and the male patient having recently appeared in the literature. These include: J. Chassequet-Smirgel (1984), "The femininity of the analyst in professional practice"; M. Goldberger and D. Evans (1985), "On transference manifestations in male patients with female analysts"; E. Lester (1985) "The female analyst and erotized transference"; E. Person (1985) "The erotic transference in women and in men: Differences and consequences"; L. Samuels (1985), "Female psychotherapists as portrayed in film, fiction and nonfiction." Except for the paper by Lester (which was available in pre-print), I was not able to include a discussion of these recent papers in this chapter.

comes: How are the experiences of men and women different? This approach commonly leads to a comparative analysis framed within a hypothesis-testing design. Valuable as this approach can be, it frequently has at its origin an inequality of understanding that the research design fails to rectify. We usually know a great deal more about the experiences of one of the sexes; hence the variables to be examined are drawn from the stock of our knowledge about the gender for whom the experience is normative or from relatively superficial observations of the gender for whom the experience is counternormative. Furthermore, as Selltiz, Jahoda, Deutsch, and Cook (1960) state in their discussion of the rationale for formulative or exploratory studies, skipping the hypothesis-generating stage of a research program commonly results in trivial findings within the hypothesis-testing stage.

Rather than beginning with a comparative study of male versus female therapists, I have chosen as my initial research strategy an in-depth interview study of women psychoanalysts, women psychotherapists, and women in training about their work with male patients. My sample has been evenly divided between social workers, clinical psychologists, and psychiatrists, with participants chosen so as to obtain the best possible informants and to sample across the range of therapist and patient characteristics rather than to meet the criteria necessary for making statistical statements about population values. The observations reported in this paper are based on a preliminary analysis of thirteen interviews conducted during the pilot phase of the research and on published case material.

BRIEF REVIEW OF THE LITERATURE

The empirical research that has considered the gender of the therapist has been concerned largely with the effects of same versus opposite sex dyads on the outcome of psychotherapy. The consistent conclusion of researchers who have reviewed these studies is that the studies have been contradictory in their findings; have overlooked a number of important variables including therapist experience, therapeutic orientation, and length of treatment; and have contributed very little to our understanding of either psychotherapy or of the differences between men and women (Orlinsky and Howard, 1980; Cavenar and Werman, 1983).

Yet, as Mogul (1982) notes in the conclusion of her overview of the literature on the sex of the therapist, therapist gender clearly makes a difference to both patients and clinicians. Furthermore, there is some evidence that the dyad of the woman therapist with the male patient is particularly problematic. Abramowitz (Abramowitz, Abramowitz, Roback, Corney, and McKee, 1976; Abramowitz, Davidson, Greene, and Edwards, 1980; Abramowitz, 1981) has reported a widespread underrepresentation of male patients in the caseloads of women psychotherapists and has suggested that male patients may pose certain countertransferential problems for women therapists.[4]

The classic psychoanalytic position has been that the sex of the analyst does not significantly effect the analytic process in general or the transference in particular.[5] As Karme (1979) points out, resistance to the idea that there may be differences in the transference to men and to women therapists is in part motivated by a fear that any acknowledgement of the impact of reality aspects of the analyst would undermine the concept of transference. Lurking behind this argument, however, one can read a subtextual fear that women analysts might have certain advantages in the analysis of preoedipal material. Freud (1931), in fact, approached this dangerous territory in his paper, "Female sexuality," in which he suggested that his women colleagues might be better able to analyze the preoedipal attachment of women patients to their mothers. Yet, the obvious corollary that women analysts might also have easier access to such material with male patients was not drawn, and the question of what is distinctive about the work of women analysts was "ghettoized" into questions concerning the woman patient.

In the last decade, a number of women practioners have shifted from asking questions concerning women as patients to questions concerning women as therapists (Carter, 1971; Chappell, 1981). Consistent with the formulations of Chodorow (1978) about the difficulties that girls have in fully separating from their mothers and

---

[4]There are clearly alternative possible interpretations to these findings. In the clinic populations that were studied, however, Abramowitz et al. ruled out the hypothesis that requests of women patients for women therapists had resulted in a disproportionate number of women in the caseloads of women therapists. Similarly, the interpretation that men are more likely to cancel appointments with women therapists was not supported by an examination of the no-show rate, which was the same for male and for female patients. In addition, the findings of Abramowitz et al. — that women clinicians see significantly fewer male patients than their male colleagues — are in accord with the reports of the women therapists and analysts whom I have interviewed, and with reports by Pendergrass (cited by Goldberg, 1979) and Surrey (cited by Kaplan, 1984) that women therapists see primarily women patients.

[5]For a comprehensive review of the literature on the effect of the sex of the analyst on the transference, see Kulish (1984).

with Stoller's (1975) claim that masculinity requires "ever-vigilant defenses against succumbing to the pull of merging again with mother" (p. 149), Benedek (1973) and Mogul (1982) have observed that women therapists are more likely to trigger both primitive wishes for reunion with the preoedipal mother and fears of either engulfment or abandonment by the mother. Similarly, Goldberg (1979), arguing from a frustration-aggression paradigm, suggests that whereas the nonresponsive style of psychoanalytically oriented treatment is consonant with the traditional male role, it is dissonant with expectations that women therapists will be nurturant and emotionally expressive and, consequently, evokes aggressive feelings towards the woman therapist.

By suggesting that paternal transferences do not occur with women analysts, Karme (1979) has challenged the notion that the transference will unfold blind to the sex of the analyst. Karme's claim is that whereas a maternal transference will develop toward either a male or a female analyst during the preoedipal phase of the analysis, during the analysis of the oedipal complex the patient's transference to the analyst is same-sexed, so that a paternal transference will develop towards male analysts and a maternal transference will develop towards women analysts.

Karme's explanation of her observations is based on the claim that the recognition of sex differences and the development of gender identity do not occur in preoedipal aged children and that, consequently, during the preoedipal phase of the analysis, "the sex of the analyst would not interfere with the illusion necessary for the development of a mother transference" (p. 259). As Lewis (1976) notes, however, current findings suggest that perception of sex differences occurs even among young infants. Furthermore, research on the formation of gender identity indicates that the child's self-designation as male or female is in place by twelve to eighteen months (Person and Ovesey, 1980) and that gender identity is, therefore, not the outcome of the oedipal period but, instead, precedes it.

Because the oedipal phase involves a triangle of mother, father, and child, Karme contends that analysis of this material can occur equally well with the analyst in either of the parental positions. It is therefore possible to claim a sex-linked transference in the analysis of the oedipal complex and still finesse the question of whether or not women have certain advantages as analysts. A sex-linked transference during the analysis of preoedipal material would, however, prove to be problematic for male analysts in that psychoanalytic theory posits for the most part a delimited or absent preoedipal father. Whereas in the triangular oedipal relationship feelings about the mother or the father can be worked through with either a maternal or paternal transference — in that there is a complementary relationship (or, as Freud wrote, a "correlation") between hostile feelings for one parent and affectionate feelings for the other parent — this is not so for the essentially dyadic preoedipal relationship.

Karme's observation that maternal transferences are found towards women analysts as opposed to both maternal and paternal transferences towards male analysts might, therefore, be explained not by a lack of perception of sex differences during the preoedipal period, but, rather, by the impossibility of working through preoedipal material without a maternal transference. Given the absence of a preoedipal father in most psychoanalytic accounts, in order for male analysts to work with preoedipal material, they must "construct"[6] a maternal transference. In other words, the asymmetry in the "traditional family" between the role of the mother and the role of the father — with the importance of the father coming into play during later phases of the separation-individuation process and during the oedipal period — implies that the maternal transference is more developmentally inclusive than the paternal transference and consequently, that women analysts, unlike their male colleagues, are able to work within a same-sex transference throughout the treatment.[7]

THE WOMAN THERAPIST:
DISTINCTIVE ISSUES

Authority: A Contradictory Terrain

It has been frequently suggested that the unconscious image of the psychotherapist/analyst is male identified (Redlich, 1950). Auerbach (1981), in an analysis of the "looming men" of the 1890s, has suggested that Freud's creation of the analyst, like the creation of

---

[6]See Schimek (1983) for a discussion of the "construction" of the transference.

[7]As Morris (1980) notes, Freud (1909) recognized the relationship of the problem of the perpetual uncertainty of the father — "that *'paper semper incertus est'* (paternity is always uncertain), while the mother is 'certissima' (most certain)" — to the (reaction formation) exaltation of the father by children. Similarly, one might argue that the centrality in Freudian psychoanalysis of the oedipal complex, which represents the transfer of authority from the mother to the father with a concomitant increase in the importance of the role of the father, is a reaction to the uncertain role of the father in development. Moreover, unlike alternative preoedipal narratives, the male analyst can easily work with oedipal material from the position of the paternal transference.

Svengali and Dracula, drew upon the imago of the dark magician who arrogates to himself "the virtually limitless powers" (p. 114) of science, myth and magic, and whose aim, like the aim of all romantic heroes, is "to save and subdue mutable womanhood" (p. 124).

Although it can certainly be argued that this is a narrow reading of the psychoanalytic tableau that rests heavily on Freud's early case studies, there are male associations to the interpretive method, such as the analogy between interpretation and penetration and the link with the usually masculine trait of intellectuality. Furthermore, as many writers have noted (Perlman and Givelber, 1976; Benedek, 1973; Kaplan, 1979), the authority of women therapists is routinely called into question. Women therapists are more frequently called by their first name, challenged regarding scheduling of the therapy hour, and asked about their age, level of experience, and previous training. Berman (1972) reports that many patients assume that there must be a special reason for their having been assigned a woman therapist, and Benedek (1973) suggests that women therapists should assume that their patients will have concerns about having a therapist who is a woman that need to be directly addressed in the treatment.

The most material instantiation of the power differential within the therapeutic encounter concerns who looks at whom. In analysis, the looking is literally unidirectional, and in vis-à-vis therapy this attitude is psychologically created in that both therapist and patient turn their gaze onto the patient. Yet, despite Freud's (1913) now infamous claim that he could not "put up with being stared at by other people for eight hours a day" (p. 134) and therefore positioned himself outside the view of his patients, there has been very little discussion of the meaning of looking and being looked at in the therapeutic encounter. This may in part be explained by the normativeness of men looking at women. As Stoller (1975) notes, "In our time and culture, looking is far more intricate and stylized for males . . . and being looked at is more so for females" (p. 98). For women to look at men is, in fact, explicitly forbidden in many cultures. Who can look at whom is frequently taken to symbolize the power relationship, as in de Sade's depiction of a master-slave relationship in *The Story of O* in which O is explicitly forbidden to look at her captors.[8]

What happens, then, when, as in the case of the woman therapist and the male patient, the positions are reversed so that the woman becomes the bearer of the gaze and the man the object of study? One

---

[8]For a feminist analysis of *The Story of O*, see Benjamin (1983).

possibility is that this reversal raises the spectre of the "phallic mother." Film critic Ann Kaplan (1983) has argued that the conventional structure of spectatorship in which men look at women is "part of men's strategy to contain the threat that the mother embodies, and to control the positive and negative impulses that memory traces of being mothered have left in the male unconscious" (p. 324); similarly, Fenichel (1945) suggested unconscious associations between the experience of being looked at and childhood fears of being devoured. Providing some clinical support for these claims are Lester's (1985) account of a male patient who associated the fantasy of "a big predatory bird perched somewhere high up watching the little chicken down on the ground" with being looked at by his woman analyst while he lay on the couch, and Socarides' (1974) report of a male rapist who would cover the eyes of his women victims during intercourse for fear that their gaze would "rob and deplete him of strength and masculinity" (p. 193).

As with the act of looking, there are asymmetries by gender concerning speech within the therapeutic dialogue. Inhibition of speech in front of women is deeply ingrained in our culture; there is talk between men (real talk), and there is polite, civilized talk that occurs when women are present. Since it is women who in the aim of socialization usually inhibit children's aggressive and sexual behavior and are therefore more likely to be associated with childhood feelings of shame, this inhibition may in part be a projection of shame. For example, Lewis (1976) reports a case of a young man in treatment whose feelings of shame about childhood experiences of spontaneous ejaculations in front of women teachers were converted into worries that his talking about this subject in front of his woman therapist would embarrass her. Furthermore, whereas the male clinician speaks from the position of "a man of science" (with all the concomitant authority), it is counternormative for women to be in the position of speaking to men about the meaning of natural and social events.

Perhaps the most fundamental distinction, however, between the male and the female clinician concerns the relationship between power and sexuality. For men, power and sexuality are complementary: the powerful man is perceived as sexually desirable, and being sexually desirable both reflects and enhances men's sense of power. In contrast, for women the relationship between power and sexuality is much more complicated and certainly not simply complementary. For women, sexuality is often equated with being the object of desire — that is, of someone else's agency. To be powerful frequently means rejecting a receptive position and refusing to be regarded as a sexual object.

Thus, when a woman assumes a professional role, she often either literally or metaphorically puts on a coat of authority that signals that she is not to be approached as a sexual object. The woman therapist or analyst must, however, simultaneously put on and take off the coat of authority; she must, while maintaining her position of authority, invite her male patients to reveal their feelings about her — which, because of both transferential and nontransferential reactions of the patient, often include sexual feelings. Although a patient's sexual feelings may elicit multifaceted reactions in both male and female therapists, because power and sexuality have a different relationship for women than for men and because (as will be argued later) the erotic transference may serve a different function for male than for female patients, we should expect significant differences between the experiences of male and female therapists in working with sexual material.

Intimacy with Women: The Threat of Merging

The second theme that is distinctive for the woman therapist concerns the meaning for men and women of being intimate with women given a history of separation-individuation from a female caretaker. According to object relations theory, the child separates from the mother, who is not originally understood as having a separate identity. The child comes to have a separate sense of self through learning that the mother is not always available — which is a secondary process that overlays the primordial experience of the mother as always available. Because the separation process is conflictual, individuation includes a residual fear of fusion, which, through transference mechanisms, may become an unconscious aspect of subsequent relationships with women (Guttman, 1984).

One paradox of the therapeutic relationship is that it is structured as a delicate balance between an interaction with the distant father — with distinct time boundaries and set codes of interaction (the father's "veto" [Loewald, 1980, p. 14] of regression) — and the intimacy and dependency first experienced with the mother. Whereas maintaining this balance requires great skill for both male and female clinicians, because of the different associations to male and female deriving from the different roles that mothers and father play in the process of separation-individuation, men and women as analysts or therapists negotiate this balance from different positions.

The work of Stoller (1968, 1975) on the establishment of gender identity among boys suggests that for men intimacy with women is in certain aspects fundamentally different from intimacy with men. Stoller's argument hinges on his claim that both girls and boys experience a primary phase of "protofemininity" as a result of the original symbiosis and identification with the mother.[9] Developing a masculine identity is, therefore, a secondary process that requires a traumatic repudiation of the original intimacy with the mother. Because this repudiation is conflictual, there remains among men "the ubiquitous fear that one's sense of maleness and masculinity are in danger and that one must build into character structure ever-vigilant defenses against succumbing to the pull of merging again with mother" (Stoller, 1975, p. 149). Greenson and Stoller both suggest that the common difficulties that men have in establishing intimate relationships with women are in part due to this threat that women pose to masculinity. As Greenson (1968) states, "women feel at their most feminine in the company of the opposite sex, whereas men feel at their most masculine in the presence of men" (p. 371).

These claims about the fragility of masculinity raise many questions about the dyad of the woman therapist and the male patient. First, whereas women therapists may stimulate greater fears of regression for both male and female patients, is the fear of regression further intensified for male patients because it threatens masculine identity? Second, Stoller's and Greenson's claim that masculine gender identity is more fragile than feminine gender identity suggests that masculinity requires more environmental support. In our culture, a woman entering a masculine domain does not usually experience her sense of 'femininity' as threatened; in contrast, men entering traditionally feminine domains (be it the kitchen, the nursery, or the typing pool) are frequently assumed to be less masculine. How, then, do male patients experience being in the 'feminine' domain of the woman therapist's office, and is entering into this domain experienced as a threat to masculinity? (Anecdotal evidence suggests that some male patients may, indeed, have strong reactions to their therapist's 'feminine' domain: one male patient fantasized about soiling his woman analyst's white couch and about smearing the walls of her office with excrement; another male patient referred to his woman therapist's office as "the clean room," which he associated with femininity, as opposed to "the dirty room" where he might drink and smoke.) Third, if masculine identity is based on a disidentification with the mother, how does the male patient identify with his woman therapist, and is the process of internalization of the woman therapist

---

[9]For a critique of Stoller's argument, see Person and Ovesey (1983).

experienced in part as a threat to defenses against "succumbing to the pull of merging again with mother?" (Stoller, 1975, p. 149).

TRANSFERENTIAL ISSUES: THE MALE PATIENT AND THE WOMAN THERAPIST

In this section, I discuss four transference themes common to the dyad of the male patient and the woman therapist, which, because of the different developmental histories of men and women as well as because of their different positions in our culture, may have a distinctive meaning in this dyad: the preoedipal maternal transference, feelings of shame in response to the woman therapist's authority, the erotic transference, and the hostile transference.

The Preoedipal Maternal Transference

From the interviews I have conducted and the case material I have reviewed, I can tentatively identify two patterns that characterize the maternal transference. Both patterns are consistent with the observations of Mogul (1982) and Benedek (1973) that women therapists are more likely to trigger both primitive wishes for reunion with the preoedipal mother and fears of engulfment or abandonment by the mother, and with the theoretical formulations of Stoller (1975) and Greenson (1966).

The first pattern concerns the beginning of treatment. Several women therapists and analysts have reported accounts of their treatment of male patients that began with an initial intense maternal transference, including dreams about the woman therapist that preceded the first session. It is as though for certain male patients, seeing a woman therapist acts as a stimulus for the development of an intense transference that may take off like a brush fire. Because the transference precedes the development of a working alliance, both therapist and patient may struggle with fears that the therapy will "get out of control." In these cases, as well as in cases reported by Karme (1979) and Lester (1985), contrary to the classical expectation that the course of treatment will work backwards so that earliest conflicts are addressed later in treatment, the course of treatment mirrored the developmental history.

Whereas for some male patients the beginning of treatment with a woman therapist seems to stimulate a "regressive pull," a second pattern that characterizes this dyad is the activation of vigilant defenses against the emergence of feelings of dependency. For example, Paul and Anna Ornstein (1975) report the analysis of a male patient by a woman analyst in which the struggle against the emergence of primitive affect is a central theme. Toward the end of the first year of treatment, the patient expressed for the first time how angry he felt that his analyst removed the tissue from the pillow while he was still in the office. These feelings were associated with his having felt as a child that he was in his mother's way; distaste for his own "childish concerns" (p. 252) had inhibited his expressing his feelings about the tissue earlier. The Ornsteins suggest that the long delay in expressing his feelings was due in part to the patient's humiliation at having infantile feelings that were unacceptable to his adult self. Whereas women certainly also feel shame at expressing infantile feelings, the degree of shame, I am suggesting, is greater for men, who are forced from early childhood to suppress affect and to assume a stance of independence.

In sum, given the differences in the relationships of men and women to their mothers, we might expect not only the content of feelings about the mother but also the defenses against this content to be different for men than for women. If masculinity is predicated on a repudiation of the closeness and comforts offered by the original symbiosis and identification with the mother, then entering into a nonsexual intimacy with a woman therapist or analyst might lead those men with weaker defenses to feel overwhelmed and those men with stronger defenses to feel a greater need for vigilance.

Issues Concerning Power For Men

The second aspect of the transference that we might expect to be distinctive for the male patient with the woman therapist involves feelings about the authority of the woman therapist. Horney (1932) suggested that the most primitive feelings of boys about their mothers revolve around the recognition of maternal power and the consequent dread of women. As a defense against this dread of women, men reverse the perceived situation and impose their power on women. Whether or not one accepts Horney's explanation of the origin of male dominance over women, it remains the case that in our culture, as in most cultures, it is assumed that men will be in positions of authority over women. Freud and his colleagues, in treating their women patients, worked within (and, some have argued, actually strengthened) this assumed social order. In contrast, the woman therapist working with a male patient reverses the expected structure.

A fundamental aspect of this reversal concerns age; in general, psychoanalysts and advanced psychotherapists are older than their patients. Whereas the pairing of an older man and a younger woman is an accepted coupling within our culture, the pairing of an older woman with a younger man is considered aberrant and raises the spectre of incest. In a popular account of romantic relationships between older women and younger men, Sunila (1980) concludes that "they are cast as a couple of losers consoling each other for not being able to lay their hands on the real prizes — the older men and younger women" (pp. 94–95). From an examination of literature and films about such pairs, Sunila describes the cultural stereotype of the relationships of older women with younger men as involving a grotesque woman who is either desperately battling a fading youth or who conforms to the spider-woman motif of "indulging a purely genital sexuality," and a younger man portrayed as a gigolo or as a naif seeking a mother.

Although women are accustomed to adult relationships with male authority figures, men are not accustomed to adult relationships with female authority figures. For many men, the last intimate relationship with a woman in a position of authority was with their mother. Because maternal authority is usually employed in the service of socialization, it leaves in its wake a residue of shame. Furthermore, as Lewis (1971) argues, all illnesses evoke feelings of humiliation, and both men and women experience shame at having to be in psychological treatment and at having to reveal to another person thoughts that are deemed unacceptable to the self. For the male patient, however, seeing a woman as a therapist can be doubly shaming — the shame of being a patient as well as the shame of being in a subordinate position to a woman.

Lewis (1976) suggests that in the case of the woman patient with a male therapist, the woman patient "is not only the sick one, but a member of the inferior sex as well" (p. 312). Consequently, Lewis argues, "the shame of being a patient (and a woman)" may be left unanalyzed "because both take for granted not only her doctor's greater wisdom as a therapist, but his superiority as a male" (p. 307). In contrast, "when a male patient is in treatment with a male psychotherapist, both are dealing with each other as members of the superior sex" (p. 312).

In an analysis of the behavior of working class boys, Willis (1977) interprets the rampant sexism as a defense against feelings of social inferiority; the 'lads' can console themselves with the thought that "At least I'm better than a girl." For the male patient with a woman therapist, however, there is no such consolation. Not only must he manage the feelings of humiliation at being a patient, he must also manage the humiliation of being shamed in front of a woman, that is, of being weak in front of one who should, according to the dominant ideology, be weaker than himself.

Clara Thompson (1938) observed that a woman patient's preference for a woman therapist may reflect an underlying devaluation of herself and of other women. Similarly, Mogul (1982) notes that men may choose a woman therapist "but might actually use belittling of the therapist to maintain their own sense of superiority and fragile self-esteem" (p. 6). What happens, then, when, as inevitably occurs in the process of therapy, the male patient feels belittled by the woman therapist? In the next section, I suggest that for the male patient with a woman therapist the development of an erotic transference may be one solution to this problem — serving to "turn the tables" and to restore in fantasy the man to the dominant position.

The Erotic Transference

Freud's writing on the erotic transference assumes more or less explicitly that the patient is a woman and that the analyst is a man. In his one paper devoted to the topic of transference love (1915), he opens by stating, "What I have in mind is the case in which a woman patient shows by unmistakable indications, or openly declares, that she has fallen in love, as any other mortal woman might, with the doctor who is analysing her" (p. 159). It is of course striking that the discussion of the erotic transference is limited to the case of a woman patient and her male physician. What is most curious, however, about the defining conditions is the phrase "as any other mortal woman might." What seems to be implied is that it is expected that a woman would fall in love with her male physician and that this falling in love is not "sick" — that is, a nonneurotic woman would also covet her attractive, powerful doctor. On the other hand, given the cultural proscriptions against men's erotic relationships with women in either authority or maternal positions, a male patient who fell in love with his woman analyst would not be like "any other mortal man"; to the contrary, relationships in which women are in some way in the dominant position are pathologized and set apart from what any "normal" man might enter. Thus the shared expectation of patient and therapist that the patient will fall in love with the therapist rests on radically different terrain given the gender match. Whereas falling in love in the case of the woman patient with the male therapist is congruent with normative romantic patterns, the male patient who falls in love with his woman therapist breaks from the romantic template.

In "The Dynamics of Transference," Freud (1912) distinguished between the positive and the negative transference and then stated that the positive transference could be further divided into two varieties: "friendly or affectionate feelings which are admissible to consciousness and transference of prolongations of those feelings into the unconscious . . . which invariably go back to erotic sources" (p. 105). Furthermore, Freud's claim that "transference to the doctor is suitable for resistance to the treatment only in so far as it is a negative transference or a positive transference of repressed *erotic* impulses" (p. 105) assumed that the erotic is a subset of the affectionate.

It is the basic assumption that the erotic transference is a variant of affectionate feelings that perhaps needs to be questioned across the board and, given the *Zeitgeist* of male conquest with rape as the unacceptable perimeter of male sexuality, most certainly is problematic in the case of the male patient with the woman therapist. The problem may lie in the tendency to view the postive–negative distinction of the transference as having some sort of ontological basis. For the male patient with the woman therapist (and perhaps in all dyads), the distinction positive–negative is obfuscating since feelings of love and desire are nearly always mixed with feelings of hostility. Furthermore, as discussed earlier, the normative pattern of male development, in which boys must, to borrow Stoller's (1975) term, "repudiate" the first loved object (the mother), insures that men's erotic and affectionate feelings toward women will be ambivalently experienced. Consequently, to talk about the positive maternal transference versus the negative maternal transference suggests a conceptual polarity in feelings that we would predict, instead, to be developmentally interwoven and phenomenologically intertwined.

The second difficulty with transposing the conception of the erotic transference that Freud developed from his observations of the transference love of women patients to male analysts to the case of the woman therapist and the male patient concerns the degree of objectionableness of the feelings. Freud (1912) viewed the erotic transference as "a positive transference of repressed erotic impulses" (p. 105) — repressed because they were objectionable. Those elements of the transference that were conscious and unobjectionable were, he instructed, to be left untouched. For men, however, although having erotic thoughts about a woman authority figure may be incongruent with traditional pairings in our culture, having erotic thoughts about women is not only unobjectionable, it is expected.

The erotic transference has continued to be discussed primarily vis-à-vis the woman patient and the male therapist. In Greenson's (1967) classic psychoanalytic primer, he states that "all cases of eroticized transference I have heard of have been women patients in analysis with men" (p. 339). Recently, however, the question of the frequency and intensity of the erotic transference of male patients to women analysts has been the subject of panels at the annual meetings of both the American Psychoanalytic Association and the American Academy of Psychoanalysis. At both forums, Eva Lester presented papers in which she reported that in her experience there has been "only mild, transient, muted erotic Oedipal transference from male patients" (Szmarag, 1982, p. 11). Lester questioned whether her experience is typical and the erotic transference is, therefore, less frequent and less intense with male patients and female analysts than with female patients and male analysts. According to Szmarag's reporting of the panel and the subsequent discussion, although there was some concurrence among members of the audience suggesting that Lester's experience is not atypical, several women analysts and several male analysts who had been analyzed themselves by female analysts disagreed with Lester's claim, stating that it was not consistent with their own experiences.

Lester (1985) argues that the erotic transference of male patients toward their women analysts might be less intense than is the case with the opposite cross-sex dyad because: "The working through of pregenital struggles with the vengeful, overpowering, phallic mother is played out over dominance–submission or sadistic–masochistic issues. These overshadow erotic genital impulses toward the oedipal mother" (p. 284). Lester claims that because the preoedipal material is worked through first, the oedipal material comes at a more advanced stage of the analysis and is therefore less potent. Furthermore, during the working through of the preoedipal material, "the passivity and receptive stance engendered by regression in the male patient will be dystonic to his active male sexual role; concomitantly, the culturally sanctioned empathic nurturing role of the female analyst, in active position vis-à-vis the regressed male patient, will be dystonic with that of the 'seductive' oedipal mother" (p. 185). Similarly, Guttman (1984) suggests that "it is culturally deviant to openly express one's sexual feelings to an asexual mother figure who is our authoritative confidante" (p. 189) and, therefore, that "it is easier for male patients to be direct in expressing their dependency needs and that their sexual feelings for the therapist remain veiled and indirect, often finding expression in acting out or displacement" (p. 196).

Although I don't disagree with the formulations of Lester and Guttman, I would like to suggest that they have located only one of the possible scenarios that occur in the transference of male patients to women therapists/analysts. This scenario of the phallic preoedipal

mother with whom sexual contact would destroy or engulf is consonant with Freud's (1912) original view of the erotic transference as
involving erotic wishes that are repressed because they are objectionable—in this case, because they are fearful. However, as Blum
(1971) has pointed out, the erotic transference—rather than being
repressed because forbidden — can be ego-syntonic, functioning as a
defense against other forbidden feelings. Thus the erotic transference
is a dual-edged sword: it may be incestual, forbidden, and threatening, or, to the contrary, it can be an attempt to fantasize a triumphant
outcome in the face of feelings of shame or fearful longings for nurturance.

The disagreement among the members of Lester's audience as to
the typicality of her experience that the erotic transferences of male
patients to women analysts are muted, less intense, and infrequent —
as well as the many cases of intense erotic transferences reported to
me by women analysts and therapists—suggest that Lester's narrative about the dominance of struggles with the overpowering phallic mother is applicable to a limited number of cases, and that a
second narrative needs to be developed to account for the frequency
of cases in which male patients do indeed develop consciously elaborated erotic transferences towards their women therapists. Although,
as Guttman (1984) suggests, it may be more difficult for some male
patients to express sexual feelings than to express dependency needs,
for many male patients the opposite is true: it is more forbidden to be
in a passive, dependent position vis-à-vis a woman than to express
sexual feelings. As Lester points out, the passive, receptive stance of
the male analysand in relation to the authoritative woman analyst is
dystonic to an active male sexual role. Whereas Lester suggests that
the consequence of this is that erotic feelings will be muted and
repressed, another solution for the male patient may be to retreat
into the active male sexual role. What is dystonic, after all, for the
male patient is not the active male sexual role, but the regressed
position. In other words, for the male patient, the erotic transference
can function as a defense against the shame evoked by being in a
passive position vis-à-vis a woman, and against the fear that this
regression—which goes against the original repudiation of the mother, which is, according to Stoller (1975), the foundation of masculinity—will lead back to a protofeminine, emasculated state.

The development of an erotic transference by a male patient to his
woman therapist can, therefore, "turn the tables" and restore in fantasy the man to the dominant position. Because in our culture sexual
behavior is viewed as diminishing women (women are "taken") and
augmenting men (men are "on top"), when a woman patient has erotic
fantasies about her male therapist, she is extending rather than alter-

ing the structure of their relationship. In the erotic transference, the woman patient extends the male therapist's psychic power to the sexual sphere. For the male patient, however, the erotic transference can serve to alter in fantasy the structure of the relationship — undoing the shame-evoking power of the woman therapist by restoring the man to a fantasized dominance in the sexual encounter. In other words, because of the deeply rooted meaning of sexuality in our culture as an expression of male dominance, the erotic transference of male patients to their women therapists can serve to "turn the tables,"—functioning as a defense against feelings of humiliation evoked by the therapy situation or against threats to masculinity spurred by the regressive pull of the preoedipal transference.

Several clinical examples illustrate the sequence in which an erotic transference in the dyad of the woman therapist and the male patient may allay feelings of shame evoked by the therapy situation.

A young man in his early thirties managed the end of each hour, in which he became acutely aware that it was his woman therapist, not he, who set the formal boundaries of the relationship, by frequently asking his therapist as she escorted him to the door if she would like to go for a drink or to continue talking over dinner. He telephoned repeatedly between sessions and in the third year of treatment suggested that they attend a sports event together in a nearby city. In his fantasy, he imagined them sleeping together, side by side, on the return train trip. The fantasy revealed the fuction of the erotic transference: to break the structure of the relationship in which the woman therapist was in authority and to establish a relationship in which they would instead be "side by side."

In a second example, Lewis (1971) reports an analysis that she conducted with a young man who had sought treatment for impotency. Five months into the treatment, following relief from his symptoms, he expressed a wish to terminate the treatment. After being counseled by his analyst that this would be unwise, he decided to continue. Nonetheless, he felt "put down" and humiliated by his analyst's reminder that he still needed treatment. Lewis reports that the following night, the patient had a dream in which he "buggered" a woman, whom he associated with the analyst, and that they then walked around town with his penis inside her anus. In the dream, the sexual act worked to reverse the "put down" feelings. As Lewis interpreted the dream:

> The shift in position of the self into the position of the other was contained in the dream's first image of the woman seen from behind. The dream image turned things around, i.e., it is I who sit behind the patient. . . . The fury which was underneath a

"put down" became available to him from the content of the dream. We were able to understand that what had been evoked was retaliatory scorn of me for siding with his doubts [p. 483].

In a third case, a thirteen-year-old boy seen in psychotherapy following extensive sexual abuse by his stepfather with collusion by his mother developed an intense erotic transference to his woman therapist. He became preoccupied with wondering about what it would be like to be her boyfriend and struggled to control the therapy hours, at times insisting upon sitting in her desk chair. In the fantasy of a sexual relationship with his woman therapist, he could imagine himself in an active, dominant position and was able to avoid both the homosexual panic evoked by the sexual abuse and the rage at his colluding mother.

In a fourth case, reported to me by a woman analyst, a male patient seen in psychotherapy who was extremely concerned with his masculine image during a period of marital conflict began to make remarks to his therapist that she was a "foxy lady." When she would get him from the waiting room, he would insist upon holding the door open for her in an exaggerated form of chivalry. An analysis of his seductive behavior revealed it to be a displaced attempt by the patient to manage his feelings of having been humiliated by his wife.

In the cases just described, the erotic transference was a defense against feelings of shame and as such was not itself a source of anxiety. In other cases of erotic transference of male patients to women therapists, the erotic feelings seemed to be themselves a source of distress rather than a defense against other unacceptable feelings. Three women therapists reported cases of older male patients who developed toward them erotic feelings that were deeply painful and accompanied by anxiety and distress. In general, it seems that the reluctance to discuss erotic feelings and the association of anxiety and distress with erotic thoughts is indicative of a different meaning from the sequence of inverted humiliation described earlier.

The fantasy. In addition to these clinical examples, it is interesting to note that the fantasy of an erotic relationship between a woman therapist and her male patient has occupied three male directors who have made films in which this is a major theme: Hitchcock's *Spellbound*, in which Ingrid Bergman analyzes an amnesiac played by Gregory Peck; Woody Allen's *Zelig*, in which Mia Farrow plays the role of Dr. Eudora Fletcher, the psychiatrist of the chameleon-like Zelig, played by Allen; and Blake Edwards' *The Man Who Loved*

Women, in which Julie Andrews plays the analyst of a womaniz-er/sculptor played by Burt Reynolds. One can read these films as projections of male fantasies about women therapists, which, given the marked similarities of the themes despite their vastly different genres, can be assumed to reflect a general cultural fantasy about what occurs between a woman therapist and a male patient.

Essentially, what happens in these three films is a love-cure: the woman therapist loves her male patient to health. In all three films, the woman therapist is obsessed with the mystery of her male patient's illness in what seems to be a displaced phallic worship. Both Bergman and Andrews return to their mentors for aid with their special patients, and Farrow is seen pouring over psychiatric texts in search of a cure for Zelig.[10] The devotion to the male patient is extraordinary, with Farrow and Bergman both abandoning their other patients to search for the missing Allen and Peck. In fact, the three women therapists are only rarely seen with other patients or doing anything but treating or thinking about the revered male patient.

The punchline, of course, is that these women therapists have fallen in love with their male patients. In *Spellbound* and *Zelig,* the woman therapist cures her patient, and he then marries her — a twist perhaps on the frog who turned into a prince except that Peck and Reynolds are fairly princely even during the worst of their illnesses. Bergman and Farrow thus move from being the devoted therapist to being the devoted wife — with the implication that now that each has found her prince there is no need to work. Although Julie Andrews declines Reynolds' marriage offer, she becomes the leader of the entourage of his devoted women lovers. It is interesting to note that Julie Andrews is, in reality, director Edwards' wife and Farrow director Allen's girlfriend, and how seamlessly the transpositions from lover/wife to therapist to lover/wife occur.

In the three films, the woman therapist restores the man to power, which then becomes a power over her. This theme is most clearly developed in *The Man Who Loved Women,* in which the critical therapeutic event involves Burt Reynolds, a sculptor paralyzed by anxiety that prevents him from working, seeing up Julie Andrew's skirt. By his seeing up her skirt, her authority is undone, and he can approach

---

[10]Aficionados of Hitchcock will recognize that the case of *Spellbound* is more complex than I have portrayed in that the romance neither fully emerges from nor is fully circumscribed by the treatment. However, the underlying dynamic in *Spellbound* is, nonetheless, consistent with the tableau of male imagination painted in the other two films.

her sexually. In the pivotal scene, he rises from the analyst's couch and leans *over* her while she leans back in her chair *beneath* him. She responds by telling him that he will get a lover but lose an analyst, and then hands the decision over to Reynolds. In the transformation of their analytic relationship into a sexual relationship, the tables are turned so that the man is both literally and figuratively "on top."

It is Reynolds' conquest of his woman analyst, not the analytic work, that restores his potency, and, in the postcoital hours following the consummation of their relationship, we see Reynolds standing erect (in counterpoint to the earlier scenes of him prone on the couch) furiously chiselling at a piece of marble. This theme of the conquest of the powerful woman is, of course, a common cultural current that ranges from the tales of Cleopatra to the exploits of the Star Trek crew; similarly, the transformation of autonomous woman into wife is itself a genre.[11] In these tales, however, female power is an impediment to male power; men need to conquer women in order to gain domestic comforts or additional kingdoms. The logic is additive: a man's conquest of a woman increases his own sphere of influence. What is unique about the three films that take as their subject the woman therapist and the male patient is the imputation that the demise of female power is the condition upon which male power is predicted. Dethroning women (in more psychogenic terms, righting past humiliations in the hands of women) is not simply aggrandizing, it is therapeutic. In the fantasies of Hitchcock, Allen, and Edwards, the logic is that of a zero-sum game: the woman therapist must give up her position of power so that her patient can become a man.

It is striking that these male fantasies of psychotherapeutic treatment by a woman clinician as a love-cure — in which, out of devotion to her male patient, the therapist will breach professional ethics and become ultimately his wife or lover — invert the reality about sexual contact between therapists and patients. Conservatively estimated, four times as many male therapists have sexual contact with their patients as do women therapists (Pope, Levenson, and Schover, 1979). As in all relationships that involve significant power disparities (parent–child, teacher–student, employer–employee, therapist–patient), it is men, by and large, who abuse the power differentials for sexual ends. In these films, however, the eroticization of the therapeutic relationship does not take on the meaning of an abuse of power by the woman professional, who is presumably in a dominant

---

[11]See Molly Haskell's *From Reverence to Rape* for a discussion of the sacrifice of career for love in the "woman's film" of the thirties and forties.

position. To the contrary, the erotic contact undoes her authority and restores the man to the dominant position.

Schmideberg (1938; cited by Abend, 1979) suggested that patients' fantasies about being completely analyzed often replicate childhood fantasies about the libidinal gratifications that will be available once one is fully grown up. Parallel to the childhood fantasy that being fully grown up will mean being able to sleep with the desired parent is the patient's fantasy that being cured will mean being able to sleep with the therapist. In Freud's (1915) discussion of the erotic transference of women patients to their male analysts, he commented on the frequency of the fantasy "that if she behaved well she would be rewarded at the end by the doctor's affection" (p. 169). What is distinctive about the fantasies revealed in the films and in the erotic transference of the male patients discussed earlier is that the love of the analyst is not simply a reward but is itself the solution to a dramatic problem. By eroticizing the relationship, the male patient is transported from the unacceptable position of the passive analysand into the acceptable position of the active male suitor. Contrary to the standard reading given to cross-status sexual contact, in which the sexual contact is viewed as a transgression by the higher status person that augments power over the lower status person, the fantasy of eroticization places the male patient in the dominant position and, therefore, solves the problem for men of the incompatibility between a dependent relationship with a maternal authority figure and the masculine role.

The Hostile Transference

Although Freud (1915) considered the erotic transference to be an aspect of the positive transference, which required restraint on the part of the analyst and which might be misconstrued by the analyst as a "conquest," he also recognized the hostile wish that can exist behind the erotic feelings "to put the analyst in an awkward position" or "to destroy the doctor's authority by bringing him down to the level of a lover" (p. 163). Wishes to "defeat, undermine, and ridicule the would-be-helper" (Appelbaum, 1972, p. 152) are ubiquitous and, according to Lewis (1971), structurally assured, given the inevitability of shame-rage as a by-product of the therapeutic interaction. Similarly, Schafer (1983) suggests that the hostile transference is unavoidable, since attempting to understand the patient is in itself disorganizing and can easily be experienced as an attack upon the analysand's stablity.

The question arises, then, What does it mean for a man to have hostile feelings towards a woman? Whereas hostile feelings by a male patient towards a male therapist may revive castration anxiety and other fears of retalization, the hostile transference of a male patient to his woman therapist has its own set of dangers. First, hating a maternal figure can raise fears of the annihilation of the source of basic needs. Second, from the adult position, there is the cultural prescription that men should protect and take care of women. Third, there is the problem of violence — that irrespective of the realities of physical strength, it is assumed that men could physically harm women.

Women therapists and analysts frequently point to the intensity of the hostility of their male patients. Prado (1976) notes the frequency with which male patients come to women analysts with "an unconscious desire to crush" the analyst. Other women analysts report long periods during which their male patients seem motivated primarily by a desire to berate the analyst. As is frequently argued (Horney, 1932; Chodcrow, 1978), our current childrearing practices make anger at women normative. Stoller's (1975) conceptualization of male development as requiring a repudiation of the original intimacy with the mother suggests that rejection of women is a necessary precondition for masculinity, and that normal gender development creates a reservoir of hatred for women. Stoller further states that gender disorders in men involve "a triad of hostility: *rage* at giving up one's earliest bliss and identification with mother, *fear* of not succeeding in escaping out of her orbit, and a need for *revenge* for her putting one in this predicament" (p. 99, emphasis in original). According to Stoller's description of the treatment of transsexual boys (who, he argues, fail to break the blissful union with the mother and consequently retain a "protofeminine" identification with the mother), with the development of what are considered in our culture to be "masculine" traits, hostility towards the mother emerges for the first time.

Although aggressive and sexual impulses are linked for both men and women, the link is particularly strong for men, with rape the extreme form of violent impulses expressed through sexual behavior. Stoller (1975) argues that there is a continuum between, at one end, the sadistic "perversions" (which he terms the "erotic form of hatred"), in which the desire to harm the erotized object can be viewed as a fantasy of converting childhood trauma into adult triumph, and, at the other end, men's common difficulty with being tender and faithful — that both the pathological and nonpathological ends of this continuum are reaction formations to the fear of the regressive pull experienced with women.

In the transference of male patients to their women therapists, the merging of hostile and sexual feelings is common. Lester (1985) reports a pivotal dream of a male patient that began with the patient hitting his woman analyst and concluded with sexual contact between them. Another woman analyst described a male patient who imagined violent sexual contact between them in which he would cut off her breasts. In a more displaced example, a third woman analyst described a male patient's fantasy that women in tight jeans were having their genitals cut.

Guttman (1984) suggests that women's fear of being viewed as seductive is paralleled by men's fear of being viewed as dangerous. Many male patients worry that they will lose control and hurt their woman therapist. More frequently, male patients worry that talking about their violent sexual thoughts will harm their woman therapist. Prado (1976) reports cases of male patients who interpreted the passive stance of their woman analyst as evidence of having harmed her. Similarly, Lester (1985) describes a male patient who worried that his sadistic impulses would harm or debase his woman analyst, and therefore, needed to be kept outside of the sessions. In a third example, a male psychotherapy patient avoided discussing violent rape fantasies because of his fear that my hearing this material would upset me. In general, as Guttman (1984) points out, there is a conflict for men between the social acceptability of expressing hostility toward women in a sexualized manner and the fact that it is a woman to whom they are talking. Thus, while women therapists seem to act as a stimulus for male patients' hostile erotic feelings (in part as a defense against more regressive and threatening maternal longings), the fact that it is a woman to whom they are talking may inhibit direct expression of these feelings.

CONCLUSION

When Freud wrote about Katharina, he was following in the tradition of men writing women's histories. During the past twenty years, women have begun to reclaim this power and to write their own stories. The woman therapist with the male patient advances this trajectory a step further by writing a man's history. As the most recent rupture in Lacan's institute following Michèle Montrèlay's attempt to organize a seminar on male sexuality suggests, (see

David-Menard, 1982) the gaze of women upon men can raise fears not only in the consulting room, but institutionally as well.

Nonetheless, the potential advantages of examining the therapeutic process and male development from the vantage point of the woman clinician are great. First, stepping back from the master narrative of the male doctor with the woman patient makes it possible to examine certain pretheoretical assumptions and theoretical elisions concerning gender within psychoanalytic theory. In particular, the case of the woman therapist and the male patient throws into relief the ways in which psychoanalytic method relies on male authority and suggests that for the woman practitioner, the therapeutic process (including struggles about power and the difficulties of the shame that is inevitably induced) needs to be conceptualized in new terms. Moving away from the case of the male practitioner yields heuristic benefits as well by providing a new vantage point for examining certain commonly reified theoretical distinctions (such as oedipal-preoedipal and the negative versus positive transference), which may be less critical or take on a different meaning when the clinician is a woman rather than a man. In addition, the case of the woman therapist with the male patient raises the question whether the major narrative line of the oedipal conflict, while well suited to the male analyst in its concerns with the point of entry (in the psychoanalytic account) of the father in development, is universally the most fruitful guiding framework.

Second, the case of the woman therapist with the male patient can be viewed as a particularly translucent microcosm for addressing a variety of broader questions about gender arrangements in our culture. Examination of the themes of the transference of male patients to their women therapists opens a unique window for looking at male development — in particular, the relationship of boys to their mothers and the ways in which this conditions other relationships to women. Similarly, the countertransference of women therapists to their male patients provides an unusually self-reflexive account of the experiences of women in assuming positions of authority over men in a culture that renders problematic the coexistence of sexuality and power in women.[12]

Finally, without a literature that specifically addresses the distinctive transference and countertransference issues that may arise in

---

[12]Manuscript based on interview data concerning countertransference themes in the work of women therapists with male patients is currently in preparation.

the dyad of the woman therapist and the male patient, the woman therapist or analyst will be at a disadvantage in conceptualizing the process of treatment. Schafer's (1983) account of the theory and practice of psychoanalysis as interrelated narrative activities mediated by the analyst's "narrative competency" provides a link between the state of the theoretical literature and actual clinical practice in that a critical aspect of narrative competency involves drawing upon the theoretical constructs in the literature. By adopting a strategy of differentiation (as opposed to the more common agenda of the human sciences to find laws and commonalities) in which the case of the woman therapist is not subsumed under the case of the male therapist, not only do we open up the possibility of fulfilling Freud's hope that psychoanalysis might provide a foundation for the study of culture, but, more practically, we can also begin to construct narrative accounts upon which women psychotherapists and psychoanalysts might draw in their work with male patients.

REFERENCES

Abend, S. (1979). Unconscious fantasy and theories of cure. *J. Amer. Psychoanal. Assn.*, 27:579–596.

Abramowitz, S. (1981). Sex and case assignment: Further evidence of a phenomenon in search of an explanation. *Psychol. Rep.* 48:644.

———Abramowitz, C., Roback, H., Corney, R., & McKee, E. (1976). Sex-role related countertransference in psychotherapy. *Arch. Gen. Psychiat.*, 33:71–73.

———Davidson, D., Greene, L., & Edwards, D. (1980). Sex-role related countertransference revisited: A partial extension. *J. Nerv. Ment. Dis.*, 168:309–311.

Appelbaum, A. (1972). A critical re-examination of the concept 'motivation for change' in psychoanalytic treatment. *Internat. J. Psychoanal.*, 53:51–59.

Auerbach, N. (1981). Magi and maidens: The romance of the Victorian Freud. *Crit. Inq.*, 8:111–130.

Benedek, E. (1973). Training the woman resident to be a psychiatrist. *Amer. J. Psychiat.*, 130:1131–1135.

Benjamin, J. (1983). Master and slave: The fantasy of erotic domination. In: *Powers of Desire*, ed. A. Snitow, C. Stansell, & S. Thompson, New York: Monthly Review Press, pp. 280–299.

Berman, E. (1972). The woman psychiatrist as therapist and academician. *J. Med. Educ.*, 47:890–893.

Blum, H. (1971). On the conception and development of the transference neurosis. *J. Amer. Psychoanal. Assn.*, 19:41–53.

Breuer, J., & Freud, S. (1893–1895). Studies on hysteria. *Standard Edition*, 2. London: Hogarth Press, 1955.

Carter, C. (1971). Advantages of being a woman therapist. *Psychother. Theory, Res., Prac.*, 8:297–300.

Cavenar, J., & Werman, D. (1983). The sex of the psychotherapist. *Amer. J. Psychiat.*, 140:85–7.

Chappell, A. (1981, March 15). Male patients seeking female psychiatrists. *Frontiers of Psychiatry*, p. 14.

Chasseguet-Smirgel, J. (1984). The femininity of the analyst in professional practice. *Internat. J. Psycho-Anal.*, 65:169–178.

Chodorow, N. (1978). *The Reproduction of Mothering: Psychoanalysis and the Sociology of Gender*. Berkeley: University of California Press.

David-Menard, M. (1982). Lacanians against Lacan. *Soc. Text*, 6:86–111.

Fenichel, O. (1945). *The Psychoanalytic Theory of Neurosis*. New York: Norton.

Freud, S. (1909). Family romances. *Standard Edition*, 10:235–241. London: Hogarth Press, 1959.

―――― (1912). The dynamics of the transference. *Standard Edition*, 12:97–108. London: Hogarth Press, 1958.

―――― (1913). On beginning the treatment. *Standard Edition*, 12:121–144. London: Hogarth Press, 1958.

―――― (1915). Observations on transference love. *Standard Edition*, 12:157–171. London: Hogarth Press, 1958.

―――― (1931). Female sexuality. *Standard Edition*, 21:225–243. London: Hogarth Press, 1961.

Goldberg, J. (1979). Aggression and the female therapist. *Mod. Psychoanal.* 4:209–22.

Goldberger, M., & Evans, D. (1985). On transference manifestations in male patients with female analysts. *Internat. J. Psycho-Anal.*, 66:295–309.

Gove, W. (1972). The relationship between sex roles, marital status and mental illness. *Soc. Forces*, 51:34–44.

Greenson, R. (1967). *The Technique and Practice of Psychoanalysis*. New York: International Universities Press.

―――― (1968). Dis-identifying from mother: Its special importance for the boy. *Internat. J. Psycho-Anal.*, 49:370–374.

Guttman, H. (1984). Sexual issues in the transference and countertransference between female therapist and male patient. *J. Amer. Acad. Psychoanal.* 12:187–197.

Haskell, M. (1973). *From Reverence to Rape*. New York: Holt, Rinehart and Winston.

Horney, Karen. (1932). The dread of women. *Internat. J. Psycho-Anal.*, 13:348–361.

Kaplan, A. (1979). Toward an analysis of sex-role related issues in the therapeutic relationship. *Psychiat.*, 42:112–120.

―――― (1984). Colloquium: Female or male psychotherapists for women: New formulations. *Work in Progress*, 83–102.

Kaplan, E. A. (1983). Is the gaze male? In: *Powers of Desire*, ed., A. Snitow, C. Stansell, & S. Thompson. New York: Monthly Review Press, pp. 309–327.

Karme, L. (1979). The analysis of a male patient by a female analyst: The problem of the negative Oedipal transference. *Internat. J. Psycho-Anal.*, 60:253–261.

Kulish, M. (1984). The effect of the sex of the analyst on transference. *Bull. Menn. Clin.*, 48:95–110.

Lester, E. (1985). The female analyst and the erotized transference. *Internat. J. Psycho-Anal.*, 66:283–293.

Lewis, H. (1971). *Shame and Guilt in Neurosis*. New York: International Universities Press.

———— (1976). *Psychic War in Men and Women*. New York: New York University Press.

Loewald, H. (1980). *Papers on Psychoanalysis*. New Haven: Yale University Press.

Malcolm, J. (1983). Annals of scholarship: Psychoanalysis — Part I. *The New Yorker*, 59:59–152.

Masson, J. M. (1984). *The Assault on Truth: Freud's Suppression of the Seduction Theory*. New York: Farrar, Straus, & Giroux.

Mogul, K. (1982). Overview: The sex of the therapist. *Amer. J. Psychiat.* 139:1–11.

Morris, H. (1980). The need to connect: Representations of Freud's psychical apparatus. *Psychiat. & the Humanities*, 4:309–344.

Orlinsky, D., & Howard, K. (1980). Gender and psychotherapeutic outcome. In: *Women and Psychotherapy*, ed. A. Brodsky & R. Hare-Mustin. New York: Guilford Press.

Ornstein, A., & Ornstein, P. (1975). On the interpretive process in psychoanalysis. *Internat. J. Psycho-Anal. Psychother.* 4:219–271.

Perlman, C., & Givelber, F. (1976). Women's issues in couples treatment: The view of the female therapist. *Psychiat. Opin.*, 13:6–12.

Person, E. (1985). The erotic transference in women and in men: Differences and consequences. *J. Amer. Acad. Psychoanal.*, 13:159–180.

———— & Ovesey, L. (1983). Psychoanalytic theories of gender identity. *J. Amer. Acad. Psychoanal.*, 11:203–226.

Pope, K., Levenson, H., & Schover, L. (1979). Sexual intimacy in psychology training: Results and implications of a national survey. *Amer. Psychol.*, 34:682–689.

Prado, M. (1976). Feminism and women analysts. *Amer. J. Psychoanal.* 36:79–84.

Redlich, F. (1950). The psychiatrist in caricature: An analysis of unconscious attitudes towards psychiatry. *Amer. J. Orthopsychiat.*, 20:560–571.

Samuels, L. (1985). Female psychotherapists as portrayed in film, fiction and nonfiction. *J. Amer. Acad. Psychoanal.*, 13:367–378.

Schafer, R. (1983). *The Analytic Attitude*. New York: Basic Books.

Schimek, J. (1983). The construction of the transference. *Psychoanal. Contemp. Thought,* 6:435–55.

Schmideberg, M. (1938), After the analysis. . . . *Psychoanal. Quart.,* 7:122–142.

Selltiz, C., Jahoda, M., Deutsch, M. & Cook, S. (1960). *Research Methods in Social Relations.* New York: Holt.

Socarides, C. W. (1974). The demonified mother: A study of voyeurism. and sexual sadism. *Internat. Rev. Psycho-Anal.,* 1:187–195.

Spence, D. (1982). *Narrative Truth and Historical Truth.* New York: Norton.

Stoller, R. (1968). *Sex and Gender.* London: Hogarth Press.

———— (1975). *Perversion.* New York: Pantheon.

Sunila, J. (1980). *The New Lovers.* New York: Fawcett Gold.

Szmarag, R. (1982). Special panel: Erotic transference and countertransference between the female therapist and the male patient. *Acad. For.,* 26:11–13.

Thompson, C. (1938). Notes on the psychoanalytic significance of the choice of the analyst. *Psychiat.,* 1:205–16.

Willis, P. (1971). *Learning to Labor: How Working Class Kids Get Working Class Jobs.* New York: Columbia University Press.

12   The Pregnant Therapist
Transference and Countertransference Issues

_____LINDA S. PENN

One situation that is unique to the female analyst is the possibility that she may become pregnant during the course of therapy. This event can dramatically affect every aspect of an analytically oriented treatment. The therapeutic climate inevitably shifts as personal facts of the therapist's life are revealed through the pregnancy, violating her relative anonymity to her patients. Suddenly the therapist's private life is in public view, and she is exposed as a mother, a sexual being, a person with a separate life, intimately involved with others for whom she is more constantly available. This exposure tends to be a stimulus for very powerful transference and countertransference reactions. Early and highly charged issues from a patient's past are often highlighted during the pregnancy as they are reexperienced through the transference, offering new opportunities for understanding and growth. In the countertransference, the therapist must deal both with her own reactions to her pregnancy and with her responses to the intense and sometimes primitive transferential reactions of her patients.

In some ways the therapist's pregnancy is similar to other unusual events that take place in a therapist's life and are unavoidably visible to the patient. For instance, the therapist's sudden use of crutches or her extended absence due to illness, like the therapist's pregnancy, unexpectedly brings aspects of her private life into view. These, too, often elicit strong, frequently highly transferential reactions from patients. Whether the private meanings the patient attributes to these "special events" (Weiss, 1975) result in a negative disruption of the therapeutic work or a positive opportunity for new integration and growth through the highlighting of the transference depends in part on the way this material is heard and dealt with in the therapy.

Although the pregnancy of the therapist is only one of those life events which interferes with her relative anonymity to her patients, it is unique in the highly charged content of what is exposed and, therefore, unique in the scope and intensity of the transferential reactions. Pregnancy invariably exposes many of the very aspects of the therapist's life that the analytic situation aims to dim. While the therapeutic process is one in which attention is focused almost exclusively on the patient, with the therapist often experienced by the patient almost totally in reference to himself, the therapist's pregnancy dramatically reminds that patient of her separate existence and of an intense and far-reaching relatedness to others. It is a declaration of her sexuality, sexuality with some unknown figure. It is a statement of her intense connectedness to a yet unborn child, with whom she is now sharing even the boundaries of her body. The pregnancy may be a reminder of the patient's own early attachment to mother, of the disappointments in his or her imperfect relationship with that mother, and of the terror of potential loss or abandonment. It is reminiscent of the discovery of mother as a sexual being and father as having exclusive rights. For many, it is a reminder of the loss of the undivided attention that was given up with the birth of a sibling. And so it is not surprising that these and other issues that are alive for our patients in our nonpregnant times tend to become mobilized, intensified, and highlighted in response to the stimulus of our pregnancy.

What is surprising and dismaying is the extent to which some pregnant therapists had not listened for these themes and so did not hear them when they arose. These therapists claim their patients never "noticed" their pregnancy throughout; hence, it and their associations to it were never discussed. Or they found their patients politely pleased and looked no further. Equally distressing are those supervisors who chastise pregnant therapists as narcissistic if they interpret other than the most direct statements as potentially related to their pregnancy. These lapses in dealing with the material in a truly psychoanalytically oriented way is very worrisome, both for the patients who missed the opportunity to work through and integrate important early issues and for those whose therapy was prematurely aborted because of intense and painful transferential feelings that were unattended and therefore unresolved.

Although innumerable therapists have been sensitive to the transference (and countertransference) issues that arose during their pregnancies and have orally shared these experiences, there has, unfortunately, been a scarcity of information in the psychoanalytic literature, where it might sensitize a wider audience to the common themes a pregnancy evokes. In a time when increasing numbers of women are combining their professional and family lives, it is particularly important for all psychoanalytically oriented clinicians, male and female, to be made aware of these issues because of the likelihood of their at least supervising a female therapist during her pregnancy.

PRIOR CONSIDERATIONS

Early Observations

The earliest paper written on the effects of a therapist's pregnancy was by Hannett (1949), who described various patients' transferential responses to her miscarried pregnancy. It was fifteen years before a second paper on this topic appeared (Van Leeuwen, 1966). In this the author focused on one male patient's response to her pregnancy as a reflection of "pregnancy envy." In 1969 Lax, in her landmark paper, presented an important discussion of the impact of a therapist's pregnancy and offered six extensive case vignettes. She described how each patient responded to her pregnancy "with a reactivation of those aspects of the infantile conflict which were most significant for the development of his pathology" (p. 364) and thus was offered a "singular opportunity to re-experience many of his pregenital and oedipal struggles" (p. 363). She then focused on the differences in the responses of male and female patients and speculated on the developmental differences that account for these. Lax further addressed potential countertransferential reactions stemming from the therapist's own history.

Case Vignettes

Most of the papers that followed Lax's discussion consist of case vignettes offered to elucidate common reactions to the therapist's pregnancy. Paluszny and Poznanski (1971) presented eight vignettes. They divided them according to the patients' tendency to (1) reenact a childhood conflict in relation to the pregnant therapist, (2) respond primarily defensively to the pregnancy, or (3) integrate into the therapy the new material and affects stimulated by the pregnancy, thus leading to new insights and therapeutic gains. Ulanov (1973) discussed three female patients who had particularly intense transference reactions to her pregnancy and illustrated how her pregnancy was instrumental in helping them to relinquish their daughter-role in the transference and in their broader interpersonal relationships. Browning (1974) presented a typical pattern found in the reactions of three child patients to her pregnancy. The reactions included denial, displacement, and fears of abandonment accompanied by anger and transient regressions. She also discussed how the transference material was used productively for the therapy in each case. Schwartz (1975) focused on the impact of pregnancy on the casework of social workers. Breen (1977) presented an interesting discussion of the reactions she observed in patients she saw in group therapy. She contrasted the reactions and themes evoked by the pregnancy in the context of individual therapy with those noted in a group therapy situation and related these differences to the different transference pulls of the two situations. Barbanel (1980) pointed to the counterproductive tendency toward a denial of pregnancy by therapist, society, and individual patients. She then presented four clinical case vignettes, two for whom the therapist's pregnancy led to greater integration and growth and two for whom it resulted in greater disruption. She also contributed a discussion of patients' reactions to a therapist's miscarriage. Clarkson (1980) discussed the need to look behind a "pronatalist facade" to find the impact of pregnancy on each individual patient and presented five brief case vignettes demonstrating the diverse meanings a therapist's pregnancy can have for different patients. Cole (1980) offered three cases sketches focusing on the different ways these patients handled their angry feelings toward the therapist during her pregnancy. Domash (1984), in a more theoretical context, discussed two cases in which the therapist's pregnancy highlighted selfobject transference issues.

Benedek (1973) and Butts and Cavenar (1979), rather than focusing on patients' reactions to the therapist's pregnancy, discussed the reactions of staff and colleagues to the pregnancy. Butts and Cavenar concentrated particularly on the intrapsychic conflict created for the pregnant therapist by negative or unhelpful reactions from colleagues and supervisors.

Empirical Studies

Berman (1975) and Naperstak (1976) have reported the only empirical studies in the area. Berman collected data on the acting-out behavior of 129 outpatients of nine female psychiatrists, covering the time of the pregnancy of the therapists and during a six-month control period. She found a higher level of acting-out behavior during the therapists' pregnancies, especially among the group of patients diagnosed as borderline. Naperstak reported the results of an open-ended questionnaire sent to 32 recently pregnant therapists. The questionnaire gathered information on practical, procedural issues as well as attempting to ascertain the most prevalent themes that arose during the therapist's pregnancy. Without reporting specific data, Naperstak pointed to the fear of abandonment and loss as the strongest theme across groups. Other themes mentioned included increased maternal transference, mobilization of sexual and procreational conflicts, and increased positive identification or competition with the therapist.

Common Treatment Issues

While the sharing of case vignettes and anecdotal material is very important in sensitizing pregnant therapists to common themes during pregnancy, there is also a need for a more organized discussion of the treatment issues; there are many fewer papers in the literature which attempt this. Balsam (1974) made the first such contribution, focusing in depth on potential countertransference reactions experienced by the therapist and pointing to typical transference reactions in patients. She examined each of the three trimesters of pregnancy, attempting to elucidate the issues most central to each phase of the treatment. Nadelson, Notman, Arons, and Feldman (1974) presented some common concerns experienced by therapists during their pregnancies and examined major transferential themes seen in patients during this period. They briefly discussed, with case illustrations, such issues as the intensification of maternal transference, sexual identity, fears of abandonment, and feelings of loss and envy. Rubin (1980) organized common reactions to the pregnancy by separating those that relate to the impending separation from the therapist from those that are "uniquely related to the psychological and physical event of the pregnancy" (p. 210). She also touched on some common countertransference issues. No entire book has yet been devoted to the topic of the pregnant therapist although one is forthcoming (Fenster, Phillips, and Rapoport, in press).

It is my hope in this chapter to expand this portion of the literature with a more comprehensive presentation of the major treatment themes seen during a therapist's pregnancy. Toward this end, I have drawn on the treatment experiences during my own two pregnancies, on information drawn from many colleagues and students, and on the information and experiences related in the current literature in the area.

COMMON TRANSFERENCE REACTIONS

The pregnancy of the therapist can act as a powerful transferential stimulus, mobilizing in patients an emotional reliving of early, significant issues from their own histories. Transference reactions that have only obliquely shown themselves prior to the pregnancy may now be intensified and highlighted, as may the childhood memories and affects that are the bedrock of the transferential reactions.

As would be expected, patients' reactions to the therapist's pregnancy are highly individual. Personal variables that shape the reactions include the patient's character structure, level of pathology, family history, and current life situation. In addition, such treatment variables as the nature of the therapeutic relationship, the length and frequency of treatment, and the type and intensity of previous transference constellations all influence a patient's response. Yet, there are definitely common themes the therapist's pregnancy tends to evoke, within which one sees the wide range of individual reactions.

Therapist as a Maternal Object

As the therapist's pregnancy openly proclaims her potential motherhood, there seems to be an intensification and highlighting of the maternal transference. Powerful conflicts and affects related to early experiences with mother are often reenacted, and important memories and associations involving that early relationship tend to surface more easily. Issues of attachment and separation, fears of abandonment or loss, and sibling rivalry very commonly arise.

Patients' reactions often focus earliest on the new baby as a potential sibling. Deep feelings of competition are frequently stirred. Terror or conviction surfaces that the therapist will prefer the baby, that the baby will be smarter, better looking, more interesting, more lovable. Fears of being rejected or cast aside in favor of the other can be felt during the pregnancy or projected into the future. The very intensity of these feelings often surprises patients even as they experience them and so facilitate the process of anchoring these reactions in their own personal history, where they clearly have their roots. Memories, often deeply buried, can return, articulating for the patient significant issues revolving around their envy of and competition with their own siblings. One patient, Richard L, found himself reacting to my prenancy with particularly intense feelings of competition, similar to feelings he inferred he must have experienced with his fraternal twin but of which he had no affective memory until the time of my pregnancy. As he began to experience fears of not being my favorite, of not being special or good enough, of the fetus "never leaving us alone" (he nicknamed and referred to the unborn baby as "the intruder"), he was also flooded with new memories of his experience as a twin and the impossibility of ever feeling really special and unique in his family. As he found himself trying to entertain me as a way of competing for love and attention he remembered similar attempts with his mother. His feelings of sad resignation that he should "wait his turn" vis-à-vis my baby, that "there's not room for two cars on any track" opened up for him the pain he had felt being one of two cars (twins) growing up, how often he had given over that track to his twin, and how frequently he reenacted this drama in his broader interpersonal relationships.

Common among first children is the reexperiencing of the acute sense of loss that followed the birth of a sibling. The mother of an only child is indeed not the same mother once a second child's needs must also be met. The sadness of having to share the attention that once had been felt to be exclusively their own comes back to haunt these patients. More than one patient assumed that once my baby was born, I would have to care for it periodically during the session rather than be able to continue to focus on them, even during their own sessions. As their fantasies were developed they led to important associations and memories. One of the patients anticipated that she would have to rock my baby's cradle during the session to soothe him. While describing this fantasy she suddenly recalled her resentment at having to do that with her baby sister, and an avalanche of memories and affects followed of experiences with her mother and sister that were highly conflictual for her.

Memories of the experiences of the actual physical loss of mother after childbirth are also stirred by the therapist's pregnancy. For one patient in a large family, dread of my childbirth led to memories of mother's departure with the baby to grandmother's house for four weeks and having to deal with that felt abandonment at a highly vulnerable time. For another, it led to the much more traumatic experience of the mother's postpartum depression, which culminated in mother's hospitalization and the physical and emotional loss of mother. It would indeed be surprising if the intense anxiety and pain associated with these experiences had not been triggered by my pregnancy.

The defensive reactions patients use in responding to the therapist's pregnancy are sometimes reflective of the very defenses used in response to the birth of their siblings. One patient with four younger siblings had no memory of any of her mother's pregnancies or of her siblings as young babies. In fact, her childhood memories were typically devoid of any image of siblings despite their inevitable presence. Just as she had tried to deny and repress their existence, she tried to do the same with my pregnancy. She had fantasies of missing sessions for the first time, which she related to avoiding seeing my pregnant body so she could continue to maintain the image of me as not pregnant. Another patient, who tended not to repress the conflictual memories of experiences with her sibling but rather the intense affect attached to them, noticed my pregnancy but denied any reaction to it at all. "Why should it affect me? I may be in Afghanistan by then for all I know." Other patients, who became the overly solicitous good little children to ensure mothers continued love after the birth of a sibling, tended initially to show similar solicitous reactions to their therapists' pregnancy.

Patients who are prone to separation difficulties because of an overly enmeshed relationship with mother may experience heightened separation anxiety during the therapist's pregnancy. Both the impending disruption in treatment and the separate existence of the therapist that the pregnancy implies intensify their anxiety. Lax (1969) describes one patient whose inability to separate from mother so powerfully transposed onto her during her pregnancy that there was a decrease in the patient's ability to differentiate the therapist from the actual mother. In this case, as is not uncommon, symbiotic yearnings for fusion and the conflicts over those wishes increased as a defense against the separation anxiety. Her particular patient, certain of abandonment, acted out a primitive identification with her therapist/mother by precipitously marrying and becoming pregnant.

Another common transference reaction to the therapist's pregnancy involves an identification with the baby, often with fantasies of how the baby will be treated. At times the therapist is viewed as a potentially hateful and neglecting mother, a fantasy stemming sometimes from the patient's experience with her own mother and at other times from the patient's anger toward the therapist and hostile wishes toward the baby. Envy of or identification with the baby resulting from an image of the therapist as an idealized mother is also frequently encountered. The therapist is then used as a counterpoint against which the inevitable disappointments in the patient's relation with his or her own imperfect mother are highlighted. Or a surge of tender memories of close moments with the patient's mother may resurface. Symbiotic yearnings and anxieties in some patients may intensify as they envy the symbiotic sharing of the pregnant mother's body boundaries with the fetus, and they are reminded of their own early attachment to mother.

In addition to identifying with the baby, patients tend also to identify with the therapist as the good mother. For some patients, identification with the pregnant therapist may be a facilitating factor in the emergence of a more clearly articulated feminine ego ideal (Domash, 1984) or in differentiating themselves from a negative maternal introject in part through identification with the pregnant therapist as a more benign identification model (Ulanov, 1973; Nadelson et al., 1974; Barbanel, 1980). However, apparent identification with the pregnant therapist, especially in cases where the patient attempts actually to become pregnant, can sometimes have a much more pathological base. Such primitive identification can represent an increase in lack of differentiation as a protection against a heightened sense of separation, can be an expression of hostile and envious competitive feelings, or can be a guise for narcissistic identification with the baby (see Lax, 1969; Nadelson et al., 1974; Rubin, 1980).

The Therapist as a Separate Being

The one experience that therapists describe as the most widespread transferential reaction to their pregnancy is their patients' sense of "abandonment." That sense of abandonment in many cases is overdetermined and is often related to real and fantasized losses of the past. It seems also however, to be a response to the loss of an illusion, the illusion that one's therapist exists only in her office for oneself. Although intellectually our patients know that we have "normal" lives apart from our work with them, emotionally they often experience us almost totally in relation to themselves. They are shocked if they see us at a movie, unnerved at running into us at a professional conference. In our offices, they have our undivided attention — they are the "only child" on an unshared center stage. It is reminiscent either of the earliest of times with mother or of a fantasied time never experienced. Our pregnancy, highly visible over a long period of time, flies in the face of the fantasy of us as an extension of themselves. They are forcibly reminded of our separate existence and our intimate relatedness to people other than themselves. Clearly, with the most narcissistic patients, the use of us as a selfobject is potentially threatened. But even with healthier neurotic patients, there is often a sense of real loss.

For some patients, then, the pregnancy not only mobilizes anxiety related to early experiences with mother and siblings, but heightens their sense of being existentially alone, even when in the room with us. It evokes not just a fear of abandonment to come once the baby is born, it is felt as evidence of current abandonment and betrayal. While such a heightened sense of separate self can lead to important insights in exploring the anxiety that accompanies it, initially the patient is most acutely aware of the psychic pain it evokes. These patients often feel convinced that they had fooled themselves into thinking we were concerned with them at all. Suddenly they see us only as our "outside" selves, interested only in the money they pay; they see themselves as a "job" to us, nothing more.

One patient described her initial reaction in this way: "I had a very strong reaction to your pregnancy — I spent two days not able to leave my house or function in any real way — I felt incredibly intense pain and then I consciously pulled back my involvement. I had been feeling increasingly involved here, really able to open up for the first time, and your pregnancy is proof that that can only lead to pain . . . it's concrete proof that I am totally insignificant to you and that I can't depend on you — someone else will always come first. . . . It's a replay of all my other relationships where someone I need is not available to me in the total way I want. . . ." Often patients become obsessed with the certainty that we will not return after giving birth despite our assurances to the contrary; they are convinced we are already absent emotionally. In these cases, resistance soars, and it is essential that such feelings be aired, explored and to some extent worked through if treatment is to continue in a meaningful way. Lax (1969), in another context, quotes one patient's reactions during her pregnancy: "I felt I was one with you, what I thought would bounce back from you to me. Now, you have the baby all the time and I am here only one hour. So the baby is here and not I. You don't like me any more now that you have your baby and I can't count on you" (p. 368).

Therapist as a Sexual Being

A woman's pregnancy inevitably displays to the world that she is an actively sexual being and that she carries a baby that is the result of a relationship with a particular man. When that woman is a therapist, whose personal life until that point has remained ambiguous, the "announced" fact of her sexuality is fertile ground for highly charged transferential reactions.

One common reaction shared by both men and women is a remobilization of their oedipal issues. With the reminder of the presence of a husband in the therapist's life, patients can find themselves feeling excluded from an oedipal triangle. Suddenly they are focusing in the transference on being outside an intimate relationship between two adults, which they can only view and envy, but not be a real part of. One patient relived the pain of not being the most significant figure in the life of someone he loved and who was most significant for him. He saw me as "coupled like everyone else" and therefore unavailable to him; he wished it could be our baby, that he, not my husband, could be central in my life. And he yearned again for a relationship "like my parents had with each other" — he had found that week an old love letter from his father to his mother — "they had a good thing." One female patient, immediately following the birth of my baby, began a sexual affair with the father of a newborn. Although she didn't particularly like the man and didn't feel the affair was in her own best interest, she felt compelled to meet him, calling their sex "grudge-fucking."

The highlighted sexuality of the pregnant female therapist can intensify erotic elements in the transference. For some patients it will mean an increased awareness of their sexual feelings toward the therapist and perhaps talking about these for the first time. For others, however, sexual feelings for the therapist at this time are particularly threatening and may lead to strengthened defenses against experiencing these feelings, thus appearing as a retreat from an erotic transference. For these patients, a once safe and neutral object for sexual fantasies has become not only a dangerously real sexual being, but also the oedipal mother belonging to someone else and toward whom sexual impulses are unacceptable. Thus, the increased awareness of the therapist's sexuality can either lead to a heightened awareness or repression of erotic aspects of the transference.

Hidden attitudes toward sex itself are often revealed in response to the pregnancy. Revulsion at the therapist's sexuality can lead to a patients' coming to realize the disgust with which they have been viewing their own sexual activities. These and other reactions open the door to an exploration of the historical roots of their attitudes toward sex and thus the reexamination of current attitudes. One patient, who had berated himself for his initial "nonliberal assuming" that his therapist was married just because she was pregnant, was able later to connect this preoccupation with his highly conflictual feelings over his father's illegitimacy.

Other patients, instead of viewing the therapist's sexuality as "dirty" or "bad," may see the pregnancy as a statement of unconflicted sexual identity, against which they highlight their own conflicts and concerns over their own sexual identity. For male patients, this may translate into fears about their own sexual potency or identity. Or it may lead to fantasies involving womb envy. For female patients, the therapist may be seen as the female prototype leading to a focus on their own ambivalence and insecurities about their feminine identity. For lesbian female patients in particular, the therapist's implicit statement of heterosexuality may be quite difficult. One lesbian patient, Jane H, found herself feeling increasingly angry and much less trusting of me after she noticed my pregnancy. Suddenly she felt as if I belonged to that group of women she had spent her life actively rejecting — I was the comfortable, middle-class professional woman, married, with two and a half children. As a straight woman, I had a "script" for life that was unavailable to her, while she both yearned for such a script to help find her way and was disdainful of stereotypic ones. She was angry that I and the therapy process were at least implicitly encouraging her "to take a harder road, one without a script or at least one that has to be written and rewritten" while I "apparently take the well-trod road." Once she openly talked about her resentment and envy of my "script," and her sadness at our differences, her resistance in that period of treatment diminished considerably. Further, those feelings helped her subsequently to deal more openly with the anxiety and ambivalence she felt about the road she did choose without feeling unduly frightened that she would have to give it up.

The Therapist as a Parent

Although a therapist's pregnancy is a strong trigger for early childhood material, it can also tend to underscore current life concerns. Intense envy of the therapist at this time, for instance, although based partly on earlier envy, can also reflect strong feelings about one's childless or single state, especially in patients who are childless beyond child-bearing years. Nadelson et al. (1974) describes how for some patients a therapist's pregnancy becomes the time to "mourn losses" associated with abortion, death, lost custody, and the like or to face sadness about children never conceived.

For those patients who have their own children, fantasies about the therapist as parent can often lead to a reexamination of their feelings about themselves as parents and their relationships with their own children. For patients not yet parents, one sometimes sees a highlighting of conflicts about potentially raising a family. The therapist's decision to combine career and motherhood seems to offer a model for some patients that such a road is possible. Other patients may experience it as a pressure to follow a similar path.

Therapist as an Object of Anger

Because of the tremendous range of reactions to a therapist's pregnancy depending on the particular patient's unique dynamics and situation, one cannot easily generalize about which issues will most prominently surface for that patient. However, one issue that almost inevitably presents itself at some point, because it is triggered by so many otherwise different transferential reactions, is dealing with one's anger. Beneath the polite (and on one level often sincere) happy congratulations offered by patients lie the myriad of transferential reactions discussed above. Many of these feelings toward the pregnant therapist are very angry ones: anger over anticipated or experienced abandonment, anger over perceived rejection, anger over an unacceptable sexuality, anger over a perceived greater intimacy with others, anger at the therapist's seeming to have what they do not, anger over an unexpected break in their treatment. Whatever the trigger for their anger, it offers one more opportunity in the treatment for them to view through the transference how they express (or do not express), experience, and handle their anger. Often one is faced first with the defense against the anger, due to the guilt and conflict it evokes, rather than a direct statement of the feeling. Once explored, the experience of anger, as well as the concerns over its expression, tend to reignite the memories of earlier angers and the ways they were dealt with by parents.

For many, their negative reaction to the therapist's pregnancy also offers another opportunity to experience anger toward their therapist without that anger destroying the therapist or their relationship together, as these patients anticipate. In Winnicott's terms (1954a), the therapist "survives" their rage and so facilitates an integrated sense of self and other and a more realistic perception of the power and effects of their anger. The wildly enraging therapist is still the same person as the quietly caring one, and the intensely angry patient is the same person as he is in his nonangry, tender times. Such expressions of rage within a steady holding environment can be crucial for the treatment of many patients.

Heightened Resistance

During the height of transferential fantasies and feelings related to the therapist's pregnancy, there are likely to be periods of strong transference resistance. Indeed, if the patient is experiencing the therapist as abandoning or rejecting, for instance, the atmosphere is not conducive to a relaxing of defenses and a sharing of private, painful experiences. Instead, the patient might show an increase in characterological defenses and maneuvers.

A distancing from therapist and therapy to camouflage a deep caring and felt wound is not uncommon. Denial of the pregnancy itself well beyond its becoming highly visible is often a sign of such a defensive posture, as is emotional indifference once the pregnancy is noticed. Until the defensive denial or the emotional withdrawal from therapy are recognized and worked through, little work can be accomplished. One patient, after revealing a powerful and highly painful reaction to my pregnancy, described her conscious withdrawal in this way: "I felt incredibly intense pain and then I consciously pulled back my involvement. I had been feeling increasingly involved here, really able to open up for the first time, and your pregnancy is proof that that can only lead to pain . . . but for once I can pull back before it's too late." [and after coming fifteen minutes late the following session]: "The task is now how to perform in a way that satisfies your wish to uncover and mine to remain covered."

Another form resistance commonly takes during the therapist's pregnancy is acting out rather than discussing and exploring highly charged emotions. Some typical forms of acting out are missed or late sessions, precipitous termination of treatment, sudden and untimely pregnancy of a patient or a patient's partner, unplanned stopping of birth control measures, or suicidal gestures or attempts.

The Effect of Different Levels of Pathology

Patients at all levels of pathology can be prone to intense and extensive transference reactions in response to their therapist's pregnancy. It does not seem that healthier patients necessarily respond primarily with later, more oedipal issues, while only the more disturbed patients play out the earlier mother–child conflicts; early maternal transference issues arise for both groups. There does, however, seem to be a significant difference related to the depth of the pathology. In the healthier patient, even with very strong transferential reactions, the "as if" quality of the transference is more often maintained; with the borderline or schizoid patients, at times this "as if" quality is lost, and the experience for the patient is one of actual abandonment by the person of the therapist. The result is a different quality in the interaction, which is often first perceived by the therapist through the intensity of the countertransference reactions it can engender. These are the patients who will be most prone to acting out or to leaving treatment precipitously if the transference is not at least partially worked through.

One would expect particularly intense and early derived trans-ference reactions from the more disturbed patients for a number of reasons. A weaker ego naturally results in a lesser capacity to defend adequately against the emergence of conflict-laden material and the handling of that material; one would expect the more disturbed patient to feel more overwhelmed and to experience more ego dis-ruption in reaction to the strong stimulus. Further, a less differenti-ated patient, without a firm sense of object constancy, will have a more primitive and intense reaction to separation and abandonment issues.

The ongoing transference of the patient with deeper pathology may be of a particular kind that especially lends itself to a highly intense reaction to a therapist's pregnancy. Balint (1968) discusses the difference between patients at two different levels of analytic work, distinguishing between the primarily oedipal-level patient — for whom the transference is primarily triangular in nature, where conflict is inherent in the situation, and where adult language is an adequate means of communication — and what he calls the patient at the level of the "basic fault." For the second group of patients, only two-person relationships really exist, the quality of the relationship is an intense dependency on a not-fully-differentiated other, conflict is not central, and adult language is often misleading. For these, more disturbed patients, he suggests that the analyst's every gesture or casual remark matters enormously and assumes an importance far beyond anything realistically intended. Interpretations are experi-enced either as attacks, demands, or insults, or as exciting, soothing, or loving. Thus, for these patients, intensely involved in a dyadic transference where every movement of the therapist is overin-terpreted in reference to themselves, a pregnancy, seemingly flaunt-ing the separateness of the therapist and the therapist's relatedness to others, can be expected to become the central focus of the trans-ference. It is likely to be experienced as an especially difficult blow and to lack the "as if" quality that is present for the patient function-ing on an other than dyadic level.

Similarly, the patient whose problems stem from the earliest stages of emotional development may be involved in the transference in a therapeutic regression to dependency (Winnicott, 1954b). In such cases there is a reliance on a therapeutic setting whose action as a holding environment minimizes impingements to which the patient must react and provides a type of adaptation to the patient. The therapist's pregnancy can certainly be seen as an impingement. Win-nicott speaks of the likelihood of a patient's acting out under circum-stances where such an impingement is experienced in the treatment and of the important therapeutic gains possible if the acting out and the underlying anger and disappointment are understood and experienced by the patient in relation to the "original environmental failure situation" (p. 289).

Finally, one might expect a particularly intense transferential reaction from borderline and schizoid patients precisely because their difficulties so often stem from internalized, highly negative early-life experiences with mother that can be reignited for them through the highlighting of the maternal transference during the therapist's pregnancy.

WORKING WITH THE TRANSFERENCE

Since the therapist's pregnancy can be such a powerful transferential stimulus, working productively with the transference material during this period is particularly important. The therapist needs to be alert to subtle transference communication so she can both be empathically attuned to the patient's distress and help him or her to more fully express, explore, and utilize the thoughts, feelings, and associations that arise.

Recognizing Transferential Responses

The first task in dealing with the transference reactions that arise in response to the therapist's pregnancy is to be aware of potential reactions and to recognize them when they occur in the patient's material, often in an indirect or oblique way. Very often the first expression of this transferential material occurs in a dream. One patient, with characterological denial, had not consciously noticed the therapist's pregnancy even by the end of its fifth month. He reported a dream reflecting both his unconscious awareness of the pregnancy and his defensive denial. In the dream he and his therapist were sitting talking, and the therapist was smoking and looking off into the air, very preoccupied. There was something about separation; he thought she was making him separate from mother. The therapist looked darker, her eyes looking half masked. When he looked at her, only the top half of her was there, as though he were looking at a picture of her. It didn't seem strange to be looking at her this way. She was talking very softly; he asked her to repeat but he couldn't hear. Finally she said, "You want to ruin this lovely thing," but he couldn't hear because of the noise outside.

Another patient, Sandra T, very early in my pregnancy produced a complex dream that reflected an early unconscious awareness of the pregnancy despite a lack of conscious recognition. It included many apparent references to my pregnancy, including fish swimming in a pond, seeing me naked from the waist up, an imagined daughter of mine reminding Sandra of her place as "only a patient," and a building about to topple, which she couldn't see as well as could a chubby woman, who had a much better view. This dream was followed by two weeks of disassociated experiences of rejection and abandonment, accompanied by increasing resistance, until the unconscious awareness of my pregnancy was interpreted to her, an interpretation she readily accepted and that led to a dramatic diminishing of the resistance.

Reactions to the therapist's pregnancy are often expressed metaphorically. Patients may express intense feelings toward figures in life outside the treatment that are applicable to the patient's response to the pregnancy. For instance, there is often an increase in themes of felt abandonment, competition, loss, betrayal, and the like or, more directly, of others' pregnancies even before there is conscious recognition of the therapist's pregnancy. Balsam (1974) notes the additional themes of dress, physical appearance, birth control, abortion, gardening, reincarnation, and rejuvenation.

Rigid denial, either of the perception of the therapist's pregnancy after it has become clearly obvious or of any feelings or reactions in response to that pregnancy at all, is usually an indication of a felt need to defend against particularly threatening transferential reactions. Likewise rigid adherence to any single response, whether it be a happy, congratulatory one or an angry experience of rejection, suggests the defense against the emergence of other, less comfortable reactions. The reactions and fantasies that are directly expressed are often overdetermined and can contain aspects of a number of different feelings. For instance, the expression of intense fears that the therapist will die through childbirth may represent for a particular patient a condensation of rage at the therapist, fears of abandonment, and memories of earlier losses (equated with deaths).

In watching for the possibility of transference resistance at this time, it is important to be particularly aware of shifts in the general level of resistance. One would want to note increased withdrawal, increased anger at "other" things the therapist is doing that are ostensibly unrelated to the pregnancy, increased acting out in the form of lateness or missed sessions, thoughts of cutting back hours, and so on. Some acting out is more subtle. One patient, who had previously had great difficulty ending sessions on time, began immediately after noticing my pregnancy to end each session after 45 minutes to the second. Exploration led to fruitful material around her reactions to the pregnancy.

It is to be noted, however, that while it is unlikely that any patient will have no transferential reactions to the therapist's pregnancy, the reaction of some will not necessarily be the area of strongest affect at that particular point in time. Just as one would not want to overlook indirect expressions of the transference material, neither would a therapist want to focus excessively on them when the patient's material is indeed leading to important conflict areas not related to the pregnancy. The transference material must be recognized as one hears it from the individual patient, not assumed in advance and projected onto the material.

Facilitating Exploration

As is often true of transferential material, patients are frequently embarassed by the presence of intense feelings toward the therapist and feel threatened by the potential consequences of expressing them. Especially in as highly charged an area as the therapist's pregnancy, with its sexual and regressive stimulus pull, many patients will not, without considerable encouragement from the therapist, explore their feelings and fantasies on their own. Once the pregnancy is openly acknowledged by the patient, it is important that the therapist attempt to go beyond the patient's "pronatalist facade" (Clarkson, 1980) to elicit the patient's more individual reactions to the pregnancy. If this is done in a climate of technical neutrality and personal empathy, patients often will express a much wider range of reactions than is initially reported.

While exploration of patients' feelings as soon as the pregnancy is recognized should be encouraged, it will probably be at some later point in the pregnancy that much of the transference material is focused on and utilized. Once the reactions are expressed and flushed out in detail, they may stop functioning as a resistance to treatment even without full understanding of their source. However, the transference reactions to the pregnancy, even when not functioning as a resistance, often provide a valuable entre to a better understanding of the patient's internal object world. The misplaced intensity, or the distortions, involved in the patient's reactions to the therapist offer the unique opportunity (as any intense transference manifestation does) to trace the reactions to their sources in childhood experiences and to understand the impact those experiences have on current intrapsychic and interpersonal life.

Timing of interpretations will, of course, vary with each patient. If the therapist facilitates the patient's expressing reactions to the pregnancy and allows them to grow in intensity with time rather than prematurely interpreting them, it will be much easier both to demonstrate them and to enlist the patient's curiosity in understanding their sources. As with any transference material, when focusing on the reactions to the pregnancy, one would want to pursue the details with the same objectivity and interest as one would with other material, implicitly communicating that the patient's reactions are not being experienced by the therapist as personal attacks or intrusions that are too uncomfortable for her to hear.

Some patients, who are particularly threatened by their transferential feelings, may not be able to acknowledge even seemingly transparent connections between their feelings or behavior and the therapist's pregnancy. Although those patients may need to deny the therapist's impact on them at that time, it does not mean that a transference interpretation necessarily went unheard or unused. It may be that despite a current inability to explore these sensitive issues further, patients may be relieved by the interpretations' in some way making sense of their confusing experiences. For some, unable to express the feelings themselves, the permission for the feelings granted by the therapist's nonpunitive interpretation may be enough to allow them to move on with work in other areas. Further, it may be possible for patients to use interpretations more fully later in treatment, either after surviving the birth of the therapist's baby without their worst fantasies having been met or simply because the patients are at a different point in treatment. Similarly, for some patients who have dramatic and stormy responses to the pregnancy, interpretations may prove ultimately helpful despite an apparent inability to explore the transferential dimensions at the time. Nonetheless, there will be some, particularly among the group of less differentiated patients with more primitive reactions, for whom the transference material may prove disruptive to the treatment despite every attempt to facilitate understanding.

Acknowledging Nontransferential Reactions

Not all reactions, or even all intense reactions, to the therapist's pregnancy are primarily transferential in nature. There can be difficulty sorting out transference-dominated reactions from those where the patient is correctly picking up subtle nuances of communication from the therapist. For instance, a patient who begins to express a feeling that the therapist would rather not be seeing her now that she is pregnant, and expresses this thought just as the therapist is feeling intense nausea from early pregnancy and wishing the session were over, is not necessarily basing that thought primarily on her own early maternal/sibling experiences. However, once the therapist can acknowledge that the patient's thought had some foundation in a communication from her, it is then possible to explore the thoughts, feelings, or fantasies that communication might have triggered for the patient.

Of course, not all reactions to the therapist are dominated by transference. Neurotic patients are simultaneously responding to their therapist transferentially, on the basis of a therapeutic alliance, and as one person to another. Just as Greenson (1969) reminds us that it is appropriate and important to comment sympathetically to a tragic event in a patient's life, we must allow our patients to express some reactions to this clear event in our lives without immediately interpreting it as transference. Even strangers on the subway sometimes smile a congratulatory smile or express some protective urge toward the obviously pregnant woman. It is almost disrespectful to patients not to accept some of their less intense reactions at face value, a caring response of one person for another. While advice to the therapist by a seasoned mother may have competitive or hostile roots, it may also offer an opportunity for patients to feel a greater sense of competence in their interactions with the therapist (Rubin, 1980). An untimely interpretation can be an unnecessary narcissistic blow.

PRACTICAL CONSIDERATIONS

Given the strong impact that pregnancy is presumed to have on the transference, careful thought must be given to how the pregnancy is initially discussed and the manner in which the break and resumption of treatment is determined and communicated.

Initial Discussion

While some therapists choose to inform patients of their pregnancy directly, before it is recognized, most analytically oriented therapists wait for some signal of the patient's awareness. One can then deal with the patient's reactions to the pregnancy much as one would with any other analytic material. Patients will vary in their timing in responding to the pregnancy; by waiting, one allows patients to deal with the issue at their own pace and when it has indeed become an issue of their own. Further, premature discussion of the pregnancy — before the patient has noticed and reacted — could cut off the intensity of early reactions and defenses that would have otherwise spontaneously occurred.

While waiting for individual patients to react to the pregnancy thus has some clear advantages to the work, of course communications and responses in analytic work are not always direct or even conscious. A patient need not directly initiate the topic of the therapist's pregnancy for the therapist to hear the patient's reactions in the material of the session. Indeed, early responses are often oblique and indirect, appearing in dreams or in issues ostensibly unrelated to the pregnancy. Once there is adequate evidence of the patient's reacting to the pregnancy, the therapist should facilitate its expression or interpret it as she would other transference material. The issue of her pregnancy and the patient's reaction to it are thus brought to the forefront, where they can be more directly discussed and explored.

For those patients who give no sign of "noticing" or responding to the pregnancy by the time it is visibly obvious or by the beginning of the last trimester, the therapist must broach the topic to insure that there be enough time to work through feelings about the pregnancy and the break in treatment before the break is upon them. Even at that point, however, the initial focus should be on exploring the patient's apparent denial rather than being a mere announcement by the therapist of her pregnancy and its ramifications for the treatment.

Scheduling the Break

Setting a tentative date for the break in treatment rather than planning to work right up to the birth can be very helpful for patients. Selecting a date some time prior to the due date can relieve patients of the anxiety that each session might be the last, can allow them a greater sense of control and some sense of temporary closure before the break. Further, patients whose therapists inform them that they will work right up to the birth, whenever that might be, may feel further burdened by the anxiety that the therapist could well go into labor during one of their own sessions. The set date, of course, even when planned prior to the actual due date, can only be a tentative one as there is always the possibility of an early delivery. In such a case, it is important that someone call the patients as soon as possible to inform them of the early delivery, cancel subsequent appointments, and assure them of the health of mother and baby.

Setting a specific date for the therapist's return is also very important. A specific appointment time can be a concrete reassurance that fears and fantasies to the contrary, the therapist will return. Naparstek (1976) describes a tendency for some therapists to underestimate the length of time they may need before returning. In her study, therapists who responded to her questionnaire took leaves of between zero and forty weeks with the largest group returning after eight weeks.

Contact During Maternity Leave

If the therapist does not want to be contacted during her leave, patients who may need to speak to someone during the interim can be given the name of a therapist they can contact.

Many therapists have found it useful to send birth announcements to patients after the birth. In this way, they acknowledge the patient's interest and concern, communicate that the therapist has survived the birth and patient's anger, make contact while not actually having a session, and reconfirm the date of return.

COMMON COUNTERTRANSFERENCE REACTIONS

So far we have focused on the significant impact the therapist's pregnancy can have on the patient in treatment. Clearly the therapist herself is in the midst of a major life event that can potentially affect every aspect of her functioning. Pregnancy is a time of significant physiological and emotional changes and a time during which one's role identifications are in the process of flux. For the pregnant therapist, the awareness of her particular reactions to the stresses and the excitement of her pregnancy become important if she is to understand and to some extent control the ways these will affect her patients and her work. In addition to monitoring her reactions to her own pregnancy, it is equally important for her to explore potential countertransferential reactions that may arise in response to the intense and often primitive transferential reactions of her patients.

A Time of Significant Physiological and Emotional Changes

Perhaps one of the most common experiences during a pregnancy is the increased sense of physiological and emotional vulnerability (Nadelson et al., 1974). Physiological reactions to the pregnancy, such as nausea or increased fatigue during the early months, can certainly interfere with the ability to concentrate as the therapist's attention is directed to her own body. Further, primary maternal preoccupation (Winnicott, 1956) in later months may result in increased self-involvement and possible withdrawal of libido from patients and work.

In addition to a sense of greater physical vulnerability, many women describe a sense of greater emotional vulnerability where their affect is much more easily aroused. For some therapists this may translate into a more empathic responsivity to their patients, while for others it may mean potentially more susceptibility to personal countertransference reactions. Further, as their own sense of firm body boundaries is lessened by the experience of sharing their body with the fetus, a greater sensitivity to certain patients' symbiotic desires may emerge and can result either in a defensive distancing or in greater empathy for the patient's experience.

Many pregnant women, especially during the second trimester, experience a sense of self-fulfillment and calm that may lead to greater openness to material. Balsam (1974) points out that this may "help her to withstand the many ungratifying passages in therapy, and . . . allow the patient more leeway to express his or her painful emotions without requiring evidence of improvement to give the seal of approval to her work" (p. 268).

Emotionally, as so aptly put by Paluszny and Poznanski (1971), the pregnant therapist is "existing in two worlds simultaneously" (p. 274). And although frequently this may enrich her work, there are invariably times when it interferes with the optimal therapeutic response. Thus, the sense of rejection and loss felt by many patients may have some basis in realistically perceived cues from the therapist.

A Time of Significant Role Change

Especially for the therapist bearing her first child, the pregnancy is a time of important role changes. The maternal role is a new one, which needs to be integrated with other, more familiar roles such as the therapist's professional identity. Conflicts and concerns about how these will meld or interfere with one another are very common. Sometimes the therapist's own anxiety and doubts about her ability to combine these aspects of her life, despite her decision to do so, can collude with her patients' concern that she may not return after the birth of the baby.

Another way the significant role changes can trigger countertransferential experiences is more related to the increased emphasis on her female sex role. Prior to pregnancy, the female therapist
functions in her work much as the male therapist does. Suddenly her
female capacity to become pregnant is in the spotlight of the transference, often leading to transferential storms. If the female therapist
views this as a liability due to her sex differences from her male
counterpart, there may be some tendency toward countertransferential acting out. The therapist might tend to deny or minimize the
impact of her pregnancy on her patients, thus leaving subtle transference communications unexplored. Or she may choose to interpret
only those aspects of the transference related to the impending break
in treatment, a transference issue shared by all therapists, while
avoiding more primitive transference material in reaction to the pregnancy itself. The therapist might find herself denying its impact on
herself and taking on too much at a time when her body is more
easily fatigued. In contrast, the therapist might feel guilt over her
pregnancy and overemphasize to herself and her patients the real
aspects of its intrusion on the therpeutic work, thereby overlooking
the transferential aspects of her patients' reactions. Finally, concern
over her pregnancy as a potential liability may result in the need to
prove herself as still competent and involved, potentially leading to
premature interpretations or excessive gratification.

In addition to personal role changes, during the course of the
pregnancy there are often moments of role reversal with patients that
may be experienced with discomfort by the therapist. Especially as
the due date grows close, patients may experience some wish to take
care of or care for the therapist, who appears vulnerable to them,
perhaps for the first time.

Counterreactions to Transference

Perhaps the most dangerous countertransferential responses are
those that are in counterreaction to patients' reactions. If the primitive and early nature of some of the transference reactions are particularly anxiety provoking for the therapist, they may be avoided or
denied. On the other hand, as the therapist becomes aware of patients' painful reactions to her pregnancy, she may feel intense guilt,
experiencing herself as indeed the abandoning object or the impinger
of her own personal issues. This guilt can lead to the danger of
underemphasizing the transferential elements because of an exaggerated focus on the reality aspects of her pregnancy's intrusion.

Highly charged angry countertransferential feelings may arise in response to patients' negative reactions. Especially when the therapist feels very vulnerable herself or concerned about the welfare of her baby, patients' expressions of hostility may evoke very angry feelings in her. For instance, patients' veiled death wishes for the baby or "concerns" about miscarriage or dangerous deliveries (often accompanied by detailed accounts of others' traumatic miscarriages or stillbirths) are not uncommon. A therapist's anger can show itself through hostile interpretations, acting out through missed appointments (especially if these are related to the pregnancy in some way), or unconscious collusion with the patients' dropping out of treatment. When anxiety rather than anger is the primary response to patients' negative fantasies, rather than offering hostile interpretations, the therapist is more likely either to avoid the negative transference material or to withdraw from that patient during the session, often into her own fantasies about the baby.

In contrast to reacting angrily or anxiously, a therapist might find herself overidentifying with some aspect of the patients' transference that coincides with her own experiences with mother or siblings. Or, indeed, a therapist could project such experiences onto the patient whose transference reactions to the pregnancy are ambiguous.

Barbanel (1980) points out that countertransference issues will differ for each therapist based on aspects of her "real" personality. "For one therapist it is the stormy angry feelings of the patient that are the most difficult to relate to, for another, the tender protective feelings evoked in the patient may be intolerable" (p. 244).

Utilizing Countertransference

It is important for the therapist to be aware of countertransference experiences that may occur during the pregnancy so she can more easily recognize them in herself if they arise and therefore have more control over their effect on the treatment. Countertransferential feelings are to be expected and need not negatively affect treatment so long as they are brought to awareness to avoid unconsciously acting on them in the therapy.

Countertransference responses, once recognized and under the therapist's control, can be a valuable tool in understanding a particular patient's transference. In addition to the countertransference reactions arising from the therapist's own internal experiences, they also arise in response to something communicated by the particular patient. A therapist is likely to find herself feeling, for instance, more guilty about her pregnancy with some patients, more angry with others; and these feelings may be early cues to the content of patients' transferential reactions. The therapist should assess the intensity of her response, as particularly intense countertransference reactions may sometimes indicate a particular intensity or a primitive quality in the transference.

REACTIONS OF SUPERVISORS

During any difficult period of therapeutic work, it is helpful to have supervisory input. This is especially true when the therapist is particularly susceptible to countertransference reactions in response to intense transference material. Supervisors and colleagues of the pregnant therapist can be an invaluable source of help in attempting to recognize and disentangle the transference, countertransference, and reality elements in patients' responses to the pregnancy. While, indeed, many supervisors and colleagues have been extremely helpful in these ways, therapists have described experiences with supervisors during their pregnancies that were, to the contrary, unhelpful and sometimes destructive.

Just as the therapist's own history of maternal and sibling experiences, her attitude toward combining professional and family roles, and her general attitude toward pregnancy can affect her perceptions during pregnancy, so can these issues affect the perceptions of a supervisor. Moreover, many supervisors, despite their greater experience, find themselves in this situation facing an area of treatment for which they have no personal frame of reference.

A common supervisory response reported by pregnant therapists is the tendency of the supervisor to focus on other, more familiar areas and to deemphasize the potential and actual impact of the pregnancy on patients. These therapist described finding themselves unprepared for the onslaught of material that did arise in response to the pregnancy, often missing or denying early indirect references or feeling unprepared to handle the intensity of the more direct responses. Even when fairly clear transference reactions surfaced, many therapists described the puzzling experience of having supervisors only rarely suggest a linkage between the patients' reaction and the therapist's pregnancy. Some described situations where supervisors, never initiating such a hypothesis themselves, would nonetheless acknowledge the probable accuracy of these hypotheses when suggested by the therapist, as if the linkage had never occurred to them (this from supervisors who in other areas were actively helpful).

Others described a much more potentially destructive situation in which supervisors tended to view the pregnancy as something that would not and should not affect the treatment unless the therapist, for her own neurotic reasons, shifted the focus to herself. When therapists reported hearing patient material as related to their pregnancy, it was viewed by their supervisors as the therapists' own narcissistic self-involvement projected onto the patients rather than viewing the pregnancy as a powerful transferential stimulus. It was assumed that those patients who made no direct comment about the pregnancy either had not noticed or had no reaction. Butts and Cavenar (1979) report a personal experience in which the therapist suggested exploring why her patient by the seventh month had never mentioned her pregnancy. "The supervisor responded that the resident perceived the lack of attention to her pregnancy as a narcissistic injury and that the patient should pay no more attention to the pregnancy than he might new shoes or glasses that the resident might have" (p. 158). Butts describes beginning to fear at that time that perhaps she was too absorbed in her pregnancy; she began to deny many fantasies and references to the pregnancy that came up in other patients' material.

Butts and Cavenar (1979) offer another example in which supervisory input negatively affected the therapist's work, in this case by overemphasizing rather than minimizing the impact of pregnancy. A clinical case conference group agreed that a patient should be immediately transferred to a nonpregnant therapist, as the therapist's pregnancy might lead the patient to decompensate, although they did not point to any evidence for this concern in the patient's dynamics. The therapist's own supervisor overruled this recommendation. The patient did not decompensate, but as a result of the conference's quick panic, the therapist felt a great increase in countertransferential anxiety and guilt in working with this patient.

Benedek (1973) describes similar experiences with staff and supervisors at an inpatient setting during her four pregnancies. She noted that after initial denial of her pregnancy and its potential impact, many staff members shifted to viewing all changes in the patients as related to the pregnancy, ignoring other essential determinants they otherwise would not be likely to ignore.

While many therapists have reported experiences in supervision during a pregnancy that were unhelpful, others have pointed to supervision during this period as especially useful. Supervisors who are attuned to the treatment issues during a pregnancy can facilitate the exploration of both transference and countertransference reactions within a supportive context. Male supervisors may be able to shed additional light on some of the specific concerns of male patients, as well as being particularly helpful in mitigating the female clinician's countertransferential guilt over her pregnancy. Female supervisors, as successful professional women, may provide a role model at a time when it is especially needed.

REFERENCES

Balint, M. (1968). *The Basic Fault.* London: Tavistock.

Balsam, R. (1974). The pregnant therapist. In: *Becoming a Psychotherapist,* ed. R. Balsam & A. Balsam. Boston: Little, Brown, pp. 265–288.

Barbanel, L. (1980). The therapist's pregnancy. In: *Birthing and Bonding,* ed. B. Blum. New York: Human Sciences Press.

Benedek, E. (1973). The fourth world of the pregnant therapist. *J. Amer. Med. Women's Assn.,* 28:365–368.

Berman, E. (1975). Acting out as a response to the psychiatrist's pregnancy. *J. Amer. Med. Assn.,* 30:456–458.

Breen, D. (1977). Some differences between group and individual therapy in connection with the therapist's pregnancy. *Internat. J. Grp. Psychother.,* 27:499–506.

Browning, D. (1974). Patients' reactions to their therapist's pregnancies. *J. Acad. Child Psychiat.,* 13:468–482.

Butts, N. T., & Cavenar, J. O. (1979). Colleagues responses to the pregnant psychiatric resident. *Amer. J. Psychiat.,* 136:1587–1589.

Clarkson, S. (1980). Pregnancy as a transference stimulus. *Brit. J. Med. Psychol.,* 53:313–317.

Cole, D. (1980). Therapeutic issues arising from the pregnancy of the therapist. *Psychother.: Theory, Res. Prac.,* 17:210–213.

Domash, L. (1984). The preoedipal patient and the pregnancy of the therapist. *J. Contemp. Psychother.,* 14:109–119.

Fenster, S., Phillips, S., & Rapoport, E. (in Press). *The Therapist's Pregnancy.* Hillsdale, NJ: The Analytic Press.

Greenson, R. (1967). *The Technique and Practice of Psychoanalysis.* New York: International Universities Press.

Hannett, F. (1949). Transference reactions to an event in the life of an analyst. *Psychoanal. Rev.,* 36:69–81.

Lax, R. (1969). Some considerations about transference and countertransference manifestations evoked by the analyst's pregnancy. *Internat. J. Psycho-Anal.,* 50:363–371.

Nadelson, C., Notman, M., Arons, E., & Feldman, J. (1974). The pregnant therapist. *Amer. J. Psychiat.,* 131:1107–1111.

Naparstek, B. (1976). Treatment guidelines for the pregnant therapist. *Psychiat. Opin.,* 13:20–25.

Paluszny, M., & Poznanski, E. (1971). Reactions of patients during the pregnancy of the psychotherapist. *Child Psychiat. & Hum. Devel.,* 1:266–274.

Rubin, C. (1980). Notes from a pregnant therapist. *Soc. Work*, 25:210–215.

Schwartz, M. C. (1975). Casework implications of a worker's pregnancy. *Soc. Case.*, 56:27–34.

Ulanov, A. (1973). Birth and rebirth: The effect of an analyst's pregnancy on the transference of three patients. *J. Anal. Psychol.*, 18:146–164.

Van Leeuwen, K. (1966). Pregnancy envy in the male. *Internat. J. Psycho-Anal.*, 47:319–324.

Weiss, S. (1975). The effect on the transference of special events occuring during psychoanalysis. *Internat. J. Psychoanal.*, 56:69–75.

Winnicott, D. W. (1954a). The depressive position in normal emotional development. In: *Through Paediatrics to Psychoanalysis*. New York: Basic Books, 1975.

———— (1954b). Metapsychological and clinical aspects of regression within the psycho-analytic set-up. In: *Through Paediatrics to Psychoanalysis*. New York: Basic Books, 1975.

———— (1956). Primary maternal preoccupation. In: *Through Paediatrics to Psychoanalysis*. New York: Basic Books, 1975.

Epilogue

JUDITH L. ALPERT

There are within psychoanalysis three distinct phases in the revisions of Freud's conceptualization of feminine development. First, there was the "cultural phase" in the 1920s and 1930s, when the importance of cultural factors in neurosis were identified. Horney and Thompson, two of the conscious feminists associated with this phase, were concerned with the depth and persistence of patriarchy, psychoanalysts' acceptance of women's derogated status, and Freud's views of women as lacking and morally underdeveloped. Feminine issues during this phase were among the underlying causes of the first major schism in the American psychoanalytic movement. Later, there was the "adversarial phase," from the 1950s through the mid-70s, when there was an adversarial relationship between psychoanalysis and feminism. While there was some dispute over traditional psychoanalytic views of female psychology (e.g. Blum, 1977; Chasseguet-Smirgel, 1970), generally during this second phase, there was continued acceptance of Freud's views about women, and psychoanalysts were attacked by feminists for encouraging women to accept their traditional roles.

Currently, psychoanalysis is in a state that might be described as "ferment." A major aspect of this ferment is the intense focus on female development. We are in a "resurgence-alliance phase"—a resurgence of interest in female development and a growing alliance between psychoanalysis and feminism. We are witnessing an integration of feminist thinking into mainstream psychoanalysis. Karen Horney, Clara Thompson, and Erich Fromm were among the few early feminist voices; today there are within psychoanalysis many voices, representing many different theoretical orientations yet making important advances in understanding women. The establishment of a section on women within the Division of Psychoanalysis of the American Psychological Association, the existence of committees on women within other professional organizations, the paper sessions and discussions in this area at our professional meetings, and the developing body of literature on psychoanalysis and women signifies a proliferation of activity.

Clearly, the changing role of women is impacting on the field. There is a growing number of analysts with a feminine orientation, some of whom are contributing to the analytic literature. Further, these men and women have gone beyond critiquing psychoanalytic theory or indicating that it is based on male development. Rather, they are writing about their analytic experiences, identifying treatment issues, reformulating definitions and conceptualizations, and placing new ideas into analytic currency. In essence, they are attempting to develop a theory about women that is relevant to their lives.

THE MYTH OF ANALYTIC NEUTRALITY

While Freud (1912) indicated that the physician should maintain "the rule of giving equal notice to everything" (p. 112) and should "show them nothing but what is shown to him" (p. 118), most of the chapters in the present anthology share the conviction that some of women's experiences have received little or no attention and have been devalued as well. Further, they hold that analytic neutrality is a myth — a truism that is neither new nor specific to our work. Sherif (1979), for example, focuses on the neutrality myth in her consideration of the bias in psychological research. She indicates that although research appears to be objective, rigorous, and scientific, it is nonetheless open to bias with respect to who is studied and how they are studied. Citing numerous examples from research in psychology, Sherif reports that the nonconscious ideologies of researchers influence their description and discussion of research findings, the choice of research topics, the selection of sample, the initial formulation of problems, and the interpretation of information.

Schlachet (1984) makes a similar point with respect to psychoanalysis. She notes:

> Analytic theory and the technique based in it can never be politically neutral, any more than can any other scientific theory, whether in the "hard" or the "soft" sciences; all of what we look at, whether or not we choose to look at it, and what interpretation we give to what we look at is necessarily based on a complex interactional system of which we, ourselves, are a part [p. 12].

The point is that our recognition of the incorporation of unconscious ideologies into our work has contributed to the integration of feminist thinking with psychoanalysis. We are aware that analysts, like other societal members, hold beliefs and stereotypes of which we may be unaware and which mirror the values of our society. Our focus needs to be on how biased views keep analysts from understanding patients. Biased views had an impact on the "adversarial phase." While we move from the androcentric model of that phase, we must attempt to articulate and evaluate contemporary biased views even while recognizing our limitations here. We should even question whether it is possible or desirable to be neutral.

Thus, our task is to construct an understanding of women's development based on the study of female development and experiences. There is a need to discover new phenomena, redefine concepts, and to reformulate theories. These attempts have implications for our work with both men and women, as the present anthology indicates.

THEMES

Many theoretical perspectives within psychoanalysis, including Freudian Theory, Interpersonal Theory, Object Relations Theory, and Self Psychology, are represented in this volume. The contributors share a commitment to help crystalize questions and stimulate answers about female development, and a belief that their theoretical orientations can be revised to be more reflective of what we know and are learning about women. This book demonstrates that multiple perspectives within psychoanalysis can acknowledge differences between women and men without equating difference with female inferiority. Further, it acknowledges that multiple perspectives within psychoanalysis can coexist with feminism.

If a broad perspective is taken, a number of general and overlapping themes emerge from a reading of this book. These themes indicate that the contemporary conceptualization of feminine development, rather than comprising a diversity of views, are tied together by common threads.

Theme One: Importance of the Preoedipal Experience

The contributors do not hold that anatomy, as defined by genital differences, is destiny. There is agreement that Freud's developmental theories of femininity are the weakest component of his thought. Freud's theories are seen as demeaning women and reflecting the androcentric model and patriarchal aspects of his culture. The contributors concur however, that some of his objectionable views can be revised:

Although there is acknowledgment of the validity of the oedipal experience and the oedipal father, penis envy is no longer viewed as a critical determinant of female development. In those cases in which it is a major problem, it is usually in connection with such other issues as extreme envy, early deprivation, and problems in separation.

The importance of the preoedipal experience and implications of a female-dominated infancy are points of focus. There is consideration of separation-individuation in the mother–child relationship and of the male repudiation of mothering. There is discussion of the influence of the early preoedipal relation with the mother on the private, unconscious experiences of both women and men, as well as how these experiences interact with objective reality and lead to the female's tendency to be more affiliative and nurturing and the male's tendencies to be more concerned with separation and autonomy.

Theme Two: Women and Men Are Different
and Are Perceived Differently.

Several of the contributors here acknowledge in some way that although certain qualities are more characteristic of one gender than another, individuals vary enormously, and individual histories are more telling than gender. While some characteristics more common in women are found in men and vice versa, men and women *are* different and analysts must understand and work with this difference in order to attain analytic goals. Further, there needs to be work toward valuing the feminine aspect of both men and women, which until recently has been derogated, and toward encouraging those human capabilities in both women and men that have been undeveloped.

This anthology stresses the content of the differences and their analytic implications. In general, women are more intimate, personal, connected, and related; men are more detached, abstract, and reasoned, and approach problems in a more objective fashion. Further, men and women engage in and think about relationships differently. The experience of men and women differ, and they frequently bring different concerns and raise different issues within the analytic session. Males, for example, have more difficulty with relationships, while females have more difficulty with individuation. Males and females, as practicing analysts or as analyst-theoreticians, differ also in how they view issues or what they engender in patients. Clearly, gender plays a role in the analytic experience. For example, Gornick points out in the present volume that some theoretical issues, such as preoedipal–oedipal and the negative versus positive transference, may take on a different meaning when the therapist is a woman. She indicates further that examining the themes of the transference of male patients to their women therapists or analysts increases our understanding of boys relationships to their mothers and consequently their relationship with other women. Pregnant therapists also provide a new vantage point for learning about feelings toward pregnancy and birth, as Penn suggests. Moreover, countertransference themes can throw light on the experience of women in power within our present society, as Gornick's and Schachtel's chapters suggest. Thus, the experiences of female and male analysts do differ, and a continued study of gender difference and transferential and countertransferential themes is indicated.

Theme Three: The Experience of Women and the Circumstances of Women's Lives Need Consideration

There is agreement that there is a need to discover new phenomena, redefine concepts and reformulate theories based on female development and experiences. We need to take a view of women that is positive and explicit rather than deal with women by indirect implication and with negative connotations. There is a complicated interaction between the internal reality and the social circumstances in which women live, and these particular circumstances are considered. The concerns of several of the authors exemplify this. Moulton, for example, indicates that while professional success enhances men's sense of masculinity, it threatens women's sense of femininity. Schachtel considers such concepts as authorization, power, and status as she revolves how gender interacts with and affects the analytic work role. And, as another example, Formanek considers physical changes that attend age and the psychological meaning of these changes to women. Thus, the contributors, like Horney and Thompson before them, recognize the importance of considering intrapsychic as well as social factors in the lives of women.

Theme Four: A Feminine Orientation Can Enrich Men's Lives

As the contributions here indicate, women approach life differently than men, as intimacy, caring, and connectedness are more central to their lives. An emergent theme is that men might experience less alienation if they were enabled to develop their more feminine characteristics.

Theme Five: A Feminine Orientation
Can Enrich Psychoanalytic Theory and Practice.

Western society devalues women's affiliative tendencies and reinforces men's autonomy and power as successful and acceptable standards. Psychoanalysis seems to mirror Western society: the structure of and values underlying psychoanalysis are masculine and reflect male's needs, capacities, and orientations. Within analytic theory, there is a focus on difference and distance, and the thinking is dualistic, linear, and in this way, inaccurate, as Spieler, Spencer, and I all indicate. Analytic theory focuses more on separation, autonomy, individuality, self-assertion, and independence than on attachment, or the maintenance and improvement of interdependency, intimacy, empathy, nurturance, or the caring for others. An issue raised in several of the chapters concerns changes in the structure and technique of psychoanalysis if it is to be more reflective of women's nurturing, empathic, and relational needs and capacities.

Several of the contributors urge women and men to enrich psychoanalysis by accepting and valuing feminine characteristics and visions. And others consider — and exemplify — women's contributions to psychoanalysis. Their contributions include, for example, more attention to the preoedipal issues of separation-individuation in the mother–child relationship. Also, this anthology poses some important questions. Litwin, for instance, acknowledges that relationships are vital to women and questions how relationships can be restructured in order to promote growth.

The present historical time is one of rapid individual, social, and cultural change. It is a time when many women perform multiple roles and face new problems within these roles and their intersection. Analysts are affected by the social change because the concerns of women have changed concomitantly. Whereas issues of the adversarial phase included problems in finding husband and difficulties in raising children, women now raise such issues as conflict around professional and personal identity and anxiety around professional performance and assertion. As analysts, we can either approach women's concerns from a perspective, in which male development and behavior is the norm from which all else deviates, or from a perspective derived from the study of female development and experience. The contributors to this volume have made the latter choice.

REFERENCES

Blum, H. P., ed. (1977). *Female Psychology.* New York: International Universities Press.

Chasseguet-Smirgel, J., ed. (1970). *Female Sexuality.* Ann Arbor: University of Michigan Press.

Freud, S. (1912). Recommendations to physicians practicing psycho-analysis. *Standard Edition,* 12:111–120. London: Hogarth Press, 1958.

Schlachet, B. (1984). *Relativism Revisited: The Impact of Life on Psychoanalytic Theory.* Paper presented at the New York University Postdoctoral Conference.

Sherif, C. (1974). Bias in psychology. In: *The Prison of Sex,* ed. J. Sherman & E. T. Back. Madison: University of Wisconsin Press, pp. 93–133.

Author Index

Subject Index